# GRAND HOTEL ABY

# FIGURES OF THE UNCONSCIOUS 15

# GRAND HOTEL ABYSS

Desire, Recognition and the Restoration of the Subject

Vladimir Safatle

LEUVEN UNIVERSITY PRESS

Original title: *Grande Hotel Abismo. Por uma reconstrução da teoria do reconhecimento*

© 2012 Portugese language edition by Editora Martins Fontes, São Paulo (Brazil)
© 2016 English language edition by Leuven University Press / Universitaire Pers Leuven /
Presses Universitaires de Louvain. Minderbroedersstraat 4, B-3000 Leuven (Belgium)

ISBN 978 94 6270 062 8
D/2016/1869/5
NUR: 777

Translation: Lucas Carpinelli
Cover design: Griet Van Haute
Cover photo: Ralph Baiker, 'Ancient Weather', in *Pan's Cave*, Schaden.com, 2009
Lay-out: Friedemann bvba

To my daughter, Valentina
and her wonderful metaphysical questions.

# Contents

# An indistinct picture

*Impossible things should not be tried at all.*
Ismene

*One step forward, two steps back.*
Vladimir Lenin

*I am the conflict. [...]*
*I am not one of those taking part in the conflict –*
*I am both combatants,*
*I am the conflict itself.*
Hegel

## *A general description*

One might say that the concept "game" is a concept with blurred edges [*verschwommenen Rändern*].—"But is a blurred concept a concept at all?"—Is an indistinct [*unscharfe*] photograph a picture of a person at all? Is it even always an advantage to replace an indistinct picture by a sharp one? Isn't the indistinct one often exactly what we need?[1]

In a certain sense, it is the intention of the present book to provide a long-form answer to the above questions, posed by Wittgenstein, by showing how, when it comes to human beings, an openly indistinct image is preferable to a falsely sharp one. Accurately recognizing the moments where indistinct pictures become necessary, however, might be the greatest challenge yet posed for philosophical reflection. For indistinct pictures are elusive: in them, the contours of a familiar image may be discerned, yet must not be completely determined. Such an image is pervaded by something that incessantly corrodes it from within, and yet stops short of destroying it.

---

[1] WITTGENSTEIN, Ludwig; *Philosophical Investigations* I, § 71, translated by G. E. M. Anscombe. Oxford: Basil Blackwell, 1986, p. 34.

To put the issue in such terms seems profitable in view of the fact that a certain hegemonic current within contemporary philosophy understands the category of subject, in the sense bequeathed to us by modern thought, as an ontological foundation at once self-identical and substantially determined. Among the illusions that fall out of these thoughts on identity, the category of subject becomes a representative, *par excellence*, of a "historical-metaphysical period" that ought at all costs to be brought to a close.

It is from Heidegger that the assessment of the category of subject as the central concept of modern metaphysics and all its attending illusions undoubtedly stems. As a foundational category, the subject was seen as a hub from which the constitutive laws underlying all objects known and all possible experiences could be revealed. Hence affirmations such as: "Within the history of the modern age, and as the history of modern mankind, man universally and always independently attempts to establish himself as midpoint and measure in a position of dominance; that is, to pursue the securing of such dominance."[2] The dominance in question is what defines a certain mode of being, a regime of determination of experience apparently derived from the way the subject founds its own relations of unity and self-identity. As a locus for operations of rational deliberation, the category of subject reveals the nature of rational normativity.

On the other hand, Heidegger knows well what he does when he refers to "man" as subject, thereby emphasizing how the formal determinations that constitute the foundation of one's knowledge are dependent on (in the sense of having their genesis in) a certain anthropology, one which stands as the very normative core orchestrating one's form of life. Still, if one can say as much, that is out of the aforementioned anthropology that modes of acting, judging, desiring and knowing develop – that is, all the expected regularities in the cognitive, expressive and judicative abilities of subjects. In this sense, a critique aimed at the category of subject might find itself successfully assailing this anthropology that often refrains from revealing the full extent of its reach, yet ultimately colonizes our modes of thinking. Therefore, an attempt at such a critique is an attempt at awakening us from what others have termed our "anthropological sleep."

---

[2] HEIDEGGER, Martin; *Nietzsche, Volumes III & IV*, translated by J. Stambaugh, D. F. Krell & F. A. Capuzzi. San Francisco: Harper Collins, 1995, volume IV, p. 100. Also: "Man is the distinctive ground underlying every representing of beings and their truth, on which every representing and its represented is based and must be based if it is to have status and stability. Man is *subjectum* in the distinctive sense. The name and concept 'subject' in its new significance now passes over to become the proper name and essential word for man. This means that every nonhuman being becomes an *object for* this subject." (*ibid.*, p. 119)

Hence, the purpose of the present book is twofold. First, it aims to demonstrate the feasibility of an alternate reading of the modern subject, at least if one of its fundamental theoreticians is to be taken seriously, namely Hegel. The interpretive strategy that understands the Hegelian notion of subject as the culmination of those foundationalist and self-referential tendencies that hearken all the way back to Descartes is well known. Let us once again recall Heidegger's words: "it is not until Hegel thinks into the word 'experience' that what the *res cogitans* is, as the *subiectum co-agitans*, finds expression. Experience is the presentation of the absolute subject [unfolding into] representation and [therefore] is the self-absorbing absolute subject."[3] The crucial effort here, then, is to demonstrate that interpretations of this sort (and they are legion) do not do justice to Hegel's thought. Rather than the safe notion of an absolute subject self-referentially unfolding within the objects of knowledge, Hegel presents us with something quite different: the idea that "subject" denotes the process of reflexive synthesis that takes place between socially recognized modes of determination and events that are indeterminate or, to use Hegel's terms, *marked by negativity*. There is a tense recognition of indeterminacy and negativity that only occurs once a subject is present. On account of that, the essential attributes of this concept of subject simply cannot be immediate self-identity and unity (the latter always presupposed, and always ready to undo any and all effective sundering). Thus, the Hegelian subject will always, in its own way, be an indistinct picture.

To recall as much sheds light on how woefully misdirected he critique of the subject that one finds within certain hegemonic sectors of contemporary philosophy really is. Furthermore, identifying this particular mistake is more than simply a historiographical pastime, as it leads to a reflection on the need for some mistaken *parti pris* to be revised regarding what a subject can do, how it expresses itself, and what it produces.

The point allows us to discuss an additional purpose. The last two decades of philosophical reflection have seen the theme of recognition return to the foreground, a revisiting on account of which philosophical concepts whose normativity sought transcendental justification could be retraced to their social ground. This was, as has been emphasized by certain commentators, a significant sector for strategies of detranscendentalization. Contrastingly, through the problem of recognition efforts were made to unbridle contemporary reflection from the foundationalist aspirations of the philosophy of

[3] HEIDEGGER, "Hegel's Concept of Experience", in: *Off the Beaten Track*, translated by J. Young & K. Haynes. New York: Cambridge University Press, 2002, p. 139 (with alterations in brackets).

consciousness (without us having been thereby forced to follow those trails leading to the Black Forest, and to the attending critique of metaphysics).

Still, this departure from the philosophy of consciousness did not lead to an abandoning of the anthropology underlying the communicational turn in Critical Theory. The anthropology in question makes itself implicitly present in the way authors such as Habermas and Honneth ground the empirical process of one's acquisition of cognitive, judicative and desiring abilities in the developmental psychology of Jean Piaget and Lawrence Kohlberg, and in the maturational theory of Donald Winnicott. In other words, such loans are fundamental components of a project dependent on a normative anthropology. Said anthropology, while never clearly thematized, ultimately constrains us to preserve what could be termed "the current figure of man," a figure through which the individual is held up as an insurmountable model of subjective maturation. This result is far from surprising, given that one would be hard pressed to find a developmental psychology not endowed with a theory of progress aimed at setting a normative horizon for the fulfillment of those conditions that ensure the humanity of man.

Nevertheless, it seems worthwhile to insist that this anthropological figure of subjectivity presupposed by certain takes on intersubjective processes defines, in addition, a normative horizon capable of determining the general outline of a successful process of recognition, and likewise that of the suffering and sense of failure that ensue in the absence of said recognition. To change such a figure would therefore imply also changing what we understand as both success and failure regarding recognition. Taking that into consideration, it may be said this book aims to show how, from a Hegelian perspective, one may conceive of a figure of the subject that is not reducible to an anthropology the main outcome of which is the entification of the entirety of subjective activity in the figure of the individual 'I.' Towards that end, an exploration shall be undertaken of the consequences of Hegel's reflections concerning the structuring of self-consciousness through the notion of desire, the institutional mode of subject recognition within the modern state, and the nature of the relations between subject and infinitude through the modes of synthesis pertaining to time. Jointly considered, they provide the framework for a conception of subject whose main features will be revisited by some of the most significant intellectual experiences of the twentieth century. Such experiences come into involuntary association in denouncing the consequences of an *egological reduction of the subject*, and yet provide (and this is their most marked peculiarity) important coordinates in what regards a renewed notion of subjectivity.

A theory of recognition no longer dependent on the preservation of the current figure of man, or on some form of egological reduction of the subject: to furnish such a theory with a solid foundation is the main goal of this book. An essential move in the strategy employed towards the attainment of said goal consists in showing how problems present in the critique of humanism – a critique that, from the look of things, seems to have outstayed its welcome – could allow for an increase in the political applicability of the concept of recognition, freeing it from the bonds of the communicational paradigm. A much needed liberation, this, since the paradigm in question, being highly dependent on the entification of limits imposed by the grammar of common sense, is subsequently dependent on the normative horizon present in our forms of life. Such a horizon, in turn, is one which we have more than sufficient reason to make an object of criticism, as it is excessively dependent on the limits of an anthropology we cannot but term "humanistic."

For that reason, the point to be defended is that the problem of recognition ought to gradually pass from the *recognition of alterity* to the *recognition of that which suspends the regime of social normativity that renders us entirely dependent on the reiterated reproduction of the current figure of man.* This passage (which, deep down, is but the passage from alterity to abnormativity) furthermore allows for a reconstitution of the notion of freedom, delivering it from the juridical-normative paradigm that preferably conceives it as a predication of positive rights potentially enunciated via juridical ordinance. It clears the way, that is, for an understanding of freedom as being inextricably linked to the unconditionality of a non-substantial universality.

This entire discussion has yet another facet that is of considerable interest. As previously suggested, when modalities of successful recognition are defined, so is the sense-giving framework that elicits suffering and feelings of failure whenever recognition is unsuccessful. Thus, a diagnostic reflection is possible that may be of great value for a better understanding of the nature of psychic suffering in our time. The systematic clinical understanding that psychic suffering is connected to deficits in social recognition originates with Jacques Lacan. The question, then, would be to follow Lacan's perspective and demonstrate how a redirection of psychoanalysis to a Hegelian matrix may be helpful in exposing the nature of the different modalities of psychic suffering. This is an important redirection, in that it could pave the way for a deeper exploration of a fruitful psychoanalytic notion: as generally admitted, psychic suffering is connected to failure in the process of individuation, of the socialization of desires and drives, of the constitution of the I. Failures of this sort would suffice to prevent an individual from being capable of social orientation when it came to personal conduct and judgment. Without for a minute ignoring this existing matrix of suffering, however, it should be remembered that one might also suffer on account of being *merely* an I, that is, on account of one's having an overly strong attachment to an entification of individual identitary structure. This is an important dimension in the reflections of three authors that play central roles in the present work, namely Hegel, Lacan and Adorno. The suffering in question may manifest in the form of a complete incapacity to experience non-identity and indetermination (which in turn may render one incapable of receiving experiences as actual *occurrences*), in the form of that isolation that assails an individual who can no longer find traces of otherness in his or her own experience of time (loss of historicity), or, finally, in the form of a compulsive attachment to the current figure of man. These three figures of suffering shall be duly analyzed in this book.

## Gameplay

Still, before the book gets fully underway, a few remarks on the presuppositions that have guided its elaboration seem in order. The first of these concerns what is meant by the metaphor we have employed at the outset of this introduction, that is, man as an indistinct picture. Indeed, said metaphor is very expressive of our understanding of just what normativity is.

So as to properly approach the issue, let us take as a starting point the overly familiar metaphor in which the logic underlying the functioning of language is referred to as the playing of a game, as well as the equally familiar distinction between regulative rules (which regulate forms of behavior that have existed independently, before the establishment of such rules) and constitutive rules (which create or define new forms of behavior).[4] It is commonly accepted that games follow constitutive rules, and that these provide us with relative certainty concerning in-game behavior and how to evaluate situations that arise therein. The clarification of the status of some ambiguous or conflicting element would depend, then, on a *comparison* between previously determined rules and particular cases. Whether or not a specific chess move constitutes a checkmate may be ascertained, for instance, by recourse to the relevant rule: "a checkmate occurs when a king is attacked in such a manner that evasion or defense are no longer possible."

---

[4] Cf. the distinction advanced by SEARLE, John; *Speech Acts*. Cambridge: Cambridge University Press, 1999, pp. 33-35.

Still, the game of language seems rather unlike a chess match (having, as the linguist Ferdinand de Saussure once wrote,[5] players that are "largely unconscious," that is, devoid of strategy). Instead, let us conceive of a game in which only the most elementary actions are subjected to rules, elementary actions that found a domain we may term (fully aware of the weight the expression has attained within contemporary philosophy, and the polysemy its use necessarily entails) "common sense." As the game progresses, however, individual moves grow in complexity. Some hold that these more complex moves likely follow the same rules that constrained the earlier, simpler ones. That is to say, they take the grammar of common sense to be a principle against which any normativity intended as rational may be evaluated, thus naturalizing it. However, there is no absolute guarantee of that being the case. It is far from clear which particular rules should apply to which particular moves. The picture we possess of what a game consists in is not alone in being indistinct: the same is true of our picture of how it ought to be played. After a certain degree, it all takes place as though that which is founded no longer had to bear any resemblance to that which lies at its foundation. And yet, that may very well be the fundamental experience of language: the experience of playing a game the rules of which all of a sudden appear obscure. Here, a tentative answer may be put forward as to which experience has led a particular dialectical tradition to favor an indistinct image of thought over a sharp one: said tradition might be driven by a critique of *the reduction of the founding of rationality to the problem of the conditions for the clarification of normativities*. Its purpose would be to criticize the notion that to act rationally is to necessarily operate on the basis of normative structures capable of establishing and ensuring ideal regulative conditions for the determination of any experience aspiring to intersubjective validity.

After all, one could easily appeal to elementary social operations and say: common sense provides me with enough certainty regarding which actions to undertake should I wish to go grocery shopping, or how to share simple sensations I have experienced. In such cases, a kind of deep consensual bedrock may be found. Nothing of the sort exists, however, when it comes to sharing the meaning of judgments on complex values (such as, for instance, "is this a fair situation, or is it not?" or "have I acted in a way that is morally valid, or have I not?" or, finally, "is such and such a social formation free, or is it not?"). All certainty is lost in the transition from the consensual sphere of common

---

[5] SAUSSURE, Ferdinand; *Course in General Linguistics*, translated by W. Baskin. New York: McGraw-Hill Book Company, 1966, p. 72.

sense to the social-dissent-ridden sphere of complex values and principles and their modes of application.

And yet, criticisms of this nature seem to perforce lead to a zone of complete *anomie* – how else, after all, could one understand or term a situation in which no normativities remain to which one might appeal?[6] And, in a sense, was it not something very much like said anomie that threatened to overtake Aristotle if, for instance, the principle of non-contradiction were to be suspended, that is, if one were to question that cornerstone of the naturalized grammar of common sense? "We shall no longer be able to tell the difference between a man and a ship." As the philosopher suggests, walking to Megara or staying at home would amount to very much the same thing, meaning antinomies would proliferate to such a degree we would no longer be able to play the language game, nor find orientation regarding our thoughts and actions.

But the better question might perhaps be: what does it even mean to come to a decision within a context where significations have become obscure, and presuppositions are no longer immediately legible, at least not on the basis of one's previous reading knowledge and experience? Should the game be suspended and all players fall silent, or limit themselves to the most elementary and primary moves, in the conviction that after a certain point no further gameplay is possible? Such an outcome would echo Ismene's statement, "Impossible things should not be tried at all." Or should one simply leave the game to pure, sovereign will, whatever that may ultimately mean?

It is my intention to argue that an answer may be found in that lineage that goes from Hegel to Lacan and Adorno. It consists in stating that instances in which one encounters moves that are openly recalcitrant to rules are instances in which one is confronted with the potency of something not completely determined. Or, to put it differently, one finds oneself standing before the very *impotence of the rule*. In such a case, the relation between the rule and the instance it refers to is one of negation, as the instance presents itself as the bearer of a different, potential order; however (and the reservation should be given its full weight), this other order will not simply be an alternative rule. Rather, it will be an order that necessarily appears as an indistinct picture, and just as necessarily the problematization of the very notion of "abiding by a rule," or "acting on the basis of a principle." Unfortunately, these propositions can only be truly clarified (in the sense of having their full implications disclosed) later, near the end of this book.

---

[6] The term "anomie" has been adequately defined as "the effects of a weakening of the tacit norms and conventions that regulate mutual expectations, leading to a degradation of so-cial ties" (BOLTANSKI, Luc & CHIAPELLO, Eve; *Le nouvel esprit du capitalisme*. Paris: Gallimard, 1998, p. 504).

Some questions may be posed at this point: who is the speaker of such a language? Who seeks to make it his or her own irrevocable means of *expression*? What manner of subject is this, who will favor an indistinct picture over a sharp one? What manner of subject is this, who no longer finds normative effectiveness (there being no sense in speaking of "normativity" without inquiring into the conditions surrounding its current effectiveness) in "abiding by a rule" or "acting on the basis of a principle?"

These are important questions. They serve to remind us that the entification of the rational potential of the structures, present in ordinary acts of language, that validate judgment and action is and could only be founded on the promotion of the current figure of the subject – with its cognitive, practical, judicative and linguistic competencies – to the status of a regulative ideal. Similarly, others before us have insisted on the need to "reveal the moral-pedagogical dimension of common sense as an *ideal.*"[7] Indeed, to speak of a "moral-pedagogical dimension" is unavoidable, as the issue revolves around structuring judgment, as well as the normative ideals of rationality, on the basis of the behavioral dispositions of a rational subject, a *vernünftig Mensch* that is set as a paradigm for the processes of formation and maturation of empirical individuals in their multiplicity. The compound adjective "moral-pedagogical" is particularly apt, as it implies that what is at stake here is "the teaching of self-conduct," which in our case does not necessarily mean the mere adoption of value hierarchies from action-oriented contents, but "learning how to abide by a rule" or, to put it even more bluntly, "submitting one's will to a principle that may function as a universalizable rule."[8] As Nietzsche has quite clearly demonstrated, no theory of language exists that is not dependent on some kind of anthropology, on some kind of reflection on what determines the humanity of that which is human. Deep down, the question revolves around finding out *which* anthropology we actually

---

[7] PRADO JR., Bento; *Alguns ensaios*. São Paulo: Paz e Terra, 2000, p. 157.

[8] On this particular point, it may be of interest to recall how madness is seen, in the early nineteenth century, as a phenomenon fundamentally connected to the *alienation* of one's will, that is, to one's experiencing of one's own will as something that is outside oneself. Yet if the need arose to ascertain exactly what is meant by this experience of one's will as existing "outside oneself," one could do worse than appeal to the words of Foucault, for whom "It is a certain anarchic form of will which consists in never wanting to submit to the will of others [*making it, therefore, fundamentally asocial*]; it is a will which refuses to organize itself in the mode of the individual's monarchical will, which consequently refuses any order and any kind of integration within a system" (FOUCAULT, Michel; *Psychiatric Power: Lectures at the Collège de France 1973-74*, translated by G. Burchell. New York: Palgrave Macmillan, 2006, p. 215, our brackets). The problem, in other words, largely concerns the modes available for the constitution of synthetic units.

want. Taking that into account, it could be said that – to refer back to the vocabulary of the remarks of Wittgenstein's which opened this text –, "once we have abandoned our belief in language as a clear image, accepting man as an indistinct picture becomes all but unavoidable." Thus, it could be said that the critique of rationality's adequacy to determine the conditions for the clarification of normativity necessarily brings with it a problematization of the concept of subject. After all, the moment one becomes persuaded of its critical validity, understanding the rational subject as being capable of positing itself as a privileged source of modes of judgment, volition and action, on the basis of aprioristically deduced normative structures, simply becomes an untenable proposition.

In this sense, the present book seeks to confront problems that have been addressed, albeit in preliminary fashion, in my previous book, *Cynicism and Critical Failure*. Its purpose was to expose a specific social pathology,[9] namely cynicism, through an analysis of modes of interversion between normativity and anomie. In that context, the term "cynicism" was meant to denote a process of decomposition of values and normative criteria that seemed like the most valuable outcome of our modern expectations concerning social rationalization. In the analysis attempted therein, I have attached special importance to the fact that the decomposition in question was responsible for the reconfiguration of processes of socialization and individuation. "Socialization" subsequently attains the sense of *the constitution of individualities capable of handling the generalization of situations of social anomie*, whether in the sphere of language, of labor or of desire, with anomie paradoxically becoming an essential condition for the normal functioning of current capitalist societies.[10]

While the aforementioned analysis will indeed be carried forward here, it will follow a different path. The discussion will be centered on the conditions of possibility for the development of a concept of subject able to provide us with the initial coordinates (and the provisional character of something that

---

[9] This particular acceptation of the concept of "pathology" owes much to the works of Axel Honneth, in particular HONNETH, Axel; *La societé du mépris: Vers une nouvelle Théorie critique* (Paris: Découverte, 2006), and *Pathologies of Reason: On the Legacy of Critical Theory* (translated by J. Ingram. New York: Columbia University Press, 2009). Nevertheless, our usage bears a significant dissimilarity from the conception advanced by the German philosopher, in that its normative horizon is defined by recourse to a theory of intersubjectivity inspired by the discussions surrounding communicative rationality. Its application, thus, has little parallel to the one proposed by Honneth.

[10] Cf. e.g. the chapter "Para uma crítica da economia libidinal" ["Towards a critique of libidinal economy"], in SAFATLE, Vladimir; Cinismo e falência da crítica ["Cynicism and Critical Failure"]. São Paulo: Boitempo, 2008, pp. 113-146.

merely aims to provide "initial coordinates" cannot be stressed enough) for a restructuring of the notion of rationality, with a view towards its emancipation from the notion of intersubjectively-shared normativity and all its possible interversions. How can one conceive of an *overcoming* of this figure of rational normativity that amounts to more than a mere reversal of *perversion*? Put differently, on what grounds are we to reconsider our usual understanding of "rational action"?

## A differently conceived subject

At this point, a justification for the intellectual effort expended in what follows to establish a developmental through line linking Hegel to Lacan and Adorno seems fitting. The earliest iteration of said effort could be found in my first book, *The Passion of the Negative: Lacan and Negative Dialectic*, where I have argued that, at a given moment of its history, psychoanalysis – a clinical practice of fundamental importance for the constitution of the contemporary framework for reflections on the structure of subjectivity and its processes of recognition – arrived at elaborations harking back to the category of subject as found in Hegel. As I have attempted to demonstrate, the impact of this confluence extended beyond its localized appearance, laying new grounds for and urging fresh development in regards to fundamental clinical problems, such as properly defining notions such as "mental illness," "treatment," and "cure." In the present work there will be occasion to engage with a number of these issues, that they may subsequently provide a firm footing for additional developments.

In the final segment of that book I endeavored to present the general coordinates for an approximation between Lacan and a contemporary of his who, similarly attempting to articulate Hegel and Freud, arrived at conceptions that converged significantly with the French psychoanalyst's, even while privileging the sphere of the aesthetic over that of the clinical for confrontations with empiricity – namely, Theodor Adorno. The ensuing approximation between aesthetic issues and clinical ones had a precedent, to an extent, in Lacan's repeated attempts to rethink *the modes of subjectivation available to the psychoanalytic clinic through a certain configuration of the aesthetic reflection on the arts*, as if processes of subjectivation could be thought in tandem with mechanisms of aesthetic formalization.

However, this attempt at a comparative study of Lacan and Adorno did not have as its sole impetus the realization that, regardless of how dissimilar their traditions might have been, a similarly creative (if tense) articulation between

Hegelian and Freudian notions could be found at the basis of their intellectual experiences; it seemed equally significant to point out how these two attentive readers of the problems that arose in the wake of Hegelian dialectics managed to renew the modes available for sustaining the principle of subjectivity *by means of strategies that were absolutely convergent.* Rather than proclaiming the death of the subject, or promoting a return to the immanence of being, to the archaic, to the ineffable, both were willing to sustain the principle of subjectivity, even while stripping from it any identitarian notions.

In their hands, the subject ceases to be a substantial entity that grounds processes of self-determination, and becomes *the locus of non-identity, and of sundering.* This is an operation that grows in intelligibility as one recalls how the Hegelian root shared by Lacan and Adorno allows for a fundamental articulation between subject and negation that evinces an important strategy for the sustaining of the figure of the subject in contemporaneity.[11] Thus, non-identity – that is to say, an irrecoverable negativity that is fundamental for the structuring of a sustainable subjectivity within the universal medium of language – can feature as a utopian horizon for Adorno while simultaneously representing that which must be recognized by the subject at the end of the Lacanian psychoanalytic process. This non-identity features most prominently, in the particular case of the subject, in the latter's confrontation with experiences of depersonalization, experiences which have their manifestation mainly within the spheres of desire, the body and sexuality. If due importance is given to such experiences, it may be said – and the precise meaning and implications of the assertion is something the present book aims to clarify – that the "subject" must not be taken to be a self-identical substantial entity capable of self-determination through reflexivity, an entity among whose fundamental predicates one would supposedly find potential autonomy of action and behavior (leading to the imputability of legal persons), coherent unity in both representations and personality, and the capacity for reflexive thinking. Instead, *the possibility ought to be entertained, and the consequences weighed, of applying the term "subject" to the reflexive process of confrontation with the impersonal as manifested, in particular, in desire, in the body and in sexuality.* The reasons that might convince us to give a process of that nature the name of "subject" shall be dutifully disclosed, of course, and in detail.

---

[11] This common Hegelian root ought to be given its full import, Hegel being a central reference – as well as a source of much conflict – for Lacan and Adorno both; indeed, it would be a mistake to consider the Hegelian slant of Lacan's thought as being solely derived from the impact of Kojève and Hyppolite's conceptions on Lacan's early writings and seminars.

So as to make this notion sufficiently clear, the starting point of this book will be an attempt to show how the origins of the latter conception of subject may be found in Hegel's reflections on the process of individuation. Adequately conducted, this should allow us to pose the following questions: to what an extent does a defense of this conception of subject – one found in both Lacan and Adorno – allow for a systematic and (in this context, the qualification seems justified) *faithful* development of reflections present in Hegel's intellectual experience? And yet, how could two authors that never missed an opportunity to openly criticize both Hegel and the horizon of reconciliation presupposed by his system be said to be in any way *faithful* to Hegel? And, last but not least, what is there to be gained from an insistence on such faithfulness?

## Reading strategies

Here, it may seem worthwhile to point out a few presuppositions that have generally oriented my reading and, consequently, the elaboration of not only this book, but the entirety of my textual production thus far. Towards that one may wish to recall a brief remark of Kant's on the reading of philosophical texts:

> When we compare the thoughts that an author expresses about a subject, in ordinary speech as well as in writings, it is not at all unusual to find that we understand him even better than he understood himself, since he may not have determined his concept sufficiently and hence sometimes spoke, or even thought, contrary to his own intention.[12]

This seemingly innocent passage points to a reading program apparently at odds with the accepted rules of interpretive rigor. After all, Kant himself seems to acknowledge that his reading is, so to speak, *symptomatological*: a search across the surface of a text for instances where letter and spirit clash, where the author *thinks against his own intentions*, where *the text thinks against the intentions of its own author*. Still, what does admitting of a thought that comes unglued from the very intention that gives rise to it, and that leaves traces of this separation in the texts it then produces, ultimately amount to?

More than anything, it seems to suggest there is a need for greater and renewed attention when it comes to textual regions in which the project of a philosophical system is driven by the implacable concatenation of its concepts

---

[12] KANT, Immanuel; *Critique of Pure Reason*, translated by P. Guyer & A. W. Wood. Cambridge: Cambridge University Press, 1998, A 314/B 370, p. 396.

to branch out in unforeseen directions; attention, that is, to structures that break through the conscious aspect of the text and leave behind discordant traces among the paths blazed by the writing. On this point, at least, it is rather difficult to agree with Victor Goldschmidt, for whom "the assertions of a system cannot have causes, whether they be immediate or imaginary, that are not known to the philosopher, and by him claimed as such."[13] The history of philosophy shows, on the contrary, that it is entirely possible to base a reflection on something an author has given thought to without knowing or realizing he or she was doing so. One could even argue that *a text, and most of all a philosophical text, invariably consists in a tense process of negotiation* – as though a true philosophical text were always and necessarily a field composed of divergent and competing "lines of force," its writing a ceaseless history of abandonments, restrictions and surprises. As though every philosopher, when writing, unavoidably set in motion conceptual machinery he or she could barely control.[14] Inside the text there is something at work that exceeds what its author *intends* to say, unless we agree to decouple this "intending to say" from the notion of *conscious intentionality*, from "causes… known to the philosopher," and from all such devices still connecting the figure of the author to themes inherited from a philosophy of consciousness. Within the text, the tense dynamic of previous texts still presses on.

Thus, our attention may be profitably directed at that which a philosopher has produced without knowing why he or she did so; in addition to logical time, some form of *transversal time* should be admitted, allowing the present to articulate fresh questions and revise past answers. The *fundamental transversality* of philosophical time suggests that, without disregarding the tension inherent to operations of the sort, the present may successfully search those texts of which the philosophical tradition is composed in the attempt to locate the remnants of potential elaborations that have been abandoned along the way. In other words, *there is much to be gained from the reading of a text in the philosophical tradition that bears in mind its ultimate fate.* In such a text, read retrospectively, traces may be found of later debates; its autonomous trajectory

---

[13] GOLDSCHMIDT, Victor; "Tempo lógico e tempo histórico na interpretação dos sistemas filosóficos" ["Logical and historical time in the interpretation of philosophical systems"]. In: *A religião de Platão* ["Plato's Religion"]. São Paulo: Difusão Européia do Livro, 1963, p. 141.

[14] In this sense, our assent should be given to the following remark by Adorno: "The art of reading [Hegel] should take note of where something new begins, some content, and where a machine that was not intended to be a machine is simply running and ought not to keep on doing so. At every moment one needs to keep two seemingly incompatible maxims in mind: painstaking immersion in detail, and free detachment" (ADORNO, Theodor; *Hegel: Three Studies*, translated by S. W. Nicholsen. Cambridge: the MIT Press, 1993, pp. 94-95).

being properly mapped, it may be possible to pinpoint its later reappearance in, and appropriation by, debates to which it would at first seem to bear little relation. The implication being that later philosophical programs have been constituted on the basis of contentious disagreements regarding the meaning of the letter of said text, a text which has steadfastly refused to remain in the past. Such disagreements are often of the silent variety, and (the expression, here, is being employed in a very precise manner) *unconsciously played out*, like a structure subjects at once support and have their choices determined by, with no elaboration being necessarily required on their part. This, on account of philosophical texts having a significant peculiarity: their processes of negotiation do not merely involve the actors present at the scene of their composition, but relate to actors that will not come along until a future date.

This reading strategy seeks to justify a procedure that is central for the realization of this book's project: a consideration of how major problems stemming from the Hegelian theory of individuation, as presented in the first three chapters of this book, reappear in Lacan and Adorno's grappling with certain core Freudian concepts, including his notions of drive, fantasy and development. These remarks should not be understood to mean that, aware of the problems Hegelian philosophy had given rise to, Lacan and Adorno sought their resolution in a haphazard amalgamation of Hegel's thought and Freudian theory; rather, Lacan and Adorno's recourse to Hegel brought them not only greater familiarity with certain themes and procedures peculiar to the German philosopher, but, most of all, allowed for their subterraneous development of possibilities hidden among Hegel's notions. Through such possibilities, in turn, they were able to creatively confront questions connected to the problem of the constitution of individualities in Freud.

## *A* caveat

Before the book gets underway, it should be said the provisional, indicial character of a number of its elaborations is by no means lost on their author. Additionally, some of the actual results the investigation has yielded have surprised and disturbed me, a state of affairs to be expected, perhaps, given my growing disbelief in the personalistic illusions of the author function and waning sense of authorship in relation to that which I write. It could be argued that some of the ideas the present book entertains could benefit from additional maturation; the suggestion, however, fails to take into consideration the existence of two classes of writer: those who set down the systematic elaboration of a long-pondered, fully-assured intellectual experience, and those who write as though to exorcize a hypothesis that has caused them great torment, a hypothesis that cannot but appear "too early," and is only thenceforth refined. And if the author of the present book feels something of a kinship to those of the latter sort, he could perhaps be excused for making his own the following words, originally uttered by Michel Foucault:

> As to those for whom to work hard, to begin and begin again, to attempt and be mistaken, to go back and rework everything from top to bottom, and still find reason to hesitate from one step to the next – as to those, in short, for whom to work in the midst of uncertainty and apprehension is tantamount to failure, all I can say is that clearly we are not from the same planet.[15]

---

[15] FOUCAULT, *The History of Sexuality, Vol. 2: The Use of Pleasure*, translated by R. Hurley. New York: Vintage Books, 1990, p. 7.

# I.
# Desire

# CHAPTER I

# Love is colder than death

*Of course all life is a process of breaking down,*
*but the blows that do the dramatic side of the work [...]*
*don't show their effect all at once.*
Scott Fitzgerald

At a time when the universality of Spirit has gathered such strength, and the singular detail, as is fitting, has become correspondingly less important, when, too, that universal aspect claims and holds on to the whole range of the wealth it has developed, the share in the total work of Spirit which falls to the individual can only be very small. Because of this, the individual must all the more forget himself, as the nature of Science implies and requires. Of course, he must make of himself and achieve what he can; but less must be demanded of him, just as he in turn can expect less of himself, and may demand less for himself.[1]

These remarks – taken from Hegel's *Phenomenology of Spirit* – stand as an adequate synthesis of all that has been imputed to the German philosopher by multiple hegemonic strands in twentieth-century philosophical thought: the philosopher of Absolute Knowledge in its totality, who is nevertheless unable to account for the irreducibility of difference, or of individual aspirations for recognition, through his strategies of conceptual synthesis. In him one finds the most highly refined expression of the philosophical belief that thinking is not possible save through the articulation of strongly hierarchical systems, as well as a subsequent disregard for the ontological dignity of contingency – that very contingency that "can expect less" of itself, and "may demand less" for itself. He is the defender of a notion of history wherein the present evinces a strengthened "universality of spirit" – a teleological history which is, at the same time, incapable of grasping a time in which any occurrences remain possible.[2]

---

[1]  HEGEL, G.W.F.; *Phenomenology of Spirit*, translated by A. V. Miller. Oxford: Oxford University Press, 1977, § 72, p. 45.

[2]  Even among Young Hegelians, suggests Habermas, those may be found who "insist on the

Common to all such accusations is the perceived failure of Hegelian thought to adequately account for a particular that could not and should not be reduced to the condition of mere particularity. It is as if, in Hegel, the particular were nothing but the occasion for the concrete actualization of the universal, and thus having in itself no reality. All these indictments seem to resonate with Adorno's diagnosis:

> If Hegel had carried the doctrine of the identity of universal and particular farther, to a dialectic in the particular itself, the particular – which according to him is simply the mediated universal – would have been granted the same right as the universal. That he depreciates this right into a mere urge and psychologistically blackens the right of man as narcissism – like a father chiding his son, "Maybe you think you're something special" – this is not an individual lapse on the philosopher's part.[3]

"Not an individual lapse in the philosopher's part" in the sense that it ought to be regarded as a flaw pervading the entirety of his system.

Yet one may be justified in questioning the viability of such interpretations; did Hegel simply ignore the preconditions required for the recognition of individuality? Or could it be that his was, instead, an attempt at setting up conditions for a renewed understanding of processes of individuation? Are we here confronted with the limits of Hegel's philosophy, or is it rather the pivotal point of a vast project whose aim is to conceive individuality anew, an aim we have yet to measure up to?

We know that Hegel developed his concept of individuality with recourse to the notion of self-consciousness. What we often forget is that Hegelian self-consciousness is not a mentalist concept, that it does not merely refer to the reflexivity of a self-sufficient subjectivity whose limits are established in relation to that which is external to it; rather, Hegelian self-consciousness is a relational concept, the function of which is to describe certain ways the subject and the other overlap, and which therefore has constitutive value for one's experience of self. As a relational concept, the most significant among the practically applicable attributes of self-consciousness (such as determinacy,

---

*desublimation* of a spirit that merely draws the real oppositions emerging at a given time into the suction of an absolute relation-to-self, so as to de-actualize them, to transpose them into the mode of the shadowy transparency of a remembered past – and to strip them of all seriousness" (HABERMAS, Jürgen; *The Philosophical Discourse of Modernity: Twelve Lectures*, translated by F. G. Lawrence. Cambridge: The MIT Press, 1990, p. 54).

3   ADORNO, *Negative Dialectics*, translated by E. B. Ashton. New York: The Continuum Publishing Company, 1983, p. 329.

freedom and accountability) can only be truly understood once one abandons the belief that the experience of ipseity rests upon the entification of formal principles of identity and unity. Self-consciousness, after all, is not founded on an immediate apprehension of self-identity, but rather on an apprehension of precisely that which negates its immanent determinacy. To employ a more contemporary terminology, one could say that Hegelian self-consciousness is the locus for a fundamental experience of non-identity that is manifested through the material relations between the subject and the other, such relations being understood through the figures of labor, desire and language. The consequences of this conception of non-identity for reflections on the practical dimension of action shall be gradually sketched throughout the remainder of this book.

Yet to say self-consciousness is a relational concept is to say very little, since that might mean no more than that subjectivity is, from the very first and without exception, dependent on an intersubjective structure of relations by which it is both preceded and constituted. Still, Hegel seems to be getting at something more. If we are to uncover exactly what, we must better understand *who this other is* one finds oneself in relation to in constitutive experiences that take place in the fields of labor, language and desire. Could it be merely another self-consciousness? Or does it consist in a deeper alterity, one that stands beyond what an individuality is able to determine as an object of mental representation and, as such, leads to one's confrontation with something that is, from the perspective of consciousness, entirely indeterminate? And what exactly should be understood, in this context, by the rather vague expression "a deeper alterity"?

Regardless of what the answers to such questions may ultimately be, following the second hypothesis might prove useful in gaining a better understanding of why, for Hegel, free individuality (that individuality that has completed its process of formation) is *that which brings to the sphere of determinacy the disruptive force of a confrontation with indeterminacy*, and, therein, has the ability to weaken all manner of limiting adherence to finite determinateness. Perhaps this is what Hegel meant by such statements as "freedom lies neither in indeterminacy nor in determinacy, but is both at once,"[4] or "'I' is the transition [*Ubergehen*] from undifferentiated indeterminacy to *differentiation*, *determination*, and the *positing* of a determinacy as a content and object."[5] Let us not forget that, as a transition, 'I' preserves those moments

---

[4]  HEGEL, *Elements of the Philosophy of Right*, translated by H. B. Nisbet. Cambridge: Cambridge University Press, 1991, § 7, p. 42.

[5]  Ibid., § 6, p. 39.

it brings into relation with one another in its movement towards its opposite – which is to say that it must preserve something of that which is not yet an 'I,' something pre-individual.

This confrontation with indeterminacy as a fundamental process for the constitution of individuality shall become clearer once we inquire into the purpose of *limit experiences* such as those concerning death, or the anguish involved in the formation of self-consciousness. We shall see that, far from providing support for an "existentialist" take on Hegelian phenomenology, or justification for a moralizing approach centering on resentment and resignation as the inevitable consequences of one's confrontation with finitude (the latter being Deleuze's perspective and, to an extent, Gérard Lebrun's[6]), death and anguish have very precise and logical functions in the formation of self-consciousness. What they point to is the necessary process of opening up to that which – from the perspective of a self-consciousness caught up in a mode of thinking marked by the finitude of representation and of the modes of categorization available to the understanding – can only appear as a lack of determinacy. In this sense, Kojève's intuition concerning the centrality of the confrontation with death in the formation of self-consciousness was, ironically, not entirely mistaken; his work simply lacked an adequate account of the phenomenological function of the processes in question.

To insist on this aspect should allow us to see how, from a Hegelian perspective, the recognition of individuality cannot be restricted to the mere recognition of demands for positive individual rights, even those rights that do not easily fit into determined, normative contexts. This is something Honneth seems to imply when expressing his difficulty in understanding why "the anticipation of one's own or the other's death is supposed to lead to the recognition, in particular, of the claim to individual rights"[7] – the same Honneth who sees experiences of indeterminacy mostly as a source of suffering, a state of "agonizing emptiness" for consciousness.[8]

---

[6] Cf. DELEUZE, Gilles; *Nietzsche and Philosophy*, translated by H. Tomlinson. London: Continuum, 2002, as well as LEBRUN, Gérard; *L'envers de la dialectique* ["The reverse of dialectics"]. Paris: Seuil, 2004. Both authors – each in his own particular way – confront Hegel with themes derived from the Nietzschean critique of morality. My appreciation goes out to professor Ernani Chaves, who first pointed out to me the deep structural similarities to be found in their individual critiques of Hegel.

[7] HONNETH, *The Struggle for Recognition: The Moral Grammar of Social Conflicts*, translated by J. Anderson. Cambridge: The MIT Press, 1995, p. 48.

[8] HONNETH, *Suffering from Indeterminacy: An Attempt at a Reactualization of Hegel's Philosophy of Right: Two Lectures*, trans. by J. Ben-Levi. Assen: Van Gorcum, 2000, p. 57.

Indeed, if we restrict our understanding to the idea that individual rights – singular expressions of autonomy and freedom – demand recognition, the issue shall remain unresolved. This, however, does not seem to be what Hegel had in mind. So much so that he does not hesitate in affirming that, while one may attain recognition as a person without risking one's life, the same cannot be said for recognition as an autonomous, independent self-consciousness – as if the true autonomy of self-consciousness could only manifest itself in a terrain that lies beyond (or perhaps beneath) the person conceived as a legal entity, as a bearer of positive rights and individualizing determinations. The facts persuade us, therefore, that Hegel meant to uncover the affinity between the constitution of subjects and confrontations with that which cannot be found save in experiences of negativity and uprooting; these, in turn, are profoundly similar to confrontations with that which weakens our particularized contexts and overdetermined worldviews. Hegel's cunning, then, consists in demonstrating how lingering before such negativity may be the condition for the constitution of a thought imbued, as concerns subjects, with universal applicability.[9]

That being the case, the tensions intrinsic to Hegel's theory of recognition cannot be understood through dualities such as the one advanced by Habermas:

> "I" understand myself simultaneously as "a person" [*Person überhaupt*] and as an "unmistakeably unique individual" [*unverwechselbares Individuum*]. I am a person in general, sharing personhood – the constitutive features of knowing, speaking, and acting subjects – with everyone else, but I am also an unmistakably unique individual who is shaped by, responsible for, and irreplaceable in a unique life history.[10]

Interpretations of this nature rely on a personalistic notion of individuality, a notion connected to the 'I' as the figure of complete determinacy. This precludes the possibility of a more fluid conception of individuality, where all determinacy is corroded by a backdrop of indeterminacy that weakens its identity and its fixity. Moreover, such interpretations tend to frame universality

---

[9] In this sense, the perspective presented here has much in common with statements such as the following: "We might consider a certain post-Hegelian reading of the scene of recognition in which precisely my own opacity to myself occasions my capacity to confer a certain kind of recognition on others. It would be, perhaps, an ethics based on our shared, invariable, and partial blindness about ourselves" (BUTLER, Judith; *Giving an Account of Oneself*. New York: Fordham University Press, 2005, p. 41).

[10] HABERMAS, *Truth and Justification*, translated by B. Fultner. Cambridge: The MIT Press, 2003, p. 186.

as a normative, essentialist concept by defining it through a determined set of "essential personal properties" that are never up for questioning, and never a source of conflict, but the engine driving the network of demands within social conflicts. This is a path that necessarily leads to the substantialization of an anthropological conception of subject. As we shall see, it is precisely in order to prevent deviations of this kind that Hegel so obstinately insists that the path towards universality must unavoidably go through the "labor of the negative" and the "way of despair."

## Ontogeneses and conflicts

If we were to reconstruct the fundamental structure of Hegel's theory of the development of self-consciousness, we would find that it entails a consideration of the ontogenesis of the practical-cognitive capacities of subjects; an ontogenesis that occurs through processes of socialization and individuation. These are conceptions that ultimately pertain to an investigation of the empirical genesis of our cognitive abilities and of our schemes for rational determination of action. However, instead of beginning with an analysis of practices of socialization effected through identifications within elementary nuclei of social interaction (family, civil society, institutions, state), Hegel instead begins with something akin to a general phenomenological matrix to allow for the intelligibility of such processes. The matrix in question is the Master-Slave dialectic (hereafter referred to as MSD).

We are well aware of contemporary attempts to invalidate the central role the MSD plays in the formation and recognition of self-consciousness. Robert Williams, for instance, writes that "it is not the full process of reciprocal recognition but the failure to achieve such reciprocal recognition that receives emphasis. For this reason, the figure of master/slave tends to dominate the *Phenomenology's* account of intersubjectivity."[11] For the commentator, it is only in the system developed by Hegel in his maturity that the "full process" is finally presented. However, such critiques fail to recognize that the *Phenomenology* is indeed the full version of the system, albeit merely *from the perspective of consciousness*, in the same way that the *Science of Logic* is the full version of the system *from the perspective of objective knowledge*. Thus, it is never prudent to ask the *Phenomenology* for more than it claims to offer.

---

[11] WILLIAMS, Robert; *Hegel's Ethics of Recognition*. Berkeley: University of California Press, 1998, p. 47.

The uneasiness a number of Hegelian commentators feel relative to the MSD stems mainly from the fact that it reveals processes of social recognition as mediated by a desire that posits conflict as an ontological substratum; which is to say that said desire appears from the very beginning as something that constitutes relations solely through dynamics of domination and servitude (later we will examine the consequences of conferring ontological dignity to conflict). Through desire one seeks to submit the other to the condition of object; devoid of all autonomy, the essence of the latter is a blank canvas upon which one may exercise one's desire. Still, as desire is the very first mode of relating to the other, the conflict it initiates presses upon self-consciousness with all the weight of an ontological fact.

If that is indeed the case, there would seem to be an inconsistency in the scheme propounded by Hegel; for, as Siep puts it, "according to Hegel, the process of recognition begins with the fact that the self is 'outside of itself,' that it is cancelled as being-for-itself, and intuits itself only in the other. However this structure is not one of struggle, but of love ..."[12] A conflict with the other only makes sense insofar as it presupposes that the other *must be, and is* capable of recognizing me. Were I to believe the other incapable of doing so (on account of, say, being insane), or have reason not to want the other to recognize me (for example, someone I despise), then there would be no demand for recognition, no attempt to submit the other's system of interests to my desire. Yet if I believe the other must be and is capable of recognizing me, then that is on account of there being a sort of pre-established connection one might indeed term "love"; such a connection functions here as an initial, unproblematic ground for intersubjective relations. In this way, Hegel would have been justified in introducing the conflictual processes of recognition between subjects with a discussion of love as a normative foundation for social demands for recognition that are present in processes of interaction – an introduction which, incidentally, he attempted as a young lecturer.[13]

In revisiting the MSD, however, it is clear that Hegel could not give his assent to contemporary attempts to reinstate love as an "intersubjective structure of reciprocal recognition"[14] that ought to be presupposed as a

---

[12] SIEP, Ludwig; "Der Kampf um Anerkennung. Zur Auseinandersetzung Hegels mit Hobbes in den Jenaer Schriften." In: *Hegel-Studien*, Bd.9, Bonn 1974, p. 194 *apud* WILLIAMS, *op. cit.*, p. 20.

[13] Cf. HEGEL, *The Jena System 1804-5: Logic and Metaphysics* (lectures at Jena, 1804-5), tr. J. Burbidge & G. di Giovanni. Montreal: McGill-Queen's University Press, 1986; and HEGEL, *Hegel and the Human Spirit: A Translation of the Jena Lectures on the Philosophy of Spirit* (1805-6), trans. by L. Rauch. Detroit: Wayne State University Press, 1983.

[14] HABERMAS, *Truth and Justification*, p. 205. The most systematic – and celebrated, justly so – among such attempts is Axel Honneth's, in his *The Struggle for Recognition*.

primary intersubjective ground for the safe, normalized development of any and all processes of social determination of individuality – or at least not insofar as we understand love through the communicational paradigm of mutually complementary, mutually dependent relations. For there is a strong possibility that Hegel meant to advance a rather different position: processes of interaction and socialization are mediated by a form of desire whose opacity and negativity compromise the primacy of intersubjective love.[15] This is a desire that cannot attain gratification unless it recognizes itself in an individuality where the I is (and, in a certain sense, shall always and irreducibly be) outside of itself – a desire the gratification of which even leads to forsaking the I as a highly individuated form.

It is beyond dispute that desire, as a negative relation towards an object, must be overcome; however, this overcoming does not imply the recovery of some form of reciprocal interaction between strongly individualized and determinate subjects, nor that pre-personal processes of symbiotic indifferentiation should be set as a horizon for the development of social relations. As I would like to demonstrate, the experience of the negativity of desire may, to a certain extent, be preserved as the basis for a reconstruction of the modes of relation with the self and with the other; this is a position that, ultimately, demands the problematization of every conception of love in terms of communicational paradigms of any sort.[16]

A return to the context in which desire is introduced in Hegel's *Phenomenology* is rather enlightening: a discussion concerning the conditions required for self-consciousness and consciousness of an object to attain unity. Recalling that the notion of "phenomenon," understood as a difference which has no being of its own (in that it is merely an appearing-for-the-Other), was not a figure of the unity of self-consciousness with itself, but rather the

---

[15] It should be recalled that one finds in the *Phenomenology of Spirit* an explicit critique of love as a founding principle for intersubjective relations, in the section named after the notions employed towards that end, "Pleasure and Necessity." Additionally, insists Hegel, self-consciousness' End is "seeing itself *as this particular individual* in another, or seeing another self-consciousness as itself" (§ 359). This intuition, however, cannot be fulfilled save through the submission of the other to the negative essence of a completely restless enjoyment, or *jouissance*. The point, then, is not to confusedly collapse "love" and "pleasure," but rather recall that Hegel's approach to hedonism may provide us with a model through which we may put into question the possibility of social actualization of a notion of love founded on the communicational paradigm of mutually complementary, mutually dependent relations.

[16] This may explain why Jacques Lacan – an early reader of the MSD – developed a notion of love that cannot be regarded as a figure of some form of primary intersubjectivity, but requires one to operate, instead, with concepts such as "subjective destitution": it was perhaps the only strategy allowing for the recovery of a notion of love able to meet the philosophical demands of Hegel's experience of negativity.

very nexus of separation (as essentiality must ever reside in an inaccessible Other, the thing-in-itself), Hegel writes that "this unity must become essential to self-consciousness, i.e. self-consciousness is *Desire* in general [*Begierde über-haupt*]."[17]

Yet what does this introduction of what Hegel terms "desire in general" – not desire for this or that particular object, but understood in a general sense as a mode of relation for interactions between subject and object – ultimately entail? It may be inferred that the unity of self-consciousness with that which had become "embedded in things" as an essence beyond phenomena, the unity between knowledge and the essential determination of objects, only becomes possible once we understand relations between subject and object to be more than mere relations of knowing; but rather, and primarily, relations of desire and gratification.

An assertion of this nature may at first seem rash; could it be Hegel was setting in motion some form of wild psychologism aimed at submitting cognitive expectations to practical, teleological interests? Or was he instead insisting, in the best tradition of reflection on desire, such as may also be found in Nietzsche or Freud, that reason determines its procedures (that is, defines what may be termed rational or legitimate) on the basis of interests directed at the accomplishment of practical ends, interests that thus lead to a restoration of the philosophical category of "desire" to a condition of dignity?

The second alternative seems to be the case. Here we may follow the lead of a commentator who clearly agrees with such an interpretation, Robert Pippin:

> Hegel appears to be saying that the problem of objectivity, of what we are willing to count as an objective claim in the first place, *is* the problem of the satisfaction of desire, that the "truth" is wholly relativized to pragmatic ends. [...] It looks like Hegel is claiming, as many have done in the nineteenth and twentieth centuries, that what counts as a successful explanation depends on what practical problem we want solved, [...] that "knowledge" is a function of "human interests."[18]

However, this would also imply that Hegel was fully committed to a form of relativism that subjects universalizing aspirations to truth to the contingency of contexts marked by particular interests and desires – unless, of course, Hegel's work can be found to demonstrate that practical interests are not guided by the particularity of appetites and inclinations; but that by engaging

---

[17] HEGEL, *Phenomenology of Spirit*, p. 105.
[18] PIPPIN, Robert; *Hegel's Idealism: The Satisfaction of Self-Consciousness*. Cambridge: Cambridge University Press, 1989, p. 148.

with the sphere of practicality towards the gratification of their desires, subjects necessarily actualize the universalizing aspirations of reason. Let us recall, furthermore, that as he does not admit of strict distinctions between the empirical and the transcendental, Hegel is unwilling to allow for a strict distinction between pathological desire and that free will whose recognition was held as the required foundation for the constitution of the universe of rights. There is something of that universality of free will already to be found within desire.

Statements of this nature seem to go against hegemonic tendencies present in twentieth-century critical thought. One might recall, for instance, the question – inspired by Freudian psychoanalysis and its description of the conflictual nature of the processes of socialization that take place within the family unit, or that depend on the internalization of social law – that recurred among theoreticians of the Frankfurt School: what do we sacrifice in fully adjusting to the demands for rationality and universality of hegemonic processes of desire socialization? And at what cost do such demands become viable? What is the price of upholding assertions such as "true freedom is ethical life [*Sittlichkeit*], where the will has for its purposes a universal content, not subjective, i.e. self-centred content"?[19] Are we not merely confronted with a perspective that, as Adorno once put it, "psychologistically blackens the right of man as narcissism"?

The significance of these questions should not be underestimated. Let us consider the case of Adorno, for whom the modes available for organizing reality within advanced capitalism, as well as the regimes presiding over its social-interaction dynamics and socialization hubs, were dependent on the implementation of a metaphysics of identity: a metaphysics responsible for guiding the ontogenesis of the practical-cognitive abilities of subjects through an internalization of demands for unity that orient the formation

---

[19] HEGEL, *Enzyklopädie der philosophischen Wissenschaften*, § 469. English language version. *Encyclopedia of the Philosophical Sciences, Part III: The Philosophy of Mind*, translated by W. Wallace & A. V. Miller, revised by M. Inwood. Oxford: Oxford University Press, 2007, § 469, p. 206. It is interesting to consider how distant such statements are from perspectives such as Freud's, who – more congenially, as far as contemporary sensibilities go – wrote that "a good part of the struggles of mankind centre round the single task of finding an expedient accommodation – one, that is, that will bring happiness – between this claim of the individual and the cultural claims of the group; and one of the problems that touches the fate of humanity is whether such an accommodation can be reached by means of some particular form of civilization or whether this conflict is irreconcilable" (FREUD, Sigmund; "Civilization and Its Discontents." In: *The Standard Edition of the Complete Psychological Works of Sigmund Freud, Volume XXI (1927-1931): The Future of an Illusion, Civilization and its Discontents, and Other Works*, edited and translated by J. Strachey. London: The Hogarth Press and the Institute of Psycho-analysis, 1961, p. 96).

of the I and repress whatever belongs to the order of the body, of drives and of sexuality (that is, whatever pertains to desire). If Adorno feels justified in writing that "the identity of the self and its alienation are companions from the beginning,"[20] that is mainly because that mode of socialization that seeks to constitute individualities follows a logic derived from the internalization of a repressive law of identity. Hence, statements such as the following:

> The dawning sense of freedom feeds upon the memory [*Erinnerung*] of the archaic impulse [*Impuls*] not yet steered by any solid I. The more the I curbs [*zügeln*] that impulse, the more chaotic and thus questionable will it find the pre-temporal [*vorzeitlich*] freedom.[21]

These remarks suggest that analyses of social reality, critiques of the metaphysics of identity and critiques of the ontogenesis of practical-cognitive abilities are entirely inseparable; moreover, it is precisely their essential connectedness that led Adorno to feel legitimately justified in opposing Hegel, that same Hegel that could not bring himself to see that the actualization of the violence of the Universal is not identical to individual essence, but rather contrary to it.

We must insist, however, that Hegel was sensitive to that which is not entirely and positively determined by processes of socialization and individuation; he was aware that a complex path must be traversed in order that the potential of such processes to meet universalizing demands be actualized. In this sense, the ontogenesis of the subject is, in Hegel, the recognition of the ontological anteriority of conflict; a conflict pre-eminently manifest in this necessary connectedness of subjectivity and negativity.

Concerning this logical anteriority, let us recall how Hegel's philosophy of nature "naturalizes the notion of conflict" by making conflict intrinsic to the notion of "life" employed therein, a notion of life the movement of which shall ultimately be recovered in a reflexive manner as part of the determination of self-consciousness. A notion of life, in other words, that provides a model for the reflexive process of self-positing peculiar to self-consciousness. To insist on this complementariness may also help us recall that what initially appears to self-consciousness as sheer exteriority (meaning nature, which Adorno will regard as a sign of the emancipation of the subject through the suspension of his subjection to reason) will ultimately provide the model for the constitution of the notion of individuality.

---

[20] ADORNO, *op. cit.*, p. 216.
[21] Ibid., p. 221.

## *The absolute fluidity of life*

As we are well aware, for Hegel's generation it was incumbent upon modern philosophy to overcome that system of dichotomies so perfectly represented by Kant's definition of the faculty of understanding as supreme among the cognitive abilities of consciousness. Hegel shares in the diagnoses of post-Kantians such as Fichte and Schelling for whom the primacy of reflection and understanding within Kantian philosophy engendered irreparable conceptual fractures, which explains the remark that "the sole interest of Reason is to suspend such rigid antitheses" as those leading to distinctions between subject and object, form and matter, receptivity and spontaneity, or nature and subjectivity.[22]

One of the initial solutions Hegel advanced towards the annulment of such dichotomies was to posit a sort of common ground or primal foundation for both the subject and the object – a position with obvious roots in Schelling. This "primal foundation" was taken to be life itself, allowing the young Hegel to remark that "to think pure life through, that is the task," given that "consciousness of pure life would be consciousness of what the man *is* [...]."[23] In this sense, to regard life as the object of desire is to recognize in desire itself the substance that shapes self-consciousness. For this and no other reason the section of the *Phenomenology of Spirit* dedicated to self-consciousness opens with a presentation of the notion of life. As a consciousness that is aware of the dichotomies within which reason – that model of reason derived from the confrontation of subject and object – had become trapped, self-consciousness seeks an intersubjectively-shared, normative background from which all modes of interaction between subject and object emerge. Life, at least at first, is taken to be just such a background.

Life, however, is still an incomplete figure, in that its movement is not *for itself*: it is not reflexively posited and apprehended. One must be careful not to regard this as a simple negation of what Hegel's reflections on life

---

[22] Cf. HEGEL, *The Difference Between Fichte's and Schelling's System of Philosophy*, translated by H. S. Harris & W. Cerf. Albany: State University of New York Press, 1977, p. 90.

[23] HEGEL, *Early Theological Writings*, translated by T. M. Knox. Chicago: University of Chicago Press, 1948, p. 253-254. As well remarked by Jean Hyppolite, "pure life transcends this separation [*produced by the primacy of understanding*], or this appearance of separation; it is concrete unity, which, in his early works, Hegel was not yet able to express in dialectical form" (HYPPOLITE, Jean; *Genesis and Structure of Hegel's Phenomenology of Spirit*, translated by S. Cherniak & J. Heckman. Evanston: Northwestern University Press, 1974, p. 149). Also: "Against the authoritarian embodiments of a subject-centered reason, Hegel summons the unifying power of an intersubjectivity that appears under the titles of 'love' and 'life'" (HABERMAS, *The Philosophical Discourse of Modernity*, p. 30).

have yielded. Indeed, there is a certain continuity between life and self-consciousness very clearly posited by the philosopher, in the following terms: "[self-consciousness] is the unity *for which* the infinite unity of the differences is; [life], however, is only this unity itself, so that it is not at the same time *for itself*.[24] All this is to say that the difference between self-consciousness and life is affirmed over a backdrop of similarities.

Still, how does Hegel understand life in its movement, through its cycle? Somewhat schematically, it may be said that his understanding of life centers on the tension between the universality of the substance that defines the living being and the particularity of the individual, or of that multiplicity of differentiated living forms (species). This tension between unity and the individual produces an opposition Hegel termed, in his early *The Difference Between Fichte's and Schelling's System of Philosophy*, the "life factor" (*Faktor des Lebens*) – a concept coming out of his description of that movement in life that seeks to overcome this very opposition. Because it tends towards this overcoming, life appears as the first figure of infinity. This explains the following statement by Hegel, found in his presentation of the notion of infinity in the chapter of the *Phenomenology of Spirit* devoted to a discussion of the understanding: "This simple infinity, or the absolute Notion, may be called the simple essence of life, the soul of the world, the universal blood ..."[25] Hegel describes the life cycle thus:

> Its sphere is completely determined in the following moments. Essence is infinity as the supersession of all distinctions [*life is that which, through the multiplicity of differences to be found in that which lives, always returns to itself*], the pure movement of axial rotation, its self-repose being an absolutely restless infinity; independence itself, in which the differences of the movement are resolved, the simple essence of Time which, in this equality with itself, has the stable shape of Space. The differences, however, are just as much present as differences in this simple universal medium; for this universal flux [*allgemeine Flüssigkeit*] [*of life as a unity*] has its negative nature only in being the supersession of them; but it cannot supersede the different moments if they do not have an enduring existence [*Bestehen*].[26]

---

[24] HEGEL, *Phenomenology of Spirit*, § 168, p. 106.
[25] Ibid., § 162, p. 100.
[26] Ibid., § 169, p. 106 (our brackets).

This cycle reveals a sundering (*Entzweiung*) within life. Indeed, Hegel suggests that life only knows an absolute negative unity (*absolut negative Einheit*) in relation to itself. On one hand, life is the universal substance that permeates all living beings – hence the importance of fluidity as a metaphor for that which cannot become stable in fixed determinacy, and tends to manifest as a principle of indeterminacy. Yet on the other hand, life is a tendency towards increasingly perceptible differentiations given increasingly determined *self-standing forms* (*selbstständigen Gestalten*). Clearly, there is a conflict between indeterminacy and determinacy that is intrinsic to life; a conflict that makes the positing of individuality dependent upon the sundering of an undifferentiated fluidity (*unterschiedslosen Flüssigkeit*), which in turn can only be posited through the dissolution of individuality. With this conflict in mind, Hegel writes:

> The *original disease* of the animal, and the inborn *germ of death*, is its inadequacy [*Unangemessenheit*] to universality. The annulment of this inadequacy is in itself the full maturing of this germ [...]. In nature however, universality makes its appearance only in this negative way, which involves the sublation of the subjectivity within nature.[27]

Hegel's intention seems to be to insist that, in nature, life cannot attain universality – this fundamental fluidity – save through the dissolution of individuality, which would explain why the organism dies from intrinsic causes: it is unable to reconcile itself with universality. And it is precisely because it cannot reconcile the individual and the universal that nature is an imperfect figure of the Spirit. While it does achieve a certain form of reconciliation, it is but an imperfect one: the genus (*Gattung*). That is, from the perspective of the genus, all individuals are already dead. In other words, one's understanding of oneself – an individual instance of the genus – *as* genus is a reconciliation that once more relies on a simple negation of individuality. Thus, "The purpose of nature is to extinguish itself, and to break through its rind of immediate and sensuous being, to consume itself like a Phoenix in order to emerge from this externality rejuvenated as spirit."[28] This ultimately led Hegel to affirm that life "consists [...] in being the self-developing whole which dissolves its development and in this movement simply preserves itself."[29]

---

[27] HEGEL, *Enzyklopädie*, § 375. English language version from HEGEL, *The Philosophy of Nature vol. III*, trans. and ed. by M. J. Petry. London: George Allen & Unwin Ltd., 1970, pp. 209-210 (with alterations).

[28] Ibid., § 376, p. 212.

[29] HEGEL, *Phenomenology of Spirit*, § 171, p. 108.

It may even be said that self-consciousness is capable of experiencing this conflict inherent in life without its individuality being dissolved; such an experience would be that of negative universality, of absolute fluidity, but in the guise of a trembling before death whose function is formative. In other words, the movement that is proper to self-consciousness is, in a certain sense, already present in nature; it is as if the germ of that motion animating the medium within which self-consciousness acts (history) were already at work in nature. And it could not be otherwise for the man who once wrote that "Spirit has [...] issued forth [*hervorgegangen*] from nature"[30] – an issuing forth that did not prevent him from also stating that Spirit was present *before* nature (in that it is one with the movement of nature).

Oddly, Hegel seems to claim that the divide between nature and history is not an absolute rupture; instead, we are confronted with a reflexive deepening of a conjoined movement, a reciprocal structure that complicates modern dichotomies between nature and freedom.[31] This is a movement that is most of all defined through paradigms of conflict and struggle – not a Darwinian struggle between living beings, but a struggle taking place within each biological individuality, within each natural singularity, and between determinacy and indeterminacy.[32] The bulk of Hegel's effort, then, comes in demonstrating how the natural singularity, rather than an immediately self-determining reality, is and always has been the proper sphere for the operation of the negative. Thus, the overcoming of a natural singularity is, in the final analysis, the fulfillment of its "natural" destiny.

---

[30] HEGEL, *Enzyklopädie*, § 376, as *Philosophy of Nature III*, p. 212.

[31] In this sense, it is not possible to accept without reservations statements such as "the fulfillment of freedom is when nature (here society, which started in a raw, primitive form) is made over to the demands of reason" (TAYLOR, Charles; *Hegel and Modern Society*. Cambridge: Cambridge University Press, 1980, p. 84). To a certain extent, the very reverse could be argued: the absolute fluidity of nature offers a model based on which reason and its restlessness ought to be made over. To insist on a "making over" is merely to continue, albeit slightly more carefully, to regard the relation between nature and history in terms of a sundering that subtracts from the former all ontological dignity. It would be more appropriate to say, as Malabou does, that "the passage from nature to spirit does not occur as an overcoming, but as a duplication [*redoublement*], a process through which the Spirit is constituted as a *second nature*. This reflexive duplication is, in a sense, analogous to the 'mirror stage' of Spirit, in which the first form of its identity is constituted" (MALABOU, Catherine; *L'avenir de Hegel: plasticité, temporalité, dialectique* ["The future of Hegel: plasticity, temporality and dialectic"]. Paris: Vrin, 1996, p. 43).

[32] As we shall see later on, the same type of conflict between determinacy and indeterminacy in biological individualities may be found in Freud, as a consequence of his theory of life and death drives. As the Freudian theory attempts to account for processes situated at the threshold between the somatic and the psychic, it, like Hegel's, pertains at once to nature and to history.

This can help us understand why the movement of Spirit seems to follow so closely the aforementioned structure of the dissolution of determinacy and subsequent manifestation of the fluidity that animates nature; Spirit is, after all, both the circumscribing of this fluidity in a finite figure and the incessant disappearance of said figuration.[33] Gérard Lebrun understood this clearly, as the following passage attests:

> If there is any certainty to be had regarding the fact that this progress is not repetitive, but renders explicit what had been hidden, that is because Spirit does not come to be through the production of finite formations, but, on the contrary, by refusing them one after another. It is not the strength of empires that endows History with its 'reason,' but their downfall. [...] The only type of becoming that the movement of the Notion espouses has nothing in common with the indifferent transition from one form to another. The only kind of becoming it can be is one that sanctions the instability of the figure to be transgressed against, an *expressly nullifying* type of becoming.[34]

It is because of this shared relation to negativity, incidentally, that both life and Spirit will be animated by one and the same "universal fluidity," one and the same "restlessness" (*Unruhe*).

Finally, it must be said that this tension within biological individualities is present, albeit reflexively, in the movement of recognition that orients processes of socialization and individuation; this explains why reflections on the structure of social dynamics of recognition are, in the *Phenomenology*, preceded by a description of the life cycle. After all, if for self-consciousness life is the primal object of desire, this is because the truth of desire – its gratification – appears in its confrontation with an object marked by universal fluidity. In other words, if the truth of desire is to actualize the universalizing aspirations of reason, that is on account of the convergence of such a truth with the Hegelian notion of experiences of indeterminacy that are universal in character. Such experiences do not disappear with the transition from abstract universality to concrete universality. With this in mind, let us turn our full attention to the notion of desire in Hegel.

---

[33] Which has to be the case once we accept that "the dialectical process is plastic in that, as it unfolds, it creates connections between total immobility (fixity) and vacuity (dissolution), and between these extremes and the vitality of the whole that is a reconciliation of the two, effecting the union of *resistance* (*Widerstand*) and *fluidity* (*Flüssigkeit*)" (MALABOU, *op. cit.*, p. 26).

[34] LEBRUN, *L'envers de la dialectique*, pp. 28-29.

## *What is it desire truly lacks?*

For Hegel, it is as desire (*Begierde*) that self-consciousness, in its earliest degree of development, first emerges. In this sense, it is at once a mode of social interaction and a mode of relating to objects. Along with desire, Hegel introduces at least two other reflexive operations that determine self-consciousness: labor and language. These three operators are intimately interconnected, as work is "desire held in check," and language, in regards to expression, follows the same dynamics as labor.

At this juncture, one would do well to recall that Hegel belongs to a long tradition – one stretching all the way back to Plato – that understands desire as the manifestation of a lack. As an example, let us dwell for a moment on the following excerpt, taken from the *Encyclopedia of Philosophical Sciences*:

> In the object, the subject beholds its own lack [*Mangel*], its own one-sidedness, sees in the object something belonging to its own essence and yet missing from it. Self-consciousness is in a position to sublate this contradiction since it is not just being, but absolute activity.[35]

The statement could not be any clearer: that which motivates desire is the lack intuited when one beholds the object – an object which, for this very reason, can posit itself as that which determines the essentiality of the subject. Discovering one's essence in something that is other (the object) is a contradiction that consciousness easily suppresses, on account of its having no being to speak of, exactly; that is, in being an activity in the sense of a *positional* reflection that takes itself for an object and, through the very same movement, assimilates the object into itself. This experience of lack is so central in Hegel's philosophy that a living thing (*Lebendiges*) is defined in terms of its ability to experience lack, to experience an excitation (*Erregung*) that inexorably drives it towards movement. Likewise, he will define the subject as something endowed with the capacity to withstand (*ertragen*) the contradiction of itself (*Widerspruch seiner selbst*) deriving from a desire that places the essence of the subject within the object. Hegel considers lack to be so fundamental in characterizing the condition of subject that he contends

> the deficiency in a stool which has three legs is in us [*it being a lack pertaining to our concept of stool*]. In life, the deficiency is in life itself however, although to an equal extent it is also sublated, for life is aware

---

[35] HEGEL, *Enzyklopädie*, § 427, as *Philosophy of Mind*, p. 155.

of the limit as a deficiency. Thus it is a privilege of higher natures to feel pain, and the higher the nature, the more unhappiness it feels. A great man has a great need, as well as the drive [*Trieb*] to satisfy it, and great deeds proceed only from profound mental [*Gemütes*] anguish. It is here that we may trace the origin of evil etc.[36]

But even this remark does not go far enough; if desire is indeed the expression of a lack, and the object is that which essentially determines this lack, then one ought to be able to say that in the consummation of such an object consciousness finds gratification. That is not the case, however:

> Desire and the self-certainty obtained in its gratification [*and this articulation, it should be noted, is fundamental: self-certainty is strictly linked to the modes available for the gratification of desire*] are conditioned by the object, for self-certainty comes from superseding this other: in order that this supersession can take place, there must be this other. Thus self-consciousness, by its negative relation to the object, is unable to supersede it; it is really because of that relation that it produces the object again, and the desire as well.[37]

The contradiction that arises here seems to result from a misunderstanding concerning the structure of desire: desire is not merely an intentional function related to the fulfillment of animal needs, such as would be the case were lack inextricably linked to the positivity of a natural object. Rather, it consists in the self-positing operation of consciousness: through desire, consciousness seeks to intuit itself in its apprehended object, to apprehend itself as an object. That is the true motor force behind gratification. In other words, what consciousness desires is nothing other than itself. This is especially true considering – it is imperative that the point be clearly understood – that lack is *a way of being* for consciousness; not only that, it is a way of being of a consciousness that insists that determinations will always be in a condition of lack in relation to being itself.

It is widely known that this understanding of desire as lack has been the object of fierce criticism within the last few decades, such as we find in the work of Gilles Deleuze and Felix Guattari. The target of their objections was not simply the appropriation of Hegel's notion by Lacanian psychoanalysis, but also the metaphysics of negativity proper to the Hegelian conception of desire. As they saw it, it was the very manner in which psychoanalysis attempted to

---

[36] Ibid., § 359, as *Philosophy of Nature III*, p. 144 (our brackets).
[37] HEGEL, *Phenomenology of Spirit*, § 175, p. 109 (our brackets).

socialize desire that *engendered* a notion of desire marked by negativity, by loss, by conflict – a desire understood as lack and, thus, ultimately harkening back to Hegel. And yet "desire does not lack anything," wrote the French authors, "it does not lack its object. It is, rather, the subject that is missing in desire, or desire that lacks a fixed subject; there is no fixed subject unless there is repression."[38] Their point seems to be that this conception of desire as lack was nothing but the fruit of a metaphysical delusion concerning the reality of the negative, founded upon a negative theology that dared not speak its name.

By way of response, let us recall that there are three different ways to understand the proposition that lack is the essence of desire. First, lack may be regarded as a manifestation of the dearth or privation of a specific object of need. This is clearly not Hegel's position, as it would imply a naturalization of systems of needs quite untenable within his philosophical system, wherein nature is not a closed system of laws.

Second, lack may be a way of being for consciousness due to the fact that – following Plato's lead – it indicates the transcendence of desire in regards to empirical objects.

We ought to recall here Plato's Socrates in *The Symposium* pointing out that "he who desires something is in want of something,"[39] suggesting both that which is not present as well as that which one is not. Due to this double sense of lack, Eros may be seen as a mediator between opposites: it embodies that lack of things both beautiful and good that is the driving force of desire (*epithumia*), and yet one has a measure of knowledge concerning what is lacking. In other words, the object of my desire is at once that which I do not possess and that which may be found within me. The intermediary character of Eros – somewhere between a presence and an absence – is more obvious from the perspective of the lover (*erastes*), rather than that of the beloved (*eromenos*).

Still, the lack that drives desire does not quite belong to the sphere of sensuous objects, as "the beauty of one form is akin to the beauty of another; and then if beauty of form in general is his pursuit, how foolish would he be not to recognize that the beauty in every form is one and the same!"[40] Through this utter rejection of the sensuous one begins one's ascent towards the "essence of beauty," which lies beyond all that which is mortal and corruptible. To

---

[38] DELEUZE, Gilles & GUATTARI, Felix; *Anti-Oedipus: Capitalism and Schizophrenia*, translated by R. Hurley, M. Seem & H. R. Lane. Minneapolis: University of Minnesota Press, 1983, p. 26.

[39] PLATO, "The Symposium," 200a. In: *Dialogues of Plato Vol. II*, translated by Benjamin Jowett. Oxford: The Clarendon Press, 1875, p. 51.

[40] Ibid., 210b, p. 61.

behold such an essence would amount to unleashing the beautiful in its purity, clearing the way for the unalloyed expression of the unity of its formal nature. It may even be said that this ascetic process is one through which "a person leaves his particularity behind,"[41] as if the point were to negate the specificity of whatever might belong to the order of mortal nature and instead affirm the essentiality of something that "somehow belongs to it, but is not immediately available".[42] In these terms, the negativity of desire would ultimately consist in intentionally bringing to expression the inexhaustible transcendence of being out of all that is empirical in nature.

Deleuze and Guattari have this philosophical strain in mind when they develop their critique of the notion of desire as lack. From their perspective, Hegel appropriated this transcendental scheme and set it in motion within a negative theology where the transcendence of the Idea no longer excludes the sphere of the sensuous, but instead the "pure negativity" that does not manifest save through the infinite reiteration of the supersession of finite sensuous determinacy – the infinite sacrifice of a finite determinacy that must always and continuously disappear so that negativity can be realized.

However, it may be countered that the issue at stake in Hegel's definition of desire in all its negativity is a very different one. After all, the negativity of desire is not exactly an outcome of the negating pressure of transcendence, as Kojève believed (an author who, unsurprisingly, was of primary importance for Deleuze's reading of Hegel).[43] Such an unrestrained appeal to transcendence would be incompatible with a system like Hegel's, where absolute knowledge is understood as a reconciliation that renews the sphere of the empirical. On this point, it may suffice to recall that Hegel, discussing this reconciliation produced by absolute knowledge, describes an infinite judgment capable of producing a synthesis of subject and object: "*the being of the 'I' is a Thing* [*das Sein des Ich ein Ding ist*], and, moreover, a sensuous immediate Thing [*ein sinnliches unmittelbares Ding*]." Hegel continues: "that judgement, taken just as it stands, is non-spiritual or rather is the non-spiritual itself," for, if we take the sensuous Thing to be a simple predication of the 'I,' then the

---

[41] LEAR, Jonathan; "Eros and Unknowing: the Psychoanalytic Significance of Plato's *Symposium*." In: *Open minded: Working Out the Logic of the Soul*. Cambridge: Harvard University Press, 1998, p. 163. It is precisely this disqualification of both the sensible and all particularity that led Lebrun to remark that "Socratic training submits the individual to an authority that is merely the simple negation of every drive" (LEBRUN, *L'envers de la dialectique*, p. 128).

[42] MORTLEY, Raoul; *Désir et différence dans la tradition platonicienne*. Paris: Vrin, 1988, p. 81.

[43] As Paulo Arantes points out in ARANTES, Paulo; "Um Hegel errado, mas vivo" ["A mistaken but living Hegel"]. In: *Revista Ide* n. 21, São Paulo, 1991, pp. 72-79.

'I' must disappear in the empiricity of the Thing. The predicate posits the subject: "in its Notion [...] it is in fact the most richly spiritual,"[44] in that its Notion leads us to a renewed understanding of the sphere of the sensuous that goes beyond its domestication by the finite identitarian structures of transcendental aesthetics.

## *An appeal to the concept of infinity*

If we are to truly understand what Hegel was getting at with his notion of desire as lack, the latter must not be understood as mere want or privation, nor as a form of transcendence pure and simple, but rather as the *manifestation of infinity*. This infinity may be *bad*, for instance in those cases where the gratification of desire is a continual consumption of objects for the purpose of enjoyment (*Genuss*) that is little more than a narcissistic (or "selfish," to employ a Hegelian term) submission of the other to the I. Conversely, it is to be regarded as a *true* infinity whenever confronted with objects that have been freed from finite determinations.

Let us recall that lack initially appears in Hegel as a way of being of consciousness within a precise historical context, a context marked by the problematization of the very foundations underlying modern forms of life. Hegel understands modernity as a historical moment in which Spirit has "lost" the immediacy of its substantial life; which is to say, nothing appears to him as being substantially founded on a power capable of unifying the values of the various social spheres.[45] From such considerations stem classic diagnoses, like the following:

---

[44] HEGEL, *Phenomenology of Spirit*, § 790, pp. 480-481.
[45] Indeed, this "loss" should be understood in a relative sense, given that, in a way, what is implied that consciousness lost is something it had never had to begin with. This allows Hegel to write the following, concerning ethicity: "But from this happy state of having realized its essential character and of living in it, self-consciousness, which at first is Spirit only immediately and in principle, has withdrawn [*herausgetreten*], or else has not yet realized it; for both may equally well be said. Reason must withdraw from this happy state; for the life of a free people is only in principle or immediately the reality of an ethical order." (ibid., §§ 353-354, p. 214) Hegel is telling us, in other words, that consciousness has lost its happiness *and* has never once achieved it – in the end, to lose and to never have had amount to one and the same thing. Furthermore, it *must* lose that which it has never had. All of this merely brings to light the illusory status of that immediacy that is peculiar to ethicity in its initial manifestation; at this particular point, consciousness is yet unaware it is a "pure singularity on its own account," meaning its condition as self-consciousness is yet to be recognized.

> [*In modern times*] Spirit has not only lost its essential life; it is also conscious of this loss, and of the finitude that is its own content. Turning away from the empty husks [*as once did the prodigal son*], and confessing that it lies in wickedness, it reviles itself for so doing, and now demands from philosophy, not so much knowledge of what it is, as the recovery through its agency of that lost sense of solid and substantial being.[46]

Decades after Hegel, the sociological efforts of Émile Durkheim and Max Weber would constitute converging frameworks that characterized modernity as an age where a certain subjective feeling of indeterminacy prevailed, resulting from a general loss of stable horizons for socialization. The autonomization of value-based social spheres in modern life, as well as the erosion of that traditional authority sedimented through ritualized customs and habits, was taken to have destroyed reference points for the structuring of relations with the self and, therefore, an irreversible problematization of acting subjects.[47] Under such conditions, the subject can only appear as

> that night, that empty Nothingness, which contains everything in its undivided simplicity; the wealth of an infinite number of representations, of images, not one of which comes precisely to mind, or which [moreover], are not [there] insofar as they are really present. [...] That is the night that one perceives if one looks a man in the eyes: then one is delving into a night which becomes terrible; it is the night of the world which then presents itself to us.[48]

---

[46] Ibid., § 7, p. 4 (our brackets).

[47] It is not by coincidence that both authors will reflect on such phenomena through an alteration of the sociological sense of the confrontation with death. On this particular regard, Weber wrote: "the individual life of civilized man, placed into an infinite 'progress', according to its own imminent meaning should never come to an end; for there is always a further step ahead of one who stands in the march of progress. And no man who comes to die stands upon the peak which lies in infinity. Abraham, or some peasant of the past, died 'old and satiated with life' because he stood in the organic cycle of life [...]. Whereas civilized man, placed in the midst of the continuous enrichment of culture by ideas, knowledge, and problems, may become 'tired of life' but not 'satiated with life'" (WEBER, Max; "Science as a Vocation." In: *From Max Weber: Essays in Sociology*, trans. and ed. by H. H. Gerth & C. W. Mill. New York: Oxford University Press, 1946, p. 139).

[48] HEGEL, *Jenaer Realphilosophie*. Hamburg: Felix Meiner, 1967, pp. 180-181. English language version taken from KEENAN, Dennis King (ed.); *Hegel and Contemporary Continental Philosophy*. Albany: State University of New York Press, 2004, p. 187.

Hegel was unwilling to settle for mere socio-historical diagnoses, however; his intention was to provide an ontological foundation for the historical condition peculiar to modernity, as though this loss of stable horizons had not simply resulted from contingent historical processes, but had rather been the fulfillment of a destiny prompted by the necessity of that which has ontological dignity. In order to accomplish this, Hegel required a particular notion of individuality, conceived as something inhabited by a potency for indeterminacy; that is, an individuality that did not entirely submit to identitarian determination through the synthetic unity of an 'I.' And it was the theory of desire as lack – or, more precisely, as the negativity that drives agency – that provided him with the ontological foundation he sought. In this context, that is, lack describes a capacity for indeterminacy and depersonalization with which every subject is endowed.

This potency for indeterminacy, in turn, is an alternate expression for what Hegel terms infinity, in that the infinite reveals the instability and inadequacy of all finite determinations. And it could not be otherwise: after all, for Hegel the infinite is not tied to quantitative determinations. Instead, one ought to regard as infinite *all that which bears in itself its own negation and, rather than self-destruct, preserves itself in a condition of determinateness that is the very figure for the instability of all determinations.* Hence, the following key sentence: "infinity, or this absolute unrest of pure self-movement, in which whatever is determined in one way or another, e.g. as being, is rather the opposite of [...] determinateness."[49]

Here, one can clearly see how the concept of infinity is erected on the basis of Hegel's notion of contradiction. Let us recall Kant's definition of contradiction: "The object of a concept that contradicts itself is nothing because the concept is nothing, the impossible, like a rectilinear figure with two sides (*nihil negativum*)."[50] Contradiction is an *empty* object, as in bereft of concept, since no representation is possible when two contrary propositions are applied to the same object, as in the example of the impossible figure at once two-sided and rectilinear. Hegel's intention is not, of course, to successfully conceive of a two-sided rectilinear figure, but to insist upon the existence of objects that cannot be apprehended save when two contrary propositions – two divergent series – are applied to them. This may help us see how the recourse to infinity is not a cunning strategy towards the disqualification of the sensuous, but a fundamental condition for a critique of the submission of the sensuous to the grammar of finitude.

---

[49] HEGEL, *Phenomenology of Spirit*, § 163, p. 101.
[50] KANT, *Critique of Pure Reason*, B348, p. 382.

However, as *the subject is essentially a locus for the manifestation of infinity*, it may be argued that the vocabulary of negativity of desire serves the purpose of stressing the nature of *the discrepancy that exists between subjects' expectations for recognition and the possibilities for social self-determination available to them*.[51] This is tantamount to saying that the positivity of reified reality and its finite representations has established itself as the "natural representation of the act of thinking" to such a degree that nothing less than a mighty effort of negation could break the cycle of alienation. In other words, the vocabulary of negativity has nothing to do with forms of judgment concerning life that amount to little more than resignation, as if it were imperative that life be devalued as the sphere of finitude, as Lebrun's interpretation suggests.[52] Quite the contrary: the vocabulary of negativity derives from an awareness of the disparity between the modes available for the determination of *social life* and the potentialities of a life that has fulfilled its destiny as Spirit.

Be that as it may, Hegel would find this equation of the negativity of desire with the positivity of a potency that expresses itself immanently, like the relation between Spinoza's substance and its modes, simply incorrect. From a certain perspective, after all, desire is always destructive (it always affirms its inadequacy in relation to finite determinations); and, from another, it is always productive (its truth is to affirm itself as that free will that constitutes institutional frameworks allowing for its recognition through relations of labor and language). Hegel was so acutely aware of that constitutive entanglement of negativity and productivity that, in the context of discussing the need for revolutionary terror as a historical internalization of negativity capable of decimating all phenomenal determination, he wrote:

---

[51] Monique David-Ménard, in a pivotal text for discussions on the critique of the notion of desire as lack, reminds us that psychoanalysis was favorable to the idea that "there is a truth in the experiencing of the inadequacy of the object of the drives [*l'objet pulsionnel*] to the gratification of drives pursued by a subject." To think otherwise would compel philosophy to revisit "the medieval idea that truth lies in the adequacy between concept and object, as well as the Spinozan idea that a true thought unfolds its determinations immanently and un-ambiguously, and that there can be no possible truth in inadequacy" (DAVID-MÉNARD, Monique; *Deleuze et la psychanalyse,* Paris: PUF, 2005, p. 22). However, David-Ménard suggests that said inadequacy cannot be understood through a "logic of negation" applied to desire, as such a logic would be dependent on an opposition between the universal and the particular where the latter appears as a negativity that exceeds the universal. Yet, at least in Hegel's case, it could be argued that, given that the concept at play seems to be infinity or infinite determinacy, the logic of negation is not a logic of opposition or contrariness, but one of *determined negation* (as I have attempted to demonstrate in SAFATLE, Vladimir; *La passion du négatif: Lacan et la dialectique* ["The passion of the negative: Lacan and dialectics"]. Georg Olms, 2010).

[52] Cf. LEBRUN, *L'envers de la dialectique*, p. 222.

But for that very reason [negation] is immediately one with self-consciousness, or it is the pure positive, because it is the pure negative; and the meaningless death, the unfilled negativity of the self, changes round in its inner Notion into absolute positivity.[53]

## The formative character of the "sheer terror of the negative"

That is the necessary Hegelian introduction to a reflection on one's confrontation with death in the path towards the constitution of self-consciousness. At this juncture, a significant consequence of the preceding considerations should be noted: if a theory of desire as presented above animates Hegel's work, then the conflict this desire produces – a conflict that appears as the motive force behind the MSD – is no mere collision between the individual systems of interests of two separate consciousnesses, as certain commentators, Terry Pinkard and Jürgen Habermas among them, suggest.[54] In other words, it is not a conflict where one (the synthetic 'I') seeks to attain dominance through the subjugation of the other's system of values and interests to one's own – where one seeks to submit the desire of another to his or her own. On the contrary: if Hegel can state that one's development towards universal free will goes through a moment of submission to a master, that is because a master simply cannot represent a different individual determination of interests.

A closer look at the MSD reveals Hegel's insistence that, once the struggle for recognition has taken place, the essentiality of the slave or bondsman is given over to the master. Insofar as the master consumes the product of the slave's work, he asserts dominance over the slave's production. The slave, as a result, sees his or her own actions as something foreign to him- or herself. And yet, this sense of estrangement also suggests an elevation of the individual beyond particularity; as Hegel puts it, "since the bondsman works for the master and therefore not in the exclusive interest of his own individuality, his desire acquires the breadth of being not only the desire of a particular individual but containing within itself the desire of another."[55] This entanglement of desire, however, is not enough to provide the universality of recognition consciousness yearns for. In order that such a condition not be

---

[53] HEGEL, *Phenomenology of Spirit*, § 594, p. 362.
[54] Cf. PINKARD, Terry; *Hegel's Phenomenology: The Sociality of Reason*. Cambridge: Cambridge University Press, 1994, as well as HABERMAS, "From Kant to Hegel and Back Again: The Move toward Detranscendentalization," in *Truth and Justification*, pp. 175-211.
[55] HEGEL, *Enzyklopädie*, § 435, as *Philosophy of Mind*, p. 161.

one of simple submission, this other must necessarily possess something of that unconditional universality of the essential; that is, this other must be an "absolute master" who, once internalized, allows for recognition of a sort that transcends any and all context. It is with such considerations in view that the following, pivotal passage must be interpreted:

> It is only through staking one's life that freedom is won; only thus is it proved that for self-consciousness, its essential being is not [just] being, not the immediate form in which it appears, not its submergence in the expanse of life, but rather that there is nothing present in it which could not be regarded as a vanishing moment [*verschwindendes Moment*], that it is only pure being-for-self. The individual who has not risked his life may well be recognized as a person, but he has not attained to the truth of this recognition as an independent self-consciousness.[56]

If the confrontation with death is an essential condition for the attainment of freedom, that is because death is the privileged figure of this unconditional and absolute universality; a universality that, precisely on account of being unconditional and absolute, is also the negation of all that is conditioned and finite. In this way we are better equipped to approach the following remarks:

> This subjugation [*Unterwerfung*] of the bondsman's egotism forms the *beginning* of genuine human freedom. This quaking of the individuality of the will, the feeling of the nullity of egotism, the habit of obedience [*Gehorsams*], is a necessary moment in the education of every man. Without having experienced the discipline [*Zucht*] that breaks self-will [*Eigenwillen*], no one becomes free, rational, and capable of command. To become free, to acquire the capacity for self-government, all peoples must therefore undergo the severe discipline of subjection to a master.[57]

Statements of this nature often give rise to a number of misunderstandings. Hegel certainly does not mean that freedom is just another term for will as constituted through the internalization of "disciplinary apparatuses" disguised as practices for self-mastery. Not all forms of submission produce freedom: only submission to a master capable of actualizing unconditional demands for universality can do so. That explains why, for Hegel, those great individualities capable of submitting entire nations to their every whim necessarily inspire

---

[56] HEGEL, *Phenomenology of Spirit*, § 187, p. 114.
[57] HEGEL, *Enzyklopädie*, § 435, as *Philosophy of Mind*, p. 161.

the feeling that the true work of Spirit is incompatible with finite politics, with utilitarian calculations based on an individual's own system of selfish interests. Indeed, it would be the height of folly to characterize Hegel's scathing critique of egoism as an astute strategy to effectively empty the particular. When considering Hegel's critical take on egoism, one ought to recall that no individuality remains in the "ego" in question, as nothing individual can remain within a system of interests constructed on the basis of identifications with, and an internalization of, principles of conduct whose origin is a separate, determinate consciousness.[58] That is why the "quaking of the individuality of the will" may be seen as a form of "liberation."

Lebrun will employ these aspects of Hegelian philosophy to contend that the formation of self-consciousness is reducible to the dissolution of an individual, the latter understood as that which obliterates itself – unceasing self-renunciation, permanent ascesis. After all, "the attainment of determinateness always depends on the renunciation of an individuating difference, and my becoming my true being a little more and my ego a little less."[59] In this sense, to tremble before the absolute master is to become aware of the essential impotence of natural singularity. It is as though Hegel's proposed liberation were a sort of magic trick, transforming one's feelings of weakness into an utter inability to resist. Thus, "in exchange for its sorrows, it is the enjoyment of the universal that is offered to consciousness – a rather nice gift."[60] This is a position not entirely unlike the one espoused by Deleuze, for whom Hegelian dialectics is "the idea that suffering and sadness have value, the valorization of the 'sad passions,' as a practical principle manifested in splitting and tearing apart."[61]

I would argue that a different interpretation remains open to us, one that would only require a closer examination of the exact sense Hegel gives to this self-dispossession produced by the internalization of death as the absolute master. On this reading, death is by no means the destruction of consciousness – all confusion in this regard ought to be seen for the crude mistake that it is, and cleared up accordingly; it is not simply one's demise, one's *running aground* (*zugrunde gehen*), but rather one's admission to the very

---

[58] This intuition of Hegel's was given material confirmation through Lacanian psychoanalysis and its description of the genesis of the ego through the internalization of the image of an Other whose function is to serve as an idealized type for behavior and the orientation of desire. On that regard, cf. the chapter entitled "Desire without images" in SAFATLE, *Lacan*. São Paulo: Publifolha, 2007.
[59] LEBRUN, *L'envers de la dialectique*, p. 100.
[60] Ibid., p. 211.
[61] DELEUZE, *Nietzsche and Philosophy*, p. 195.

foundations: the way one *goes to the ground* (*zu Grund gehen*). For, ultimately, the confrontation with death, as a phenomenological experience, grants access to the initially indeterminate character of ground in the following fashion: "In determining itself as ground, essence determines itself as the not-determined [*Nichtbestimmte*], and only the sublating [*Aufheben*] of its being determined [*Bestimmtseins*] is its determining."[62] This may be understood as follows: the ground's indeterminacy comes from the fact that it serves as a common substratum for opposed determinations. Hence, Hegel can affirm that such foundations imply the existence of a unity – an *identity*– between identity and difference (what he terms *die Einheit der Identität und des Unterschiedes*). Still, as the 'I' is the synthetic principle that provides the foundation for this experience, as well as the connective, unifying principle that determines the mode of articulation between *ground* and *grounded*, to regard the true essence of ground as that which has its being in another (*sein Sein in einen Anderen hat*) will require a confrontation with a state of differences that have not been constrained to the form of 'I.'[63]

Let us linger on this point for a moment. We gather that to ground is to determine the existent on the basis of its relation to a standard, thus allowing thought to orient itself. For instance, by mobilizing categorial structures such as causality – the modality that ensures the intelligibility of phenomena – one determines the form of the existent. Through this recourse to form as ground one ensures and clarifies the criteria for truth and falsity, correctness and incorrectness, adequacy and inadequacy. The application of these structures to phenomena is dependent on a previous, tacit decision concerning the general logical principles of connection and unity that constitute the objects of experience, and provide a ground for propositions of identity and difference. The principles of connection (*Verbindung*) and unity in question are derived from the 'I' as the synthetic unity of apperceptions, which is thus revealed as the true ground of all determination. The proper object of dialectics, however, is precisely the problematization of such principles. For instance, when wittily stating that, for consciousness, "Being means what is its own" (*das Sein die Bedeutung das Seinen hat*)[64], Hegel is alluding to the fact that being an object of consciousness is tantamount to being structured on the basis of

---

[62] HEGEL, *The Science of Logic*, translated by G. di Giovanni. Cambridge: Cambridge University Press, 2010, p. 386.

[63] Longuenesse understood this well, as the following remark makes clear: "Hegel's 'ground,' like his 'concept,' is the heir to Kant's transcendental unity of apperception in the *Critique of Pure Reason*" (LONGUENESSE, Béatrice; *Hegel's Critique of Metaphysics*, translated by N. J. Simek. Cambridge: Cambridge University Press, 2007, p. 88).

[64] HEGEL, *Phenomenology of Spirit*, § 240, p. 145.

an internal principle of connection and unity that is a way for consciousness to appropriate the world: to constitute the world after its own image. This, of course, allows Hegel to safely ignore Kant's relevant distinctions between receptivity and spontaneity.

Dialectics must then accede to a ground no longer dependent on the self-identical form of the 'I', which only becomes through overcoming naturalized modes of determination; that is to say, made possible through the enfeeblement of the images of the world that orient and constitute our structured field of experiences.[65] This enfeeblement is phenomenologically described by Hegel as anguish and as the confrontation with death.

We now see how the confrontation with death enables self-consciousness to understand that Spirit only finds expression in the multiplicity of its determinations, rendering all of them provisional, and confronting them with a pre-personal potency for indeterminacy – a potency that prompts us to reconsider our understanding of difference. Difference, from this perspective, cannot be equivalent to that which establishes distinctions between conceptually articulated entities, as Deleuze understood Hegel's contention. Rather, difference in Hegel is this inner potency for in-difference that corrodes all determinacy. It is the expression of being that echoes Scott Fitzgerald's sentiment that "all life is a process of breaking down," a breaking down which occurs once we part the "fringe of indetermination which surrounds individuals."[66] What we have here is not exactly a gain in determinacy and positivity, but rather an assumption of risk associated with our confrontation with something purely indeterminate. Under such conditions, submission to an "absolute Lord" that dissolves all that had seemed fixed and determined bears no relation to a psychological dynamic of resignation, resentment, or the need for repression.

## Determinacy through work

A few remarks on the essential point responsible that stabilizes this dialectic seem to be in order. The fear experienced by the enslaved consciousness is not, after all, restricted to a

---

[65] This is our take on the thesis developed by Ruy Fausto, for whom if *grounding* is necessarily a form of *clarification*, "only those discourses whose first foundations are in some way 'obscure' (meaning marked by negation) can be effectively clear statements (in the dialectical sense)" (FAUSTO, Ruy; *Marx: logique et politique*. Paris: Publisud, 1986, p. 35).

[66] DELEUZE, *Difference and Repetition*, translated by P. Patton. New York: Columbia University Press, 1994, p. 258.

dissolution of everything stable merely in principle; in his service [*Dienen*] he *actually* brings [said dissolution] about. Through his service he rids himself of his attachment to natural existence [*Dasein*] in every single detail; and gets rid of it by working on it. However, the feeling of absolute power both in general, and in the particular form of service, is only implicitly this dissolution, and although the fear of the lord is indeed the beginning of wisdom, consciousness is not therein aware that it is a being-for-self. Through work, however, the bondsman becomes conscious of what he truly is.[67]

Hegel goes on to present an extremely significant gradation of the acting consciousness in its expressive potentialities. He writes of service (*dienen*), work (*arbeiten*) and formative activities (*formieren*, "forming"). This triad marks a progressive actualization of the possibilities available for the self-positing of consciousness through the object of its actions. Service is dissolution itself (*Auflösung an sich*), in the sense of being the complete alienation of the self from its own activity, which at this phase appears as pure acting *for-another* and *as-another*. Work, conversely, implies reflexive self-positing. However, Hegel does not operate with an expressivist notion of work, the most perfect realization of which would be aesthetic production or a manifestation of the expressive capabilities of singular subjects. The working consciousness does not express the positivity of its affections in an object destined to circulate within the social fabric – work is not a straightforward transfer of one's interiority to the external world. To a certain extent, the Hegelian category of work is – at least initially – a defense against the feelings of anguish awakened by the negativity of death; or, better yet, a dialectical sublation of said anguish, in that it is the self-positing of a subjectivity who has felt the evanescing of all its immediate connections to natural *Dasein* and, thus, has quiveringly experienced intimations of its own dissolution. In this respect the following, central statement of Hegel's gains new relevance.

Work [...] is desire held in check [*gehemmte Begierde*], fleetingness staved off; in other words, work forms and shapes the thing. The negative relation to the object becomes its *form* and something *permanent*, because it is precisely for the worker that the object has independence. This *negative* middle term or the formative *activity* is at the same time the individuality or pure being-for-self of consciousness which now, in the work outside of it, acquires an element of permanence. It is in

---

[67] HEGEL, *Phenomenology of Spirit*, §§ 194-195, pp. 117-118.

this way, therefore, that consciousness, *qua* worker, comes to see in the independent being [of the object] its *own* independence. [...] In fashioning the thing, the bondsman's own negativity, his being-for-self, becomes an object for him.[68]

Restraining the destructive impulse of desire in its consumption of the object, work is a formative activity that it enables the structure of self-consciousness to objectify itself into an object that is its own double. Therefore its function will be to do (albeit imperfectly) what desire could not: work allows the self-positing of self-consciousness in its demands for universality, insofar as it is organically connected to modes of social interaction and recognition.

The dialectical turn, then, would consist in stating that alienation in labor – the confrontation with action as a foreign essence (acting *for-an-absolute-Other*) and with object as that which resists one's projected actions (an experience of resistance that would prove fundamental for Adorno's development of the idea of dialectics as the *primacy of object*) – is formative because it opens consciousness to the experience of an internal alterity as a fundamental moment for the positing of identity.[69] This would explain Hegel's contention that both fear and forming are indispensable moments for work as a mode of reflection. Hegel does not hesitate in claiming that any formative activity devoid of absolute fear can provide nothing but an "empty self-centered attitude," as its form or negativity is not "negativity in itself" (*Negativität an sich*). Through work, the subject's place as foundation, as *ground*, is negation itself: the necessary consequence of a philosophy of subject where "subject" is merely *a name for the negative character of ground*.

To say that there is a negative aspect to be found therein implies, among other things, that one's relation to the existent is not a repetition of what has been potentially posited in said ground. The determination of the existent can no longer be understood as the mere subsumption of a particular instance under a general rule. Indeed, *there is no complete determinacy, in the sense of a fully-formed identity, to be extracted from the relation between determinations and*

---

[68] Ibid., §§ 195-196, p. 118.

[69] As I intend to argue elsewhere, this particular understanding of work bears deep connections to a certain aesthetic-expressive paradigm. In order to demonstrate this, however, a full reconstruction of the category of "expression" seems unavoidable, a reconstruction that might successfully address significant issues that have arisen in contemporary aesthetic production. The way I see it, this would allow for a recovery of certain aspects of Hegel's system that is as unexpected as it is peculiar, and somewhat at odds with the very nature of that system as a whole, given the relatively reduced status aesthetic work receives therein. It is a recovery, nonetheless, and (as I would like to contend) a much needed one.

*ground.* This is the realization self-consciousness comes to along its difficult path.

Finally, we need to account for the fact that work, as presented in the *Phenomenology of Spirit*, does not point us, as might be expected, towards an "institutionalization of ego-identity."[70] Contrary to all expectations, labor does not launch a dynamic of recognition that finds actualization in the juridical regulation of one's relations with the other through the assumption of one's rights as a subject who contributes to the wealth (*Vermögen*) of society. Or, rather, it *does*, but only after a thorough overhaul of the accepted interpretations of "identity," "rights" and "subject." After all, Hegel's true interest in work is as a form of positing that negativity which the subject confronts in its path towards assuming indeterminacy: the very condition allowing self-consciousness to exist "in the universal." From that, Hegel tells us, one may derive modernity's most pressing problem, one that lies at the very foundation of his philosophy of right: How are we to make institutional recognition viable for subjects conceived as singular modes of confrontation with indeterminacy? Suffering is not produced by indeterminacy, but by the incapacity of institutional structures and processes of social interaction to acknowledge indeterminacy as the real foundation of the existential condition of each and every subject. Only when these structures are able to provide general outlines for processes of recognition that confront the potency for indeterminacy within every subject will we be able to grope towards a renewed concept of love as a regulating horizon for practices of social interaction. Such love, in a manner that is still unclear, must bear within itself those experiences of infinitude and depersonalization that Hegel associated with the confrontation with death. To paraphrase Fassbinder, then, and to take more than poetic license, here looms the promise of a love that is colder than death.

---

[70] HABERMAS, "Labor and Interaction: Remarks on Hegel's Jena *Philosophy of Mind*." In: *Theory and Practice*, translated by J. Viertel. Boston: Beacon Press, 1974, p. 160.

# Chapter II

# On how law becomes freedom

*Even if Immanuel Kant, the arch-destroyer in the realm of ideas,*
*far surpassed Maximilien Robespierre in terrorism ...*
Henrich Heine

If we take seriously the definition of desire outlined in the previous chapter, important questions remain concerning its ultimate social application. Still, it is a useful starting point for unpacking the concepts of individuality and intersubjectivity underlying the reflection on the modern subject conducted by one of its most definitive theoreticians – namely, Hegel; Hegel's efforts in this direction turn on a critique, buttressed by the concept of negativity, of that which some have termed the "analytics of finitude." In this sense, a return to Hegel allows us to ask what was truly at stake in his complex, polyphonic movement towards the constitution of the category of subject. Given that he understands the modern subject as a potential locus for the manifestation of infinitude – a manifestation which compels us to abandon any notions of individuality dependent on the subject's egological reduction – a significant number of contemporary critical efforts directed at the subject appear misguided. Ultimately, they evince a deliberately poor, reductive appreciation of previous philosophical approaches to the subject. They create a strawman and the price of such a stubborn forgetfulness must be paid on a variety of fronts.

First of all, this kind of dismissal makes it harder to reflect on the nature of social institutions and the formative processes they must undergo to attain socialization; very quickly, one is left with little choice but to describe institutions using the vocabulary of coercion, of discipline, or of even more elaborate modes of enforced control. And yet it is clear there must be more to these institutions, if for no other reason than that they allowed for the development of perspectives openly critical of the hegemonic nature of their functioning. While their coercive dimension must not be ignored, a proper theory of institutions should be able to explore their ambivalences and contradictions.

Secondly, the reductionist reading makes it harder for us to get a handle on the suffering and constant risk of collapse that necessarily occurs in the development of all individualities. The articulation between subjectivity and infinitude that negativity can provide is, in a sense, the *articulation of a tension* whose equalization, while invariably difficult and uncertain, is necessary. It provides us with a key to understand matrices of suffering that have become generalized within our hegemonic ways of living.

Finally, without a more careful reading, we lack the means to ponder the rationality of moral judgments. Because moral judgments are not simply founded on the answer to the question "what ought to be done?" but, most importantly, "what kind of life do I wish to lead?" confusion surrounding the category of subject ends up obscuring our apprehension of those forms of life that stand as our regulatory horizon. Each of these three points shall be dealt with in this book, starting with the first one.

The previous chapter concluded with the claim that modernity's greatest problem, for Hegel, concerns the viability of the institutional recognition of subjects a viable proposition; further, these subjects were defined as particular modes of confrontation with that which presents itself as indeterminate. The problem ought to be explored further, so that we may understand what is truly at stake in the institutional structures peculiar to those forms of life that, again according to Hegel, can serve as attainable horizons for modernity.

At this juncture, we would do well to turn to Hegel's *Philosophy of Right* so as to better identify potentialities inherent to the concepts of negativity and indeterminacy, as well as any impasses that may result from their use. The universe of the philosophy of right should help us better understand how such concepts provide a regulatory foundation for Hegelian freedom; subsequently, we shall gain a deeper understanding of both the model of individuality Hegel wants to put into circulation and the dynamics of recognition such a model requires. Towards that end, the best course of action is to begin with some general remarks on the Hegelian definition of "right" and its relation to the notion of will.

## Right and freedom

> The basis [*Boden*] of right is the *realm of spirit* in general and its precise location and point of departure is the *will*; the will is *free*, so that freedom constitutes its substance and destiny [*Bestimmung*], and the

system of right is the realm of actualized freedom, the world of spirit produced from within itself as a second nature.[1]

The above remark by Hegel might well sounds naïve to contemporary ears; with our current sensibilities, we feel more at ease defending right as the most visible facet of a disciplinary apparatus that perpetuates certain material conditions of life in conformity with the interests of hegemonic powers within the state. In other words, we feel more comfortable defending statements such as the following, by Theodor Adorno:

> In large measure, the law is the medium in which evil wins out on account of its objectivity and acquires the appearance [*Schein*] of good. Positively it does protect the reproduction of life; but in its extant forms its destructiveness shows undiminished, thanks to the destructive principle of violence. [...] That the individual is so apt to find himself in the wrong when the antagonism of interests drives him into the legal sphere – this is not, as Hegel would persuade him, his own fault because he is too benighted to recognize his own interest in the objective legal norm and its guarantors. It is the fault of constituents of the legal sphere itself.[2]

And yet it is worth exploring more carefully Hegel's claim – that the object of right is free will, and, hence, proper juridical order could be nothing other than the actualization of freedom: a spiritual second nature turned to institutionalized habit in man. His shrewd adoption of "second nature" and related expressions like an insistence, against contractualism, on the existence of freedom as a natural, inalienable, non-renounceable right – a natural right founded on a "second nature" that is the fruit of a long historical process and on a naturalization of habits that weighs heavily and irreversibly upon the issue.

It may be said that the central concepts at play in Hegel's philosophy of right are "freedom" and "free will," in that they define the scope of the rationality of right. The goal, then, would be to demonstrate how Hegel's perspective offers a nuanced elaboration of the necessary relation between the recognition of free will and the constitution of modern institutions. We would begin from the following line of questioning: What should our conception of institutions be if they are to meet those demands for recognition that have

---

[1]  HEGEL, *Philosophy of Right*, §4, p. 35 (emphasis ours).
[2]  ADORNO, *Negative Dialectics*, p. 309.

been entrusted to the concept of "freedom"? And is it even possible to think freedom in the absence of some guarantee of institutional recognition? These are questions that inevitably lead to a third, and a rather crucial one, namely: what is meant by "freedom" in this particular context?

Before we delve into such discussions more directly, Hegel's peculiar sense of "right" should be noted: by "right," Hegel understands more than the mere ordering of the state in regards to the regulation of social life. Under the concept of "right" Hegel includes "all the social preconditions that can be shown to be necessary for the realization of the 'free will' of every individual subject."[3] Such preconditions encompass the current juridical ordering and its conflicting internal dynamics, the political institutions that constitute the modern state, the intersubjective relations of love that take place within the family unit, the subjective disposition that results from the internalization of moral precepts, and the dynamics of the free market, among other things. Furthermore, they must be somehow guaranteed (or in the process of becoming so) within the current frameworks of the modern state.

Therein resides a large portion of the complexity of the Hegelian project: the state cannot merely be an ideal conception, an ought-to-be. If the purpose of Hegel's philosophy of right is "*to comprehend and portray the state as an inherently rational entity*,"[4] that is because it must be capable of presenting, through the necessity of its own inherent rationality, *the state that is in the process of becoming actual* as a result of the project of modernity. In other words, the state in question is neither the one currently realized, nor an ideal one – the latter being but an idea, lacking any and all relation to an actuality –, but a state *imbued with the potential to become actual*, in the sense of something capable of exploring current social conflicts towards its own actualization.

The juridical ordering of a state is not, after all, something organically cohesive and monolithic. Rather, it is the heteroclite outcome of the sedimentation of social struggles between several contrary – even contradictory – dispositions within society. A state's juridical ordering bears the mark of such conflicts. In this sense, it is the role of the philosophy of right to uncover which particular struggles or conflicts have impressed their rational tendencies upon a given juridical ordering. It is perhaps on account of this that Hegel felt it appropriate to conclude his prefatory remarks to the *Philosophy of Right* with the beautiful metaphor of philosophy as the owl of Minerva, who will not take to wing until the coming of twilight, and the gathering of "the shades of night." Philosophy, after all, seeks to show how those social conflicts that give

---

[3] HONNETH, *Suffering from Indeterminacy*, p. 29.
[4] HEGEL, *Philosophy of Right*, p. 21.

the notion of right its shape, that impress upon it their various tendencies, are mobilizations of Spirit in its attempt to actualize the concept of freedom within social life. As actualizations go, this is hardly a linear one, and must remain vulnerable to the tactical and strategic dimensions of thought, as well as the configuration of localized situations. According to Hegel, this actualization has already left an indelible mark on our juridical ordering, particularly after the establishment of the Napoleonic Code and in the aftermath of the French Revolution.

Hence, by insisting that free will can only be conceived as the actualization of preconditions that must be undergoing a process of institutionalization within social life, it becomes necessary for Hegel to advance a critique of two hegemonic models of freedom: one based on the hypostatization of demands for *authenticity*, and the other based on the hypostatization of demands for *autonomy*. The hypostatization at work in these two models perpetuates a state of contradiction between the notions of freedom and institution, which Hegel found unacceptable. After all, when authenticity is hypostatized, it can only produce a *negative freedom* that, when employed as a guide for political action, leads directly to terror. The hypostatization of autonomy, on the other hand, engenders a notion of *free will* that, when guiding political action, ultimately leads to a profound social atomization, which ensues whenever the category of "individual" attains undue centrality in social life. Let us ponder each of these distortions of the concept of freedom, which are not entirely unrelated, so that we may better grasp the Hegelian concept in its specificity.

## From negative freedom to terror

> If the feelings of the heart, [personal] inclinations, and arbitrariness are set up in opposition to positive right and laws, philosophy at least cannot recognize such authorities. That force and tyranny may be an element in positive right is contingent to the latter, and has nothing to do with its nature.[5]

This is a decisive statement from Hegel, reminding us that freedom must not be confused with the presumed *authenticity* of the unmediated spontaneity of feelings – an authenticity that would find, in the body of laws, nothing but institutionalized coercion and violence in the form of positive right. These laws

---

[5]   Ibid., §3, p. 28.

could never correspond to that which Hegel termed, in the *Phenomenology of Spirit*, "the law of the heart," that law for which the course of the world is necessarily perverted. Against such a hypostatization of authenticity, from the perspective of which every right is but a form of veiled violence, Hegel will defend affirmations such as the following: "Freedom is nothing but the recognition and adoption of such universal substantial objects as Right and Law, and the production of a reality [*Wirklichkeit*] that is accordant with them – the State."[6]

A statement of this nature easily becomes the object of the direst confusion. "Free is that will which yearns for the Law": it is hard not to hear, in such an Orwellian turn of phrase, the confession of a philosophy that cannot grasp the meaning of experiences – so common in our societies – where right and justice have become dissociated. What is one to say when faced with unjust laws? And, most importantly, why speak of such things at a time when the Prussian state seemed animated by the impetus behind the Congress of Vienna (1814-1815) and the anti-liberal Restoration that sought to eliminate once and for all any influence exerted by the ideals of the French Revolution? It ought to be remembered that more than a few have read into the *Philosophy of Right* ample proof of Hegel's support for the Restoration (a perspective the foremost example of which is Rudolf Haym's book, *Hegel and His Time*).

However, a fundamental point must be emphasized: there was no philosopher *in his time* more clearly committed than Hegel to setting the French Revolution in its proper place among the pivotal events of modernity.[7] As Domenico Losurdo, a fine commentator, once wrote, "every revolution in the history of humanity was supported and celebrated by Hegel, despite his reputation as an incorrigible defender of the established order,"[8] whether it be the American revolution, the Haitian revolution led by Toussaint L'Ouverture, the Plebeian revolt against the Patricians, the revolt of slaves under Spartacus, the Great Peasants' Revolt in the days of the Reformation, or, as previously mentioned, the French Revolution. Concerning the latter, it should suffice to recall how it is described in the *Lectures on the Philosophy of History*:

---

[6] HEGEL, G.W.F. *The Philosophy of History*, translated by J. Sibree. Kitchener: Batoche Books, 2001, p. 75.

[7] Cf. RITTER, Joachim; *Hegel and the French Revolution*, trans. by R. D. Winfield. Cambridge: The MIT Press, 1982.

[8] LOSURDO, Domenico; *Hegel and the Freedom of Moderns*, translated by J. & M. Morris. Durham: Duke University Press, 2004, p. 99.

Not until now had man advanced to the recognition of the principle that Thought ought to govern spiritual reality. This was accordingly a glorious mental dawn. All thinking beings shared in the jubilation of this epoch. Emotions of a lofty character stirred men's minds at that time; a spiritual enthusiasm thrilled through the world, as if the reconciliation between the Divine and the Secular was now first accomplished.[9]

Still, Hegel will suffer from no shortage of harsh words when writing against Jacobinism and revolutionary terror. Specifically, "he does criticize the Jacobin Terror, even sternly at times, but he never demonizes it or reduces it to a mere orgy of blood. [...] The Jacobin leader was not the savage beast referred to by the political press of the Restoration as well as by the liberal political press."[10] Hegel knows terror to be the disastrous result of the first manifestation of a concept of freedom that harbors in its core the moment of *negative freedom* proclaimed in the name of an enthusiastically-felt emotional authenticity. It is "absolute freedom" made *destructive wrath*, in that it is a freedom that does not, under any circumstance, recognize its own institutionalization as a possibility: it sees every right as a loss of that free spontaneity of revolutionary enthusiasm and, as a consequence, turns against anything that seeks to determine it: that is, against all government. As Hegel writes in the *Phenomenology of Spirit*, for this absolute freedom "what is called government is merely the *victorious* faction, and in the very fact of its being a faction lies the direct necessity of its overthrow; and its being government makes it, conversely, into a faction, and [so] guilty."[11] Jacobin terror, after all, bore no resemblance to the simple, totalitarian violence perpetrated by the state against discontented sectors of civil society. In fact, it was a self-devouring movement of societal destruction and, from the perspective of the state, of self-destruction – at least until the Jacobin leaders themselves came to an untimely end on the guillotine. Jacobinism is the reflexive figure of that *terror that turns against itself*.[12]

---

[9] HEGEL, *Philosophy of History*, p. 467.

[10] LOSURDO, *op. cit.*, p. 105.

[11] HEGEL, *Phenomenology of Spirit*, § 591, p. 360. As Charles Taylor writes, "the curse of vacuity haunts this enterprise as well. Its aim is to found society on no particular interest or traditional positive principle, but on freedom alone. But this, being empty, gives no basis for a new articulated structure of society. It only enjoins destruction of the existing articulations and any new ones which threaten to arise." (TAYLOR, *Hegel and Modern Society*, p. 179).

[12] In this sense, it is unlike that other figure of revolutionary terror, Stalinism. While in the latter one finds the constitution of an apparatus of state violence that is legitimized by revolutionary violence and constantly turned against society and against sectors of the state itself, it is nevertheless able to ensure the perpetuation of a power nucleus sustained by the figure of a despot, which is not the case in Jacobinism.

However, and this is often forgotten, Hegel stresses that this negative moment of freedom is a necessary stage in the history of Spirit. So that this is properly understood, we need a more precise definition of what Hegel terms "negative freedom". The following statement is from the fifth paragraph of his *Philosophy of Right*:

> The will contains ($\alpha$) the element of pure indeterminacy, or of the 'I''s pure reflection into itself, in which every limitation, every content, whether present immediately through nature, through needs, desires, and drives, or given and determined in some other way, is dissolved; this is the limitless infinity of *absolute abstraction* or *universality*, the pure *thinking* of oneself.[13]

"Negative freedom," as the first moment of will, thus appears as a possibility for complete release from all determinacy, for one to be absolutely for oneself, as expressed in the famous opening to the Master-Slave dialectic. Hence the notion of "absolute abstraction," which posits an unconditionality that is a first manifestation of universality; this unconditionality, in turn, seeks at every moment to reaffirm its inadequacy to posited determinations. It is almost as if Jacobinism were the political actualization of desire conceived of as pure negativity. On account of that, the hypostatization of that negative moment of freedom is described by Hegel in very harsh terms:

> This is the freedom of the void, which is raised to the status of an actual shape and passion. If it remains purely theoretical, it becomes in the religious realm the Hindu fanaticism of pure contemplation; but if it turns to actuality, it becomes in the realm of both politics and religion the fanaticism of destruction, demolishing the whole existing social order, eliminating all individuals regarded as suspect by a given order, and annihilating any organization which attempts to rise up anew. Only in destroying something does this negative will have a feeling of its own existence.[14]

Still – and the point is worth emphasizing – Hegel reminds us that the ability to abstract oneself from everything else and thus transcend all posited determinations belongs to humans alone. The philosopher is therefore compelled to insist that

---

[13] HEGEL, *Philosophy of Right*, §5, p. 37.
[14] Ibid., p. 38.

this negative freedom or freedom of the understanding is one-sided, but this one-sidedness always contains within itself an essential determination, and should therefore not be dismissed; but the defect of the understanding is that it treats a one-sided determination as unique and elevates it to supreme status.[15]

In light of this, a reconstruction of the historical context that leads Hegel to see negative freedom as essentially determined is in order. As discussed in the previous chapter, Hegel understands modernity as a historical moment in which Spirit has "lost" the immediacy of its substantial life: things no longer appear to him as being substantially founded on a power capable of unifying the values of the various social spheres. The philosopher, in other words, characterizes modernity as a time in which freedom has led to a loss of those substantial connections allowing for shareable forms of life – hence his idea of modernity as producing a type of feeling where the subjective experience of indeterminacy is a by-product of processes of socialization.

As we have seen, Hegel was not willing to settle for socio-historical diagnoses; rather, he wanted to provide an ontological foundation for the particular historical situation of modernity, as if the erosion of stable horizons in the latter were not merely the outcome of contingent historical processes, but the fulfillment of a destiny marked by ontological necessity. Due to that necessity, negative freedom appears essentially determined. There was no other outcome to be had, of course, given the centrality of the experience of negativity for the determination of the nature of subjects in the philosophical thought in question.

Indeed, Hegel will acknowledge that the pure indeterminacy of will can only lead us to an impasse that is at once political and existential. It may be said that both aspects promote little beyond an "aestheticization of violence," whether it be the violence against the self that is actualized in one's absolute dissatisfaction and in recurring inadequacies in acting and judging, or the political violence that is indiscriminately perpetrated against any and all

---

[15] Ibid., pp. 38-39. It is not without interest to recall that the understanding that modern freedom requires, for its attainment, a moment of *negative* freedom may already be found in Descartes, at least if we are to believe what Sartre tells us; as the latter will himself write, on the topic of Cartesian transcendence, "we recognize in this power to escape, to move, to withdraw, a prefiguring of Hegelian negativity. Doubt reaches every proposition that dares affirm the existence of anything outside of our thought, which is to say, I can put every single existent between parentheses, and am in the full exercise of my freedom when I, myself null and void, turn all there is into nothing" (SARTRE, Jean-Paul; *Situations philosophiques*. Paris: Gallimard, 1990, pp. 71-72).

institutions. Be that as it may, it is worth remembering that one of the main problems facing modernity – and this is an issue at the very foundation of Hegel's philosophy of right – may be stated as follows: how can the institutional recognition of subjects, conceived of as particular modes of confrontation with that which presents itself as indeterminate and negative, be made viable? We could, after all, invert Durkheim and Weber's diagnoses and affirm that it is not only indeterminacy that produces social suffering, but also the failure of institutional structures and processes of social interaction to recognize the reality of the foundational role of indeterminacy in the existential condition of each and every subject. In this sense, the Jacobin impasse demonstrates, among other things, the difficulties inherent to the constitution of an institutional structure capable of recognizing said foundational reality. Following such notions to their logical end, one is perhaps unavoidably led to admit that "the terrorist past has to be accepted as *ours*, even – or precisely because – it is critically rejected."[16]

That being the case, reflections on the politics of the French Revolution, and on the continuation of its ideals, would do well to address the period that comes *after the Jacobin impasse*. As Ritter puts it, "the Revolution brought forth the problem to be solved [...], that of the concrete political realization of freedom."[17] Towards that end, the possibility of reconciliation between freedom and state law must be set as a task for thought.[18]

---

[16] ZIZEK, Slavoj; "Introduction." In: ROBESPIERRE, Maximilien; *Virtue and Terror*. London: Verso, 2007, p. ix.

[17] RITTER, *Hegel et la révolution française*, p. 25

[18] We know how, in Hegel's *Phenomenology*, the issue presented by the Jacobin impasse is overcome by subjective freedom, as the autonomy of moral consciousness. Marcos Müller provides us with a precise description of the process in question: "Things take place as if the experience of the political actualization of absolute freedom and its self-destruction in the Jacobin attempt to promote – through political equality and republican virtue, despotically imposed – social equality, were, in the phenomenological progression of figures, the indispensable condition for Spirit's full access to the consciousness of freedom as both its fundamental principle and final destination. It all takes place, therefore, in the order of presentation (*Darstellung*), as if, before freedom is allowed to unfold within moral interiority – that "ineffectiveness" that assumes, then, the "value of truth" (§595) – it were required to go through an attempt at political realization and the experience of its impasse and self-destruction in Terror." (MÜLLER, Marcos; *A liberdade absoluta entre a crítica à representação e o terror* ["Absolute freedom between the critique of representation and terror"]. In: *Revista Eletrônica Estudos Hegelianos*, Ano 5, n° 9, dezembro de 2008, pp. 77-78). It may be said, then, that by also criticizing the autonomy of moral consciousness in the *Philosophy of Right*, it is as if Hegel were reinstating the question of the full access of Spirit to the consciousness of freedom, but doing so within the political-institutional sphere.

So that its negative moment does not become hypostatized, freedom must be able to determine its own objects within a social life institutionalized through a just state. Hegel had in his favor the fact that Jacobinism consisted not only in a merely negative impulse, but also sought to define conditions for participation in the modern state through unrestricted demands for *universality*. For this and no other reason we have Jacobinism to thank for the egalitarian slant of the *Declaration of the Rights of Man and Citizen* of 1793, as well as for the extension of the rights of man to the colonies, and for the end of slavery. Only after such demands for concrete universality could the egalitarian foundations of the modern state be established. It may even be said that, in a sense, the articulation of concrete universality becomes possible only after the experience of negativity, as the latter presupposes a capacity for abstraction and transcendence – *an indifference to differences* – that is essential for the constitution of the modern conception of the citizen.[19]

As we shall see, this is not an easily analyzed issue. Freedom must be capable of determining its own objects within social life and ensuring their recognition without, in doing so, annulling the negative moment that is immanent to the modern conception of freedom whose initial expression was greatly deformed by Jacobin terror. Thus, in a rather peculiar way, the state Hegel attempts to conceive of is the *post-revolutionary, constitutional state*: a state capable of addressing those demands for recognition and universality that were put into circulation by the French Revolution.

## *The formalism of free will*

For now, let us return to Hegel's critique of hegemonic models of freedom. As pointed out previously, models of freedom that hypostatize the notion of *autonomy* were also targets for the philosopher's criticism. When hypostatized, autonomy produces an idea of *free will* that, employed as a guide for political action, leads to a deep social atomization resulting from the elevation of the category of "individual" to the status of central element in social life. Let us attempt to understand this point a little more clearly.

---

[19] A problem arises, here, that others have pointed out before: the "abstraction" that finds its footing with the French Revolution runs the risk of becoming one of those "morbid aspects of a state of permanent disengagement," as Paulo Arantes once put it, with the deterritorialized formation of the modern intellectual as one of its fundamental figures. On that regard, cf. the first two essays in ARANTES, *Ressentimento da dialética* ["Resentment from dialectics"], São Paulo: Paz e Terra, 1996. To provide said abstractive force with its proper territory is, deep down, the challenge faced by the Hegelian state.

We are aware that autonomy, in a modern context, denotes the ability of subjects to freely place themselves under the authority of their own moral law, thus proving themselves to be moral agents capable of self-rule.[20] Originating with Rousseau, for whom "obedience to a law that we prescribe to ourselves is liberty," it is with Kant that this conception of autonomy attains its decisive contours.

This law – on the deliberate subjection to which a subject's self-affirmed autonomy depends – is not, as we know, a particular law connected to the selfish interests of the private individual. Rather, it is unconditional, categorical and universal. It is a law that clears the way for the recognition of an intersubjective sphere of rational conduct validation, one with the potential to lead the subject to guide his or her own actions towards the construction of a systematic connectedness of rational beings effected through common laws. If such a potential is to become a reality, it is essential for something other than private and "pathological" desires to be found within subjects: they must be endowed with a *pure will* that acts according to the universality of the Law *out of love*. The pure will presents itself as a *duty*, for, through a sense of duty, consciousness can impose upon itself its own law as well as judge its own actions as though it were split into a consciousness that acts and a consciousness that judges. As Hegel reminds us, however, the perpetuation of morality in the form of duty leads to nothing so much as an impasse; after all, "'morality' does not consist in a perpetual confrontation between man as he is and man as he 'ought to be'."[21] This confrontation, if unduly perpetuated, results in the complete disarticulation of the capacity for action.

Hegel insists, at several points, that this paralysis, part and parcel of the conception of autonomy in question, has a name: "formalism." In this context, formalism means that the founding of moral action upon the pure form of duty does not provide us with a reliable decision-making procedure as to what concerns the moral content of our actions. To found morality "upon the pure form of duty" is to fundamentally define the moral nature of the actions of an individual in terms of their conformity to certain formal procedures articulated as a categorical imperative (meaning a categorical and unconditional universalizing procedure, free of all contradiction). We shall return to this point in a more systematic fashion in the third part of this book; for now, it should suffice to recall that Hegel does not believe that the transcendental founding of a moral principle is enough to ensure the proper

---

[20] For a thorough discussion of the genesis of the concept, cf. SCHNEEWIND, J. B.; *The Invention of Autonomy*. Cambridge: Cambridge University Press, 1998.

[21] FLEISCHMANN, Eugène; *La philosophie politique de Hegel*. Paris: Gallimard, 1992, p. 118.

clarification of its modes of application. Quite the opposite, in fact: Hegel will often insist that a merely formal definition of duty results in a tautology, an "identity without content."

The point may be understood in the following way: duty, while apparently formal, in fact has a "content" of sorts, which is ultimately the Hegelian term for the "particularization of action contexts" – a nice reminder that the determination of the meaning of a moral action does not stem exclusively from procedural considerations, but requires a complex articulation with the actualization of particular contexts for action. Duty, after all, is manifested within particular action situations in which there is a clearly defined content ("should I or should I not steal this, if I am hungry and have no money?"; "should I or should I not leave my spouse if I have fallen in love with someone else?"). That goes to show how duty is an *activity* directed at becoming externally actualized. It accedes to the calculations of a *contextualized and intersubjectively structured pragmatism*. Only then can the activity in question set particular ends for itself. This explains Hegel's definition of morality:

> The concept of morality is the will's inner attitude towards itself. But not just *one* will is present here. On the contrary, its objectivization also contains the determination whereby the individual will within it is superseded; and in consequence, since the determination of one-sidedness disappears, two wills with a positive reference to one another are now posited.[22]

In other words, morality only finds its foundation when it is capable of positioning itself not as the will of an individual, but as a will bearing a reference to "the will of others" (a far more obscure expression than it may at first seem). Thus, Hegel writes: "Action contains the following determinations: ($\alpha$) it must be known by me in its externality as mine; ($\beta$) its essential relation to the concept is one of obligation; and ($\gamma$) it has an essential relation to the will of others."[23]

Hegel had already stressed the same point in his discussions of moral intentionality that may be summarized as follows: subjective will is more than simply will, it is a motive force for action. The action performed is by necessity the alteration (*Veränderung*) of an existence previously given, an alteration for which I, as its agent, am responsible. Still, there are predictable alterations and unpredictable alterations; there are consequences I could

---

[22] HEGEL, *Philosophy of Right*, §112, p. 140.
[23] Ibid., §113, p. 140.

easily form representations of, and others I could not. How far, then, does my responsibility extend? Who is to define, on the basis of my action, what is predictable or easily represented? Which elements ought to be taken into consideration when such a definition is attempted?

To entirely disregard consequences or, conversely, to measure the nature of an action based on its consequences alone are two complementary mistakes. Yet if one is to define what, in the consequences of an action, is *necessary*, a general representation is needed of what follows when a particular intended purpose is given. This implies recognizing that *my* purpose is inextricable from consequences that are not simply defined by myself, but will necessarily follow a particular action. Which is to say, purpose is not all I am after: when I acted, I sought consequences. That was my intention. Hegel attempts, in this way, to define intention as *the ability to reconstruct the totality of the relations expected to involve, and ensue from, an action.*

In this context, intention is the recognition that one's interiority is inhabited by intersubjective considerations on the consequences of every action (hence the recourse to "the will of others"). So that they may consist in the ability to reconstruct a totality of relations, intentions must be "certain kinds of know-how,"[24] insofar as they are always connected to a socially defined network of intentional states. Hegel thus speaks of "universal character" and "value of action." Intention is, in fact, the name given by Hegel to a behavioral disposition that is a direct result of the sedimentation of social models of judgment. That explains why intention always appears in tandem with reflections on *das Wohl*, or welfare (in the sense of that which is required for the satisfaction of material needs): said social models of judgment are the outcome of a historical process, a long-term search for ways to realize forms of life that secures their normative weight.

This may explain why Hegel seems inclined to adopt the notion of a *morality of consequences* that is nevertheless able to take intentional calculations into account. Even if the notion of accountability takes intentional dispositions very much into consideration (the case of Oedipus, for instance, is deemed exemplary by Hegel), this morality of consequences removes the anticipatory meaning of moral action from centre stage, leading it instead towards the condition of something the final outcome of which can never be fully anticipated by consciousness (however founded on a calculation of

---

[24] SEARLE, *Intentionality: an Essay in the Philosophy of Mind.* Cambridge: Cambridge University Press, 1983, p. 143. Indeed, Hegel's considerations on intentionality such as they appear in the chapter of the *Philosophy of Right* dedicated to morality are not entirely unlike John Searle's.

consequences moral intentionality, thus conceived, may be), nor guaranteed in advance by means of transcendental strategies.[25]

That is the backdrop that explains why Hegel time and again insists that the deliberation of the free will is not to be understood as *arbitrariness* (*Willkür*), or as a choice that is made with a view towards the attainment of the most adequate content for the form of said will. When I choose, I do so from among possibilities that present themselves to me as possible fulfillments of my will; however, this presupposes that the self-determination of the form of my free will does not carry within itself the content through which its fulfillment, or the mode of its actualization, occurs. Hegel is therefore compelled to say that "since only the formal element of free self-determination is immanent within arbitrariness, whereas the other element is something given to it, arbitrariness may indeed be called a delusion if it is supposed to be equivalent to freedom."[26]

In other words, Hegel is telling us that in regards to a free will there is no such thing as a choice. "The nature of freedom cannot be linked to the question of freedom of choice."[27] As counterintuitive as this may seem *freedom is not a matter of individual choice* and it is extremely symptomatic that contemporary debates about freedom should focus so much on that particular aspect. Such discussions center on whether something like a free will can exist or not, as if we were in search of some sort of decision capable of suspending any and all causal determination outside of the spontaneity of individual decision, which is not subjected to external authorities of any kind and, therefore, conceived of as autonomous.[28]

In this sense, a dichotomy is quickly established where we find the notion of *external causes* on one side and a completely internalist autonomy on the other. Hegel often approaches causes that are external to autonomous action through the will-drive (*Trieb*) dichotomy, an issue he could have just as easily accessed by way of subjectivity-intersubjectivity instead. By favoring

---

[25] The morality of consequences Hegel's perspective presupposes is not entirely dissimilar from something Bernard Williams once termed "moral luck." On that regard, cf. WILLIAMS, Bernard; *Moral Luck*. Cambridge: Cambridge University Press, 1991. Additionally, the final chapter of the present book attempts to reflect on the general characteristics of this type of morality of consequence.

[26] HEGEL, *Philosophy of Right*, §15, p. 49.

[27] PIPPIN, *Hegel's Practical Philosophy: Rational Agency as Ethical Life*. Cambridge: Cambridge University Press, 2008, p. 39.

[28] However, "if freedom is to renounce all heteronomy, any determination of the will by particular desires, traditional principle or external authority, then freedom seems incompatible with any rational action whatsoever. For there do not seem to be any grounds of action left which are not wholly vacuous, that is, which would actually rule some actions in and others out, and which are not also heteronomous" (TAYLOR, *Hegel and Modern Society*, p. 80).

the former pairing, however, the philosopher was able to emphasize how the formalism of duty is also a form of ignorance concerning the manner through which drives provide free will with its content (in the sense of its motivations for action); what is ignored, ultimately, is that "nothing great has been and nothing great can be accomplished without passion. It is only a dead, too often, indeed, a hypocritical morality which inveighs against the very form of passion."[29]

## Human nature as the history of desired Desires

Such dichotomy becomes crucial in light of a modern conception of freedom deeply marked by the opposition between nature and freedom —external causality determined by vital normativity, and internal causality determined under autonomous conditions, respectively. The naturalization of this dichotomy leads us to believe that a will that is merely determined by natural drives must be entirely conditioned by that which is extrinsic to it. Hegel's strategy, however, consists in affirming that natural drives *already are* instances of free will. Thus, because it is not exactly a choice, freedom must ultimately be seen as a form of reconciliation with that which had been initially understood as an *external cause*. Hegel will insist on the point:

> The will which is free as yet only *in itself* is the *immediate* or *natural* will. The determinations of the difference which is posited within the will by the self-determining concept appear within the immediate will as an *immediately* present content: these are the *drives, desires,* and *inclinations* by which the will finds itself naturally determined. This content, along with the determinations developed within it, does indeed originate in the will's rationality and it is thus rational in itself; but expressed in so immediate a form, it does not yet have the form of rationality.[30]

In other words, drives, desires and inclinations are not limits imposed upon human freedom, irrational elements connected to whatever does not submit to my will, as if it were a question of preserving a strict separation between *humanitas* and *animalitas*; rather, they emerge from the rationality of will and can, therefore, have a rational form. Thus, if Hegel can say that "underlying the demand for the *purification of the drives* is the general idea that they should be freed from the *form* of their immediate natural determinacy and from the

---

[29] HEGEL, *Enzyklopädie*, §474, as *Philosophy of Mind*, p. 211.
[30] HEGEL, *Philosophy of Right*, §11, p. 45.

subjectivity and contingency of their *content*, and restored to their substantial essence,"[31] that is because to free the drives from the form of their natural determinacy is to reveal them to be from the first animated by a normativity that cannot be conceived of as causally closed. And it could not be otherwise, as there is no place in Hegel for a merely natural drive. If it is possible to put a stop to the "natural violence of drives" without recourse to an even greater violence – the price of which shall be ever beyond our means – that is because doing so entails more than simply repression.

Let us clarify the point. The notion of drive (*Trieb*, a term occasionally rendered as "instinct" in psychoanalytic literature) is distinct, in humans, from that which Hegel calls instinct (*Instinkt*); the latter is conceived as a "purposive activity [*Zwecktätigkeit*] operating in an unconscious [*bewusstlose*] manner,"[32] said end being internal to the organism, and mostly connected to the preservation of the genus in question. When attached to animal behavior and thus subjected to instinct, a drive appears to be an activity (*Tätigkeit*), an excitation striving to accomplish an organism's internal ends – ends, furthermore, directed at some specific, given object.

Yet in what concerns specifically human behavior, this unity of drive and instinct no longer holds. Here, a drive appears as a determination of will (*Willensbestimmung*) that produces its own objectivity, positing for itself the object required for its satisfaction (on account of it not being immediately posited by instinct). This producing is an activity of Spirit that may already be found in drives. A drive is not the throbbing of a simple vitality – it is not merely *physis* –, but preserves a vitality that, because it is socially determined, must be spiritual as well.

There is a particular understanding of spiritual vitality that may be of use in resolving certain dichotomies. It would seem but a matter of accepting that, *when one mobilizes drives, one is in fact mobilizing one's memory of the "history of desired Desires,"* to use the beautiful expression coined by Alexandre Kojève.[33] I allow desired desires that have sought to actualize a successful form of life and that have influenced my formation to act as motive forces for my actions.[34] Through drives I desire – in a manner that is at first a deep source of

---

[31] Ibid., §19, p. 51.

[32] HEGEL, *Enzyklopädie*, §360, as *Philosophy of Nature III*, p. 145.

[33] KOJÈVE, Alexandre; *Introduction à la lecture de Hegel*. Paris: Gallimard, 1947.

[34] Which seems to confer validity to the affirmation that "we need, so that we may understand *who acts*, and *why*, to inquire into the positive conditions for self-actualization, and not merely, nor necessarily, into the negative conditions for the fulfillment of our desires" (JOUAN, Marlène; *Psychologie morale: autonomie, responsabilité et rationalité pratique*. Paris: Librairie Philosophique J. Vrin, 2008, p. 13).

conflict – the desires of others that have preceded me, and that have in some sense never ceased to speak within me. Thus we encounter the problem of the relation between subjectivity and intersubjectivity anew, in the heart of the relation between drives and will.

It is a fact that natural drives are seen by consciousness as opaque, negative, irrational. However, if they appear as such that is because they are *traces of a forgotten history, one that is no longer visible for consciousness on account of not being the history of the individual.* In the first chapter of this book we have seen how Hegel's conception of "life" manifested an ontological conflict between indeterminacy and determinacy. Something of that conflict seems to be transposed to the dichotomy between drives and will. Along these lines, let us recall the way Hegel describes, in the chapter of the *Phenomenology of Spirit* entitled "Pleasure and Necessity," the impasse of a life oriented towards the immediate fulfillment of drives. Such a life uncovers that what is called *necessity [Notwendigkeit]* is "just that about which we cannot say what it does, what its specific laws and positive content are, because it is the absolute pure Notion itself viewed as [mere] *being,* a *relation* that is simple and empty, but also irresistible and imperturbable, whose work is merely the nothingness of individuality."[35] That is to say, the drives that are manifested under the form of necessity and taken as immediate vital normativity are the nothingness of individuality, an opaque principle in both its laws and its content, that is nothing other than indeterminacy, simple and empty and purely negative.

The shattering of this illusion of immediacy – an illusion that ultimately leads to nothing but collapse – seems to depend, in a sense, on a rediscovery of the history that lies within nature. That would suggest that drives are in fact the non-individual segment of the history of subjects, the history of those desires that have preceded subjects and that nevertheless constitute them. The "passions of the individual," when returned to their truest essence, reveal themselves never to have been the passions of just one individual. The task is to recognize in drives something that was weaved behind our backs by the hands of a social experience that continues to act upon us. We shall encounter more refined versions of this idea in the second part of this book.

The proper understanding of this social experience is something Hegel alludes to when he writes of the reconduction of the drives to their "substantial essence," a reconduction that reminds us that *autonomy cannot simply be understood as the possibility for one to act differently from how one currently acts,* as we find in the model that privileges free will. Rather, *autonomy is deeply*

---

[35] HEGEL, *Phenomenology of Spirit*, p. 229.

*implicated in one's capacity to desire what one wants*,[36] that is to say, to express in action the reflexive unity of two moments: the conscious enunciation of will (which must take into account the moral requirements associated to the actualization of intersubjective forms of life consciously adopted and shared) and the drive of desire. A reflexive unity between the desire I have and my desire to have that desire. In other words, Hegel provides us here with an alternative conception of autonomy no longer conceived through the figure of self-legislation that sunders the subject into pathological desire and free will, but through one's capacity to overcome said sundering and understand the rational character of the heteronomous moment of will.[37]

## The risk of social atomization

The interpretation here advanced has the merit of pointing out how autonomy cannot affirm itself unless it is reconciled with that which initially appears as heteronomy and external causality. Furthermore, it insists that the process of reconciliation with natural drives provides us with a way of relating to ourselves that might make us more open to a new form of social relation that goes beyond a mere contractual relation between individual wills. The manner in which this reconciliation with one's drives occurs shows that free will is not constructed on the model of individual will. Rather, it is the acceptance of that which is non-individual and non-personalized in the subject, that which, at least in this case, consists in the acceptance of something whose initial manifestation must perforce be in the form of a drive. It is the model for an engagement with alterity (alterity in a sense beyond that of the simple figure of another individual, of another consciousness) through the problematization of relations with the self. That being the case, its social recognition must be actualized through *a process where will is delivered from its strict dependence on the figure of the individual.*

---

[36] Which is why Hegel can write "he is happy who has conformed [*hat angemessen*] his existence [*Dasein*] to his special character, will, and fancy, and so enjoys himself in that condition" (HEGEL, *Philosophy of History*, p. 41, with alterations).

[37] On that topic, it is worth recalling that "the splitting of morality into reason and inclination sometimes factually exists, yet always as the result of an ethical *flaw*, which is disharmony in the system of social relations within which each individual lives and acts" (WOOD, Allen; "Hegel's critique of morality", in: SIEP (org.), *Grundlinien der Philosophie des Rechts*. Berlin: Akademie Verlag, 2005, p. 158).

Without this engagement, the very constitution of autonomy shall lead to the generalization of a mode of action in which motivational systems cannot be understood outside the framework of individual will. Growing out of a conception of action in connection with the self-certifying dynamics of solipsistic consciousness, such autonomy, for Hegel, can only be the autonomy of isolated individuals. Thus, demands for autonomy are politically realized as a value mobilized towards justifying the constitution of a society of individuals, one where every social relation is conceived as a contract – the latter being the most prominent manifestation of a negative agreement (ultimately, the only possible form of agreement) between individual wills. From Hegel's perspective, such conditions entail a society haunted by an irreversible process of social atomization and disaggregation.

Hegel finds it symptomatic that authors for whom individual autonomy is the touchstone of practical reason cannot think through the nature of socio-political relations save through the concept of contract. He understands that this contractualist tendency has its origin within the atomized social circumstances of individuals whose interests must be restricted by the interests of other individuals – a restriction commonly legitimized by the juridical fiction of a social contract, through which only those interests that have the potential to be socially implemented are preserved, while those that do not meet this condition are discarded. This fiction must, in turn, feed upon an *elevation of fear to the position of central affect of political enfranchisement* (fear of having one's goods dispossessed, fear of a violent death, fear that one's privacy may be invaded, etc.). The contractualist perspective is inextricable from a politics aimed at the perpetuation of fear.

Conversely, if the contract may be said to be an important moment in the actualization of freedom, in that private property is itself a necessary moment of will as it struggles to be externalized and to be recognized in its particularity, the generalized application of the figure of the contract to the entirety of social life is a pathological distortion. Far from being a model for social cohesion, the metaphor of the contract is the hallmark of a crumbling society. One's marriage, one's relation to the state, the relations established between parents and children, these are not contractual relations: These are relations of a different nature, quite unlike the sort of relation one can establish with things one owns (as is the case in contractual relations).[38] These can only be conceived

---

[38] Hegel's anecdote concerning the Kantian notion of marriage as a contract is rather famous. Kant, as we know, defined marriage as a condition of reciprocal possession between two people, a *commercium sexuale*, or, better yet, "the union of two persons of different sexes for lifelong possession of each other's sexual attributes" (KANT, *Doctrine of Right*, §24). Hegel termed this definition "barbarism," noting that, were marriage indeed a contract granting

as contractual once they have entirely lost any semblance of substantiality. Subjects, not knowing how to behave in the context of social action and bereft of the social cohesion that makes concrete relations of recognition possible, hold fast to a reified understanding of the behavior of other subjects as if a given behavior were a thing, amenable to being listed among the clauses of a contract.

This interpretive scheme was already clearly apparent in his critique of Rousseau, about whom Hegel stated:

> Rousseau considered the will only in the determinate form of the individual will (as Fichte subsequently also did) and regarded the universal will not as the will's rationality in and for itself, but only as the *common element* arising out of this individual will *as a conscious will.* The union of individuals within the state thus becomes a contract ...[39]

Setting aside the question of whether or not this is an adequate reading of Rousseau's ideas, it is worth noting how Hegel criticizes the French philosopher for reflecting on will by means of the notion of individual will; a will that does not stem from a *universal will*, exactly, but from a *common will*, understood as an association of various wills that do not seek a universal object, but rather the conditions for the fulfillment of their particular systems of interests.[40] Indeed, as Gérard Lebrun reminds us by insisting on the "ultra-individualistic root of the contract," in the *Social Contract* man is still "he who looks at himself." Man's desire to acquire civil liberties stems from a demand born of his natural independence; his entry into civil unity is exclusively conducted in the name of his love for himself.

---

one possession over the "sexual attributes" of one's spouse, one could have recourse to the police any time one's spouse refused to consent to sexual relations, in blatant breach of one's property rights. Instead, Kant's definition merely revealed the complete inadequacy of contractual relations of property to intellections pertaining to the nature of intersubjective relations.

[39] HEGEL, *Philosophy of Right*, §258, p. 277.

[40] This might explain why, in justifying the social contract, "Rousseau's language is often as blatantly utilitarian as Hobbes': this is what you must lose, but look at what you get in return!" (LEBRUN, "Contrato social ou negócio de otário?" ["Social contract or a sucker's deal?"], in: *A filosofia e sua história* ["Philosophy and its history"]. São Paulo: Cosac & Naify, 2006, p. 226). Should we accept to enter into the social contract, then, "that is on account of having read, in the second book, that the 'private people' that constitute the 'public person' remain 'naturally independent' of the latter, therefore continuing to enjoy their natural right *as men*, while 'the Sovereign, for its part, cannot impose upon its subjects any fetters that are useless to the community'" (ibid., p. 230).

Hegel cannot help but read Rousseau – one of the central theoreticians of modern political philosophy – the way he does, given that the advent of modern free-market societies is understood by the German philosopher as a movement that is inseparable from that particular way of defining social relations. Such societies, therefore, are haunted by the risk of *social atomization*. What is meant by the latter expression is a process, intrinsic to civil capitalist societies, through which the normative force of social connections is weakened, while demands for decision-making become increasingly directed at individuals. Hegel describes one of the facets of this process as follows:

> In the shapes which it more commonly assumes in history (as in the case of Socrates, the Stoics, etc.), the tendency to look *inwards* into the self and to know and determine from within the self what is right and good appears in epochs when what is recognized as right and good in actuality and custom is unable to satisfy the better will. When the existing world of freedom has become unfaithful to the better will, this will no longer finds itself in the duties recognized in this world and must seek to recover in ideal inwardness alone that harmony which it has lost in actuality.[41]

As we have seen, Hegel knows his period to be in the throes of a "legitimacy crisis" of a similar sort. However, his skepticism relative to the strengthening of the individual as an element capable of counteracting this tendency results from, among other things, his awareness of the catastrophic consequences already evidenced in the socioeconomic sphere. Social atomization does not only mean that all decisory power concerning behavioral orientation rests squarely upon the shoulders of individuals, but further implies *an atomized way of understanding the dynamics of social life* – social life, from this perspective, consisting in the juxtaposition of individual wills. This should be a rather unsurprising fact, given that models for reflection on the structure of the moral subject typically stand as general models for the understanding of value- and norm-based modes of social action. One behaves morally in the same way one behaves socially: on the basis of the same structure of judgment and orientation (this being perhaps one of the fundamental intuitions behind Max Weber's study on protestant ethics).

In light of this reciprocity, it may be said that the models of individual autonomy and free will ultimately produce an image of society as a collection of norms, institutions and rules able to ensure the full realization of particular

---

[41] HEGEL, *Philosophy of Right*, §138, p. 166.

systems of interests, each of these oriented by its own singular take on what the actualization of the good and the amassing of wealth entail. Hegel is among the first to see that, when transplanted to the sphere of economical relations, this process necessarily gives rise to poverty and social alienation. Here we can clearly see the impact of Hegel's reading of the British economists which was so fundamental for his understanding of the functional complexity of modern societies.

This transition towards political economy is justified. The concept of freedom Hegel operates with is one in which defining the social conditions that would allow for its actualization is intrinsic to the very nature of freedom in question; hence, he should be able to describe situations in which the functioning of social life no longer provides the required preconditions for the fulfillment of the aspirations of individual autonomy.[42] An elementary precondition concerns the function of the economic sphere and its labor-related dynamics as the basis of the constitution of what Hegel understands by civil society. We may state as much because, for the philosopher, problems related to alienation and the redistribution of income in the economic sphere of labor are unequivocally indicative of more generalized problems pertaining to social recognition.

Processes of pauperization, for instance, do not simply consist in "social justice" problems for Hegel, but rather as problems related to the conditions for the actualization of freedom.[43] One cannot be free, of course, in a state of extreme poverty. The freedom to choose is radically limited for one assailed by poverty and subsequently subjected to social subservience. Much like the Stoic Epictetus, who despite being a slave declared himself a free man, I may operate under the illusion that regardless of any restrictions imposed upon my person I remain a free thinker, coming to decisions through my individual free will. However, a freedom that has been reduced to the condition of pure

---

[42] As Pippin saw rather clearly, Hegel "denies that we can separate the moral-psychological, individual dimension of freedom (the possibility of the 'freedom of the will') from the social relations of dependence and independence, which are taken to be equally constitutive of freedom (the freedom to act)" (PIPPIN, *Hegel's Practical Philosophy*, p. 7).

[43] In relation to this, it is always worth remembering how Hegel will justify that *right of necessity* (*Notrecht*) that may be claimed under extreme circumstances: "Life, as the totality of ends, has a right in opposition to abstract right. If, for example, it can be preserved by stealing a loaf, this certainly constitutes an infringement of someone's property, but it would be wrong to regard such an action as common theft. If someone whose life is in danger were not allowed to take measures to save himself, he would be destined to forfeit all his rights; and since he would be deprived of life, his entire freedom would be negated." (HEGEL, *Philosophy of Right*, §127, p. 155) In other words, the problem is entirely related to the definition of the social conditions for the actualization of the concept of freedom.

thought is hardly effective, in the sense that it only minimally determines the motive force behind our actions.

Let us start, then, with the young Hegel's statement that individuals seeking to attain the good and wealth by reference to their own particular systems of interests triggered the following process:

> As manners and way of life [*Lebensart*] changed, each individual became more preoccupied with his own needs and private affairs; the overwhelming majority of free men – the middle class [*Bürgerstand*] proper – had to look exclusively to its own needs and livelihood; the states became larger, the external circumstances became more complex [*verwickelter*], and those who had to concern themselves exclusively with the latter became a class [*Stand*] of their own; the mass of things required by free men and by the nobility, by those who had to maintain themselves in their position either by industry or by service to the state, grew larger.[44]

In other words, society entered a process of multiplication of needs and of affirmation of interests. As needs escalated, the means to satisfy them grew in number and complexity, on one hand producing wealth, refinement and development, and, on the other, deepening the dependence of individuals on one another. On this point, Hegel notes: "Needs and means, as existing in reality [*als reelles Dasein*], become a *being* [*Sein*] for *others* by whose needs and work their satisfaction is mutually conditioned."[45] My work becomes a means for the satisfaction of others, while my own satisfaction depends on their labor. This is what Hegel terms a "system of needs."

However, Hegel insists that this system of needs, constituted through a multiple dependence on labor, has as its ineluctable consequence the *division* of labor. From his youth Hegel realizes that the development of modern free-market societies requires an ever-greater specialization consequent upon the increasing complexity of the objects produced and of the growth of large-scale production. Furthermore, Hegel is aware this process inevitably leads to a simplification and *abstraction* of individual work that renders the entire sphere of labor increasingly *mechanical*, ultimately leading human beings to be replaced by machines, as clearly stated in paragraph 198 of the *Elements of the Philosophy of Right*. Hegel might have been the first to understand that mechanization and automatization are inescapable consequences of

---

[44] HEGEL, "The German Constitution," in: *Political Writings*, ed. by L. Dickey & J. B. Nisbet. Cambridge: Cambridge University Press, 2004, p. 63.

[45] HEGEL, *Philosophy of Right*, § 192, p. 229.

modern society that lead subjects to suffer from social alienation due to their dependence on a mode of exteriorization which deadens them.[46] Simply put, the seeking of both the good and wealth by reference to particular systems of interests results in the obstruction of the structure of labor as a space for recognition.

In addition to this, Hegel will recognize yet another serious social problem stemming from the way labor is organized in liberal societies; it appears in the following passage, taken from the *Elements of the Philosophy of Right*:

> When the activity of civil society is unrestricted, it is occupied internally with *expanding its population and industry*. On the one hand, as the association of human beings through their needs is *universalized*, and with it the ways in which means of satisfying these needs are devised and made available, the *accumulation of wealth* increases; for the greatest profit is derived from this twofold universality. But on the other hand, the *specialization* [*Vereinzelung*] and *limitation* of particular work also increase, as do likewise the *dependence* and *want* [*Not*] of the class which is tied to such work; this in turn leads to an inability to feel and enjoy the wider freedoms, and particularly the spiritual advantages, of civil society.[47]

One's mode of insertion into the universe of labor is conditional, according to Hegel, on a relation between one's financial assets and the talents or skills one possesses or is allowed to develop. The implication is that not only is entry into the universe of labor uneven, but also that there is a tendency for wealth to be concentrated in the hands of those who are already wealthy, ensuring a deepening of the social fracture and a devaluing of all work subjected to the division of labor. Thus, at the dawn of the nineteenth century, Hegel is one of the few philosophers to clearly evince awareness of the true scope of the problems that would thenceforth orient the field of the "social question"

---

[46] As may be gathered from the following statement, written in the philosopher's youth: "Work becomes... absolutely more and more dead, it becomes machine-labour, the individual's own skill becomes infinitely limited, and the consciousness of the factory worker is degraded to the utmost level of dullness [*Stumpfheit*]" (HEGEL, *Jenaer Realphilosophie I: Die Vorlesungen von 1803/4*. Leipzig, 1932, p. 239 *apud* AVINERI, Schlomo; *Hegel's Theory of the Modern State*. London: Cambridge University Press, 1972, p. 93). For this and other reasons, our assent ought to be given to the following remark by Shlomo Avineri: "Hegel accepts Smith's view that behind the senseless and conflicting clash of egoistic interests in civil society a higher purpose can be discerned; but be does not agree with the hidden assumption which implies that everyone in society is thus being well taken care of" (ibid., p. 148).

[47] HEGEL, *Philosophy of Right*, §243, p. 266.

in western societies. For him, the tendency towards growing inequality and pauperization – which leads him to consider that however wealthy civil society may become, it shall never be sufficiently wealthy to eliminate poverty – is a threat to all possibilities for the actualization of a form of life regulated by the concept of freedom. Because of that, reflections pertaining to the structure of modern labor societies are not external to reflections on free will, or on the fate of freedom as a notion derived from a hypostatization of the concept of individual autonomy.

## Ethicity and the dual role of the state

Hegel's proposed solution against both of these hazards to the cohesiveness of social life, driven by the hypostatization of models of freedom based on autonomy and authenticity, respectively, involves the strengthening of the state. In order to secure increased state power without mere violence, something must be preserved from each of these models.

The state ought to provide an object for negative freedom; that is, it should confer an institutional form to negation that prevents individuals from becoming petrified within fixed social determinations (as "members of a class" or "representatives of the interests of a class"). This is a notion Hegel will advance in the context of his reflections on war. Through war, the state will bring to term an intricate process of constituting individualities through the internalization of the formative character of the experience of the negativity of death. This is a recurrent theme in Hegel's works; we may find it, for instance, in the *Phenomenology of Spirit*, where confronting death appears as a movement towards the very foundation of existence. Turning to a different section of the same work, the one titled "Spirit," one finds statements such as the following:

> In order not to let [individuals] become rooted and set in this isolation, thereby breaking up the whole and letting the [communal] spirit evaporate, government has from time to time to shake them to their core by war. By this means the government upsets their established order, and violates their right to independence, while the individuals who, absorbed in their own way of life, break loose from the whole and strive after the inviolable independence and security of the person, are made to feel in the task laid on them their lord and master, death. Spirit, by thus throwing into the melting-pot the stable existence of these systems, checks their tendency to fall away from the ethical order,

and to be submerged in a [merely] natural existence; and it preserves and raises conscious self into freedom and its own power. The negative essence shows itself to be the real power of the community and the force of its self-preservation.[48]

If government does not rest on a promise of peace, that is because the formative process that began within the family must also animate processes of social interaction as means towards the actualization of subjectivity as a universality bereft of all adherence to the natural *Dasein*: a subjectivity actualized in the work of confronting the increasing fragility of static images of the world.

It should be noted that this war of which Hegel speaks is not the outburst of rage that results from damage done to one's private property, or to one as a private individual. War is the sphere of the "sacrifice of the singular to the universal as an accepted risk."[49] If in Greece war, understood in this sense, was indeed a feature of the ethical life of the population (given that taking part in war was required of every citizen), it is nevertheless true that Hegel conceives of the state here as something that dissolves the security and fixity of finite determinations. War is the name of that process that reveals how the annihilation of the finite brings about the manifestation of its essence. Hegel is unequivocal on this point: there is an "ethical moment of war." Furthermore,

war should not be regarded as an absolute evil [*Übel*] and as a purely external contingency whose cause [*Grund*] is therefore itself contingent [...]. It is necessary that the finite – such as property and life – should be posited as contingent, because contingency is the concept of the finite. [...] War is that condition in which the vanity of temporal things and temporal goods – which tends at other times to be merely a pious phrase – takes on a serious significance, and it is accordingly the moment in which the ideality of the particular attains its right and becomes actuality.[50]

---

[48] HEGEL, *Phenomenology of Spirit*, p. 272-273.

[49] SOUCHE-DAGUES, Denise; *Liberté et négativité dans la pensée politique de Hegel*. Paris: Vrin, 1997, p. 26. Furthermore, "as war enfeebles the safety and fixity of finite determinations, it renders them in-finite. Their annihilation is the manifestation of its essence. This twofold manifestation of war follows the twofold manifestation of negation and infinity. War, as pure annihilation, as a destructive form of leveling, is directed against the materiality of finitude; the war that blooms within ethical life is the element by means of which this life acquires its infinite spiritual essence" (*ibid.*, p. 28).

[50] HEGEL, *Philosophy of Right*, §324, p. 361.

The attempt being made here is not, of course, to provide an argument in defense of belligerent states; rather, it is to go beyond the literality of such remarks and seek their actual function. In fact, the hypothesis I would like to defend is that these statements on war are of central importance for working out the necessary configuration of any institutions and social practices that aim to truly and properly meet the demands of modernity. Perhaps the most essential aspect of these reflections on war is Hegel's claim that institutions willing to recognize non-substantial subjects must be founded on social practices that can acknowledge the sovereignty of a figure of negation whose phenomenological manifestation may be that of a symbolic death. This is the proper figure for *social institutions whose function has ceased to be the identification of subjects within fixed determinations and identities.* Were our purpose merely to reflect on this process, it could have been done in several ways that do not involve Hegel's apology of war, an apology that is certainly questionable and hardly defensible – not merely in our day and age, but even back in the philosopher's time. Still, to go beyond the letter of Hegel's work is to attempt a recovery of his intention to, in the final analysis, expose the necessary relation between the notion of negativity and the state. We shall return to the point later on.

If the problem of demands for authenticity can be regulated in this fashion, the problem of autonomy will in its turn require a state capable of providing the necessary social conditions for autonomy within social systems of judgment. This much is present in Hegel's considerations on "ethicity" (*Sittlichkeit*), which must furnish the institutional structure for the actualization of individual aspirations to autonomy. Said structure also encompasses the requirement that the state oppose the social divide inherent to the functioning of civil society within the capitalist dynamic of development. Ethical life cannot be indifferent to the social question, or evade the mandatory institutionalization of policies aimed at combating poverty (a consequence easily derived from the *Philosophy of Right,* even if the letter of the work does not state as much). Still, the type of consolidation of customs and modes of judgment that can be expected from the application of the notion of ethicity to modern life is something that deserves a more thorough analysis.

Let us begin by noting that *the modern state has a dual function that is apparently contradictory. It must embrace the experience of indeterminacy that is present in individualities and yet provide the determinations required for the actualization of autonomy through the constitution of a set of positive laws amenable to universalization.* It provides a collection of social rules while also providing the means for the expression of that which, in subjects, is recalcitrant to determination in the context of social rules. *It at once creates institutions and manages indeterminacy.* To clarify, for Hegel the state is an institution that possesses the ability to manage indeterminacy, which is to say, to overcome it without outright negating it.

Finally, we may begin to understand why Hegel feels compelled to criticize the liberal conception of state, insofar as the latter is viewed as an institution responsible for ensuring the functioning of those principles that are intrinsic to civil society, such as the right to property, individual liberties, and respect for contracts. While the state may be rather adept at incorporating such demands, there is more to it than this subordinate function. It must do what civil society cannot (such as implementing policies of redistribution through which social demands for recognition may be actualized), and, most of all, must shake subjects from a state of complete immersion in their condition as individuals endowed with particular systems of interests. In a sense, the state de-individualizes its subjects. Such de-individualization, however, is a necessary condition for freedom, as it bears the potential to open up the subject to something other than his or her isolated, atomized condition as an individual. Hegel knows, after all, that while much suffering can ensue on account of our failure to be individuals – that is, our failure to attain actualization as individualities capable of making themselves recognized within social life – there is also much suffering to be had in being *just* an individual: a form of suffering that manifests as isolation, as a feeling of growing emptiness, and as the utter inability to adequately orient one's actions in a social context.

With this paradoxical potential in mind, one of the most important ideas in Hegel's philosophy of right may be more clearly understood. If at various instances the philosopher insists that individual interests must not be repressed (*unterdrückt*), but rather brought into concordance with the universal, that is because

> individuals as a mass [*Menge*] are themselves spiritual natures, and they therefore embody a dual moment, namely the extreme of *individuality* [*Einzelheit*] which knows and wills *for itself*, and the extreme of *universality*, which knows and wills the substantial. They can therefore attain their right in both of these respects only in so far as they have actuality both as private and as substantial persons.[51]

---

[51] Ibid., §264, p. 287.

The importance of this statement should not be underestimated, as it reminds us that the conflict between the particular and the universal is not a conflict between the individual and the state (as Adorno's remarks, reproduced above, seem to presuppose), but a conflict taking place within individuality itself. The conflict is intrinsic to every individual, thus allowing the state to appear as a form of overcoming that, at the same time, is able to preserve individuality. In a certain sense, one's relation to the state is, for Hegel, a relation of individuality with itself, an internal relation that attains externality.

As they have the moment of substantiality inside them, individuals actualize a fundamental aspect of their will through the creation of institutions and laws (laws which, in turn, have in the establishment of a constitution their most fully-realized manifestation). The conditions for this are prepared by the particular way an individual is engendered through his or her relation with normative institutions, such as the family unit or civil society. In this way, the transition to state institutions makes ample use of processes already put in circulation in the other two spheres of social life. This may be termed the *strong* sense of Hegelian institutionalism, where even substantial self-relations must be actualized through the constitution of institutional structures both visible and active within social life.

At this juncture, however, it might be appropriate to bring the issue to a close by inquiring into *what an institution can actually do*. We normally think of institutions as markedly normative and disciplinary structures that perpetuate clearly defined modes for the functioning of social life. In these terms, their normative force would be indissociable from the material reproduction of hegemonic values and forms of life, or from the attendant blocking of the development of alternatives to such values or forms. Yet it seems quite possible that the essential aspects of the Hegelian theory of the state may nevertheless be preserved if we instead regard institutions as potential modes for *the management of conflicts* pertaining to norms and values. Even if this is not the exact formulation that appears in Hegel's texts, it seems to adequately address the particular way Hegelian themes feature in reflections on the challenges endemic to a contemporary theory of the state.

We know that, on one hand, there are normative laws, while, on the other, there are laws that attempt to create institutional frameworks for the politicization of conflicts pertaining to values and norms. These "second-order laws" teach us that we do not have to be in agreement on fundamental values; rather, *we must be in agreement on forms of politicizing value-based conflicts*, which is something altogether different.

When considering that Hegel grounds his conception of the state in ethicity, we must not forget that modern ethicity is radically unlike that ancient ethicity peculiar to the substantial relations of the Greek polis, or of the first Christian communities based on love. Modern ethicity is deeply conflictual, in that it is the social sedimentation of a long history of conflicts relative to the concepts that organize our modes of living, such as "freedom," "autonomy," the "common good" and so forth. Likewise, the history of Spirit is, at bottom, the history of human conflict. We should bear this in mind, suggests Hegel, whenever we consider what to expect from the modern state; it reveals – at least according to the philosopher –, that *the modern state is born as an attempt at creating a way to institutionalize value-based conflicts.*

It may even be said that the modern state should be capable of actualizing the history of Spirit, in the sense of making contemporary struggles surrounding values resonant with the echoes of previous struggles. This way, political subjects engaged in social conflict could attain unprecedented historical density, and become modes of actualization for a past that has never fully passed. In this fashion, as shall be seen in the following chapter, subjects, as *political* subjects, may once again experience infinitude.

Let us note, finally, that this form of institutionalization potentially allowable in the modern state is the very condition required for the production of social normativities of low prescriptive potential that are nonetheless strong enough to ensure social cohesion. Such normativities are qualified as having "low prescriptive potential" in that they do not dictate exactly what one must do, or exactly how one should interpret a given set of values, but rather how one should negotiate both the interpretations one aims to defend and the legitimacy of what one intends to do. The success of such negotiations depends on understanding that one's transformation into a political subject is connected to one's ability to transform one's own political gestures into manifestations of a trans-individual multiplicity of desires. In formulating these conditions, the best line of inquiry might be the following: two hundred years after Hegel, can we conceive of a better regulative idea to orient our political struggles? And are we truly justified in abandoning the struggle for a state model of this nature?

# CHAPTER III

# Not all things are destined for transience

*In the first place we must here banish from our minds
the prejudice in favor of duration, as if it had
any advantage as compared with transience.*
Hegel

*The tradition of all the dead generations
weighs like a nightmare on
the brain of the living.*
Karl Marx

Let us dwell for a moment on the suggestive closing lines of the preceding chapter: the transformation of individualities into political subjects implies their having the ability to convert subjective gestures into manifestations of a trans-individual multiplicity of desires. Were that to be the case, political subjects could conceivable attain a historical density of such great proportions within social struggles that they would in effect become modes for the actualization of a past never entirely gone, and, subsequently, points of contact for experiences scattered throughout time. This is unequivocally grasped by Walter Benjamin, as evidenced in the following statement:

> History is the subject of a structure whose site is not homogeneous, empty time, but time filled by the presence of the now [*Jetztzeit*]. Thus, to Robespierre ancient Rome was a past charged with the time of the now which he blasted out of the continuum of history. The French Revolution viewed itself as Rome reincarnate. It evoked ancient Rome the way fashion evokes costumes of the past.[1]

This notion – which, I would contend, may already be found in Hegel – could be systematically explored in several different ways. One approach

---

[1]  BENJAMIN, Walter; "Theses on the Philosophy of History". In: *Illuminations*, translated by H. Zohn. New York: Schocken Books, 2007, p. 261.

stands out as being of particular importance to my concerns here, insofar as it establishes a point of articulation between notions such as subject, infinitude, and temporality. An articulation of this sort should allow for greater insight into the nature of that negativity found in the subject, specifically through an understanding of how said negativity has the temporal actualization of infinity as its ideal figuration, and of how "subject" may be correctly employed as a term to denote the location where said actualization occurs. If it is indeed proper for this temporal actualization of multiple "nows" to be termed "infinity" – as if the actual now were merely the contraction of a series of nows pointedly refusing to go by –, that is because the question of infinity, in Hegel, is connected to that which refuses to be circumscribed by, or intuited through, the forms of space and time in our transcendental aesthetics. Put differently, the conundrum in Hegelian thought is not connected to ways of conceiving that which is infinitely large or infinitely small, but rather that which is infinitely *other*. And this, of course, is precisely what time is: the dimension of that which is infinitely other.

At the same time, this articulation of subject, infinitude and temporality allows for a renewed understanding of Hegel's "historical teleology," clearing the way for a reconsideration of the modalities of reconciliation between dialectics and history. A new conception arises, then, in which reconciliation with historicity no longer depends on the suspension of dialectical movement nor on the reinstatement of the utter stillness of the speculative.

Such investigations demand, at their very inception, a more precise definition of "infinitude" and related difficulties. This leads us, unhesitatingly, to certain passages that are central to Hegel's *Science of Logic*. In order to demonstrate how *considerations on which specific problems the category of subject is meant to solve are dependent on a given ontology*. The ontology in question does not obstruct reflections on the dynamic character of historical processes, however, but better equips us to consider the unavoidable instability of all determination, or the universal prevalence of internal movement in historical situations. In what follows, the restoration of this ontology will feature as an important strategy for reflections on what should take the place of a non-normative anthropology.

## Conflicts in Dasein

One of the first categories Hegel presents us with in the *Science of Logic* is that of *Dasein* ("being there," often given in English as "existence"), which is the very first category of determinate, qualitatively differentiated being.

Hence, it confronts us for the first time with the problem of what the nature of determination must be if it is to integrate an ontology that starts from the affirmation that, paradoxically, an ontology of being is impossible (as "being and nothing are the same"[2]), and that one should understand becoming (*Werden*) as "the first concrete thought and thus the first concept."[3]

This explains why the core statement of Hegel's definition of *Dasein* is "Existence [*Dasein*] proceeds from becoming" (*"Aus dem Werden geht das Dasein hervor"*).[4] This is a fundamental claim not merely because it establishes the concept's provenance – a point of origin, of sorts –, but also because it clarifies its destination. Emerging from becoming, *Dasein* is destined to establish the mode of determination of whatever has its reality in restlessness and movement. This determination, originating as it does from becoming, will be ever marked by continuous alteration (*Veränderung*). Thus, *Dasein* reminds us that whatever is determined is determined to be a figure of transformation.

The establishment of becoming as the first among concepts is indicative of Hegel's overarching project of replacing the static character of being with temporality; he will speak of the moments of becoming as "rising and falling" (*Entstehen und Vergehen*), and define becoming as that potent restlessness that corrodes being to the point of evanescence. This is made clear by statements such as "becoming is the vanishing of being into nothing, and of nothing into being, and the vanishing of being and nothing in general [...]. This result is a vanishedness [*Verschwundensein*], but it is not *nothing*."[5] In other words, "becoming," as a category, establishes the meaning of "being" and of "nothing" as a transition towards their own constitutive thresholds, thus prodding us to overcome the limited character of these categories through a problematization

---

[2]  HEGEL, *Enzyklopädie*, § 88, as *Encyclopedia of the Philosophical Sciences in Basic Outline, Part 1: Science of Logic*, trans. and ed. by K. Brinkmann & D. O. Dahlstrom. Cambridge: Cambridge University Press, 2010, p. 140. Hegel will also remark that being is "pure inde-terminateness and emptiness," (HEGEL, *Science of Logic*, p. 59) that is, thought bereft of object. Defining nothing – "pure nothingness" – as "simple equality with itself, complete emptiness," (*ibid.*), Hegel acknowledges that it may exist within our intuition or thought. In this sense, it may seem reminiscent of the Kantian notion of *ens imaginarium*; the differ-ence, here, is that being, understood to be the form of empty, objectless intuition, is more than just a formal condition on which phenomena depend (although it does fulfill this role, so to speak). More precisely, its function is not determining the general formal conditions allowing an object to be; rather, *it is the excess that indicates that the structuring of every object will invariably be haunted by indeterminacy.*

[3]  HEGEL, *Enzyklopädie*, § 88, as *Encyclopedia Part 1: Science of Logic*, p. 143.

[4]  HEGEL, *Science of Logic*, p. 83.

[5]  *Ibid*, p. 81.

of their implied grammar, whose intended referent is a class of experience that eludes it at every turn.[6]

That being the case, the mode of determination that is particular to *Dasein*, given that it emerges directly from becoming, can never give rise to complete, fully limited determinateness. Hence, there will always be a decisive contradiction within *Dasein*. As a "concrete" existence, *Dasein* will be something (*Etwas*) both limited and finite. The expression itself suggests the limitations of which it is comprised: *Da-sein*, "there-being," that is, "being (*Sein*) in a certain *place* (*da*)."[7] This reference to space is fundamental, regardless of Hegel's own insistence on the irrelevance of this spatial representation (*Raumvorstellung*). After all, *Dasein* is that being whose presence – at least at first – accords to that of all things that exist in space; which is to say, its presence is marked by juxtaposition, by separation, by the unavoidable presence of limits between things. Two things, it is said, cannot occupy the same place in space, at least not at the same time. With that in mind, Hegel describes the mode of being-in-space as "juxtaposition" (*Nebeneinander*). In the case of *Dasein*, this appears as a form of solidarity between its position as something and its relation to another, a relation by which it is limited. Said solidarity will, as we shall see, problematize the very notion of limit.

However, time and space are not fixed categories in relation to one another, a fact which explains Hegel's insistence that we refrain from hypostatizing the special nature of the determination of *Dasein*. For Hegel, there is a movement through which space becomes time, through which it brings into itself the mode of ordering that is particular to things in time: "Time, to put it briefly, is the truth of space. Consequently, the first required step towards the attainment of a speculative notion of time is to highlight existing relations between space and time."[8] Hence, *Dasein* may be understood as the locus through which the particular arrangement of things in time can manifest.

In general terms, then, it may be said that, for Hegel, one's intuition of something *in time* is (at first) nothing other than one's experience of being in

---

[6]  In this sense, it must be said that "Every determination has its moment of being and nothing-ness. All subsequent logical determinations will bear the mark of the indeterminacy of being. The status of alterity will change, mediations will make themselves present, and so will essence and reflection, but determinations will remain forever marked by this oscillation between be-ing and nothingness at their constitution" (DRIGO, Larissa; *De la contingence dans la* Science de La Logique *de Hegel*, Mémoire, Université Paris I, 2010-2011, p. 25) – a precise reminder that the statement according to which being is in fact nothing seeks to undermine the *onto-logical assuredness* of something meant to ground the determination of objects.

[7]  HEGEL, *Science of Logic*, p. 83.

[8]  ARANTES, *Hegel, a ordem do tempo* ["Hegel, the order of time"]. São Paulo: Hucitec, 2001, p. 22.

the presence of something *right now*. This "now," however, is not a mode of presence for singular things; "now" is, in a sense, a term denoting the general negation of every instant. One may attempt to indicate the present instant by stating, "*this* instant is the *now*"; still, the now in question ceases to be before the indication has even been fully uttered, and the reference is immediately transferred to the instant that follows. And yet, the expression "now" should not be understood as denoting this other instant, but rather the incessant passage from one instant to another. This seems to be what Hegel meant when he stated that, in reality, the now is the form of the "negative in general" – a figure of the negative that should be understood as the manifestation of that which can be neither this nor that, but is, instead, "not-this" (*nicht-dieses*). In other words, the now is the form of the evanescence of every instant. This is a reading one also finds in Heidegger, as may be gathered from his remark that "the most appropriate expression which the Hegelian treatment of time receives, lies in his defining it as 'the *negation of a negation*' (that is, of punctuality)."[9] – which, finally, is equivalent to saying that one's intuition of something *in time* is an experience of something which can only be by not being (as per Hegel's proposition that "the temporal is, in that it is not, and is not, in that it is"[10]).

However, it must be remarked that, beyond what Heidegger intends, Hegel's conception also implies a mode of presence no longer dependent on the primacy of visibility that is common to whatever presents itself in space, where limits are a mode of being in exteriority. Indeed, what we find is quite the reverse: a mode of presence in which things never quite coincide with themselves. Hegel would go as far as stating that

> the *finite* present is the *now* fixed as being, and as the concrete unity, distinguished from the negative, the abstract moments of the past and the future, it is therefore the affirmative factor; yet in itself this being is merely abstract, and disappears into nothing. [...] [For] the concrete present is the result of the past, and is pregnant with the future. The true present is therefore eternity.[11]

---

[9] HEIDEGGER, Martin; *Being and Time*, § 432, translated by J. Macquarrie and E. Robinson. Oxford: Basil Blackwell, 1985, p. 484.

[10] HEGEL, *Enzyklopädie*, § 448, as *Philosophy of Mind*, p. 181.

[11] HEGEL, *Enzyklopädie*, § 259, as *Philosophy of Nature I*, pp. 233-235. As Denise Souche-Dagues puts it, "The simultaneous overcoming of both negation and that which it negates invites us to think of a *result*, namely that time is neither now, nor future, nor past, but all of these moments in their totality: it is infinite" (SOUCHES-DAGUES, *Recherches hégéliennes: infini et dialectique*. Paris: Vrin, 1994, p. 127).

Unlike the finitude of the present conceived as now, "fixed as being," the true present bears the promise of an experience of infinity. On one hand, this infinity of eternity requires renewed concepts of presence and determination; on the other, it reveals how reflections on the problem of the infinite in Hegel would also need to address the true locus from which it stems: his account of temporality.

Such considerations ought in turn to be brought to bear on a strict thematization of history, effective time being neither a devastating curse upon the "primal" experience of temporality nor its dissolution. Rather, effective time is the process through which infinity is necessarily actualized, the implication being that it would be possible to experience *temporal* becoming as *historical* becoming. An understanding of the renewed concept of presence this particular experience of time requires is, thus, the *sine qua non* condition if one is to clearly define the modes of manifestation of subjects within history, as well as the modes of constitution of objects and processes that do not appear except within history. Still, as I would like to demonstrate, such modes of manifestation can under no circumstances be reduced to the actions of an individual. For Hegel, *history is the sphere within which individuals are dissolved, and transindividual processes take shape.* And yet the dissolution in question has a peculiar character, not being the result of the outward imposition of a foreign principle on individuality; it results, instead, from awareness of the performance potency of that which inhabits individuality and yet resists total determination by the finite character of the individual.

This form of the transindividual is necessarily the form of infinity as well, on account of the latter's being the determination of *multiplicities in the process of being actualized* – the determination, that is, of something unrestricted by the limitations of individuated form. In this sense, historical subjects cannot be reduced to the form of the individual; one's understanding of oneself as a historical subject entails one's reconciliation with a temporality that is a mode of manifestation of infinity.

A historical subject, then, is the transindividual actualization of temporal infinity. Such a subject does not act on the basis of his own particular system of interests, but allows his actions to resonate with the "history of desired desires." This is something Hegel alludes to, when he remarks that historical subjects – "world-historical men" – are animated by "that Spirit which [...] is the inmost soul of all individuals [*innerliche Seele aller Individuen*]; but in a state of unconsciousness [*bewusstlose Innerlichkeit*] which the great men in question aroused."[12]

---

[12] HEGEL, *Philosophy of History*, p. 45.

A better understanding of the transindividual character of this historical subject requires that attention be given to what is possibly the least likely segment in Hegelian philosophy to deal with the issue: the considerations that appear in the *Science of Logic*. Only the logical construction of the concept of infinity can assist us in our present endeavors.

## *The problem of finitude*

Let us return, then, to the Hegelian concept of *Dasein* as it appears in the *Science of Logic*. Here, the need to reconstruct the available processes of determination first becomes apparent as a consequence of considerations on the dialectical relation between the finite and infinity. Said relation is one in which "infinity becomes an internal reason of the finite itself."[13] It seems to be Hegel's intention to show that distinctions between the finite and the infinite are ultimately untenable, particularly in view of the fact that the finite is destined to perish; to show, in other words, what it means to say that "it is the very nature of the finite that it transcend itself [*über sich hinauszugehen*], that it negate its negation and become infinite."[14]

Hegel reminds us that, when we say that something is finite, we mean its very nature is non-being. Finite things, after all, are not merely things that undergo change, but things that perish, with that being their essential determination: "the hour of their birth is the hour of their death."[15] What the metaphor suggests is that while finite things do have being, it is being characterized by a negative relation-to-self. What is essential to finite things remains external to them, in something that is not revealed by those forms of determination peculiar to the finite. Nevertheless, this negative relation-to-self is an illusion, as it consists in the attempted elevation of non-being to the status of an autonomous mode of being, one possessed of "its own legality" within the sphere of the existent.

On one hand, a legality of this sort would entail the perpetuation of the distinction between the finite and the Absolute; on the other, and despite this distinction, one could simply affirm that knowledge outside the Absolute can nonetheless aspire to validity – a position contingent on the acceptance that "cognition in general, though it be incapable of grasping the Absolute, is still

---

[13] BADIOU, Alain; *Being and Event*, translated by O. Feltham. New York: Continuum, 2007, p. 163.
[14] HEGEL, *Science of Logic*, p. 109.
[15] *Ibid.*, p. 101.

capable of grasping other kinds of truth."[16] In other words, it is as though the finite could lay claim to the truth within its own autonomous dimension. To defend the ontological sundering of the finite and the infinite is, in a sense, to defend that the finite *is*, that it has a being all its own that rules undisputed within a delimited sphere of knowledge. This is precisely what Hegel could not accept,[17] on account of the following: the finite being entitled to its own existence implies that the infinite is merely the "non-finite," or that which has its being only in contrast to the finite. This reciprocal determination between the finite and the infinite brings about the abasement of the latter, turning it into what Hegel terms a "finite infinite."[18]

What Hegel intends to show is that the opposite is true; that however much one may insist on the ontological autonomy of the finite it amounts to little more than a grammatical mistake, one that disappears once consciousness is able to thematize that which is given to experience yet lies beyond what can be represented by the understanding. Insofar as the finite does not appear save as limited, as perishable, we must ask ourselves whether, in the being of the finite, perishing remains absolutely or must be dissolved as well. On this point, Hegel is clear: "The development of the finite will show that [...] the finite is not just perishable, and that it perishes, but that the perishing, the nothing, is rather not the last of it; that the perishing rather perishes."[19] Hegel will say that the finite is merely that which infinitely perishes, that which is infinitely insufficient, and that this evanescence is the truth of its being – that aspect of it which must be repeated

---

[16]  HEGEL, *Phenomenology of Spirit*, § 75, pp. 47-48.

[17]  "In reality, one is forced to choose between the two following propositions: 1) Being is something the Finite and the Infinite both possess; 2) the Finite has a Being that is peculiar to itself. To favor one of these theses is to necessarily hold the other as untenable. And yet for the longest time Metaphysics attempted to surreptitiously favor both at once. After supporting the second thesis (the Finite has a Being all its own), and with it the mutual independence of the Finite and the Infinite, it would formulate questions pertaining to their unification. It would ask, albeit covertly: how can finite being, insofar as it is *finite*, be infinite? [...] Dialectics does not force any outcomes; it simply brings any latent sophistry to the daylight." (LEBRUN, *A paciência do conceito*, p. 185) Hence, "the philosopher has a role to play in the emergence of the idea of infinity. His role, however, is simply to *let* the infinity inherent in finitude itself come explicitly to the fore" (HOULGATE, Stephen; *The Opening of Hegel's Logic*. West Lafayette: Purdue University Press, 2006, p. 396).

[18]  After all, "[the] dualism that makes the opposition of the finite and the infinite insuperable fails to make the simple observation that in this manner the infinite is at once only *one of the two*, that it is thus made into merely one *particular* for which the finite is the other particular" (HEGEL, *Enzyklopädie*, § 95, as *Encyclopedia Part 1: Science of Logic*, p. 150).

[19]  HEGEL, *Science of Logic*, p. 103.

infinitely.[20] Finite things are thus contradictory entities whose being immediately becomes non-being. It is with this in mind that one should approach Hegel's claim: "In going away and ceasing to be, the finite has not ceased; it has only become momentarily an *other* finite which equally is, however, a going-away as a going-over into another finite, and so forth *to infinity*."[21]

Such considerations allow us to say that because it does not constitute a separate reality, *the infinite in Hegel is just the affirmation of the necessary character of the self-dissolution of the finite*. Of course, such a statement could rather easily be misconstrued, it might be taken to imply that "infinity" is just the name one gives to the finite's ceaseless confession of impotence. It would be easy to conclude as much, given a somewhat forced reading to bear on Hegel's statement that the infinite is "the nothing of the finite."[22] The end result would be our remaining stuck in the finite, now eternalized under a negative form, as though we were dealing with a speculative variation on negative theology.

What Hegel defends, however, is that while we have indeed never left the finite, that is because "finite" is just how one refers to something infinite that no longer recognizes itself as such, that no longer understands its own nature.[23] *To lead infinity to rediscover itself is, in a sense, the central task of philosophy.* Should we wish to employ a theme which Gilles Deleuze held dear, we could say that this is simply Hegel's way of stating that the non-being peculiar to the finite is an "illusion of the negative," or, more precisely, a strategy to convey the negative's illusory character.[24]

It could even be argued that there is a need for this "illusion of the finite" in Hegel, a position whose defense merely requires that the following statement be taken seriously: "Those who are too dismayed at the finite do not accomplish anything actual [*Wirklichkeit*], but instead remain trapped in the abstract and fade away into themselves."[25] That is to say, passage through

---

[20] As Lebrun puts it, "that is the angle for Hegel's attack: you claim [he seems to say] that the finite is transitory, that it is quick to drain away, and yet do nothing but make of this non-being an attribute both imperishable and absolute; therefore, neither your vocabulary nor your sorrow are in accord with your ontology" (LEBRUN, *A paciência do conceito*, p. 187).

[21] HEGEL, *Science of Logic*, p. 108.

[22] *Ibid.*, p. 110. Also: "The finite has thus vanished into the infinite and what *is*, is only the *infinite*" (*ibid.*).

[23] For "something comes together *only with itself* in its transition into something other, and this relation to itself in its transition and in the other is the *true infinity*" (HEGEL, *Enzyklopädie*, § 95, as *Encyclopedia Part 1: Science of Logic*, p. 150).

[24] As we find in the philosopher's discussion of the problem of the negative in DELEUZE, *Bergsonism*, translated by H. Tomlinson & B. Habberjam. New York: Zone Books, 1991.

[25] HEGEL, *Enzyklopädie*, § 92, as *Encyclopedia Part 1: Science of Logic*, p. 148.

the experience of limitation is a necessary condition for the attainment of actuality, and for keeping at bay confused conceptions of infinity – whether as an empty abstraction or (as we have seen in the previous chapter) as pure destructive fury. *It is as though finitude were a strategy employed by infinity in order to establish itself as a contradiction* – and a much-needed strategy at that, given Hegel's insistence that infinity can only be apprehended through contradiction.

In order to avoid characterizing the negative as purely illusory, Hegel must convince his reader that it is not impossible to conceive of something as simultaneously infinite *and* determined. The latter statement seems tantamount to a defense of the possibility of conceiving something as simultaneously infinite and limited, and, therefore, to a contradiction in terms (as something determined must also be something limited in terms of both space and time) – unless it may be shown that whatever is limited must invariably "pass over" (*Übergehen*) itself, *transition past* itself, and that a reflection on this transition is fundamental for any adequate account of infinity. In other words, it appears there is a *drive* of sorts that is *intrinsic to the finite*, and that inexorably leads it to this form of self-overcoming. This was a notion thematized by Hegel: "It is part of the concept of existence [*Dasein*] to alter itself [*sich zu verändern*], and alteration is merely the manifestation of what existence [*Dasein*] is in itself."[26]

We are all familiar with Deleuze's criticism regarding this particular use of the notion of contradiction by Hegel; in Hegel's work, he clarifies further, "the signification of the very notion of limit changes completely: it no longer refers to the limits of finite representation, but, on the contrary, to the womb in which finite determination never ceases to be born and to disappear, to be enveloped and deployed within orgiastic representation."[27] Deleuze understood this as a strategy towards the unveiling of the infinite, one dependent on allowing finite determination to subsist, and on representing the finite not as something that has disappeared or been dissolved, but as something in the process of disappearing or being dissolved – something, in other words, engendering itself to infinity.

Such considerations allow Deleuze to suggest that contradiction should not, in view of its intended function in Hegelian philosophy, be taken too literally: therein, it merely "resolves difference by relating it to a ground."[28] More specifically, it is as if contradiction were there to prevent the dissemination of difference as multiplicity, organizing difference by means of a dialectical

---

[26] *Ibid.*
[27] DELEUZE, *Difference and Repetition*, p. 43.
[28] *Ibid.*, p. 44.

relation between finitude and infinity in which the two terms function as mutually-reporting poles in their process of signification (in the same sense as diametrically-opposed terms such as One and Multiple, being and non-being, or night and day are mutually dependent as to their meaning); hence the following affirmation: "Like Aristotle, Hegel determines difference by the opposition of extremes or of contraries,"[29] as though all essential difference could be submitted to relations of opposition.

And yet, this is hardly a tenable interpretation, as it seems to disregard the fact that Hegel deliberately elaborates the notion of determinate negation (a key notion for the organization of the dialectical conception of contradiction) as a critical device poised precisely against the idea that oppositions could suffice for the structuring of relations in its entirety. For while opposition does admit of the notion that a term may only be posited once the reality of its diametrical opposite is assumed (an opposite term which functions, thus, as the very limit of signification), opposition cannot admit of the identity of a term *actually being* a transition into its opposite, cannot admit of the limit of a term – precisely because it is its limit – being conceived as a part of the extension of the term itself.

To admit as much would mean the dismantling of the very notion of identity in its capacity to distinguish among discrete elements, with the subsequent implosion of the notion of finitude itself. After all, once the possibility of distinguishing elements is gone, what can there be left of "identity"? Certainly nothing that bears any relation to the usual meaning of the term, in that it has ceased to have the organizing function one usually expects from representation. Hence, in Hegel, conceptual identity is something entirely unrelated to representational identity. To think the concept (and this is something Deleuze evinced some difficulty in understanding, as had Schelling, long before, in a letter addressed to Hegel himself[30]) is to lead thought beyond representation. In these terms, remarks such as the following, by Deleuze, are difficult to accept: "Difference implies the negative, and allows itself to lead to contradiction, only to the extent that its subordination to the identical is maintained."[31] Such statements produce the illusion that one knows what one is talking about when denouncing this "subordination to the identical"; and yet, was this not ultimately conducive to Hegel's true aim: to bring "identity" to the point of self-exhaustion, to the point where one is

---

[29] *Ibid.*

[30] "I confess I have so far failed to apprehend the meaning of the opposition you have established between *concept* and *representation*." (Schelling, in a letter to Hegel dated November 2, 1807)

[31] DELEUZE, *Difference and Repetition*, p. xix.

no longer sure what one means by it, the point where to continue to employ it would be to commit the cleverest of betrayals against those initial illusions denoted by the term?

The advantage of Hegel's perspective might reside in the fact it provides us with an explanatory principle for the following problem, which remained unsolved in Deleuze's intellectual experience: if the intellection of the univocity of being is dependent on multiplicity and difference,[32] then how is the perpetual recurrence of the illusions of finitude and identity to be accounted for? Such "illusions" must be either moments of univocity, or actual entities fully endowed with ontological dignity (for were they simply "inexistent" entities, we would find ourselves in the rather comical situation of having to explain why we have historically built veritable philosophical war machines against something which is, in the final analysis, inexistent from an ontological perspective). If they are indeed ontologically-dignified entities, then the assumed univocal character of being will be an untenable concept, and multiplicity will be revealed as being more fragile than identity, since identity would, in this case, be a strong enough "illusion" to send the experience of multiplicity into exile, to consign it to highly-restricted territories and moments.

Identity, therefore, must be understood as a moment of difference, just as the finite must be understood as a moment of infinity's strategy towards actualization. Likewise, *the failure of the finite to determine itself must be understood as a moment of the actualization of an infinity that, at first, appears as a force of indeterminacy, one only revealed as a productive force later, through the resignification of the limits of the finite.*[33] Hegel's insistence on contradiction as a central notion for reflection on the regimes of determination of the finite gives credence to the argument that this is what he had in mind.

---

[32] Which, following Alain Badiou's interpretation, seems to be the case, for Badiou, "Deleuze's fundamental problem is most certainly not to liberate the multiple but to submit thinking to a renewed concept of the One. What must the One be, for the multiple to be integrally conceivable therein as the production of simulacra?" (BADIOU, *Deleuze: The Clamor of Being,* translated by L. Burchill. Minneapolis: University of Minnesota Press, 2000, p. 11)

[33] As suggested by statements that are central to Hegel's philosophy, such as the following: "Sublating [*Aufheben*] is not [...] alteration or otherness in general, not the sublating of *something*. That into which the finite is sublated is the infinite as the negating of finitude. But the latter has long since been only existence [*Dasein*], determined as a *non-being*. It is only the *negation*, therefore, that in the negation sublates itself. Thus infinity is determined on its side as the negative of the finite and thereby of determinateness in general, as an empty beyond; its sublating of itself into the finite is a return from an empty flight, the *negation* of the beyond which is inherently a *negative*." (HEGEL, *Science of Logic*, p. 116)

## Determination through quality

For a better understanding of this particular strategy, meaning Hegel's emphasis on the productivity that is inherent to the failed determination of the finite, we would do well to revisit the chapter in the *Science of Logic* wherein *Dasein* is discussed. There, Hegel's reflections on finitude are conducted with the assistance of three pairs of opposites, that is to say, of limitations: *something* and *other* (*Etwas* and *Anderes*), *determination* and *constitution* (*Bestimmung* and *Beschaffenheit*), and *external limit* and *internal limit* (*Grenze* and *Schranke*, respectively). The first pair of opposites, on account of its thematization of the relation between identity and alterity, serves as a foundation for the latter two. The purpose of the pair determination/constitution is to accomplish an articulation between an intrinsic determination and the network of relations constituting the context required for said determination to be actualized. In this sense, it develops something that, in the defining of *Etwas* and *Anderes*, had functioned as a motor cell articulating identity and alterity. *Grenze* and *Schranke* are, in turn, figures of the notion of limit, boundary setters through which the presence in determination of the very principle leading to its alteration may be thematized.

The following two passages may assist us in understanding Hegel's conception of that limitation that is peculiar to finite things:

> Existence [*Dasein*] is *determinate* being; its determinateness is *existent* [*seiende*] determinateness, *quality*. Through its quality, *something* is opposed to an *other*; it is *alterable* [*veränderlich*] and *finite*, negatively determined not only towards an other, but absolutely within it. This negation in it, in contrast at first with the finite something, is the *infinite*; the abstract opposition in which these determinations appear resolves itself into oppositionless infinity, into *being-for-itself*.[34]

> Something, as an immediate existence [*Dasein*], is therefore the limit [*Grenze*] with respect to another something; but it has this limit *in it* and is something through the mediation of that limit, which is just as much its non-being. The limit is the mediation in virtue of which something and other each *both is and is not*.[35]

The way the first passage ends seems to suggest that infinity must be understood to be simply the internalization of a relation of opposites, one that allows, as

---

[34] HEGEL, *Science of Logic*, p. 83.
[35] *Ibid.*, p. 99.

the second passage makes clear, an external limit to appear as an internal boundary. Still, Hegel's strategy deserves a more thorough examination.

As the pure, immediate presence of a being tells us nothing in regards to what the thing in question is, Hegel starts from the admission that to apprehend an existent is to determine its qualities. Indeed, "to determine something" usually means to establish a set of defined qualities that suffice to individualize that something. Something determinate is by definition something endowed with certain colors, textures, properties, and so on. Qualitative determination is, thus, determination through a *plurality* of qualities. Only through its qualities can *something* be individualized, and, consequently, be the opposite of an *other*.

Using this somewhat trivial notion, Hegel goes on to establish that qualities are determined through oppositive negations: that which is white is not black; that which is salty is not sweet. His aim seems to be to insist on the idea that a determination is always and necessarily articulated through negations. This goes to show that the thing is not pure self-relatedness, but an excluding unity as well, that is, something which negates its identity with something other. From this, Hegel can safely state that "through its quality, *something* [here, *Dasein*] is opposed to an *other*," or, "something [is] the limit with respect to another something." We can only perceive things – that is, *determinate* things – *in their relation to other things*, that is, as things within a system of coordinates and relations. That explains why *Dasein* is, as we have seen, "something through the mediation of that limit, which is just as much its non-being," in that this limit is a mark of the externality of all that which it is not.

The determination of being in regards to quality, however, is both "alterable and finite." It is "alterable" because it is the nature of qualities to alter as a result of external interventions. Such qualitative alterations (and this is the fundamental point) are seen by Hegel as mere possibilities, whose actualization has no ground in *Dasein* itself, but are rather a result of casual transformations of the external environment. As Descartes once put it, once the temperature is altered, the sensible qualities of the piece of wax will be altered as well. This alteration is therefore not apprehended as an essential movement, but merely one particular way *Dasein* perishes.

It is "finite" because qualitative determination is by necessity incomplete: we shall never exhaust the thing by enumerating its qualities. The thing is always something more than the sum of its properties and characteristics, since one may always claim that the thing itself is yet another property, which suggests that determination is structurally mutable. "Salt" is not only that which is white, piquant, often cubiform, but also that which is found in the ocean, is astringent, and so on and so forth, with infinitely possible additions implying structural incompleteness in the possibility of stating what something in itself is. This incompleteness is the privileged figure of what Hegel terms "bad infinite," which appears here as the structural incompleteness of the act of determination through a differentiation of qualities.[36] This situation also serves the purpose of showing us how Hegel believed there would always be deep solidarity between finitude and the bad infinite, since *the essential operation of the finite is to sustain the bad infinite*. A determination marked by finitude will always be incomplete, as it will be haunted by bad infinity. In view of this, it should be recalled that *the finite is not only characterized by having a limit, by constantly establishing the very limit by which it is determined, but also by having to incessantly move past it*. This is, incidentally, the critical foundation underlying Hegel's disqualification of quantitative infinity, such as may be found in his discussion of the contradiction inherent to the idea of a progression to infinity. If Hegel can say that "[it] belongs to the concept of quantum to have a *beyond* [*Jenseits*] of itself"[37] that is an abstract moment of non-being, that is because quantitative determinations invariably posit, whether through the infinitely large or the infinitely small, the possibility of their own overcoming.

Yet how are we to understand from such considerations that, through quality, something is in itself "negative determination," pure and simple? Or that something immanently bears its own limit? Hegel claims that understanding the latter is the key to overcome the abstract oppositions that give rise to determinations, determinations which would subsequently be dissolved in an infinity where such oppositions have no being.

It should be noted that we have yet to come upon a type of alteration resulting from more than just external intervention upon a substance and its qualities. What is missing is a consideration of how "external influence does not just transform the surface of things; it goes to the very heart of things and can transform even what things are in their innermost selves"[38] – a condition that allows Hegel to argue that *it is the nature of the finite to negate itself and become infinite*. In justifying his position, Hegel stresses that

---

[36] In this conception of determination as expressed through quality we may clearly see how "Hegelian logic is the well-founded, methodical exploration of the idea of there being a unity between a critique of metaphysics and a presentation thereof" (THEUNISSEN, Michael; *Sein und Schein. Die kritische Funktion der Hegelschen Logik*, Frankfurt: Suhrkamp, 1994, p. 16).

[37] Cf. HEGEL, *Science of Logic*, p. 191.

[38] HOULGATE, *The Opening of Hegel's Logic*, p. 352.

the notion of limit must be thought under two distinct figures – *Grenze* and *Schranke* – where determination is inextricable from the defining character of external oppositions that are jettisoned in the process. The resulting scenario suggests that the structure of relations between something and an *other* is indissociable from the structure of relations that something establishes with itself. And it could not be otherwise because opposition, in Hegel, is not just a relation between beings that are external to one another, but a mode that determines a being's relation to itself. Within this process of self-reference, self-determination no longer constitutes an opposition, but rather a contradiction.

## *The ought and free will*

In the *Science of Logic*, Hegel holds that the determination of being understood as *ought* (*Sollen*) exemplifies *limit* (here, *Schranke*). This abrupt transition in the *Science of Logic* from ontological concerns to the thematization of a concept derived from moral philosophy is somewhat startling; the ought, after all, is hardly an ontological concept. And yet, it is possible that Hegel's aim was to point out that what thought encounters as a necessary form is not unrelated to attempts within the practical sphere to ground its dispositions. Hegel the "idealist" ceaselessly reminds us that *as we think, so do we act*: in this ways, he draws attention to the misguided reflections that remain exclusively concerned with thematizing pure thought, or with the constitution of a speculative science of the pure forms of thinking.

In the *Science of Logic*, Hegel states that the elevation of *Dasein* beyond finitude begins with the ought; that is, the ought establishes a diremption within determinateness, allowing a being to oppose and transcend itself. And yet Hegel does not shy away from the problematic nature of this diremption occasioned by the ought; for, above all, the ought is a norm – the imposition of a regular, constitutive generality – to which *Dasein* must conform. Yet as Kant put it, one can never be entirely sure whether one acts out of love of duty or in obedience to duty, as though the constant pain it gives rise to were a signal of something never fully actualized. Hegel clearly saw the impasses that arise in making the formal unconditionality of the ought (or of its particularized manifestation as *duty*, or *Pflicht*[39]) the sole foundation of moral action.[40] Instead, he insisted that it would be necessary for consciousness to no longer experience the causes determining its actions as a form of the ought,

---

[39] As Hegel put it, "Duty [*Pflicht*] is an *ought* [*ein Sollen*] directed against the particular will, against self-seeking desire and arbitrary interest." (HEGEL, Science of Logic, p. 107)

[40] Cf. e.g. HEGEL, *Elements of the Philosophy of Right*, § 135, pp. 162-163.

but rather as a manifestation of free will, for in a will that is free "the infinite has actuality and presence."[41]

Still, Hegel knows that there is an element of truth to the ought, for the ought annuls any immediate connection between *Dasein* and whatever the prevailing configuration of its interests and impulses may be. The ought is self-transcendence in the form of the internal relation of the self to itself, and is, therefore, a fundamental moment of the negative force of freedom. Here it is useful to recall that passage in the *Phenomenology of Spirit* where this internal diremption established by the ought is discussed in terms of the figure of *unhappy consciousness*. In Hegel's words:

> This unhappy, inwardly disrupted consciousness, since its essentially contradictory nature is for it a single consciousness, must for ever have present in the one consciousness the other also; and thus it is driven out of each in turn in the very moment when it imagines it has successfully attained to a peaceful unity with the other. Its true return into itself, or its reconciliation with itself will, however, display the Notion of Spirit that has become a living Spirit, and has achieved an actual existence, because it already possesses as a single undivided consciousness a dual nature. The Unhappy Consciousness itself is the gazing of one self-consciousness into another, and itself is both, and the unity of both is also its essential nature. But it is not as yet explicitly aware that this is its essential nature, or that it is the unity of both.[42]

Relative to the other figures of consciousness that preceded it, the peculiarity of unhappy consciousness is its internalization of the split between consciousness and essence. Essence had initially been conceived as a separate self-consciousness, one that holds itself up as the possessor of the perspective required for the universal validation of behavior and judgment, and which, therefore, represents the ought; this means that in unhappy consciousness the ought is the internalization of a self-consciousness that is Other. Having internalized the perspective derived from said consciousness, which is both Other and essential, it may intuit itself in this Other, and thus be both at once. In other words, it is precisely because this split directly affects consciousness that it may be transcended.

This universal perspective lays down no positive rules, however, but merely persists as a continuous demand for the limited determinations of

---

[41] Cf. *ibid.*, § 22, p. 54.
[42] HEGEL, *Phenomenology of Spirit*, § 207, p. 126.

finite consciousness to be transcended. The Other's perspective is always an issue for the unhappy consciousness: it cannot quite understand what the Other requires, what the ought is directed at. This seems to be the experience that gives the ought its form, at least according to Hegel. For, unlike Kant, Hegel does not believe that "judging what according to [the moral law] is to be done must not be so difficult that the commonest and most unpracticed understanding could not deal with this law, *even without worldly prudence*."[43] Instead, he believes the ought at first manifests as nothing other than an awareness of the inadequacy and fragility of one's natural models of action.

Thus, even if Hegel can describe the ought as remaining "fixed in finitude"[44] – as a perennial recurrence of bad infinity – it has the virtue of allowing contradiction to appear as an operation towards the determination of being as being-in-itself, rather than simply as being-for-another. This is a crucial step towards understanding that it is in the nature of the finite to go beyond itself (*über sich hinauszugehen*), to negate its negation and thus to become infinite. Acting in accordance with the ought is, therefore, a moment of the constitution of free will – a moment to be transcended once will *wills itself*.

The notion of a will that wills itself may first appear little more than a baroque articulation of a will that gives itself its own law, in clear accordance with traditional Kantian conceptions regarding autonomy. But Hegel's perspective, somewhat unexpectedly, is that free will is *truly infinite*:

> The will which has being in and for itself is *truly infinite*, because its object [*Gegenstand*] is itself, and therefore not something which it sees as *other* or as a *limitation*; on the contrary, it has merely returned into itself in its object. Furthermore, it is not just a possibility, predisposition, or capacity (*potentia*), but the *infinite in actuality* (*infinitum actu*), because the concept's existence [*Dasein*] or objective [*gegenständliche*] externality is inwardness itself.[45]

Hegel is openly associating free will and infinity in this passage, seemingly due to the fact that, in this particular case, the object of will is the will's own productivity *in actu*. Hence the remark that the "absolute determination or, if one prefers, the absolute drive [*absolutes Trieb*], of the free spirit is to make its

---

[43] KANT, *Critique of Practical Reason*, § 36, translated by W. S. Pluhar. Cambridge: Hackett Publishing Company Inc., 2002, p. 54.

[44] HEGEL, *Science of Logic*, p. 108.

[45] HEGEL, *Elements of the Philosophy of Right*, § 22, p. 53.

freedom into its object [*Gegenstand*]."[46] And yet, why must this productivity be described as being "truly infinite"? It goes without saying that it cannot be on account of its limitless potency. The point may be interpreted as follows: this dialectical identity of the will and its object, of a necessary volition and its content, may be understood as a figure of *infinitum actu* in that it is a volition that cannot be satisfied except through the reality and presence of objects that dissolve the limits of finite determinations entirely.

The form of the ought was usually seen as a volitional yearning for the norm in its generality and regularity, which resulted in an *experience of time* marked by repetition. Thus, the form of the ought is re-characterized as a volition directed at the repetitive, and therein that which produces uniformity. In this sense, the ought is first and foremost a determination of volition under the form of regularity, that is, of uneventful temporality. It is clear, then, that the ought is a way of organizing time; with this emphasis on the temporal structure of the ought, it is also clear that free will institutes a different volitional mode within time.

For if the development of free will requires the moment of the ought that is because the ought can sever one's bond with the immediate, breaking one's subjection to the demands of one's system of individual interests. Once this bond has been severed, the will becomes capable of willing transindividual objects. This transindividuality must not be merely understood as referring to the multiplicity of subjects that nowadays constitute a social community. Rather, it is the actualization of the virtuality of historical processes.

This is an essential point; so much so that Badiou seems more than justified in stating that "veritable infinity is subjective in that it is the virtuality contained in the pure presence of the finite."[47] In this context, however, one must refrain from conflating virtuality with unreality. Quite the opposite: the concept of virtuality (or, to employ an analogous term taken from the Hegelian lexicon, "ideality") allows us to differentiate "Being" from "being-present." The predominant conception of *presence* tends to be static, pointillistic, instantaneistic: presence is commonly understood as the instant, in the now, this location here. And yet, the notion of "determinate becoming," so intimately bound up with the Hegelian concept of finitude, requires that time no longer be defined in terms of succession (which inevitably leads to an abandonment of definitions of space that rely on contiguity); as though it were a question of amending transcendental aesthetics, the need arises

---

[46] *Ibid.*, § 27, p. 57.
[47] BADIOU, *Being and Event*, p. 165.

for determinations of an entirely different character in regards to time – determinations in which a moment is the virtual convergence of multiple temporal series.

This need becomes more evident when we consider the experience of temporality presupposed in Hegel's theory of history. Such temporal determinations put us in the position of having to affirm that free will necessarily wills objects that *are* the *sedimentation of history*. Implicit in such a position is an elaboration of Alexandre Kojève's remarkable intuition, alluded to in the previous chapter, that the object of human desire – and thus of free will – is the "history of desired desires," a history congealed into the form of an object.

## *The first Historical People are the ones who passed away*

Our concern here is to develop an adequate methodology for connecting the experience of infinity to an awareness of time. This connection is not based in the identity of time and the sphere of the limitless, but rather in the fact that "time" refers to that which is destined to be the reverse of finitude. Once we accept that "finitude" denotes ceaseless perishing and, at the same time, ceaselessly points beyond itself, the view that *time is the unceasing presence of that which does not perish* presents little difficulty. Bringing history into the heart of the experience of time, Hegel found the right approach to the problem of infinity. After all, one of the fundamental ideas supporting Hegel's concept of history is that history, rather than delimiting the sphere of that which perishes and comes to ruin, circumscribes all that persists, all that which stubbornly refuses to die. A properly historical event will, by its very nature, continue to validate a past series of events showing that, when all is said and done, such events have never ceased to occur. A truly historical event unravels the myriad layers of time into the enduring occurrences found therein. In Hegel's words:

> The life of the ever present Spirit is a circle of progressive embodiments, which looked at in one aspect still exist beside each other [*nebeneinander*], and only as looked at from another point of view appear as past. The grades which Spirit seems to have left behind it, it still possesses in the depths of its present.[48]

---

[48] HEGEL, *Philosophy of History*, p. 96.

The awareness that multiple series of steps spiral within each instant, revealing each instant to be nothing other than a compressed instance of series long past, and that the present is a time saturated with nows – the awareness that tells us, that is, that things are not destined for transience – must be anchored in a more nuanced account of infinity. A truly historical event, and this bears reinforcing, unfolds the endless layers of temporal occurrences, each and every instant imbued with the strength to endure in its very perishing. Those who affirm the reality of infinity exist in a historical moment whose every aspect is resonant with neverending things: this is but another formulation of the idea that *infinity is but the experience of the unreality of the finite*. In these terms, historical events are modes of manifestation of that which Hegel, in the sphere of logic, thematizes by means of an appeal to the notion of infinity. As suggested in the passage just cited from Walter Benjamin's, a historical event must always be the actualization, the reinstatement of temporal series derived from the past.

Before continuing, however, we need to address the usefulness of this strategy – attempting to find a model for the reconstitution of the Hegelian philosophy of history in the *Science of Logic*. Such a strategy is necessary if we are to go beyond the usual understanding of Hegelian history as a redemptive teleology deduced on the basis of the self-movement of an all-absorbing, all-justifying Spirit – a history within which no further events can be expected. Our present purposes, however, require that we consider the ambiguity inherent to the teleological determination of history in earnest. As Hegel saw it, universal history represents the gradual march of consciousness towards freedom. What must be shown, then, is how such freedom cannot be adequately conceived without developing a notion of infinity that is up to the task. If it is true that "I am free when my existence depends upon myself" ("*Frei bin ich, wenn ich bei mir selbst bin*"),[49] then we need to ask ourselves what this coincident relation-to-self consists in; that is, whether the character of this relation would not also require a model allowing for a *negative* relation-to-self, or, at the very least, a relation in which the production of states of determinateness did not annul experiences that can only manifest negatively. The notion of infinity thus seems to be a requirement for reflections on relations of this sort.

And yet, contemporary intellectual trends already associate the anthropological determination of humankind to the notion of finitude. Among these, the most strategically refined appears in the work of Michel Foucault.[50] The

---

[49] *Ibid.*, p. 31.
[50] Cf. especially FOUCAULT, Michel; *The Order of Things: An Archaeology of the Human Sciences*. New York: Routledge, 2002, pp. 340-347.

French philosopher coined the expression "analytic of finitude" in reference to the particular way modernity establishes the field of human sciences, its models of analysis directed at the modes through which the objectification and constitution of humankind takes place. "Man" appears here as an object of knowledge, one who (to paraphrase the Gospel of Luke) "knows not what he does," who knows not to which conditions of objectivity he is subjected. Consequently, a reflection on "man" can only be an "analytic of finitude," as finitude is integral to the way humankind – previously and externally determined by the regulative character of work, the systematic character of language, and the normative character of life – confronts its own limits, its own absence of freedom. Through such a confrontation, humankind gains awareness of the capacity of apparently external forces to determine the form of its consciousness.

As we have seen, what is essential to everything that is finite is of necessity found outside of it. Foucault will, in his own way, take advantage of this idea to bring attention to a certain repetitiveness, or analytical tautology, within which "man" is nothing more than the productive instance of a work that alienates him, of a language that is much older than his consciousness, and of a life that imprisons him within the boundaries set by his organism: by the spatiality of his body, by the obscurity of his desire. Work, life and language thus appear as the "concrete forms of finite existence."[51]

Within this interpretive rubric, any hopes for reflexive synthesis deposited in history as a discourse are shown to be a most cunning illusion of the analytic of finitude; from the early nineteenth century (and Hegel played a fundamental role in this particular epistemic turn) there appears "another, more radical, history, that of man himself – a history that now concerns man's very being, since he now realizes that he not only 'has history' all around him, but is himself, in his own historicity, that by means of which a history of human life, a history of economics, and a history of languages are given their form."[52] History, thus reconceived, harbored the promise of a reflexive synthesis directed at that which founded the modes of determination of humankind in its finitude.

Such synthesis was at first intended as a model for overcoming the limitations inherent to the analytic of finitude; however, it soon showed itself to be no less subjected to historical conditions, deeply rooted as it was in a society, a language and a life fully imbued with a history (a variation on the famous performance contradiction involving historicism), and thus only able

---

[51] *Ibid.*, p. 345.
[52] *Ibid.*, p. 403.

to provide "a finitude that has never finished, that is always in recession with relation to itself, that always has something still to think at the very moment when it thinks, that always has time to think again what it has thought."[53] Once again we arrive, albeit by a different path, at the criticism that states that finitude's perpetual confession of impotence does not amount to a conception of infinity.

The totality provided by history would thus be a "limited totality," unless one were willing to insert the notion of presence into a totalizing suspension of time – to anchor the present, that is, to a time capable of effecting the cessation of all occurrences. This would allow "man" to internalize the causes of his conditions and narrate the occurrences that had theretofore conditioned him: just as a traveler retroactively narrates the straightforward and uninterrupted nature of a long path traversed, one whose destination had not been fully apprehended until arrival. In this vein, Foucault says:

> Continuous history is the indispensable correlative of the founding function of the subject: the guarantee that everything that has eluded him may be restored to him; the certainty that time will disperse nothing without restoring it in a reconstituted unity; the promise that one day the subject – in the form of historical consciousness – will once again be able to appropriate, to bring back under his sway, all those things that are kept at a distance by difference, and find in them what might be called his abode.[54]

Nevertheless, Foucault left two fundamental questions concerning the problem of history in Hegel unexplored: *who* narrates (which is to say, what sort of mutation transforms one who seeks to narrate history), and *what* is narrated (meaning what sort of mutation transforms history once it is narrated)?

As to the first question, it is worth remembering that, as far as Hegel is concerned, it would be inaccurate to say that historicity is the very being of "man," given that his illusions concerning self-determination and identity depend on his being oblivious to the accumulation of past events upon his back. Like consciousness, "man" is not capable of remembering without bringing about his own dissolution. Therefore, it would be correct to say that neither man nor consciousness have a history. Indeed, historicity is the very being *of Spirit*, a claim that brings with it significant repercussions. Spirit, in

---

53 *Ibid.*, p. 406.
54 FOUCAULT, *Archaeology of Knowledge*, translated by A. M. Sheridan Smith. New York: Pantheon Books, 1972, p. 12.

Hegel, is not a concept that depends on any given anthropology, but one that only attains intelligibility once we go beyond the limits of anthropology.[55]

This conception of Spirit implies that our understanding of what the object of historical narrative is must undergo a profound mutation. Narrated history is not the self-reflexive appropriation of the conditions of determination of "man" in his finitude, but, on the contrary, the repetitious movement that renders explicit the frailty of the systems of anthropological determination and conditioning that operate within work, language and life. A close reading of the chapter dedicated to Spirit in the *Phenomenology of Spirit* reveals, for instance, the history of Spirit to be a peculiar movement that brings into relief the ruptures in and insufficiencies of systems of social determination, which accounts for why such figures as Antigone (who exposed the disintegration of the normative substance of the *polis*), Rameau's nephew (who exposed the disintegration of the normative substance of the *ancien régime*), and the "beautiful soul" (who rather tragically reveals the limits of morality) have such central roles in this particular narrative. We might recall here the words of Foucault's friend, Gérard Lebrun:

> If there is any certainty to be had regarding the fact that this progress is not repetitious, but renders explicit what had been hidden, that is because Spirit does not come to be through the production of finite formations, but, on the contrary, by refusing them one after another. It is not the strength of empires that endows History with its 'reason,' but their downfall. [...] From the perspective of the history of the world, all state formations are but evanescent moments.[56]

Lebrun's insightful remarks show us how the object of the history of Spirit is, in fact, the self-dissipating movement of finitude. This is a notion that was of course already implicit in Hegel's remark that "the Persians are the first Historical People; Persia was the first Empire that passed away" (*"Die Perser sind das erste geschichtliche Volk, Persien ist das erste Reich, das vergangen*

---

[55] We are in agreement, then, with Derrida, for whom "the *Phenomenology of Spirit* ... does not have to do with something one might simply call man. As the science of the experience of consciousness, the science of the structures of the phenomenality of the spirit itself relating to itself, it is rigorously distinguished from anthropology. In the *Encyclopedia*, the section entitled *Phenomenology of Spirit* comes after the *Anthropology*, and quite explicitly exceeds its limits" (DERRIDA, Jacques; *Margins of Philosophy*, translated by A. Bass. Chicago: Chicago University Press, 1982, p. 117). In this sense, it may even be said that the history of the *Phenomenology* is the history of the end of the finitude of "man," the history of the collapse of the analytic of finitude, from which the need for a complete reconstruction of the category of subject ensues.

[56] LEBRUN, *L'envers de la dialectique*, pp. 28-33.

*ist.*"),[57] leaving nothing but ruins behind it. This is an important statement, in that it reminds us that the ruins left in the wake of history's continual movement are actually modes of the manifestation of Spirit in its potential for irrealization. If the Persians are the first historical people, that is because they allowed themselves to be animated by the restlessness and negativity of a universal that brings particular determinations to ruin. This goes to show that history is not the reactualization of a past originating moment, *the origin* as it makes itself present once more; and that the "originating" moment had been marked from the start by restlessness and negativity. History is the cure for any illusions regarding this origin, for it exposes how the multiplicity present in time had always been capable of weakening the determination of any originating moment. And yet:

> Passing away is hardly enough when it comes to attesting the historical character of a people, it being also necessary for the downfall of the civilization in question to be the outcome of internal processes. [...] In historical peoples, the negative can only emerge from within, with outside violence never playing a determinant role towards their final collapse.[58]

## *The* valet de chambre *of reason*

It must be asked, then, what the nature of this internal process is, the emergence of the negative in history, a process indistinguishable from what we have termed the self-dissipating movement of finitude. Here, Hegel himself may offer an answer, as long as we take seriously remarks like the following:

> In world history the outcome of human actions is something other than what the agents aim at and actually achieve, something other than what they immediately know and will. They fulfill their own interests, but something further is thereby brought into being, something which is inwardly involved in what they do but which was not in their consciousness or part of their intention.[59]

---

[57] HEGEL, *Philosophy of History*, p. 191.
[58] ARANTES, *Hegel: a ordem do tempo*, p. 163.
[59] HEGEL, *Introduction to the Philosophy of History*, translated by L. Rauch. Cambridge: Hackett Publishing Company, 1988, p. 30.

This internal process, which brings to ruin those determinations that constitute the finite positivity of a historical period, is animated by something that can in no way stand for or represent individual consciousness or intention. With that in mind, we may affirm that history is not made by individuals who are manacled to the finitude of their particular system of interests – something which, furthermore, makes them ill-equipped to narrate it. And if Hegel will nevertheless speak of the "great men in history," he will do so in order to describe a subjective position: these are men whose "own particular aims [*Zwecke*] contain the substantial will that is the will of the World Spirit."[60]

From this subjective position, events take place as though desire gradually learned to trust this "something other" whose content is yet to be unearthed, yet to be realized in "present existence" (*gegenwärtige Dasein*), which is why it so violently clashes with the outer world from within, tearing through the latter as though it were a shell (*Schale*) meant for a different type of kernel (*Kern*). Desire thus discovers the strength to transform something which, at first, it apprehends only opaquely, something which appears to it as a *pathos* whose object is foreign to the regime of presence of consciousness and intention: an event bearing a new possible order. Let us say it once again: this strength discovered by desire as it appears in historical subjects derives from the unveiling of *pathos* as a means for the infinite will of the World Spirit to manifest itself.

Hegel reminds us that, as the old saying goes, "no man is a hero to his valet" – after all, one's chamber valet is privy to the salacious interests and private passions that lie behind and motivate our most glorious deeds. And yet, as Hegel puts it, "what schoolmaster" – the schoolmaster, of course, being a *compagnon de route* to the valet – "has not demonstrated that Alexander the Great and Julius Caesar were driven by such [selfish] passions, and that they were therefore immoral? And from this it immediately follows that he, the schoolmaster, is more admirable than they, since he has no such passions – the proof being that he has not conquered Asia nor defeated Darius and Porus, but that he is willing to live and let live."[61] Hence, suggests Hegel, the adage ought to be given a complement: if no man is a hero to his valet, that is "not because the former is no hero, but because the latter is a valet."[62]

What this witticism gestures at is a certain problem of perspective: a viewpoint (such as the valet's) that erases the notion of historical subject reduces sequences of events to the lesser condition of collections of random

---

[60] *Ibid.*, p. 32.
[61] *Ibid.*, p. 34.
[62] *Ibid.*

occurrences, which is to say, to occurrences bereft of history. If Hegel once remarked that nothing great had ever been accomplished without passion, it was to remind us that the perspective that imparts to passions a broad, revelatory scope is precisely a historical one. History does not erase the passions that reside within the heroism of edifying narratives. Rather, it removes from such passions their narcissistic, particularistic features. They cease to be the passions of an "I." What the sneering chamber valet fails to grasp is how one's interests lose their particularistic traits once they become integral to the unfolding of great historical processes. He cannot see that, at certain moments and even in private quarters, one's individual gestures become the actualization of a multiplicity of desires that once again strive to be given voice. Rash as it may seem, in such cases it is not the individual who desires, but *reason*. Hegel never ceased to believe in the possibility of transformations of this sort.

# II.
# Drive and fantasy

# Chapter IV

# The coupling of sex and death is not exclusive to decadent romantics

*I am the spirit that endlessly negates.*
Mephistopheles

After our initial look at how certain aspects of Hegel's account of desire might transform the concept of individuality, we turned to possible repercussions for his theories of juridical ordering and the state. Then, a third textual movement attempted an articulation of subjectivity, history and infinity, the foremost aim of which was to show that the Hegelian subject exceeds all egological reductions, analytics of finitude or anthropological limitations. That is to say, Hegel leaves us with a subject sufficiently inclusive to allow for both reflections on models of institutional association, as well as modes of determination or the process of synthesis in time.

What remains to be considered, then, is the nature and extent of the consequences of Hegelian subjectivity for the normative dispositions underlying theories of recognition; more specifically, the way in which these dispositions become something more than merely the condition for the universalization of positive rights that essentially defines a legal person. The interpretation advanced here, once accepted, compels us to affirm that contemporary societies (should we also accept the attending proposition that, in a certain sense, we may still be regarded as Hegel's "contemporaries") are driven by demands for recognition that are bound up with productive experiences of indeterminacy and negativity.

Of course, we do not want our institutions to be consolidated, disciplinary structures that produce of individuals who are, from an identitarian perspective, completely determined; but neither should institutions cultivate identities so amorphous that they culminate in social anomie—identities caught up in the perverted logic of the *infinitely bad* game of swinging between the affirmation of the law and its transgression.[1] In order to avoid these equally unpalatable

---

[1] A process I have described in great detail in the previously mentioned *Cinismo e falência da crítica* ["Cynicism and Critical Failure"].

alternatives, it is essential that these indeterminacy-producing experiences set in motion the process of restoring the historical density of our drives and desires.

Due to our focus here on the centrality of indeterminacy-producing experiences, we are no longer restricted to the mere unveiling of historical causes as though it were just a matter of reconstructing biunivocal systems of causality; rather, our aim is to learn how to engender synthetic unities out of elements which are un-identical, which must in fact be infinitely *other*. And it is for this reason that historical density primarily manifests itself as indeterminacy: indeterminacy disrupts the restrictive, identitarian character of normative determinations, as well as the model for the constitution of synthetic unities that is derived from a hypostatization of the 'I,' or ego. It does so not by instituting a new, more inclusive norm, however, but through its openness to that which can only appear as an event.

The recourse to psychoanalysis that appears in this, the second part of the present book, is ultimately a restatement of these very conclusions. This step, while it may appear unnecessary or repetitive, is necessary for demonstrating the ways in which psychoanalysis may be employed towards empirical investigations of the genesis of the experiences described in the first part of this book. With its theoretical elaborations of drive and fantasy, psychoanalysis offers a genuine and fruitful alternative to an anthropology that only serves to further entrench and reify the limits of the current figure of "man".

The advantages of psychoanalysis in this respect stem from its recognition of the restrictive character of identitarian determinations: psychic suffering is not only a result of one's inability to be an individual, but also of one's inability to successfully realize processes of socialization and individuation. In other words, we may suffer from being "just" an individual, from being compulsively chained to one's own ego. In order to bring into relief the peculiarities of this form of suffering, it is essential to return to the psychoanalytic concept of the death drive, and particularly its relation to sexuality. Once this is accomplished, the theory of drives is more clearly a potential ground for critical strategies directed at the normative structure of the moral subject in its Kantian acceptation. The importance of such efforts is directly proportional to the scope and strength of the psychoanalytic critique of both the autonomous ego and processes of maturation that have autonomy (in the Kantian sense) as their ultimate teleological horizon. The appeal to fantasy in the last chapter of this, the second part of the book, takes up the considerations offered so far on the recognition of the historical density of subjects, only now with a view to how patterns of repetition commonly found in affective life are structured.

Hence, if the concept of desire was emphasized in the first part of this book, here we shift focus to fantasy and drive (*Trieb*). The underlying intention is to show that, once these concepts ground our understanding of modes of psychic synthesis pertaining to time (by means of a complex articulation between fantasy and memory) and the character of whatever resists said processes of synthesis (a resistance that is intrinsic to the concept of drive), problems quite similar to those animating the Hegelian theory of the subject arise. For this, if for no other reason, the shift to language of fantasy and drive will be significant for Lacan's and Adorno's as readings of Hegel. The point here, then, is to arrive at an understanding of how integral the concept of drive is for the reconstitution of a thought capable of ascribing ontological dignity to negativity, and for reflecting on the material ramifications of such an ontology. An ontological reading of the theory of drives actualizes central facets of the Hegelian concept of individuality. Subsequently, it must be shown how, on the one hand, Lacan's conception of drive owes much to developments of the problem of negation whose roots lie with Hegel's philosophy; and how, on the other, an appreciation of the problem of drives endowed with a symmetrical character has a direct bearing on the inner workings of some of Adorno's most important conceptual elaborations.

## Drive and ontology

"I have my ontology – why not? – like everyone else, however naive or elaborate it may be."[2] This is an unusual, provocative statement, and especially so coming from a psychoanalyst. Jacques Lacan's admission that he has an ontology, and furthermore his suggestion that everyone else does too – in the most off-handed tone, as if to say "why shouldn't one?" – raises a number of questions. After all, what does ontology have to do with psychoanalytic praxis, the latter so closely tied to the particularity of the clinical case? Why should we look for a connection between the developments within clinical treatment and a particular ontology? And, most importantly, what sort of ontology could actually impact the direction of psychoanalytic treatment?

These questions point towards the consequences of an overarching hypothesis concerning Lacan's theoretical edifice: namely, that one of the French psychoanalyst's chief contributions to his field was a defense of psychoanalysis

---

[2] LACAN, Jacques; *The Four Fundamental Concepts of Psychoanalysis: The Seminar of Jacques Lacan, Book XI*, edited by J.-A. Miller, translated by A. Sheridan. New York: W. W. Norton & Co., 1998, p. 72.

as the site of a complex but decisive articulation between the clinical and the ontological. This is a slightly riskier re-inscription of the claim that clinical orientation in psychoanalysis is dependent on an unvarying conceptual core around which the field conventionally known as "metapsychology" has been established.

It is true such considerations are not immediately self-evident—accustomed, as we are, to simply take on the conventional discourse that elevates clinical considerations to a position of "sovereignty." Said sovereignty seeks its legitimacy in the true, urgent suffering that drives a subject to submit to analysis; as though therapeutic efficacy, relative to such a highly-diffuse collection of phenomena categorized as "suffering", were a sufficient condition to ensure the validity of clinical devices. Here, where the validity of praxis is measured against its effectiveness in actualizing variable normative dispositions in accordance with socio-historical contexts, one finds no occasion to insist on an articulation between the clinical and the ontological. In other words, insofar as the worth of a clinical procedure is dependent on how well it can "cure suffering" one needs little more than the disciplinary implementation of normative devices.[3] It would be far wiser, of course, to recognize that the genuine cause of the suffering the psychoanalytic clinic so efficiently allays, as shall be seen in the next chapter, is bound up with the manner in which the modern notion of individuality was constituted.

This might explain Lacan's peculiar insistence on there being a necessary relation between the direction given to treatment and the recognition of the ontological dignity of certain metapsychological concepts, the concept of drive (*Trieb*) in particular. His position was that *Trieb* "is an absolutely fundamental ontological notion, which is a response to a crisis of consciousness that we are not necessarily obliged to identify, since we are living it."[4] Drive theory was thus seen as providing the correct orientation for clinical efforts in their aspirations to validity, particularly in view of the theory's supposed capacity

---

[3] The "canonical" statement regarding the delusional character of this "sovereignty of the clinic" came from Michel Foucault: "Medicine had tended, since the eighteenth century, to recount its own history as if the patient's bedside had always been a place of constant, stable experience, in contrast to theories and systems, which had been in perpetual change and masked beneath their speculation the purity of clinical evidence." In other words, this particular discourse assumed that "[at] the dawn of mankind, prior to every vain belief, every system, medicine in its entirety consisted of an immediate relationship between sickness and that which alleviated it." (FOUCAULT, *The Birth of the Clinic: An Archaeology of Medical Perception*, translated by A. M. Sheridan Smith. New York: Routledge, 2003, pp. 54-55)

[4] LACAN, *The Ethics of Psychoanalysis, 1959-1960: The Seminar of Jacques Lacan, Book VII*, edited by J.-A. Miller and translated by D. Porter. New York: W. W. Norton & Company, 1992, p. 127.

to uncover the nature of the suffering at the foundation of the modes of intervention peculiar to the psychoanalytic clinic.

In this sense, the main characteristics of Lacan's reconstruction of metapsychology are well worth evaluating. Such characteristics cannot be adequately discerned, however, unless the traditional idea is abandoned that a simple structuralist reading of the unconscious and its formative dynamics lies at the center of the Lacanian project. Instead, we would do well to engage with the latter as an attempt to endow metapsychology with an ontological status beyond any and all structuralism—an ontological status that raises its head whenever Lacan speaks of the "being of the subject" (why else, after all, would a psychoanalyst feel compelled to discuss *being*?), or of the "essence of the object" of desire, to which he once added: "You will notice that I spoke of essence, just like Aristotle. So? That means that such old words are entirely usable."[5]

In order to properly conduct the intended reflection on Lacan's drive theory, however, we must first return to Freud's original conceptions for the express purpose of identifying those aspects that would directly impact Lacan's intellectual development.

## *Freudian energetics and the theory of sexuality*

As we know, Freud's appeal to a theory of drives as *Grundbegriff* ineluctably established a speculative dimension at the very heart of psychoanalytic reflection. Even if he at times defended a form of materialist reductionism, anticipating a time when "all our provisional ideas [*Vorläufigkeiten*] in psychology" would be at last "based on an organic substructure [*Trägen*],"[6] we must not forget the speculative nature of the physical-chemical energetics that served as a foundation for the scientific horizon alluded to whenever the notion of "organic phenomena" cropped up in his texts. This is a characteristic that would lead Lacan to affirm, quite unequivocally, that "energetics is also a metaphysics."[7] Briefly going over the development of the concept of drive in

---

[5] LACAN, *On Feminine Sexuality, the Limits of Love and Knowledge, 1972-1973: The Seminar of Jacques Lacan, Book XX, Encore*, edited by J.-A. Miller, translated by B. Fink. New York: W. W. Norton & Company, 1999, p. 58.

[6] FREUD, "On Narcissism: An Introduction." In: *The Standard Edition of the Complete Psychological Works of Sigmund Freud, Volume XIV (1914-1916): On the History of the Psycho-Analytic Movement, Papers on Metapsychology and Other Works*, ed. and trans. by J. Strachey. London: Vintage, 2001, p. 78.

[7] LACAN, *The Ego in Freud's Theory and in the Technique of Psychoanalysis, 1954-1955: The Seminar of Jacques Lacan, Book II*, edited by J.-A. Miller, translated by S. Tomaselli. New York: W. W. Norton & Company, 1991, p. 61.

the course of Freud's body of work should make this speculative dimension of drive theory readily apparent.

In its first explicit appearance in the *Three Essays on the Theory of Sexuality* the term "Trieb" was meant to denote those internal sources of excitation (or, as often given in English, "stimulation") from which an organism cannot escape. Among them, sexuality – while by no means construed as the only one – already has pride of place as a central preoccupation for Freud. Conversely, in Freud's unpublished manuscript commonly referred to as *Project for a Scientific Psychology* (1895), while describing the "exigencies of life" (*"Not des Lebens"*) as a form of internal excitation that counteracted the "trend towards inertia" of the psychic apparatus, he listed hunger and respiration alongside sexuality as equally significant sources of such excitation. In this early discussion of drives, Freud would insist that a defining trait was their being a constant force, rather than a momentary pang resulting from a lack experienced by the organism. From this followed the canonical definition of *Trieb*: "[The] psychical representative [*psychische Repräsentanz*] of an endosomatic, continuously flowing source of stimulation."[8]

Up to this point, nothing we have seen indicates that the concept of drive could be made a foundation for speculative concerns. If anything, Freud seems more inclined to provide a materialistic explanation for the causal processes of the psychic apparatus, and to be operating from a perspective, common to classical medicine since at least the days of Broussais, according to which *excitation* is the primordial vital fact. Problems associated with attempted definitions of the status of drives would not be long in coming, however, making themselves felt the moment Freud sought to determine the nature of this energy that produced constant internal excitation.

We know that Freud initially distinguished a libidinal energy peculiar to sexuality from "other forms of psychical energy", such as those involved in physiological processes of self-preservation.[9] This gave rise to an early instinctual dualism where sexual drives were regarded as distinct from drives pertaining to self-preservation – a dualism that would only be overcome with the appearance of the category of "narcissism," which allowed Freud to recognize how "the [drives] of self-preservation were also of a libidinal nature: they were sexual [drives] which, instead of external objects, had

---

[8] FREUD, "Three Essays on the Theory of Sexuality." In: *The Standard Edition of the Complete Psychological Works of Sigmund Freud, Volume VII (1901-1905): A Case of Hysteria, Three Essays on Sexuality and Other Works*, edited and translated by J. Strachey. London: The Hogarth Press and the Institute of Psychoanalysis, 1953, p. 167.
[9] *Ibid.*, p. 217.

taken the subject's own ego as an object."[10] From that, he would conclude that "the [drives] are all qualitatively alike and owe the effect they make only to the amount of excitation [*Erregungsgrössen*] they carry, or perhaps, in addition, to certain functions of that quantity."[11] This, as we shall see, is a highly symptomatic reduction of qualitative difference to quantitative magnitude. Instinctual dualism would reappear in Freudian thought, albeit entirely transformed, in the phase of his work beginning with *Beyond the Pleasure Principle*. At that critical juncture, where the notion of *libido* also undergoes a profound reconfiguration, Freud starts to make greater use of the reflections on the notion of *Trieb* developed in the German idealist tradition, the philosophy of Schopenhauer in particular (although the important role the concept played in the philosophical systems of Fichte and Hegel, among others, must not be overlooked).

The key concept for a correct apprehension of instinctual energy within Freud's work would thenceforth be *libido*. Freud usually defined it as a quantitatively variable force allowing processes and transpositions in the sphere of sexual excitation to be compared to one another. By defining the drive that determines the intelligibility of behavior in terms of a plastic, endosomatic, quantitatively characterized energy, Freud updates an old rationalist tradition: psychology is a "physics of external sense" that would allow us to "determine the quantitative constants of sensation, and the relations among such constants."[12]

Indeed, none of this should be too surprising, given that the theory of drives was a byproduct of Freud's long-term engagement with conceptual devices whose ostensive purpose was to marry his reflections on the psychic apparatus with notions peculiar to the *Naturwissenschaft* tradition. Furthermore, Freud's

---

[10] FREUD, "Two Encyclopaedia Articles." In: *The Standard Edition of the Complete Psychological Works of Sigmund Freud, Volume XVIII (1920-1922): Beyond the Pleasure Principle, Group Psychology and Other Works*, edited and translated by J. Strachey. London: The Hogarth Press and the Institute of Psychoanalysis, 1955, p. 257.

[11] FREUD, "Instincts and Their Vicissitudes." In: *The Standard Edition of the Complete Psychological Works of Sigmund Freud, Volume XIV (1914-1916): On the History of the Psycho-Analytic Movement, Papers on Metapsychology and Other Works*, edited and translated by J. Strachey. London: The Hogarth Press and the Institute of Psychoanalysis, 1957, p. 123. [Translator's note: So as to avoid any confusion resulting from James Strachey's famously-controversial decision to render both *Trieb* and *Instinkt* in English as "instinct" in the *Standard Edition*, I have used the simple expedient of systematically replacing "instinct(s)" with "drive(s)" (in square brackets) whenever *Trieb(e)* is intended.]

[12] "La psychologie se fait physique du sens externe [...]. Elle cherchera à déterminer des constantes quantitatives de la sensation et des relations entre ces constantes." (CANGUILHEM, Georges; "Qu'est-ce que la psychologie?" In: *Etudes d'histoire et de philosophie de la science*. Paris: Vrin, 2002, p. 370)

definition of drive as a "limit concept" (*Grenzbegriff*) separating the psychic and the somatic, and his belief that instinctual dualism was connected to the conceptual pair attraction/repulsion at work in the inorganic world, suggest, certain particulars aside, that he adhered to that tradition which sought to establish systematic relations between the physical and the moral; and, furthermore, that these relations were legitimized by the belief that the dualities action/reaction and attraction/repulsion suffice to bring phenomena to a general plane of intelligibility.[13]

On the other hand, the very idea of a limit concept capable of operating at points of intersection between the psychic and the somatic, founded on a somewhat vague use of the notion of energy, inevitably points to the psychophysics of Fechner, an influence Freud openly acknowledged. Through formulations such as the notorious "Weber-Fechner Law,"[14] Fechner sought to strictly quantify perceived correlations between perceptions (seen as mental phenomena) and bodily stimuli (understood as physical phenomena). In the final analysis, this allowed for thought to be included in a chain of bodily processes, with mental activity becoming entirely reducible to the general laws of what Fechner termed *kinetic energy* (*lebendige Kraft*), such as the principle of conservation of energy, regarded as equally valid for both so-called psychic phenomena and for those of a strictly organic nature.[15] In other words, "the general principles of psychophysics involve nothing but the handling of quantitative relations,"[16] a proposition that is also valid for thinkers such as Brücke, Helmholtz and Du Bois-Reymond, for whom organisms thrived on physicochemical forces alone, and whose influence on Freud was decisive.[17]

---

[13] Cf. e.g. STAROBINSKI, Jean; *Action and Reaction: The Life and Adventures of a Couple*, translated by S. Hawkes & J. Fort. New York: Zone Books, 2003.

[14] A logarithmic relationship between a stimulus and the ensuing perception commonly summarized as follows: "As a stimulus increases as a geometric progression, the corresponding perception increases in an arithmetic progression."

[15] "Kinetic energy employed to chop wood and kinetic energy used in thinking are not only comparable, but each can be transformed into the other, and therefore both kinds of work are measurable on their physical side by a common yardstick." (FECHNER, Gustav; *Elements of Psychophysics, Vol. I*. New York: Holt, Rinehart and Winston, 1966, p. 36)

[16] *Ibid.*, p. 9.

[17] In the words of Canguilhem, "If we add that Descartes, while not exactly being the inventor of the term reflex, or the associated concept, at least affirmed the constant character of the connection between excitation and reaction, it will be seen that a psychology understood as a mathematical physics of external senses begins with him, and reaches Fechner thanks to the assistance of physiologists such as Hermann von Helmholtz [...]." ["Si l'on ajoute que Descartes, s'il n'est pas à proprement parler l'inventeur du terme et du concept de réflexe, a néanmoins affirmé la constance de la liaison entre l'excitation et la réaction, on voit qu'une psychologie, entendue comme physique mathématique du sens externe,commence avec lui pour aboutir à Fechner, grâce au secours de physiologistes comme Hermann Helmholtz

This vocabulary of "energy" and "force," far from being an obstructive scientistic metaphor preventing psychoanalysis from revealing its true character as a practice grounded in the clinical use of processes of self-reflection (as maintained by a long critical tradition pitched against metapsychology that includes authors as disparate as Politzer, Habermas and Ricoeur), is, in reality, a means for Freud to show that drives are connected to the dimension of an irreflexive, still-unstructured ground for both thinking and behavior.

It should be stressed that the characterization of libido in terms of energy quanta did not have as its purpose any form of "measuring" of psychic processes against one another. While it is true that Freud defined the *economic* perspective of his metapsychology (which, alongside *topographical* and *dynamic* models, oriented his approach to metapsychological facts) as an effort to "follow out the vicissitudes [*Schicksale*] of amounts of excitation [*Erregungsgrössen*] and to arrive at least at some *relative* estimate [*Schätzung*] of their magnitudes,"[18] there is in fact no contradiction with the previous claim: if a relativization clause is brought to bear upon the problem of estimation, that is done so as to remind us that what is truly important in following the course of said "vicissitudes" – of the *fate* – of the drive is the quanta of libidinal energy.[19] Indeed, this goes to show how the very aim of the economic perspective is to allow Freud to accord due consideration to the plasticity of psychic energy, an energy chiefly characterized by its capacity for transposition, inversion (Freud reserves the term *Verkehrung* for such instances), deviation or repression – characterized, in other words, by how it lends itself to seemingly inexhaustible varieties of displacement. It is this principle of unceasing movement that initially led Freud to regard libido as energy that circulates unimpeded ("free energy"), energy that cannot be tamed through its subsumption (*Bändigung*) by representation.

---

[...]."] (CANGUILHEM, *op. cit.*, p. 370)

[18] FREUD, "The Unconscious," *S.E. Vol. XIV*, p. 181.

[19] Regarding the use of the term "fate" in this context, it should be recalled that "it indicates that what is at stake in what concerns a human being's drives is something properly human, and the product of entirely singular beings, while at the same time a drive, in that its components elude the subject that is a theater for said drive, seems anonymous, 'depersonalized,' a-subjective." ["[Il] indique que ce qui se joue d'un être humain dans ses pulsions est proprement humain, et produit des êtres tous singuliers, alors qu'en même temps une pulsion, parce que ses composantes échappent au sujet qui en est le théâtre, apparaît comme anonyme, 'dépersonnalisée', a-subjective."] (DAVID-MÉNARD, "Les pulsions caractérisées par leurs destins: Freud s'éloigne-t-il du concept philosophique de Trieb?," § 14. In: *Revue Germanique Internationale* [Online Edition], 18 | 2002, accessed on February 12, 2015. URL: http://rgi.revues.org/924).

That Freud's reflections on plasticity predominantly concerned phenomena connected to sexuality is an absolutely central point. In fact, his intention was to demonstrate that there is something within the subject that resists being reflexively determined through conscious representation; something that does not manifest save in a polymorphous, fragmentary way, and necessarily finds its privileged dimension in sexuality unrestrained by the logic of procreation. This would be a dimension of pure corporeal impulses entirely free of teleological considerations of that sort. For that reason, libido was initially characterized as autoerotic and inconsistent (on account of being subjected to primary processes), as well as perverse (on account of having its goals constantly inverted, deviated or fragmented).

This is an important point, in that it clarifies the Freudian understanding of sexuality. Far from attempting to establish some form of naturalized morality through the promotion of Eros to the condition of the ground of being, Freud's reflections stress that "sexuality" is the psychoanalytic term for a "radical ontological impasse."[20] In light of this, let us recall how, from the first, sexual drives were dissociated from any procreative imperatives polymorphous in tendency—that is, unceasingly amenable to deviations regarding sexual aims and objects. What results is a paradoxical scenario: the transgression of an inexistent rule. The primacy of genital sexuality in the service of reproduction is only the final stage attained by sexual organization and one that depends on deeply repressive processes. This notion underlies the following remark by Freud: "Sexual life includes the function of obtaining pleasure from zones of the body – a function which is subsequently [nachträglich] brought into the service of reproduction."[21] For this reason, it may be said that "there is indeed something innate lying behind the perversions but that is something innate in everyone,"[22] a consideration that helps account for the polymorphous perversity characteristic of infantile sexuality. It should be noted that, here, the polymorphous character is understood as an expression of the complete lack of submission of corporeal enjoyment in all its multiplicity to the teleological hierarchy of procreative imperatives and the primacy of genital pleasure that entails.

---

[20] ZUPANCIC, Alenka; "Sexuality and Ontology." In: Why psychoanalysis? Three Interventions. Uppsala: NSU Press, 2008, p. 16.

[21] FREUD, "An Outline of Psycho-Analysis." In: The Standard Edition of the Complete Psychological Works of Sigmund Freud, Volume XXIII (1937-1939): Moses and Monotheism, An Outline of Psycho-Analysis and Other Works, edited and translated by J. Strachey. London: The Hogarth Press and the Institute of Psychoanalysis, 1964, p. 152.

[22] FREUD, "Three Essays on the Theory of Sexuality," S.E. Vol. VII, p. 171.

Thus, because bodily pleasures do not immediately submit to functional hierarchies, each erogenous zone (mouth, anus, ears, genitals, etc.) appears to follow its own economy of enjoyment, with each associated object (breast, feces, voice, urine, etc.) satisfying a particular drive and producing an "organ specific" type of pleasure.[23] To drives whose satisfaction is not dependent on a unified image of the body, in accordance to which global representations of individual persons are produced, Freud assigned the name "partial drives." He also qualified the type of satisfaction as "auto-erotic," in that the objects of desire are sought and found in the desiring subject's own body, as even the breasts or voice of the maternal Other are seen by the infant as intrinsic to his or her own sphere of existence.[24]

Several psychoanalysts have insisted, however, that the process of sexual maturation through the submission of polymorphous, autoerotic sexuality to genital primacy is never realized in full. This is something well understood by Jacques Lacan, who remarked:

> The most archaic aspirations of the child are both a point of departure and a nucleus that is never completely resolved under some primacy of genitality or a pure and simple *Vorstellung* of man in human form by androgynous fusion, however total one may imagine it.[25]

In other words, genital primacy is a fragile construct continuously threatened by dissolution. The unification of partial drives is never achieved. It is as if sexuality were determined by something irreducible to the unified image of a *person*, something that, from the perspective of the person as a coherent behavioral unity, appears as a force of indeterminacy.

We shall return to this discussion in the next chapter. For now, however, some consequences may be extracted from this complex articulation of representation and libido (the latter understood as free energy). One such consequence may be easily apprehended once we bring two canonical

---

[23] One of the finest articulations of the meaning of such "organ-specific" pleasures can be found in the work of Alenka Zupančič: "In relation to the need for nourishment, to which it attaches itself at the outset, the oral drive pursues an object different from food: it pursues (and aims at repeating) the very sensation of satisfaction produced in the region of the mouth during the act of nutrition. [...] [In] human beings, all satisfaction of a need allows, in principle, for another satisfaction to occur, which tends to become independent and self-perpetuating in pursuing and reproducing itself." (ZUPANCIC, *op. cit.*, pp. 8-9)

[24] In this sense, Freud's "autoerotism" may be regarded as a stage preceding narcissism, one that points to the polymorphous character of a libido directed at deriving pleasure from organs that have yet to be submitted to the ego as a synthetic unity capable of providing a general unifying principle.

[25] LACAN, *Seminar VII*, p. 93.

statements regarding drives to bear on each other. The first of these comes from the essay "The Unconscious": "[A drive] can never become an object of consciousness – only the idea that represents the [drive] can."[26] The second, written in the same period, reminds us that the object of a drive is "what is most variable [*variabelste*] about [a drive] and is not originally connected [*verknüpft*] with it [...]. It may be changed any number of times in the course of the vicissitudes which the [drive] undergoes during its existence."[27] Clearly, if we define "object" as that which results from the procedures of categorization of consciousness in its attempt to unify the manifold of the sensible through synthetic representations, then it makes sense to say that a drive cannot appear to consciousness unless it has been tamed by object representations. Such a taming will be tenuous, however, in that it is marked by the structural variability of that which refuses to be objectified in any essential way; it is a binding process held together by a representation unfit to encompass anything evades unification—anything, that is, that does not lend itself to reflection within structured relations.

It is with such issues in mind that one must approach the questions raised by Freud's somewhat-late construction of the concept of a "death drive," a concept that would become central to Lacanian metapsychology, as may be gathered from the Parisian psychoanalyst's remark that "every drive is a death drive."[28] As shall be seen later, this declaration is crucial for any understanding of the Lacanian conception of drive, as it emphasizes the fact that Lacan's is a very particular type of *instinctual monism*; hence, the fact that *drive* invariably appears as a singular noun in his work is hardly an accident.

Following up on Lacan's claims, Jean Laplanche notes that a profound metamorphosis takes place when the later Freud, having adopted the instinctual dualism Eros/Thanatos, associates the notion of libido to the unifying potency of Eros (as described in mythical terms by Aristophanes in Plato's *Symposium*). This definition of libido as a unifying erotic potency whose aim is "to form living substance into ever greater unities [*Einheiten*], so that life may be prolonged and brought to higher development"[29] suggests that, at this juncture, the former understanding of libido as the free energy

[26] FREUD, "The Unconscious," *S.E. Vol. XIV*, p. 177.

[27] FREUD, "Instincts and their Vicissitudes," *ibid.*, pp. 122-123.

[28] LACAN, *Écrits*, translated by B. Fink in collaboration with H. Fink & R. Grigg. New York: W. W. Norton & Company, 2005, p. 719.

[29] FREUD, "Two Encyclopaedia Articles." In: *The Standard Edition of the Complete Psychological Works of Sigmund Freud, Volume XVIII (1920-1922): Beyond the Pleasure Principle, Group Psychology and Other Works*, edited and translated by J. Strachey. London: The Hogarth Press and the Institute of Psychoanalysis, 1955, p. 258.

peculiar to a sexuality both fragmentary and polymorphous no longer held sway. The abandonment of the latter conception seems to have been prompted by Freud's reflections on the centrality of narcissism and its mechanisms of projection and introjection—mechanisms capable of unifying instinctual vicissitudes under the binding image of the ego.[30] It is as if narcissism suddenly unveiled the pathos inherent to an ego conceived as the synthetic unity that provides object representations of the manifold of sensory experience with a binding principle. The interest that philosophers such as Theodor Adorno take in the field of psychoanalysis seems largely due to such considerations; that is, to what is in essence a reflection on the "pathologies of transcendental schematism."

## A metaphysics of death?

In this context, the reconstruction of instinctual dualism through the pair Eros and death-drive could be seen as satisfying the need to find a new direction for the principle of un-binding particular to the free energy that initially characterized libido. In other words, in Freud's drive theory the polarity life/death actually encompasses the distinction between energy that has been bound by representations as a result of the ego's capacity for synthesis, and the free, unbound energy that inaugurates psychical dynamics.[31]

At first, however, what led Freud to use the term "death" to describe such a principle of un-binding is far from obvious. This is a question explicitly posed by Lacan in the following passage:

---

[30] As Laplanche put it, "Eros is what seeks to maintain, preserve, and even augment the cohesion and the synthetic tendency of living beings and of psychical life. Whereas, ever since the beginnings of psychoanalysis, sexuality was in its essence hostile to binding – a principle of 'un-binding' or unfettering (*Entbindung*) which could be bound only through the intervention of the ego – what appears with Eros is *the bound and binding form* of sexuality, brought to light by the discovery of narcissism." (LAPLANCHE, Jean; *Life and Death in Psychoanalysis*, translated by J. Mehlman. Baltimore: The Johns Hopkins University Press, 1990, p. 123) That explains why, in Freud, "the ego emerges as a defensive, inhibitory structure that functions [...] to establish a restricted economy of impulses and their discharge." (BOOTHBY, Richard; *Freud as Philosopher: Metapsychology After Lacan*. New York: Routledge, 2001, p. 285).

[31] We are, thus, in agreement with the view expressed by Boothby, for whom "[the] most crucial idea, rarely stated explicitly precisely because it is so fundamental to Freud's entire outlook, is the assumption of an inevitable and irremediable disjunction between the level of somatic excitations and their psychical representation. There is always a remainder, an irrecoverable left-over, a portion of the body's energies that fail to receive adequate registration in the battery of *Triebrepräsentanzen*" (*ibid.*, pp. 286-287).

> Beyond the homeostases of the ego, there exists a dimension, another current, another necessity, whose plane must be differentiated. This compulsion [*peculiar to the death drive*] to return to something which has been excluded by the subject, or which never entered into it, the *Verdrängt*, the repressed, we cannot bring it back within the pleasure principle [*which is here indistinguishable from Eros*]. [...] We must therefore posit another principle. Why did Freud call it the death instinct?[32]

The question appears entirely justified in view of the fact that this conceptual shift initially seems disproportionate to the magnitude of the problem it aims to solve (to find a way to preserve the disruptive potency in sexuality that transcends the unifying capacity of the ego, the true extension of which could only be uncovered by Freud's theory of narcissism) – unless, of course, the problem anticipated by Freud were in fact much greater than it first seemed. Only if that were the case could we take seriously a unity of any sort among the phenomena as apparently unrelated as the ones Freud attempts to subsume under the notion of death drive, which include: the compulsion to repeat traumatic events (found most commonly in war-related neuroses); the resistance to cure and attachment to illness that psychoanalysis terms "negative therapeutic reaction"; the organization of a direction for libido, conceived as free energy; and, finally, the economic problem of masochistic fantasies, which would seem to demand a decoupling of desire from the calculus of pleasure.

In order to grasp the question this final version of Freud's drive theory was intended to solve, we should recall that the reconfiguration of the theory on the basis of the dichotomy life drive/death drive favored a redefinition of the very concept of drive. In it, a drive was no longer conceived as the psychical representation of a constant, endosomatic source of excitation, but rather as "an urge [*Drang*] inherent in organic life to restore an earlier [inorganic] state of things which the living entity has been obliged to abandon under the pressure of external disturbing forces."[33] Somewhere in the transition from the former definition to its late-period counterpart a certain *teleological* character was added, the function of which was to conduct drive-derived pressure to an operation of return. Drive, in this context, is an expression of the inertia inherent to organic life, an urge towards the reestablishment of a lost, tensionless state. This is a tendency that manifests mainly as a compulsion to repeat, understood as a movement of return directed at the annihilation of

---

[32] LACAN, *Seminar II*, p. 171.
[33] FREUD, "Beyond the Pleasure Principle," *S.E. Vol. XVIII*, p. 36.

the individual, the latter an orientation towards self-preservation through the calculation of pleasure, the symbolization of any traumatic experiences that could prevent consciousness from realizing its synthetic proclivities, and the actualization of the principle of individuation.

It is here that Freudian speculation flirts most shamelessly with a metaphysics of death, one founded in its entirety on a bona-fide philosophy of nature. It would be a mistake to regard this metaphysical inflection, essentially absent from the early version of drive theory and harking back most obviously to Schopenhauer (with additional nods to Plato, from whom the illustration of the unifying power of Eros was derived, and Empedocles), merely as a veering off-course. In fact, several principles derived from Fechner's psychophysics that would go on to influence Helmholtz, Mach and others, and later provide a theoretical foundation for Freud's drive theory, are by no means foreign to Schopenhauer's philosophy or, more specifically, to the reflections on force dynamics found therein. Such principles, furthermore, were themselves not exempt from metaphysical presuppositions, which was particularly obvious in the case of Fechner. It seems as though Schopenhauer's only role was to provide Freud with a sort of expanded intelligibility of something that had already and lastingly insinuated itself into theories of energetics.

In this sense, it would be beneficial to recall how general accounts of human and natural behavior based on force dynamics, reconceived through the figure of a metaphysics of Will as being in-itself, ultimately underlie Schopenhauer's view of death as a protocol of "return into the womb of nature."[34] For the philosopher, the death of an individual was nothing if not a perfect demonstration of the perennial character of forces and of matter, as opposed to the transitory nature of states and forms: "Thus, taken already as a force of nature, vital force remains entirely untouched by the change of forms and states, which the bond of cause and effect introduces and carries off again, and which alone are subject to arising and passing away, just as these processes lie before us in experience."[35] It may even be said that death, for Schopenhauer, is a *principle of unbinding*: through it, the binding of forces into individualization-engendering representations is suspended – hence, his use of the dichotomy between the immortality of the species as "Idea" on the one hand, and individual destructibility on the other. This dichotomy would later reappear at the very core of Freud's drive theory in the guise of the distinction between *soma* and *plasma* inherited from Weismann. It should

---

[34] SCHOPENHAUER, Arthur; *The World as Will and Representation*, Volume II, translated by E. F. J. Payne. New York: Dover Publications, Inc., 1958, p. 469.
[35] *Ibid.*, p. 471.

be noted, additionally, that said dichotomy is one that resonates with that "sundering within life" addressed in the first chapter of this book, at the occasion of our commentary on the Hegelian view of nature.

Regardless of such similarities, however, fundamental differences abound. Schopenhauer regarded death as the destruction of the individual, and insisted:

> To desire immortality for the individual is really the same as wanting to perpetuate an error for ever; for at bottom every individuality is really only a special error, a false step, something that it would be better should not be, in fact something from which it is the real purpose of life to bring us back.[36]

This is rather unsurprising given that death is at once intrinsic to the *telos* of life's cyclical renovation of nature, and a means of access (dissimilar from reflexive knowledge) to the intelligibility of a dynamic of unbound forces freely taking on one form after another without perpetuating any of them. "Death" is thus the name given to the process that reveals nature to be an incessant cycle shifting from the individuation of forces to the annulment of individuation and back again – a pulsation, so to speak, alternating between bound and unbound energy. Thus, to Schopenhauer, far from being a senseless phenomenon – mere negation, bereft of all meaning – death, through its unveiling of the mechanisms that orient vital force, is that which ultimately assures us that nature is *a positive pole of meaning attribution*.

That, of course, is not something one finds in Freud. He is in agreement with Schopenhauer that death is more than just the destruction of the integrity of the biological organism: death is also that which suspends the principles of individuation and synthetic unity at work in the ego. It is on account of this that death can appear in Freud's work as the source of the instinctual dynamic behind such processes as the repetition of non-symbolized traumatic events, and the resistance to processes of subjectivation set in motion by clinical analysis commonly known as "negative therapeutic reaction." However, there is nothing in Freud that bears the least similarity to the teleological perspective according to which life is an incessant cycle of destruction and reconfiguration resulting from some variation on the general principle of conservation of energy. The death drive is, on the contrary, more closely related to the absorption of the energetics-based concept of entropy, employed as the principle behind whatever appears strictly as *loss*, or grounding whatever

---

[36] *Ibid.*, pp. 491-492.

resists being submitted to and configured by protocols of organization.[37] Death, for Freud, is therefore the presence of precisely that which resists being absorbed into a certain conception of nature in the role of a positive pole of meaning attribution, the presence of that which resists being counted among the elements in a vitalist economy.

As it turns out, however, the conception of nature at work within Freud's drive theory is a very peculiar one. After all, it is clear that Freud's tendency to explain the principles underlying the behavior of organisms *in general* through drive theory (an "updating" of sorts of the holistic explanatory principles typical of nineteenth-century psychophysics) presupposes a non-thematized conception of nature – something akin to a nature that resists being conceived through figurations related to vital cycles, or any other form of organizing functionalism, and that only and necessarily manifests as a resistance against integration into any and all principles of positive determination.[38] Consequently, Freud ultimately naturalizes the very notion of *conflict* present in his reflections on drive dynamics. It is as if, instead of seeing instinctual conflict as an outcome of deviations in the processes of socialization and subjective formation, Freud understood it as an inert, irreducible given, one imbued with (why not state it unequivocally?) ontological weight; as if, in other words, *the only ontologically-positive concept in Freud were, in the final analysis, precisely that of conflict.*

---

[37] A statement which is in full agreement with Paul-Laurent Assoun's position: for the French psychoanalyst, the Freudian notion of energy "marks a 'passage' from one state to another which conveys a mechanical loss, itself the particularized manifestation (motion) of the general increase in disorder predicted by the second law of thermodynamics (Carnot-Clausius) – a notion expressed [...] as 'every drive, insofar as it is a drive, is a death drive'." (ASSOUN, Paul-Laurent; *Introduction à l'épistémologie freudienne*. Paris: Payot, 1981, pp. 182-183)

[38] Adorno clearly understood this eminently negative conception of nature present in Freud, as becomes evident once one recalls, for instance, the definition provided by the philosopher (writing with Max Horkheimer) for the notion of *mimetism*; this key concept for the reconciliation between subject and nature was understood by Adorno as "the tendency to lose oneself in one's surroundings [*Umwelt*] instead of actively engaging with them, the inclination to let oneself go, to lapse back into nature. Freud called this the death impulse [*Todestrieb*], Caillois *le mimétisme*." (ADORNO, Theodor & HORKHEIMER, Max; *Dialectic of Enlightenment: Philosophical Fragments*, edited by G. S. Noerr, translated by E. Jephcott. Stanford: Stanford University Press, 2002, p. 189) If, as the philosopher sees it, the death drive indeed provides coordinates for a reconciliation with nature, several consequences must be admitted. After all, the Freudian acceptance of the death drive uncovers the libidinal economy leading a subject to seek an association with nature, understood as the sphere of the inorganic, and as the ultimate symbol of the unyielding opacity of materiality to reflection. This "tendency to lose oneself in one's surroundings" Adorno describes with the death drive in mind is simply what results from one's recognition of oneself in that which is without symbolic inscription (cf. SAFATLE, Vladimir; "Mirrors without images: mimesis and recognition in Lacan and Adorno." In: *Radical Philosophy*, n. 139, 2006, pp. 9-19).

This is an essential claim. Among other things, Freud's naturalization of conflict implies, for instance, a subsumption of the myriad forms of social antagonism to a single foundational antagonism already operating within the biological individual. This may at first strike us as a paradoxical proposition, as it apparently runs counter to the fact that subjective conflicts and antagonisms result from processes of formation and socialization. What is in fact at stake, however, is the presumption that the configurations of the processes of socialization do not *produce* antagonisms, but merely *formalize* them through social-relation matrices. There is a fundamental difference between saying that conflict is *given shape* by social-relation matrices and that these are the actual *sources* of conflict. Implicit in the latter case one finds, for example, the thesis that conflict arises as a result of external, repressive demands that one's instinctual urges be curbed, and of one's subsequent introjection of such demands. In the first case, conversely, repression is merely one among many potential figures for conflict imbued, as we have seen, with ontological weight. Thus, it may be said that conflict can acquire multiple social figurations. The disruptive power of the death drive might appear, for example, in the form of a tendency towards aggression, and towards the destruction of others (a tendency often inverted into an internalized aggression against the self), but it may also appear in the guise of polymorphously perverse sexuality, or even manifest as that dimension of indeterminacy and impersonality that every subject bears within him- or herself – an impersonality very aptly described by Gilles Deleuze, who wrote of the disruptive power of the death drive as

> the state of free differences when they are no longer subject to the form imposed upon them by an I or an ego, when they assume a shape which excludes *my* own coherence no less than that of any identity whatsoever. There is always a 'one dies' more profound than 'I die.'[39]

And if, in a given historical context, the death drive appears most commonly as aggression against oneself and against others, it is the social conditions that prompted such a state of affairs that ought to be the object of one's inquiry.[40]

The attempt to found an entire clinical perspective, including protocols for cure, on the basis of a naturalization of conflict was not, of course, without

---

[39] DELEUZE, *Difference and Repetition*, p. 113.

[40] This being our understanding of Freud's essential elaborations in "Why War?," in *The Standard Edition of the Complete Psychological Works of Sigmund Freud, Volume XXII (1932-1936): New Introductory Lectures on Psycho-Analysis and Other Works*, edited and translated by J. Strachey. London: The Hogarth Press and the Institute of Psychoanalysis, 1964, pp. 197-218.

difficulties. This would account for, among other things, the symptomatic position occupied by the death drive in the Freudian clinic, a highly-complex position whose true value and import are rather difficult to ascertain. Let us simply recall how, in his late essay *Analysis Terminable and Interminable*, Freud wonders whether there could ultimately be limits for the curbing, or taming [*Bändigung*] of drives into representations – an uncertainty that pertains to the possibility of one's ever achieving mastery over, in particular, the compulsion to repeat typical of the death drive. The answer he arrives at is programmatic: only the *a posteriori* correction of the original process of repression may put an end to the effective power of the quantitative factor of the drive. Freud, of course, was the first to recognize the endless character of instinctual forces, and to stress the inexhaustibility of their rule: "One feels inclined to doubt sometimes whether the dragons of primaeval days are really extinct"[41] – a position that suggests the incapability of analytic procedures of symbolization to dissolve the compulsively repetitious character of the death drive.

Still, the negativity of the death drive would not be integrated into the Freudian clinic as a driving force behind curative processes; rather, the compulsion to repeat would be a *limit* to the effectiveness of clinical processes, including the mechanisms of remembering, verbalization and reflexive symbolization that are characteristic of Freudian modes of subjectivation. Freud cannot conceive of the manifestation of the negativity of the death drive in the psychoanalytic clinic save in the forms of sadistic or masochistic fantasies, the "negative therapeutic reaction," the destruction of the other in transference, and so on – fantasies *that ought to be annihilated if the subject is to complete the analysis.* The program for "curbing [*bändigen*] the patient's compulsion to repeat and for turning it into a motive for remembering [*Motiv fürs Erinnern*]"[42] by way of overcoming a repetition commonly mistaken for transference would never lose its validity for Freud, even though he knew there to be clear limits to its efficacy. It appears that there is a solution to this conundrum to be found among elements of Freud's own text, one (as I would like to demonstrate in Chapter VI) suggesting a deep connection between the death drive as a potency of de-individualization and the notion of fantasy understood as a process of remembering. In order to explore it, however, we need to consider the relations between drive and fantasy in a manner that Freud never explicitly took up.

---

[41] FREUD, "Analysis Terminable and Interminable," *S.E. Vol. XXIII*, p. 229.

[42] FREUD, "Remembering, Repeating and Working-Through." In: *The Standard Edition of the Complete Psychological Works of Sigmund Freud, Volume XII (1911-1913): The Case of Schreber, Papers on Technique and Other Works*, edited and translated by J. Strachey. London: The Hogarth Press and the Institute of Psychoanalysis, 1958, p. 154.

## *Lacan and the clinic of the death drive*

The most common solution adopted by psychoanalytic posterity was to disregard this peculiar amalgamation created by Freud as a result of his introduction of the death drive. The death drive was typically and insistently received as a social fact linked to destructive impulses in societies that socialized their subjects through the repressive imputation of a sense of guilt (the work of Marcuse exemplifies this position well), or as no more than metaphysical debris devoid of clinical function, especially considering clinical analysis had, supposedly, no need or use for abstract forces postulated in the antechamber of the phenomena with which it was concerned. The phenomena the death drive had been constructed to explain had already been fully understood, it was claimed, through alternative concepts such as "helplessness" and the aforementioned "compulsion to repeat."[43]

In this sense, one of Jacques Lacan's most peculiar traits as an analyst was his attempt to reorient clinical treatment around the centrality of the death drive as a perspective for clinical intelligibility. Indeed, Lacan recognized that the privileged place of the death drive was essential for both analytic progress and the direction of treatment. This, on account of the fact that, for Lacan, the true issue at the heart of clinical treatment was not finding ways to curb the destructive urges of the death drive and towards allowing life to operate increasingly broader processes of unification. Quite the contrary: the aim was to break this Eros-directed unity that, for Lacan, had a fundamentally narcissistic and imaginary character, connected as it was to the projection and the introjection of the ego's image. Indeed, Lacan's most essential contributions depend on his basic insight that the death drive is more than the compulsive repetition of a destructive impulse; this, in turn, made way for the structuring of a new mode of reflection on the figures of the negative in a clinical context.

As part of that struggle, Lacan first attempted to weave connections between the disruptive power of the death drive and a conception of "negativity" simultaneously inherited from reflections by French commentators on the Hegelian notion of *Begierde* – the first mode of manifestation of subjective individuality – and from the several confrontations with the experience of death in the *Phenomenology of Spirit*. However, philosophical loans have a rather unique characteristic: they are possibly the only kind in which the borrower receives more than he bargained for. We are thus entitled to ask whether Lacan did not accidently import, right into the heart of psychoanalytic drive theory,

---

[43] On this, cf. GEYSKENS, Tomas & VAN HAUTE, Phillipe; *From Death Instinct to Attachment Theory*. New York: Other Press, 2007.

a concept of negation that had an undeniable ontological status in Hegel—a concept of negation that bore a direct connection to the mode of manifestation of that which determines itself as essence. Such a concept helped Lacan deal with issues already present in Freud's attempt to "naturalize" the death drive, with the difference that Lacan was able to use this process to provide a true north for the intelligibility of the behavior of any and all subjects.

Before continuing with this point, it should be noted that Lacan's slant on drive theory becomes much clearer once it is seen for what it is: an outgrowth of his earlier reflections on the status of desire for the psychoanalytic clinic, that same desire which, according to Hegel, leads to the positing of conflict as an ontological ground. It may even be said that the status of the drive does not attain its central position in Lacan's theoretical framework until he finds himself forced to reconsider certain questions left unresolved by his account of desire.

In this respect, it is worth remembering how the essence of desire in Lacan is the absence of any natural processes of objectivation. His is a strange, fundamentally objectless desire, one incapable of deriving satisfaction from empirical objects and thus entirely removed from any immediate possibility of phenomenal fulfillment.

This pure negative transcendence, linked to the intentional function of a desire that persists beyond any and all object relations, is seen as an insurmountable obstacle to the Lacan of the early writings and seminars. The reason for this is Lacan's early development of an object-constitution theory predominantly based on the centrality of narcissism. Said theory was the outcome of his simultaneous recognition of the fundamental role of the ego in the binding of the manifold of sense intuition into object representations and of the *empirical genesis* of the ego-function through the logic of narcissistic identifications.

Thus, at this particular point in the course of Lacan's thought, both objects and empirical individuals are held, without exception, to be narcissistic projections of the ego; Lacan even speaks of the *egomorphic character of empirical objects*. From this, it follows that a *fundamental narcissism* guides all object relations, and that getting to the other side of this narcissistic regime of relations – through a critique of the primacy of the object in the determination of desire – is imperative.

The motif of a critique of the primacy of the object primarily appears in Lacan as a critique of relations that have been reduced to the dimension of the Imaginary, as the Lacanian conception of the Imaginary denotes, for the most part, the sphere of those relations that constitute the logic of narcissism with its projections and introjections.[44] Roughly speaking, it could be said that the Lacanian Imaginary is a type of *spatial-temporal categorization schema* operating through the subsumption of the manifold of sense intuition to the image (in this sense, Lacan's theory bears striking similarities to the theory of image and schematism present in Heidegger's *Kant and the Problem of Metaphysics*). It is through a principle of binding and identity derived from the ego as a synthetic, self-identical unity that the image unifies the manifold. Moreover, this image is precisely what is at stake in representation, at least as far as Lacan is concerned; hence, his tightly woven articulation of Imaginary, narcissism and *representation*.[45]

It is in this fashion that the *empirical object* appears as an *object submitted to the engineering of the Imaginary* – at this juncture, the possibility of libidinal fixation on an empirical, non-narcissistic object had yet to be posited. A process of freeing the subject from a fascination with objects that, deep down, are no more than narcissistic inventions, it was the task of psychoanalysis to "purify desire" of all empirical content: that is, to subjectivize desire precisely where it is most brutally emptied. After all, the taming of desire into object representations entails the alienation of a transcendent mode of being, from which necessarily follows the definition, uttered with an unmistakable Sartrean accent, of the negativity of desire as *manque d'être*: "Desire is a relation of being to lack. This lack is the lack of being [*manque d'être*] properly speaking. It isn't the lack of this or that, but lack of being whereby the being exists."[46] The goal of analytic practice was to lead the subject to the recognition of being as *lack-in-being* (*manque à être*, as Lacan would later rephrase it to differentiate his conceptions from those of Sartre).

Such is the schema at work in Lacan's initial elaborations of drive theory. In his earliest seminars Lacan already tended to view the unity produced by the life drive as a submission of the other to the logic of narcissism, describing the binding of psychic energy as "being captured by form, being seized by play, being gripped by the mirage of life."[47] This, in light of a posited unifying potency of the Imaginary connecting the subject to an other that is essentially an image of the subject's own ego. It is as if the "ever greater unities" Freud

---

[44] "We regard narcissism as the central imaginary relation of interhuman relationships." (LACAN, *The Psychoses, 1955-1956: The Seminar of Jacques Lacan, Book III*, edited by J.-A. Miller, translated by R. Grigg. New York: W. W. Norton & Co., 1997, p. 92)

[45] We have attempted to provide a more detailed description of this function of the Imaginary, as well as of Lacan's use of the notion of narcissism, in the aforementioned SAFATLE, *La passion du négatif: Lacan et la dialectique* (Georg Olms, 2010).

[46] LACAN, *Seminar II*, p. 223.

[47] *Ibid.*, p. 87.

wrote about were constructed by means of the binding of representations and affects, however great their multiplicity, in the ego's own *image*. The disintegrating power of the death drive was thus regarded as being in conflict from the first with the imaginary coherence of the ego and the imaginary object relations derived from it. In addition, the death drive was repeatedly presented as leading the subject beyond a mode of enjoyment linked to the submission of libidinal energy to a homeostatic principle which sought to attain balance through the "transference of the quantity from *Vorstellung* to *Vorstellung*"[48]: that is, through the submission of libidinal energy to representations. This might explain why the emergence of that which belongs to the order of the drive in Lacan is always enmeshed with the theme of an enjoyment that flirts with formlessness, an enjoyment that lies beyond the pleasure principle – that lies beyond the principle of submission to representation. Interestingly, it is at this point that Lacan employs a barrage of motifs and examples derived from Georges Bataille.

Bataille stressed the need for a program that was, in broad terms, similar to Lacan's: "Suppression of the subject and of the object: the only means of not resulting in the possession of the object by the subject, that is to say in avoiding the absurd rush of *ipse* wanting to become everything."[49] The driving force behind suppression is also connected to the theme of the experience of death as a means of escape from the primacy of anthropology: "He who does not 'die' from being merely a man will never be other than a man."[50] However, to associate Lacan and Bataille – a perfectly feasible proposition – is to invite a number of conceptual confusions. Most significantly, it could suggest that by making the death drive the central concept behind analytic progress, Lacan had allowed himself to be seduced by a sort of *clinical implementation of expectations regarding the aestheticizing potential of limit-experiences*, the latter conceived by means of an appeal to the themes of *formlessness* and *heterology*.[51]

---

[48] LACAN, *Seminar VII*, p. 58.

[49] BATAILLE, Georges; *Inner Experience*, translated by L. A. Boldt. Albany: State University of New York Press, 1988, p. 53.

[50] *Ibid.* p. 35.

[51] Experiences of this sort would force Lacan to accept statements such as those of Derrida's, who claimed Bataille showed us that "[t]he blind spot of Hegelianism, around which can be organized the representation of meaning, is the point at which destruction, suppression, death and sacrifice constitute so irreversible an expenditure, so radical a negativity – here we would have to say an expenditure and a negativity *without reserve* – that they can no longer be determined as negativity in a process or a system" (DERRIDA, *Writing and Difference*, translated, with an introduction and additional notes, by A. Bass. New York: Routledge, 2001, p. 327).

That such an objection could be raised was, of course, a permanent risk; it seems to depend, however, on an insufficient apprehension of what had truly been at issue in Lacan's theoretical developments. Let us recall how at first the death drive allowed Lacan to articulate some important distinctions between the dimensions of the Imaginary and the Symbolic, the latter conceived in a structuralist key, constituted by the pure signifiers that organize sociolinguistic differences. Still, Lacan never went so far as to defend any form of disaggregation of procedures of subject synthesis or suppression, however critical he may have been of their entification in the self-identical figure of the ego.

Let us reflect, for instance, on the very first sentence in the *Écrits*: "My research has led me to the realization that repetition automatism *(Wiederholungzwang)* has its basis in what I have called the *insistence* of the signifying chain."[52] Lacan seems to be saying that this compulsion to repeat – which disrupts any logic accounting for the behavior of the psychic apparatus strictly through an appeal to the notions of maximization of pleasure and avoidance of displeasure – is a manifestation of the mode of functioning of the symbolic structure that determines subjects. This is clearly a radically different claim than what Freud had in view when thematizing both the compulsion to repeat traumatic and unpleasant situations typical of certain classes of neurotic and the urge to achieve mastery over processes of loss through a symbolizing repetition (as in the notorious example of the game of *Fort-Da*).

What Lacan seems to have intended by this articulation of signifying chain and repetition automatism is, first of all, to remind us that the free energy peculiar to the death drive's power of un-binding is what produces the primary processes of condensation, displacement and figuration that provide a foundation for the dynamic of signifiers; hence, the feasibility of the articulation. This is Lacan's interpretation of what Freud termed the "network" (*Netz*) aspect of the drive and the drive in its "fluid" (*Flüssigkeit*) character. The proposition is as bold as it is fragile, since the structuring of the signifying chain, possessed as it is of the sort of organizing power common to all symbolic constructions, cannot but be entirely foreign to the mode of dissemination of something which can be characterized as free energy. In other words, the binding performed by the signifying chain must be entirely foreign to the sphere of the death drive.

---

[52] LACAN, *Écrits*, p. 11.

There is yet another facet to this articulation. In his attempt to bring death drive and signifier to bear on each other, Lacan seems to deny that the particularity of a drive or urge could be distinct from one's intersubjectively-shared sociolinguistic universe. On the contrary: the drive is somehow *constitutively enmeshed* with that which allows subjects, through their access to language, to socialize.[53] Ultimately, then, the drive is not something systematically repressed by subjective processes of socialization. Instead, it is the very force leading subjects to use language – on the condition that we confer reality to the rather peculiar regime of language alluded to here, that is. The language Lacan has in mind is, after all, absolutely anti-realist in that it is not composed of signs but of pure signifiers, exclusively composed of terms that denote no object whatsoever. This, essentially an effacement of the facticity of reference, is described by Lacan in the following terms: "[S]ignifiers only manifest at first the presence of difference as such and nothing else. The first thing therefore that it implies is that the relationship of the sign to the thing should be effaced."[54]

This allowed Lacan to state that, therefore, "we find the scheme of the symbol as the death of the thing"[55] – as if the negating impulse that characterizes the death drive were operational, or even found fulfillment, whenever the signifier revealed itself to be the effacement of the thing *as a reified object constituted by the logic of the Imaginary*. In its essence, the signifier was seen not as a denotative device, but merely as a mark of the extreme, mutual inadequacy present in the relation between words and things, the mutual inadequacy that must exist between a signifying chain articulated as a flow of unbound energy and things conceived as the outcome of a process of subjection to imaginary unities. Lacan's recourse to a language composed in its entirety by signifiers was an essential component of his efforts to fit the death drive into the *logic*

---

[53] An instructive parallel may be drawn, here, with the Hegelian concept of *Trieb*, in that, for Hegel, the urge stems from the suppressed opposition between the subjective and the objective, which means, among other things, that its satisfaction is no longer exclusively marked by the particularity of the object (as would be the case with desire), but rather appears as something that bears a universal character. In other words, the drive in question is one towards a reconciliation with the object by means of the realization of the intuition of a lack in said object.

[54] LACAN, *Identification, 1961-1962: The Seminar of Jacques Lacan, Book IX*, translated by Cormac Gallagher from unedited French typescripts. Session of 06.12.61 [Digital Version], p. 36, accessed on February 5, 2015. URL: http://www.lacaninireland.com/web/wp-content/uploads/2010/06/Seminar-IX-Amended-Iby-MCL-7.NOV_.20111.pdf.

[55] "Nous retrouvons le schéma du symbole en tant qu'il est la mort de la chose." LACAN, *Le séminaire, Livre IV: La relation d'objet et les structures freudiennes*, text established by J.-A. Miller. Paris: Seuil, 1994, p. 377.

*of inadequacy* produced by processes of socialization. He would not associate such signifiers with object denotation, but rather with the satisfaction of the drive, as though the uses of language were subordinated to practical interests of fulfillment.

As may be easily seen, the strategy employed by Lacan was ambivalent in character and, as initially constructed, quite untenable. On the one hand, the signifying chain favors processes whose binding and ordering of the world of objects is absolutely foreign to that which belongs to the order of the death drive. This is essentially Lacan's way of insisting that the death drive is not an urge of pure transgressive destructiveness aimed at the attainment of formlessness, or of enjoyment in its deadliest guise, but rather confers greater intelligibility to processes of socialization – at least in regards to whatever may be non-repressive in the processes of socialization *at work within our societies*. On the other hand, the signifying chain describes precisely that flow of unbound energy that negates whatever is amenable to being bound in the form of an object, that is to say, as a representation.

The contradiction in question is, nonetheless, quite a fertile one. It is undeniable that Lacan sought a formalization regime capable of handling the relation of the subject to a drive that resists the language of representation – a language that, in the terms of Lacanian topography, is subjected to the logic of the Imaginary; still, if he was to adequately thematize this resistance, Lacan had to provide a story as to how a subject could relate to something never organized on the basis of binding principles derived from the ego as a synthetic unity. The emphasis here is on the need to "structure relations" without falling back on some form of immediate intuition.

The aims and characteristics of this strategy – the reconfiguration of the death drive in the context of clinical analysis – should become clear once we take into consideration the status of negation within Lacanian psychoanalytic praxis. The modes proposed by Lacan for the relation between subject and drive are independent of that which Freud once defined as the binding of the drive into object representations, regardless of Lacan's insistence on the need for renewed reflections on what the "object" of the drive might be. In this context, after all, the very notion of object is dismantled—no longer defined by the binding principles derived from the ego as a synthetic unity. The object of the drive is an "object" only insofar as it provides an *obstacle*, or that which offers resistances to the processes of determination peculiar to consciousness.

This leads us to an additional question, one relevant to the direction of treatment. Lacan repeatedly insists that instances of clinical subjectivation cannot be organized from the perspective of a broadening of the consciousness' reflexive horizon of understanding, or of a reconstitution of the synthetic capacities of the ego; in other words, clinical subjectivation cannot be guided by the representational-binding imperatives that typically support the triad that structures the Freudian clinic, namely remembering, verbalization and symbolization. Still, these limitations to the scope of reflexive processes should not suggest that the subject's self-positing is a complete impossibility, nor that subjective capacities for experiential synthesis have been ineluctably blocked, no matter how much Lacanians may insist on seeing the end of analysis as the advent of an irreflexive, mute, monological enjoyment, or as the advent of some form of subjective destitution leading thought to the complete abandonment of any and all aspirations to synthesis.

Here, Lacan's theory of negation is useful in helping us ascertain more precisely what the psychoanalyst had in mind, especially given that his conception of subjectivation is founded on the recognition of the eminently negative character of the "objects" the drive is associated to, and *in which the subject must recognize him- or herself.* This goes to show how the Lacanian clinic requires a mode of negation quite distinct from the mere indication of a not-being, of a privation (*nihil privativum*), of emptiness as the pure absence of determination, quite distinct from a denial or an ejection from the self of whatever goes against the pleasure principle. It evidently requires a mode of negation that is a mode of presence for whatever has been excluded from reflexive symbolization and its protocols of identification, without this necessarily implying some form of return to the ineffable. This was quite possibly the most significant contribution from Lacan's large-scale appropriation of Hegelian philosophy. After all, for Lacan, who had always associated the analytic cure with subjective possibilities of self-objectivation that went beyond a subject's objectivation through the Imaginary, *there can only be a cure once the subject recognizes him- or herself in a negation conceived as a mode of presence of that which manifests as the essential determination of objects no longer constituted as narcissistic ego-images.* There is something deeply Hegelian to this strategy. In the case of Lacan, the point might become more evident once it is shown that there is a negation that, beyond its manifestation as a destructiveness directed at objects, can *reveal the structure of the objects* that bring the drive to fulfillment.

## Anxiety as the object's mode of manifestation

There are several ways to approach the problems raised by Lacan's reflections on the constitutive negativity of the object of the drive. The notion seems paradoxical and, at first glance, his claim that there are modes of negation capable of revealing the structure of drive-fulfilling objects is far from self-evident. One approach that seems potentially fruitful is to explore Lacan's take on a phenomenon central to clinical analysis – namely *anxiety*, given a meaning largely distinct from how the term appears in Freud.

Freud presented an important articulation between one's anxiety (*Angst*) and one's instinctual life, in that neurotic anxiety is deemed to have evident links to the emergence of drive-based demands (an articulation, incidentally, that would be preserved by Lacan). Indeed, as early as 1895 Freud, while working on the nosography of "anxiety neurosis" (*Angstneurose*), indicates that the genesis of the disturbance is connected to the neurotic's inability to psychically elaborate (that is, to *bind*) a present accumulation of endogenous excitation of a sexual nature. Later, aspects of this view would remain in his affirmation that, in a state of neurotic anxiety, one fears one's own libido, as instinctual demands are experienced as a danger emerging from within. This schema will function as the foundation for a definition of anxiety as an affect arising from a quantum of unusable libidinal energy – one, that is, that cannot be bound into object representations. This allows Freud to link anxiety to that feeling of danger stemming from the loss of connection between the drive and that which presents itself as a determined object, a relation in which the drive is sustained where the object is lacking, and which plunges the subject into a state Freud terms "helplessness."

This unbound libidinal energy undergirds the canonical definition that connects anxiety to a traumatic factor that cannot be overcome by the pleasure principle, especially given the fact that it is "the magnitude of the sum of excitation [*Grösse der Erregungssume*] that turns an impression into a traumatic moment, paralyzes the function of the pleasure principle and gives the situation of danger its significance."[56]

Lacan's reflections take as their starting point this conception of Freud's which links anxiety to situations in which there is object loss, as well as an increase in unbound libidinal energy. Hence, the following remark:

---

[56] FREUD, "Anxiety and Instinctual Life," *S.E. Vol. XXII*, p. 94.

When, due to resistance, defense, etc. – anything that can be said to be of the order of object-effacing mechanisms – the object disappears, is subtracted, what remains of it is that which can remain, that is, the *Erwartung*, the direction towards the place it is missing from, where it is nothing but an *unbestimmte Objekt*, or again, as Freud says, nothing but an object with which we have a relation of *Hilflosigkeit* [*that is, of helplessness*]. When we are at that point, anxiety [*l'angoisse*] is the final mode, the radical mode under which the subject carries on sustaining, though it may be unbearable, its relationship to desire.[57]

Still, Lacan's truly original insight would only appear later on, in connection with his attempts to associate himself with the long-standing philosophical tradition that understands anxiety as fundamental to the formation of the subject – a tradition to which Hegel, for instance, clearly belonged. Anxiety, after all, signals the occurrence of a confrontation between the subject and that which cannot be articulated on the basis of binding principles derived from the ego as a synthetic unity; and, insofar as it delivers the subject from the narcissistic illusions of the ego, it plays a role in the Lacanian conception of analytic progress that is every bit as central as the experience of the death drive.

This anxiety-inducing dimension (the existence of which does not exclude an anxiety-blocking dimension, of course) is thematized by Lacan when he insists, in opposition to both his own as well as Freud's earlier elaborations, that "anxiety is not without object." Anxiety will be conceived, here, as a mode of manifestation of objects no longer submitted to those structures of spatial-temporal categorization characteristic of the Imaginary. This is why throughout the entirety of his anxiety-themed tenth *Seminar* Lacan will demand a reconstruction of the transcendental aesthetic that would render it more adequate to the psychoanalytic experience. After all:

There are *moments of the appearance of the object* that cast us into *an entirely different dimension*, [...] which is precisely *the dimension of the strange*, of something which in no way allows itself to be apprehended,

---

[57] "Quand, pour des raisons de résistance, de défense, etc., tout ce que vous pouvez mettre dans l'ordre des mécanismes de l'annulation de l'objet, quand il ne reste plus que cela et que l'objet disparaît, s'escamote, mais non pas ce qui peut en rester, à savoir *l'Erwartung*, la direction vers sa place, la place où il fait dès lors défaut, où il ne s'agit plus que d'un *unbestimmtes Objekt*, ou encore comme dit Freud nous sommes dans le rapport d'*Hilflosigkeit*, quand nous en sommes là, l'angoisse est le dernier mode, le mode radical sous lequel il continue de soutenir, même si c'est d'une façon insoutenable, le rapport au désir." LACAN, *Le Séminaire, Livre VIII: Le Transfert*, text established by J.-A. Miller. Paris: Seuil, 1994, p. 429.

as if, before it, *the subject were made transparent to his or her own knowledge*. Before this new thing, the subject literally vacillates, and everything regarding the subject's so-called primordial relation to all effects of knowledge is called into question.[58]

This "dimension of the strange" Lacan spoke about may be identified with what Freud attempted to convey by means of his notion of *Unheimlichkeit* (*uncanniness*).[59] The phenomena Freud had in mind were indeed anxiety-inducing, phenomena in which familiar situations and objects were unexpectedly divorced from their natural matrices of identity and identification. For instance, if all of a sudden one's image in a mirror no longer appeared to be one's *own* image, but rather the image of something seemingly endowed with autonomy, as though it were the image of a double, then one would be faced with a phenomenon of *Unheimlichkeit*. Usually, situations in which the distinction between subject and object is put into question, as though there were something of the order of an acting subject where one expected to find no more than an inert object (or vice-versa), will also produce *Unheimlichkeit*.

Lacan tended to regard such phenomena as key elements in the determination of the formative role of anxiety because they are modes of apparition of objects no longer submitted to naturalized protocols of identity, difference and opposition; and that, as a result, confound one's safe distinctions between subject and object, self and other, identity and difference. Thus, by suggesting that such apparitions cause the relation of the subject to the very structures of knowledge to "vacillate," Lacan sought to bring attention to how the manifestation of objects that call into question such general principles of understanding as identification and differentiation can easily lead to the enfeeblement of a subject's ordered images of the world and of him- or herself. Yet if said objects are capable of calling certain general principles of understanding into question, that is on account of their being objects that bear in themselves the negation of their own submission to the law of identity.

This is a central point. When Lacan determines that such objects satisfy the death drive – a strange satisfaction, marked by anxiety – it is because the negativity of the death drive can find satisfaction through an object that bears

---

[58] "[C'est] qu'il existe *des moments d'apparition de l'objet* qui nous jettent dans *une toute autre dimension*, dans une dimension [...], qui est justement *la dimension de l'étrange*, de quelque chose qui d'aucune façon ne se laisse saisir, comme laissant en face de lui *le sujet transparent à sa connaissance*. Devant ce nouveau, le sujet littéralement vacille, et tout est remis en question de ce rapport soi-disant primordial du sujet à tout effet de connaissance." LACAN, *Le Séminaire, Livre X: L'Angoisse*, text established by J.-A. Miller. Paris: Seuil, 2004, pp. 73-74.
[59] Cf. FREUD, "The Uncanny," *S.E. Vol. XVII*, pp. 217-256.

its own negation within itself, an object that consists in its own destruction and in the upending of its own order of identity (protocols that, for Lacan, are fundamentally linked to the order of the Imaginary).

However, to state that an object bears within itself its own negation seems to be little more than a nebulous way of remarking that what we have here is an "empty object," an object void of all concept (*nihil negativum*)[60], a *contradictory object* and nothing more. Perhaps that is why Lacan claims that such an object "escapes the laws of the transcendental aesthetic."[61] Indeed, Lacan's position in regards to the centrality of the death drive as a device capable of providing treatment with a direction is dependent on a notion of the object that does not reduce the figure of the self-negation of identity to the status of an empty object. Such an object is marked by a negativity that will invariably be a source of anxiety on account of the enfeeblement of one's ordered images of the world and of oneself it implies – a perspective whose character seems rather Hegelian.

This explains why the experience of anxiety has a twofold function in Lacan. While anxiety may appear as a cause of symptoms and inhibitions, it will also be what may be termed the *engine* of subjective formation. In the former sense, Lacan no longer operates with the Freudian notion that deems it the outcome of desire lacking an object, remarking that, instead, anxiety manifests itself when there is a "lack of lack." There is always "a certain void to be preserved, one which bears no relation to the content of the demand, whether it be positive or negative." In the "total filling" of the void, there "appears the disturbance from which anxiety manifests."[62] Insofar as desire lacks any essential object, anxiety can only originate from the impossibility of lack being adopted not only as a condition for the operations of desire, but as their necessary byproduct.

As an example of this, Lacan speaks of a relation between mother and infant in which "there is no possibility of lack."[63] This is an apparently paradoxical proposition, given that regardless of how immediately present the mother may be whenever the baby expresses the smallest intimation of a need she will never be able to prevent him from sensing lack, from experiencing a moment of emptiness, however small it may be, between the manifestation of the need

---

[60] Cf. KANT, *Critique of Pure Reason*, A292/B348, p. 382.

[61] "*[Ce] reste, ce résidu, cet objet dont le statut échappe au statut de l'objet dérivé de l'image spéculaire,* échappe aux lois de l'esthétique transcendantale." LACAN, *Séminaire X*, p. 51.

[62] "Mais le comblement total d'un certain vide à préserver qui n'a rien à faire avec le contenu ni positif, ni négatif de la demande, c'est là que surgit la perturbation où se manifeste l'angoisse." *Ibid.*, p. 80.

[63] "[Ce] rapport est le plus perturbé quand il n'y a pas de possibilité de manque." *Ibid.*, p. 67.

and its fulfillment. However, Lacan likely had a different type of phenomenon in view. In her relation to the infant, the mother is in a privileged position, appearing as the first Other to provide organizing principles for the baby's demands for satisfaction – a time lapse preceding the experience of fulfillment, a certain mode of meeting the demand, a particular regime of presence, and even what might be termed a "transcendental aesthetic" of desire, albeit one generated within an empirical process (an idea, incidentally, which Lacan defended). To say that such organizing principles prevent "the possibility of lack" is simply to say that the recognition of any demands that fail to conform to the order posited by these principles, that elude the mode of enjoyment these principles allow for, is a complete impossibility;[64] or, to put it differently, the constitution of an object not in conformity with the rules of the symbolic organization presented by the actions of the members of the family nucleus is simply not possible. The anxiety in question is a consequence of one's inability to distance oneself from institutionalized modes of demand fulfillment.

In this sense, Lacan can act as though he were stating that the treatment of anxiety necessarily encompasses the recognition of its truth content. Hence his insistent claims that anxiety functions as a "cut" allowing us to disassemble imaginary objects. As may be seen, this association of anxiety to formative processes does not imply an acceptance of the idea – denounced by Deleuze as a consequence of his particular understanding of dialectics – that processes of emancipation need to be defenses of "the idea that suffering and sadness have value, the valorisation of the 'sad passions,' as a practical principle manifested in splitting and tearing apart."[65] What is at work here is a reflection on the conditions required for a restructuring of the field of experience; or, if we wish to be more precise, what we find here is the adoption of a renewed conception of *health*, one defined in exemplary fashion by Canguilhem:

---

[64] This is an important point as well, one that finds its full development in the Lacanian elaboration of the superego. It is clear that conformity to social modes of functioning depends largely on the acceptance of socially-approved regimes of enjoyment (and their possible transgression), which is why Lacan can confidently state: "*To enjoy on command*, that is something in which everyone senses that, if there is a source, an origin to anxiety, it must indeed be found *somewhere around there*." ["Car *jouir aux ordres*, c'est quand même quelque chose dont chacun sent que s'il y a une source, une origine de *l'angoisse*, elle doit tout de même se trouver *quelque part par là*."] (*Séminaire X*, p. 96) For an analysis of the problems posed by the Lacanian notion of superego, cf. SAFATLE, "Para uma crítica da economia libidinal" ["Towards a critique of libidinal economy"], in *Cinismo e falência da crítica*, pp. 113-145.

[65] DELEUZE, *Nietzsche and Philosophy*, p. 195.

> Because health is not a constant of satisfaction, but the a priori of the power to master perilous situations, this power uses itself up in mastering successive perils [*let us not forget how, for Freud, anxiety and danger were related notions*]. Health after healing is not the same health as before. The lucid consciousness of the fact that healing is not a return helps the patient in his search for the state of the least possible renunciation by liberating him from his fixation upon his previous state.[66]

To paraphrase Hegel, true health feels no dread before anxiety, and suffers no harm from its devastating effects; indeed, true health is able to withstand anxiety, and convert the negative into being.

## The Hegelian grammar of Lacanian negation

We have seen how, as a result of the privileged position given to the death drive, Lacan's clinical conceptions operate with a rather specific theory of negation; what becomes clear now is that such a theory requires, in turn, a figure of negation capable of determining objects irreducible to the positivity of images, or to representation-based formalizations.

We are familiar with several aspects of the conflict-laden relation between Lacan and Hegel, a relation built on disagreements and misunderstandings, as would have to be the case when one confronts "a mistaken but living Hegel," to use Paulo Arantes' happy formulation. Beyond the more obvious confusions, however, attention must be given to the Hegelian grammar of Lacan's notion of negation, with the caveat that this should not be taken to imply the latter's unconditional alignment with the consequences of the Hegelian system. In this sense, it may be said that some of the central points of Lacan's project consisted in: a) turning the theory of the drives into a *theory of the drive*; b) turning the negation characteristic of the death drive into an ontological negation, or a mode of manifestation of essence; and c) demonstrating how said negation can determine objects whose manifestation depends on a state of anxiety. These are not only negation-determined objects but also decentralized ones, on account of their carrying within themselves the negation of their own subjection to identity.

Once again, countless approaches are available for exploring possible commonalities between Hegel's concept of negation and the one present in the Lacanian death drive. It would seem best, however, for us to take a

---

[66] CANGUILHEM, Georges; *Writings on Medicine*, translated by S. Geroulanos & T. Meyers. New York: Fordham University Press, 2012, pp. 65-66.

moment here to recall the main characteristics of the phenomenological figure of negation at the heart of Hegel's philosophy, one we have already encountered in the first chapter of this book – that is to say, death. When Hegel writes of death he has in mind the phenomenological manifestation that is peculiar to the phenomenal indeterminacy of that which is never a simple *ens*. In other words, "death" points to an experience that evades the self-identical contours of representational thinking; death is that which does not submit to the determinations of the ego. For Hegel, there is a certain confrontation with indeterminacy – an instance onto which the thinking of the pure "I" cannot project its own image – that is equivalent to death. The conception of death employed here is not, as we have seen, the mere *foundering* of one's consciousness, one's *running aground* (*zugrunde gehen*), but rather a path through which one *goes to the ground* (*zu Grund gehen*) – a content-free, groundward motion that, as in the Lacanian death drive, propels the determination of objects in which consciousness can recognize its own negativity. That is why Hegel will state, in the *Science of Logic*, that essence, understood as that which determines itself as ground, determines itself as indeterminate, this determination being nothing other than the sublation of its own determinateness. Regarding this articulation between the negativity of death and the experience of a ground, let us bring to mind a central moment of the *Phenomenology of Spirit* to which Lacan was particularly attuned – the moment in which, within the Master-Slave dialectic, consciousness comes to experience anxiety (*Angst*):

> [T]his consciousness has been fearful, not of this or that particular thing or just at odd moments, but its whole being has been seized with dread [*Angst*]; for it has experienced the fear of death, the absolute Lord. In that experience it has been quite unmanned, has trembled in every fibre of its being, and everything solid and stable has been shaken to its foundations. But this pure universal movement, the absolute melting away of everything stable, is the simple, essential nature of self-consciousness, absolute negativity, pure being-for-self, which consequently is implicit in this consciousness.[67]

It would be impossible to read the excerpt above and not compare it with Hegel's personal experiences as described in the famous letter to Windischmann written on May 27, 1810:

---

[67] HEGEL, *Phenomenology of Spirit*, § 194, p. 117.

From my own experience I know this mood of the soul, or rather of reason, which arises when it has finally made its way with interest and hunches into a chaos of phenomena but, though inwardly certain of the goal, has not yet worked its way through them to clarity and to a detailed account of the whole. For a few years I suffered from this hypochondria to the point of exhaustion. Everybody probably has such a turning point in his life, the nocturnal point of the contraction of his essence in which he is forced through a narrow passage by which his confidence in himself and everyday life grows in strength and assurance – unless he has rendered himself incapable of being fulfilled by everyday life, in which case he is confirmed in an inner, nobler existence.[68]

This textual comparison suggests that the passage from the *Phenomenology* and others of a similar bent may well be descriptions of a pathological experience of suffering. And were that the case, one might be inclined to ask: to what extent could this experience of illness be seen as a condition for the advent of dialectics? Is not dialectics, after all, a mode of confrontation with the aforementioned "point of the contraction" of one's essence? That a form of thinking should be dependent on the way one experiences the enfeeblement and dissolution of one's image of the world should not be precociously discarded.[69] Let us recall, furthermore, that the term "dread" (*Angst*) is aptly employed in the above excerpt from the *Phenomenology*, given that it points precisely to that existential situation in which the subject feels as though it were standing before a desire capable of problematizing normative determinations regarding form.[70] However, if a consciousness becomes capable of understanding that the anxiety aroused by seeing the enfeeblement of its world and of its language is but the first manifestation of Spirit, of that Spirit which can only manifest through the destruction of all fixed determinateness,

---

[68] HEGEL, "Hegel to Windischmann: Nuremberg, May 27, 1810." In: *Hegel: the Letters*, translated by C. Butler & C. Seiler. Bloomington: Indiana University Press, 1984, p. 561.

[69] It should be noted that in the early nineteenth century "hypochondria" was the name given to a disease lacking a specified cause, and was seen as the masculine counterpart of female hysteria; it has, furthermore, been characterized as a form of anxiety in relation to the functioning of one's body since the days of Galen. In Hegel it is more broadly conceived as a state of being lost to indeterminacy, of confrontation with chaos.

[70] Indeed, Hegel and Lacan share an assumption regarding this: both men – each in his own fashion, yet both ultimately coming to largely convergent conceptions – associate feelings of anxiety and dread to themes derived from a philosophy of infinity. Regrettably, a thorough discussion of the structure of this notion of infinity one finds in both Hegel and Lacan falls beyond the scope of our present endeavors, and will have to be taken up on a later occasion.

then that consciousness will also become capable of understanding that, deep down, the "way of despair" is the internalization of the negative as an essential determination of essence, as suggested by such remarks as "the fear of the lord is indeed the beginning of wisdom."[71] And it is to this position that Lacan, with his reflections on the drive, seems to want to bring us as well.

---

[71] HEGEL, *Phenomenology of Spirit*, § 195, pp. 117-118.

# CHAPTER V

# An impulse toward lawlessness

*Laws are like sausages;*
*it is better not to see them being made.*
Otto von Bismarck (attributed)

*What is common to metaphysics and transcendental philosophy*
*is, above all, this alternative which they both impose on us:*
*either an undifferentiated ground, a groundlessness, formless nonbeing,*
*an abyss without differences and without properties,*
*or a supremely individuated Being*
*and an intensely personalized Form [either God or the ego].*
*Without this Being or this Form, you will only have chaos ...*
Gilles Deleuze

Thus far, our main concern has been to adequately develop notions of subject and of individuality on the basis of articulations between psychoanalysis and Hegelian philosophy. These articulations have been silently guided by a strategy which consisted in adopting as our own critical perspectives aimed at the work of both authors; this procedure in turn allowed us to ultimately conclude that the commentators in question, while to some extent right, had been right for the wrong reasons.

We know, for instance, how Hegelian thought would be seen by many as deeply reliant on the conceptual framework of a philosophy of consciousness that raises the subject's absolute self-reflection to the condition of a ground for rational normativity. Let us recall, in this sense, the words of Habermas, for whom the later Hegel (precisely the one this book is most concerned with) had been under the spell of the "presupposition of an absolute that is conceived on the model of the relation-to-self of a knowing subject."[1] And, indeed, our strategy consisted in presupposing that Hegelian philosophy establishes substantial associations between "subject" and "ground." However, for reasons discussed in the first chapter of this book, grounding in Hegel is

---

[1] HABERMAS, *Philosophical Discourse of Modernity*, pp. 39-40.

less a process of clarification than it is the positing of a process that is corrosive of all positivity involved in the determination of the modes of disposition of beings. Often, ground is even discussed as something possessed of a negative aspect, as Hegelian philosophy presents us with the figure of a ground no longer dependent on the self-identical form of the "I," or ego – a ground that could lead us to overcome naturalized modes of determination, on account of its being supportive of a progressive enfeeblement of the images of the world that orient and constitute our structured field of experience. In this context, the meaning typically assigned to the expression "relation-to-self of a knowing subject" should be revised, as it can no longer be taken to express anything like "the process of positing the self-identity of the subject."

Psychoanalysis, in its turn – and Lacanian psychoanalysis in particular – was a practice often criticized for its supposed dependence on a normative framework derived from a philosophy of subject. Among several accusations of this nature, the following, by Gilles Deleuze, may be worth recalling:

> The fact is that psychoanalysis talks a lot about the unconscious – it even discovered it. But in practice, it always diminishes, destroys and exorcizes it. The unconscious is understood as a negative, it's the enemy. *Wo es war, soll Ich werden.* In vain has this been translated as: 'There where it was, there as subject must I come' – it's even worse (including the *soll*, that strange 'duty in an ethical sense').[2]

Yet an analysis of Lacanian subject theory, and of one of its principal foundations in particular – namely, drive theory –, reveals that this negative element psychoanalysis introduces should be seen as more than a mere counter-consciousness, as more than simply a difference interpretable as an opposition to consciousness' characteristic modes of determination. What it does, in reality, is allow for an important articulation between *subject* and *negation* that can help us avoid the reduction of the category of subject to the condition of locus of identity.

In both cases, the construction of a non-substantial, non-identitarian notion of subject is the preamble for a renewed understanding of the nature of conceptualization processes and of the synthetic operations through which experiential objects are constituted (something the preceding discussions on the relation between anxiety and object have already shown us); furthermore, it significantly clarifies the processes that determine our understanding of rational

---

[2] DELEUZE, Gilles & PARNET, Claire; *Dialogues*, translated by H. Tomlinson & B. Habberjam. New York: Columbia University Press, 1987, p. 77.

normativity. The latter aspect has yet to be discussed, however; indeed, that is the main function of the present chapter. For that reason, the discussion will now encompass fundamental elements of Theodor Adorno's subject theory, a theory in which psychoanalysis and dialectics meet. They converge, more specifically, in the context of his critique of rational normativity as derived from Kant's transcendental philosophy and his reflection on practical reason in particular.

Hence, a discussion of Adorno's critique of Kantian morality shall be undertaken, with a particular emphasis on the Frankfurtian philosopher's defense of the ontogenesis of the judicative power of moral subjects. The first step towards that end is a reconstruction of Adorno's employment of Freudian drive theory, so that the constitution of this ontogenetic conception may be properly understood, and its consequences duly established. This recourse to Freud is of fundamental importance for Adorno's development of a regulatory horizon for his critique of rationality, and of a "material basis" for his subject theory. Our recourse to Adorno is justified in its turn on account of his being without question the author who most systematically explored the potential of Freudian psychoanalysis for a critique of the notion of rational normativity presupposed by Kant's moral philosophy.

Hence, a clarification of this articulation between Adorno and Freud should highlight one of the central characteristics of Adorno's bold claim— advanced, with the assistance of Horkheimer, in the *Dialectic of Enlightenment* – that Kant ought to be read alongside the perverse structure of Sade's libertine morality; that doing so would provide us with a clearer perspective regarding the consequences of the Kantian constitution of the sphere of the moral subject. In fact, it is quite possible that through this juxtaposition Adorno sought to transform the critique of rationality into an instrument for the analysis of social pathologies. In the present context, said transformation entails a transition from a critical perspective aiming to clarify the conditions of possibility for the grounding of rational normativity to an analysis of the nature of the suffering produced by forms of rationality ultimately intended as guidelines for social actions aspiring to both validation and universalization. The suffering in question is social in character, and arises whenever subjective demands for recognition and attendant aspirations towards self-actualization cannot be met. Thus, the starting point for reflection shifts from a determination of normativity conducted in advance, to the initial identification of a pathological situation involving great suffering and feelings of limitation which results from existing ideals of rationality. Precisely what form of obstruction to recognition is inherent to the Kantian take on the formation of the moral subject, however, is something we shall have to look into.

Let us first note how the use of the term "pathology," in this context, loses some of its strangeness once we adopt an interpretation of rationality as a *form of life*. From that, it may be said that a *rational* form of life would be one organized on the basis of institutionalized values and normative criteria allowing subjects to apprehend, in a purely self-reflexive manner, the foundations upon which society's non-coercive practices and their aspirations to universality have been established. This notion of reason as a form of life is one that had already been explored by Hegel, through his notion of *Geist*.[3] Yet a form of life cannot but be understood as "pathological" when it produces social suffering on account of its incapacity to meet the demands of recognition of subjects in their struggle toward self-actualization. In this sense, it seems likely that Adorno's critique was based on the idea that the conceptual structure that defines the extent of our capabilities as autonomous, rationally deliberating subjects might itself be "pathological," as though there were something of a deeply "disciplinary" nature in the figure of the *vernünftig Mensch*.[4] This mode of inquiry resembles Nietzschean genealogy, which Adorno had more than a passing familiarity with. In other words, the actual question Adorno seemed to be getting at is: *are the notion of autonomy and the model of rational deliberation present in the Kantian constitution of the moral subject not themselves pathological figurations?*

The question may seem hyperbolic, or even nonsensical; providing an adequate answer is, furthermore, dependent on a conceptual movement that runs through the entirety of this book. For the moment, then, it should suffice to point out that the moral ideals criticized by Adorno often appear as a normative horizon for processes of socialization, as well as for the formation of subjects able to orient themselves rationally in regards to judgment and action. This goes to show that the aim of this problematization of moral action is not merely providing an answer to "what ought to be done?" but addressing questions such as "what kind of person do I want to be?" and "what form of life should I adopt as my own?" Taking that into account, Adorno's peculiar use of clinical categories – such as, among others, *narcissism, paranoia* and *fetishism* – is worthy of consideration. From his perspective, after all, these

---

[3] Cf. the aforementioned PINKARD, *Hegel's Phenomenology: The Sociality of Reason*, and PIPPIN, *Hegel's Practical Philosophy: Rational Agency as Ethical Life*.

[4] Many commentators have noted the striking similarities that exist between Adorno's critical strategies and the description of disciplinary devices in Foucault; cf. e.g. DEWS, Peter; *Logics of Disintegration: Post-Structuralist Thought and the Claims of Critical Theory* (London: Verso Books, 1987), pp. 150-161.

do not describe pathological deviations relative to normative standards for intersubjectively-shared behavior; instead, they denote *the residue unavoidably left in the wake of the ontogenesis of the practical-cognitive capabilities of socialized subjects.*

In this sense, by also employing said categories (especially narcissism and fetishism) towards a critique of the Kantian moral subject,[5] Adorno acts as though he presupposed this particular conception of subject to be a regulative horizon for the ontogenesis of our practical-cognitive capabilities. This is a plausible interpretation, especially if one takes into account Freud's seemingly risky and certainly controversial remark that "Kant's Categorical Imperative is [...] the direct heir of the Oedipus complex."[6] In this respect, one might also recall how Lawrence Kohlberg's psychology of moral development details a form of ontogenesis whose final stage is the acquisition of a principle of autonomy largely convergent with the one Kantian morality advances.[7]

Once the idea is accepted that the Kantian moral subject is the regulative horizon for the ontogenesis of our practical-cognitive capabilities, a whole other dimension is added to Adorno's critique, as it then conveys how reflections on psychoanalytic drive theory can uncover the nature of the suffering that ensues from the internalization of normativities intended as rational. This is a position that raises the question of what alterations the idea of "rational deliberation" must necessarily undergo once the moral subject's empirical genesis – as conceived in the conceptual framework favored by Adorno as a reader of Freud – becomes an acceptable starting point. What could an act of rational deliberation even entail in view of Adorno's insistence

---

5   For instance: "In the abstract universal concept of things 'beyond nature,' freedom is spiritualized into freedom from the realm of causality. With that, however, it becomes a self-deception. Psychologically speaking, the subject's interest in the thesis that it is free would be narcissistic, as immoderate as anything of the kind. There is narcissism even in Kant's arguments, for all his categorial localization of freedom in a sphere above psychology" (ADORNO, *Negative Dialectics*, p. 220). He would also call Kant's moral philosophy "a model case of fetishism" (ADORNO, *Problems of Moral Philosophy*, translated by R. Livingstone. Stanford: Stanford University Press, 2001, p. 139). Regarding this "narcissistic" character of Kant's moral philosophy, one could ultimately follow Butler's lead and say that "Adorno's characterization of Kantianism as a form of moral narcissism seems to [...] [suggest] that any deontological position that refuses consequentialism runs the risk of devolving into narcissism and, in that sense, ratifying the social organization of individualism" (BUTLER, *Giving an Account of Oneself*, p. 108).

6   FREUD, "The Economic Problem of Masochism." In: *The Standard Edition of the Complete Psychological Works of Sigmund Freud, Volume XIX (1923-1925): The Ego and the Id and Other Works*, edited and translated by J. Strachey. London: The Hogarth Press and the Institute of Psychoanalysis, 1961, p. 167.

7   Cf. KOHLBERG, Lawrence; *The Psychology of Moral Development*. San Francisco: Harper and Row, 1984.

on the need for a problematization of both the notion of autonomous ego and of the leftover residue of processes of socialization, or in view of his insistence on the impossibility of establishing strict distinctions between impulses and free will, and on there being a need for what some authors have termed a "totalizing critique of reason"?

Before such questions are broached, a foundational issue must be settled: a critique of Kantian morality conducted through a defense of the ontogenesis of judicative abilities requires that the relation between the psychological and the transcendental be conceived anew.

## Recovering the "psychological"

A specter haunts philosophy – the specter of psychologism. Making accusations of falling back on psychologism was a strategy repeatedly employed to disqualify the most varied positions throughout the history of modern philosophy, beginning at least from the time of Kant's denial of the possibility of a rational psychology. Again and again it has been suggested that those who allow themselves to get caught up in such an error, cleverly wrought as it may be, show themselves incapable of grasping the unconditional ground of whatever it may be that is imbued with transcendental validity, and relativize this ground when they subject it to the psychological conditions of the thinking subject.

Still, what if behind the frequent discomfort evinced in relation to this reduction of the foundation of our rational operations to psychology a different issue had been hiding? What if it kept us from discussing the possibility that our rational structures and principles are products of empirical experiences? For it is possible that, behind psychologism, there lies a throbbing sense that nothing that aspires to unconditional validity *for us* is truly indissociable from its genesis. As if questions of *validity* and *genesis* could not be so easily distinguished; as if, that is, they could not be distinguished *at all.*

It may be said that this was precisely what that "psychologist," Sigmund Freud, understood when he sought in familial conflict the empirical genesis of moral feelings. That is, he attempted to demonstrate how the sense and significance of that which aspires to transcendental validity within the sphere of practical reason is ultimately indissociable from the determination of its genesis – a determination that ultimately provides general coordinates for critical approaches.

However, this operation is not restricted to the sphere of practical reason. Once we accept the strategy laid out by Freud, there is nothing to stop us from extending this procedure to encompass the genesis of that which appears to us as formally necessary within the field of cognitive consciousness – to encompass, more specifically, the empirical genesis of those principles that dictate, for example, that something must invariably be self-identical (the principle of identity), or that a paradoxical object cannot possibly be thought through two mutually-contradictory sets of propositions (the principle of non-contradiction), among a host of others. Are such "principles" not connected to a monumental effort to compel thought to begin there, where the machinery has already been fully assembled and the game rigged from start to finish?

Questions of this nature guided at least one philosopher: Theodor Adorno, who wrote and sought to carry through to their ultimate consequences such remarks as: "[All] the talk of an 'I' and all the other features that are claimed to be transcendental elements in Kant actually presuppose something like an empirical individuality."[8] Involved discussions of the presuppositions behind the Kantian "I think" (*Ich denke*), that formal principle regarded as "the vehicle of all concepts whatever, and hence also of transcendental concepts,"[9] allowed Adorno to, among other things, recover the sphere of the psychological as a constitutive moment in the grounding of moral reflection.[10]

Adorno's adoption of this perspective comes from his regarding the "I think" as imbued with a facticity, a concreteness, directly derived from the operational role it plays in structuring the psychic syntheses of the psychological "I," the ego. This suggests it would be impossible to effect a complete separation of the "I think" as the formal unity of the subject of representation from the "I" that is the actual unity of what has been experienced in the empirical life of consciousness. The inseparability was seen, furthermore, as symptomatic of a certain regime of dependence. With this in view, Adorno could mobilize the genesis of the psychological "I" against certain consequences of a transcendental notion of subject.

---

[8]  ADORNO, *Kant's Critique of Pure Reason*, translated by R. Livingstone. Stanford: Stanford University Press, 2001, p. 203.

[9]  KANT, *Critique of Pure Reason*, A 341/B399, p. 411. The term "vehicle" (*Vehikel*) is essential, here, in that it conveys the idea that the "I think" is the *means* through which the concept fulfills its synthetic function.

[10]  For Adorno, we ought to attempt to "move past the Kantian principle that requires there to be a separation between the 'metaphysics of customs,' seen as completely independent from experience, and the 'empirical element' of morality, essentially a collection of psychological, sociological or anthropological observations on the principles underlying morality that ultimately leads us to a confrontation with the 'dear self' and brands with the seal of inanity the very concept of duty" (JOUAN, *Psychologie Morale*, p. 11).

## Freud, Hegel and the question of genesis

In order to analyze this problematization of the relation between the psychological and the transcendental in Adorno, we begin by stressing the philosopher's conceptual reliance on strategies present in both Freud and Hegel. Particularly when it came to his dealings with Kantian morality, Adorno often employed a critique of transcendentalism that found inspiration in both Hegelian *dialectics* and Freudian *materialism*. This operation would give rise to a rather peculiar breed of *dialectical materialism*.

Concerning this, let us first recall how early in his *Science of Logic* Hegel discarded the possibility of beginning his reflections with the "I," as this would entail a promotion of the principle of subjectivity to the condition of "a beginning and foundation" for the objectivity of knowing, and thus perpetuate a line of thinking associated with what we now term "philosophies of consciousness." This is a line of thinking alluded to by Hegel when he denounced the "new time" (meaning modernity) for having elevated the "I" to the condition of a ground for knowledge.

Hegel insisted that the "first truth" from which the entire sequence of knowing is derived must be something regarding which one has immediate certainty (*unmittelbar Gewisses*). There is a structural difficulty inherent in the adoption of the "I" as the ground for this kind of immediate certainty, however, for just as the "I" seeks to affirm itself as an immediately self-certain consciousness, so is it an empirical instance enmeshed in the world's endless multiplicity – or, as Hegel puts it, "the 'I' is, as such, *at the same time* also a concrete, or rather, the 'I' is the most concrete of all things – the consciousness of itself as an infinitely manifold world."[11] If it is to be a ground, the "I" must stand separately from its empirical multiplicity. This would require an "absolute act" by virtue of which the "I," purifying itself *of itself*, could enter consciousness as an abstract "I" (or, to state it differently, as a transcendental subject), which would in turn imply an elevation to a standpoint of pure knowledge, in which "the distinction between subject and object has disappeared" (since in this scenario the "I" would function as the very foundation for the constitution of any and all experiential objects).

Hegel insists that this pure "I" is not something immediately accessible to the "ordinary I" (*gewöhnlich Ich*); nevertheless, if it is to be viewed as more than an arbitrary perspective imposed through non-reflexive means, "the progression of the concrete 'I' from immediate consciousness to pure knowledge must be demonstratively exhibited within the 'I' itself, through its

---

[11]  HEGEL, *Science of Logic*, p. 53.

own necessity"[12] – as though the grounding of knowledge were a consequence of the internal necessity peculiar to the empirical "I" (an argumentative path which, peculiarly, could be seen as characteristic of the general direction of this "science of the experience of consciousness" that is the *Phenomenology of Spirit*), and not a radical break with any empiricity found in what we now think of as the psychological ego. Still,

> inasmuch as this pure 'I' must be essential, pure knowledge [*in the sense of absolute transcendental determination*] – and pure knowledge is however one which is only posited in individual consciousness through an absolute act of self-elevation, is not present in it immediately – we lose the very advantage which was to derive from this beginning of philosophy, namely that it is something with which everyone is well acquainted, something which everyone finds within himself and to which he can attach further reflection [...].[13]

In this sense, suggests Hegel, one speaks as if of something familiar, which is to say that "I" referring to the psychological ego of empirical consciousness, and yet what is actually denoted is something that, to ordinary consciousness, is an absolute "unknown" (*Unbekanntes*); still, a pure "I" continues to be spoken of, and "[d]etermining pure knowledge as 'I' acts as a continuing reminder [*Rückerinnerung*] of the subjective 'I'" as a mode of synthesis construction.[14] This would explain why even at the level of ground one finds that "insurmountable opposition to an object" that is characteristic of the "I" as a concept. Thus, it would be better to abandon the "I" as ground and show how the unfolding of the empirical "I" reveals it to have no existence as an isolated entity, but to have always been Spirit –to have never been an absolute "I," but rather that which can only appear once the irreducible individuality of the "I" has been unmasked as an illusion. These are considerations Hegel takes up to show us that, as Robert Brandom's paraphrasing of John Haugeland so unequivocally states, "all transcendental constitution is social institution."[15]

---

[12] *Ibid.*

[13] *Ibid.*, p. 54.

[14] *Ibid.* A consideration of this issue may help us arrive at a better understanding of statements such as the following: "What results from abstraction can never be made absolutely autonomous vis à vis what it is abstracted from; because the *abstractum* remains applicable [*anwendbar*] to that which is subsumed within it, and because return is to be possible, the quality of what it has been abstracted from is always, in a certain sense, preserved [*aufbewahrt*] in it at the same time, even if in an extremely general form [*Allgemeinheit*]" (ADORNO, *Three Studies*, p. 15).

[15] BRANDOM, Robert; *Tales of the Mighty Dead: Historical Essays in the Metaphysics of Intentionality*. Cambridge: Harvard University Press, 2002, p. 216.

That is one of the reasons why Hegel can regard the *Phenomenology* as being presupposed in its entirety by the *Science of Logic*. It might also explain why, in the *Encyclopedia*, the *Psychology* is preceded by the *Phenomenology of Spirit*. Of course, far from being a mere description of the mental faculties responsible for establishing one's relationship with the world and with oneself, "psychology" here is a method of uncovering modes of relation to objects (such as intuition, representation, thinking, impulse, satisfaction, etc.), of *Vermögens*, in the sense of skills for interacting with one's environment, with said environment's intelligibility being dependent on the uncovering of the phenomenological genesis of social relations. Thus, the *Phenomenology* in a certain sense rids us of the illusion that the ground of knowledge is in the "I," and points us towards the thematization of a potential mode of synthesis no longer dependent on the solipsistic figure of an ego.

And yet, as has been stated above, the problematization of the relation between the psychological and the transcendental is an issue that also raises its head in Freud. Several instances in the psychoanalyst's work make this evident, but perhaps none more so than those occasions he looked into interactional conflicts wherein main processes of socialization take place – the family, for instance – for the genesis of moral feelings. At stake in such passages is a cogent demonstration of the fact that any assertion of *transcendental validity* in the sphere of practical reason amounts to little more than an obstruction, hindering more precise considerations on those genetic processes Freud unhesitatingly regarded as originating from feelings of "social anxiety."[16]

In other words, there are approaches to be derived from both Freud and Hegel for an inquiry into the *genesis* of what we are so willing to categorically, unconditionally and universally regard as rational – *a genesis that can be described as at once social and psychological*, given that, for the Viennese psychoanalyst as well as the German philosopher, "psychological" for the most part denotes the manner in which the subjective internalization of social processes occurs.[17] Hence, in both cases the "psychological" in question may be said to be a *psychology devoid of interiority*.

---

[16] FREUD, Sigmund; "Thoughts for the Times on War and Death," *S.E. Vol. XIV*, p. 280.

[17] Concerning Freud's perspective in particular, it may be worth recalling that his description of the ontogenesis of practical-cognitive abilities is inextricable from phylogenetic considerations that ultimately lead to an actualization of the accumulated weight of the social processes of interaction developed throughout history. Employing the phylogenetic perspective Freud could demonstrate that the process of constitution of psychic instances, of mental faculties and of intentional functions was truly indissociable from conflictual processes of socialization that take place within ever-broadening interactional nuclei, nuclei where the present and the historical past are profoundly intertwined.

Taking into account this redefinition of the term "psychological," it may be stressed, in addition, that the psychological dimension sought by Adorno was not reducible to descriptions of the intentional functions of an individual empirical consciousness. Rather, it was a psychological dimension marked at its core by an analysis of the impact of processes of socialization on the formation of one's practical-cognitive capabilities and in the direction given to one's drives, that is, by a problematization of the relations between the individual and said individual's social attachments. This is a fundamental consideration if we are to understand Adorno's particular way of problematizing the relation between the psychological and the transcendental; it is with this in mind that one ought to interpret a remark such as the following:

> Freud was the first to register the full implications of the Kantian critique of an ontology of the soul, of 'rational psychology': the soul of Freudian psychology, as part of the already constituted world, falls within the province of the constitutive categories of empirical analysis.[18]

Such considerations allow Adorno to hold Freud responsible, from the moment the latter submitted the theory of the soul to an empirical theory of infantile sexuality, for bringing to an end the ideological transfiguration of animism into the psychic. In light of the fact that Adorno's stated intention is to demonstrate, among other things, that "the implicit genesis of the logical is certainly not psychological motivation. It is a sort of social behavior,"[19] we can easily see the ways in which Freud's conceptions will be of assistance to him in his project to discern, within the transcendental subject, "society unaware of itself."[20]

Let us recall, furthermore, how since *Kierkegaard: Construction of the Aesthetic*, Adorno strictly avoided any appeals to the notion of interiority (*Innerlichkeit*) to account for whatever might be peculiar to the dimension of the subject; interiority, argued Adorno, was nothing but a bourgeois

---

[18] ADORNO, "Sociology and Psychology – II," translated by I. N. Wohlfarth. In: *New Left Review* I/47, January-February 1968, p. 81.

[19] ADORNO, *Against Epistemology: A Metacritique*, translated by W. Domingo. Cambridge: Polity Press, 2013, p. 76.

[20] ADORNO, *Negative Dialectics*, p. 177. In this sense, it may also be said that "[Adorno] accepts that psychologism is false but proposes a kind of, what we might call, 'sociologism' in its place. What he is saying is that no feature of logic – understood as a realm of pure validity – can be understood as independent of its sociogenesis." (O'CONNOR, Brian; *Adorno's Negative Dialectic: Philosophy and the Possibility of Critical Rationality*. Cambridge: The MIT Press, 2004, p. 136). Nevertheless, one must not be so careless as to forget how dependent the proposed sociogenesis is on interpretive schemes that are particular to the Freudian model of subject-formation through drive-socialization dynamics.

abstraction that sought to substantialize the impossibility of the modern subject's recognizing itself in a reified objectivity, an objectivity reduced to the condition of "a complex of senses – meanings – which has become rigid and strange, and which no longer awakens interiority; it is a charnel-house of long-dead interiorities [...]."[21] Thus, the psychological subject founded upon the notion of interiority was inadvertently responsible for endowing with ontological reality what was merely the fruit of a social situation – one that ought to be overthrown, no less.

That being the case, if "objectless [*Objektlose*] inwardness strictly excludes objective history,"[22] then the Adornian recovery of the subject and any ensuing reconciliation with a non-reified objectivity must perforce reject all entification of interiority; this, on the basis of an understanding of the psychological as a sphere that is also related to the impact of social processes in the formation of modes of relation to self and to objects. The psychological genesis of the transcendental is thus deep down a peculiar genesis of a social-empirical sort. In this context, one can easily imagine how and why an attentive reader of Freud such as Adorno can claim that "the usual distinction between social science and pure philosophy cannot be sustained because social categories enter into the very fibre of those of moral philosophy."[23]

The proposed reflection, however, must begin by addressing questions perennially found in Freud's work, which might be generally stated as "what must one give up so as to be able to conform to demands of rationality present in hegemonic processes of socialization?," and "what economic calculation must be made so as to ascertain the actual cost involved in meeting such demands?" We ought to inquire, after all, into what exactly a subject must undergo if it is to act in accordance with a regime of rationality that imposes ordering patterns, modes of organization, and institutional structures of legitimacy. These are questions Adorno would try to address.

## The critique of the ego

Through his inquiry into the actual cost of socialization processes – processes whose chief aim is the constitution of a self-referential instance, an *ego* – Adorno paves the way for critical approaches to the modern conception of

---

[21] LUKÁCS, György; *The Theory of the Novel: A Historico-philosophical Essay on the Forms of Great Epic Literature*, translated by A. Bostock. Cambridge: The MIT Press, 1971, p. 64.

[22] ADORNO, *Kierkegaard: Construction of the Aesthetic*, translated by R. Hullot-Kentor. Minneapolis: University of Minnesota Press, 1989, pp. 34-35.

[23] ADORNO, *Problems of Moral Philosophy*, p. 138.

individuality. This is not something that is entirely evident at all times, as, for instance, Adorno often insists on understanding the weakening of the ego, viewed as an instance of mediation between the demands of drives and external reality (as it stands within late capitalism), as indicative of the unraveling of subjective autonomy. However (and this particular "however" ought to be given its due regard), Adorno not once associated himself with such therapeutic demands for a "strengthening of the ego" as were fashionable among practitioners of that "ego psychology" we know the philosopher to have been acquainted with. He was aware, after all, that the ego, as the representative of the reality principle within the psychic system, is above all the instance responsible for the production of resistances to, and for repressing, the demands of the drives. In this sense, strengthening it would be akin to perpetuating a specific form of alienation.

Indeed, that is so much the case that several commentators have noted how Adorno tended to insist that the ego, as a self-referential instance, actually *prevents* us from coming to the conclusion that "some form of development toward sociability would occur in the presence of other subjects who do not exercise coercion."[24] For Adorno, that is, the formation of the ego as a psychic instance could not be understood as a gradual opening up of the subject to processes of non-coercive intersubjective interaction, nor could the relation between mother and infant be seen as some privileged empirical form of primary intersubjectivity.[25] Therefore, as a mode of psychic synthesis the ego could in no way sustain regimes of recognition of that which Adorno termed "non-identity," for it is, on the contrary, a rigid principle through which experience is constrained to adopt the general form of identity, as made clear in the *Dialectic of Enlightenment* when Adorno and Horkheimer write of an "identity of the self which cannot be lost in identification with the other."[26] This would explain the extensive use, characteristic of Adorno, of the category of narcissism in accounting for the hegemonic object-relation modes one finds in contemporary society.

At least on this point it may be said that Adorno's perspective finds additional legitimization when contrasted with the theories regarding the constitution and function of the ego one finds in the work of psychoanalysts such as Jacques Lacan. It must be remembered, of course, that Adorno did not come into contact with Lacan's theoretical work until very late in his life, as we learn through the single reference he ever made to the French psychoanalyst:

---

[24] BENJAMIN, Jessica; "The End of Internalisation: Adorno's Social Psychology." In: *Telos*, 32, 1977, p. 60.
[25] Cf. e.g. HONNETH, *The Struggle for Recognition*, p. 98.
[26] ADORNO & HORKHEIMER, *Dialectic of Enlightenment*, p. 6.

a remark that appears in his last lecture course, *Introduction to Sociology*, to the effect that he would wish to devote a seminar, in "the term after next," to French Structuralism, a strain of social thought he specifically associated to Lévi-Strauss and Lacan. It is nonetheless easy to imagine how the Lacanian conception of the ego as the principle of psychic organization – constituted by means of an introjection of one's image as seen by an other, and of a subsequent denegation of this very process – might have proved useful to Adorno.

Lacan held the ego to be an instance formed through one's recognition of one's own image in a mirror, or through one's identification with the image of another baby. This moment in the constitution of the ego, known as the Mirror Stage, consists in an operation of mimetic role-playing through the adoption of ideal images. This is a notion that allowed Lacan to hold ego-formation as only taking place through processes of identification, processes through which the baby introjects an external image provided by an other. In other words, if the infant is to get his or her bearings in relation to thinking and acting, learn to desire, and find a place within the family structure, he or she must initially reason through analogy, imitating an image elevated to the position of an ideal type and adopting as his or her own the perspective of an other. These imitative operations are important not only because they provide a direction for cognitive functions, but also on account of having fundamental value for the constitution of the ego and its subsequent development throughout mature life. Such reflections led Lacan to state that "nothing separates the ego from its ideal forms,"[27] which are fully absorbed into social life, for "[the] ego is constructed like an onion, one could peel it, and discover the successive identifications which have constituted it."[28]

By taking this into account, Lacan was able to hold that the genesis of the ego reveals how autonomy and individuality are no more than figures that betray a complete lack of knowledge concerning the ego's constitutive dependence on the other. While the ego is commonly believed to be the core of one's autonomy and self-identity, its genesis shows that, in the words of Rimbaud, "I is another" (*Je est un autre*). Hence the notion, central to Lacan's thought, that the true function of the ego is not related to synthetic processes of a psychic or representational nature, but rather connected to its lack of knowledge in regards to its own genesis and to the projection of its mental schema onto the world. That is why Lacan did not believe that this dependence between the ego and the other was enough to guarantee the existence of a

---

[27] LACAN, *Écrits*, p. 146.
[28] LACAN, *Freud's Papers on Technique, 1953-1954: The Seminar of Jacques Lacan, Book I*, edited by J.-A. Miller, translated with notes by J. Forrester. New York: W. W. Norton & Co., 1991, p. 171.

consolidated communicative relation between subjects. The multiple figures of aggression and rivalry in the relation between ego and other would in fact be structural symptoms of the ego's inability to acknowledge the other's constitutive role in that determination that is inherent to said ego's identity. The ego is, after all, an organizational principle that functions as a "rigid structure" bringing cohesion to one's behavior and beliefs, an "armor"[29] of sorts that forces any potential affirmations of that which resists submission to self-identity to manifest exclusively under the guise of conflict, of symptom, of inhibition and of anxiety.[30]

This critique of the ego provided a material foundation for Adorno's critique of identity; in this sense, it may be said that Adorno fully expected Freudian ontogenesis to be able to ground a true *critique of the repressive character of the primacy of identity*, a primacy entified not only in the figure of the psychological ego, but in that of transcendental subjectivity itself. It is with such problems in view that we must understand Adorno's programmatic use of "the strength of the subject to break through the fallacy of constitutive subjectivity [...],"[31] as, at several moments, the philosopher, like Lacan, seems to have believed there to be a need for separating the subject from ego-derived modes of psychic synthesis. The particular way in which this program was critically mobilized against Kantian morality is something we shall have the occasion to address in what follows; towards that end, however, we should begin by discussing a specific problem with the way the transcendental conception of subject is constituted.

## Synthetic unity

Should we turn our attention to the second excursus presented in the *Dialectic of Enlightenment*, "Juliette or Enlightenment and Morality," we shall easily see how it starts with Kant's canonical statement from *Beantwortung der Frage: Was ist Aufklärung?*, in which enlightenment is presented as "the human

---

[29] Cf. LACAN, *Écrits*, p. 78.

[30] Whitebook systematized well the similarities that exist between Lacan and Adorno in what concerns the critique of the ego: "[...] Adorno and Lacan advance the same three interconnected theses: 1. The unity of the ego as such is rigidified, compulsory and coercive. 2. The ego is a narcissistic (or paranoid) structure insofar as it can apprehend the object only in terms of its own reflection (or projections). 3. The rigidly integrated ego is deeply implicated in the will to power [*in the broader, non-Nietzschean acceptation of the expression*] and the domination of nature" (WHITEBOOK, Joel; *Perversion and Utopia: A Study in Psychoanalysis and Critical Theory*. Cambridge: The MIT Press, 1995, p. 133).

[31] ADORNO, *Negative Dialectics*, p. xx.

being's emergence from self-incurred minority." There, said emergence was deemed to be only possible through the constitution of an understanding not directed by another, of a law that one, in a situation of complete autonomy, imposes upon oneself. In other words, Adorno and Horkheimer begin their considerations with the modern definition of autonomy as the ability of subjects to determine their own moral law and thus become moral agents fully capable of self-rule. In a way, the authors develop their joint text as a critique aimed at inversions seen as an inevitable outcome of this notion of autonomy. Let us attempt a summarized reconstruction of the argument as it appears in the text.

Adorno and Horkheimer aim to demonstrate that the autonomy in question could not but manifest as a form of "self-control" conducive to psychological rigidity, affective inhibition, and an irreconcilable split between the demands of rationality and affective openness. Said self-control, they argue, obstructs what might be termed "self-expression" (without for a second disregarding the need for a reconstruction of the very notion of expression, of course). However, rather than discuss aspects of the *Critique of Practical Reason* that could provide support for their suggested problematization, the authors decide to begin by critically addressing the role performed by the schematism of pure concepts of the understanding that is a feature of the *Critique of Pure Reason*.

We know that Kant tried to provide an account of how pure concepts of the understanding could be applied to general phenomena by means of an appeal to the functions of transcendental schemata. Each schema was meant as a rule, a transcendental product of the imagination that allows for the production of meaning (*Bedeutung*) through the establishment of relations between the categories and the empirical material of intuition. Imagination, in Kant, invariably stands for the faculty through which the manifold of sense intuition is brought into figurative synthesis (*synthesis speciosa*). The transcendental schema is a mediating representation, homogenous both in relation to the categories (to the extent it is a universal, *a priori* rule and seeks general unity) and to phenomena (to the extent it directly unifies the *particular determinations of sensibility*, providing the object to be submitted to categorial apprehension). Kant, so as to emphasize said schema's mediating character, even described it as "the sensible concept of an object" (*sinnliche Begriff eines Gegenstandes*).[32]

---

[32] KANT, *Critique of Pure Reason*, A 146/B 186, p. 276.

Adorno and Horkheimer believe that this particular function of the schematism demonstrates that knowledge "consists in subsumption under principles."[33] This subsumption, which Kant viewed as a form of harmonization, is seen by the authors as the figure of a principle of domination over nature by the system, that is to say, of domination over the manifold of sense intuition through protocols of unity and systematicity. However, instead of directly addressing the reasons why the mediating character of the transcendental schematism should warrant criticism (as Heidegger did, to a certain extent, in *Kant and the Problem of Metaphysics*), Adorno and Horkheimer prefer to employ a psychological argument. It consists in stating that the harmonization promised by the transcendental schematism was in fact a strategy of domination over nature *aiming at the self-preservation of the subject*. Self-preservation, they hold, is the true purpose behind human beings' "emergence from minority."

Their use of this psychological category (namely self-preservation – perhaps even that "self-preservation drive" one finds in Freudian theory) is justified, they argue, on account of there being an "unclear relation" in the *Critique of Pure Reason* between the empirical ego and the transcendental ego. What they seem to be saying, albeit tacitly, is that if the transcendental ego is a formal principle of unity capable of providing the conditions of possibility required for the constitution of the objects of experience, that is only because said principle is the means through which empirical demands for self-preservation are met. In light of this the following statement, absolutely central to their argumentation, should come as no surprise: "Even the ego, the synthetic unity of apperception, the agency which Kant calls the highest point, from which the whole of logic must be suspended, is really both the product and the condition of material existence."[34] Not content to operate a complete relativization of the distinction between the empirical and the transcendental, Adorno and Horkheimer will further claim said empirical demands for self-preservation to be, in their turn, inextricable from a very specific social scenario: they are demands that are characteristic of a social form of life, historically determined by the existential conditions of capitalist society. We are thus faced with a double movement that consists in insisting, on the one hand, on the psychological genesis of the transcendental subject and, on the other, on the social genesis of the psychological conditions allowing for the transcendental subject. This in turn provides an explanation for what at first seems a somewhat risky statement: "The true nature of the

---

[33] ADORNO & HORKHEIMER, *Dialectic of Enlightenment*, p. 63.
[34] *Ibid.*, p. 68.

schematism which externally coordinates the universal and the particular, the concept and the individual case, finally turns out, in current science, to be the interest of industrial society."[35]

Still, the implications of such affirmations are far from immediately clear; after all, in what sense should we understand the deduction of the transcendental subject to be dependent on empirical demands of self-preservation? And, most of all, what are these demands that are supposedly produced within the social experience of capitalist societies?

Let us begin by attempting to understand the first issue. In his lecture course on the *Critique of Pure Reason*, Adorno stated the following: "[In] Germany the soul is too refined to have anything to do with psychology."[36] The target of the quip was Kant's disqualification of even the possibility of a rational psychology, a disqualification meant to persuade us that what belongs to the order of the psychological can tell us nothing regarding the transcendental concept of subject, which is to say the supposed ground of all rational normativity. Kant is relentless in affirming that all modes of self-consciousness in thought are simple logical functions, and that there is no sense in wondering about the empirical or psychological genesis of something that is a logical function and a form of representation in general. "Thus," wrote Kant, "from this follows the impossibility of explaining how I am constituted as a merely thinking subject on the basis of materialism."[37]

We know that consciousness, as a "form of representation in general," is the spontaneous act of unifying the manifold of sense experience on the basis of a principle of combination, or connection (*Verbindung*), that is already present in the subject. After all,

> we can represent nothing as combined in the object without having previously combined it ourselves, and that among all representations *combination* is the only one that is not given through objects but can be executed only by the subject itself, since it is an act of its self-activity.[38]

---

[35] *Ibid.*, p. 65.

[36] ADORNO, *Kant's Critique of Pure Reason*, p. 192.

[37] KANT, *Critique of Pure Reason*, B 420, p. 452. From his earliest writings Adorno had been very critical toward this impossibility in Kant. In this regard, statements such as the following spring immediately to mind: "The 'I think' means not only the formal unity of the represented subject of thought = $\chi$, but, as already stated, the actual unity of my experiences in the course of empirical consciousness" [*"Das 'Ich denke' bedeutet nicht allein die formale Einheit eines vorgestellten Subjekts der Gedanken = $\chi$, sondern, wie bereits gesagt, die tatsächliche Einheit meiner Erlebnisse im empirischen Bewusstseinsverlauf"*] (ADORNO, "Der Begriff des Unbewussten in der transzendentalen Seelenlehre." In: *Gesammelte Schriften, Band I: Philosophische Frühschriften*. Frankfurt: Suhrkamp, 1990, p. 163).

[38] KANT, *Critique of Pure Reason*, B 130, p. 245.

Said combination presupposes, however, the representation of the *synthetic unity* of the manifold, constructed through an uncritical and unproblematic acceptance of principles of identity, synthesis, unity and difference. These formal principles structuring the field of experience can only manifest to the subject in an unproblematic way because their constitutive locus is *the subject itself* – it is precisely in the subject that the operation allowing such principles to be constituted takes place. Thus, we would do well to explore to the fullest the range of consequences suggested by the fact that the synthetic unity of the manifold of experience finds its initial ground in the immediacy of the self-evidence of self-consciousness. We would do well, in other words, to explore whatever consequences can be derived from the fact that the synthetic unity of apperception is "the highest point to which one must affix all use of the understanding, even the whole of logic and, after it, transcendental philosophy; indeed this faculty is the understanding itself."[39]

Thus, Adorno could state that representations had to be structured and ordered on the basis of a principle of identity and of categorial distinctions that are, in reality, projections of the image of the "I think."[40] Furthermore, he wrote, "[the] senses are determined by the conceptual apparatus in advance of perception; the citizen sees the world as made a priori of the stuff from which he himself constructs it. Kant intuitively anticipated what Hollywood has consciously put into practice [...]."[41] We must refrain from seeing such remarks as mere witticisms.

Indeed, Adorno seems to have been rather sensitive to the fact that Kant allowed the transcendental entification of a concept of experience constructed by means of solipsistic self-reflection to take place, and also saw no issue with the elevation of unity (and, consequently, of identity) to the status of something like a metaphysical premise. The Frankfurtian philosopher's take on this is made clear in passages such as the following:

---

[39] *Ibid.*, B 134, p. 247.

[40] Which, to us, is precisely what is entailed by affirmations such as the following: "Experience, if it is to be more than a mere rhapsody of perceptions, would have to rest on a synthetic unity of phenomena. And it is precisely this unity that is understood to be produced through the categories, which Kant finds in the forms of judgment supposedly founded on the 'I think' as the synthetic unity of apperception." (HÖSLE, Vittorio; *O sistema de Hegel: o idealismo da subjetividade e o problema de intersubjetividade* ["Hegel's System: the Idealism of Subjectivity and the Problem of Intersubjectivity"]. Belo Horizonte: Edições Loyola, 2007, p. 33). This is something that had already been stated clearly in the first edition of the *Critique of Pure Reason*, where we find the following remark: "[The] unity that the object makes necessary can be nothing other than the formal unity of the consciousness in the synthesis of the manifold of the representations." (KANT, *Critique of Pure Reason*, A 105, p. 231)

[41] ADORNO & HORKHEIMER, *Dialectic of Enlightenment*, p. 65.

[The Kantian] concept of unity is never discussed or deduced from anything else. Instead, it represents the canon by which everything else can be judged. That knowledge is one and the fact that this one has primacy over the many may be said to be the metaphysical premise of Kantian philosophy.[42]

As far as Adorno was concerned, however, deep down said metaphysical premise betrayed a complete lack of knowledge regarding how an empirical experience of psychological consciousness could provide a basis for the genesis of transcendental consciousness. The philosopher believed that an appeal to Freud would allow him to demonstrate how such principles were the expression of a problematic and repressive *metaphysics of identity*, that is, the fundaments of a "damaged life" (*beschädigten Leben*)[43] which, we would add, common-sense entifies. In this sense, one could even say that through his recourse to Freudian "psychology" Adorno was able to reveal existing links between a certain social regime of *identity* and individual demands for *self-preservation*. This in turn allows us to more easily grasp the meaning of the following statement:

The backstage expectation of the Kantian system is that the supreme concept of practical philosophy will coincide with the supreme concept of theoretical philosophy: with the ego principle that makes for theoretical unity and tames and integrates the human drives in practice.[44]

In this light, the statement is unequivocal: there is, in the practical dimension of psychological consciousness, a mode of synthesis and integration of drives that is fundamentally connected to demands of self-preservation, and that

---

[42] ADORNO, *Kant's Critique of Pure Reason*, p. 196. Also: "Reason [in Kant] contributes nothing but the idea of systematic unity, the formal elements of fixed conceptual relationships." (ADORNO & HORKHEIMER, *Dialectic of Enlightenment*, p. 64) Adorno is above all referring to statements such as: "That the I of apperception, consequently in every thought, is a *single thing* that cannot be resolved into a plurality of subjects, and hence a logically simple subject, lies already in the concept of thinking, and is consequently an analytic proposition [...]." (KANT, *Critique of Pure Reason*, B 408, p. 446)

[43] For Adorno and Horkheimer's characterization of Kant's transcendental questioning as a metaphysics of identity, cf. e.g. ADORNO & HORKHEIMER, *Dialectic of Enlightenment*, p. 65. The passage in question is a crucial one, on account of their affirming that Kantian concepts "are ambiguous" (*sind doppelsinnig*). In this sense, the "transcendental, supraindividual self" was seen as additionally encompassing the idea of free coexistence through a universal subject. The point will be discussed in greater detail below.

[44] ADORNO, *Negative Dialectics*, p. 292.

provides a model for the constitution of the regime of synthesis that determines the formal processes of manifold-binding and of unification that characterize transcendental consciousness.

## Suffering from determinacy

The establishment of a connection between the concept of a "damaged life" and the adoption of a metaphysics of identity is something that provides us with a key to better understand that social suffering which, for Adorno, was inextricable from the very constitution of the Kantian moral subject. After all, the type of suffering Adorno seems to have had his sights on has a very specific character; it is not associated, for instance, to a feeling of indeterminacy resulting from the loss of stable, deeply-rooted social relations (a classic sociological motif since at least Durkheim, and one which furthermore echoes a loss of *Sittlichkeit*, in the Hegelian sense). Rather, Adorno acts as though *the most terrifying form of suffering we could be subjected to were the one resulting from the repressive character of identity*. This theme, which I have attempted to explore in the first part of this book, resonates deeply with the paths Adorno's intellectual journey would follow. It may even be said that, for both Adorno and Hegel, modernity, beyond its character as that historical moment where "Spirit has not only lost its essential life; it is also conscious of this loss, and of the finitude that is its own content"[45] – a loss implying an anxiety supposedly produced by growing feelings of indeterminacy – is also the historical period in which the ego is elevated to the condition of foundation for whatever aspires to objective validity. In this case, what that means is that in the period in question a compulsive yet rigid recourse to subjective self-identity prevails, one that provides a ground for behavior as well as an orientation for thinking. To ponder the consequences of this historically-sensitive diagnosis for reflections on the moral subject seems to be one of the main objectives underpinning Adorno's discussion of Kantian morality. In fact, it all takes place as if the diagnosis imparted by Adorno pointed to the existence of a certain "suffering from determinacy" derived from the processes that constitute our individualities.

So as to better understand this point, we should revisit the critique of the moral subject developed in Adorno's *Negative Dialectics*. There, we see the philosopher deploy a strategy that begins with a critical evaluation of Kant's tendency to conceive the self-consciousness of the moral subject as something

---

[45] HEGEL, *Phenomenology of Spirit*, p. 4.

bereft of a constitutive relation to the other (as, to him, awareness of the moral law appears to take place within self-reflexivity alone). We can see said critical approach very clearly in statements such as the following:

> The supposedly noumenal subject [*ansichseiende Subjekt*] is transmitted within itself by that from which it is distinguished, by the context of all subjects [*Zusammenhang aller Subjekte*]. The transmission makes it what in its sense of freedom it does not want to be: it becomes heteronomous.[46]

This assertion summarizes Adorno's initial and most significant objection against Kant's strategy to transcendentally determine pure will: in the sphere of action, insisted Adorno, the subject is unavoidably confronted with an intersubjective structure that throws the pole of production that provides actions with meaning entirely off center. To affirm that the subject of an action, supposedly an autonomous subject, is mediated by something from which it stands apart is to affirm that the determination of the meaning of the action is not an immediate given, but the result of a complex social mediation that takes place *a posteriori*. Intersubjectivity, after all, provides actions with meanings that, absent the reference to an other, would be pure abstractions. In other words, the other is not simply an occasion for the exercise of one's freedom, but a true condition for the constitution of the meaning of actions.[47] This echoes a fundamental idea in Hegel's critique of Kant, namely that one cannot separate the *grounding* of a moral principle from the determination of the *modes of application* of said principle in intersubjectively-shared contexts.

Yet Adorno seems to be getting at more than this; he suggests that recognition of the constitutive character of social mediation for the determination of the meaning of moral action is tantamount to an introduction of heteronomy to the very heart of those actions once regarded as free. How are we to understand this, precisely?

---

[46] ADORNO, *Negative Dialectics*, p. 213.

[47] Which is why Adorno cannot accept propositions such as: "I cannot have the least representation of a thinking being through an external experience, but only through self-consciousness. Thus such objects are nothing further than the transference [*Übertragung*] of this consciousness of mine to other things, which can be represented as thinking beings only in this way." (KANT, *Critique of Pure Reason*, A 347/B 405, p. 415) What propositions of this nature imply is that access to the other invariably occurs through a transfer of sorts of the results of a process of self-determination conducted by consciousness in the form of solipsistic self-reflection.

In this context, to speak of heteronomy invariably means to be forced to acknowledge the existence of a fundamental opacity between the transcendental principle behind the moral imperative and its empirical actualization. This would by no means be acceptable to Kant, as it would force him to conclude that it is impossible for consciousness to make *a priori* judgments regarding actions. For him, it bears repeating, "judging what according to [the moral law] is to be done must not be so difficult that the commonest and most unpracticed understanding could not deal with this law, *even without worldly prudence* [*Weltklugheit*]."[48]

It is true that Kant recognizes a limit to the cognition consciousness is capable of within the practical sphere, due to the impossibility of our *knowing* the reality of the idea of freedom and, consequently, knowing the reality of *das Gute*, as consciousness of freedom is not founded on any form of intuition. This would lead us to accept the moral law as a fact (*faktum*) of reason. And if the objective reality of freedom cannot be known, then it is clear that "in experience no example could be hunted up where [moral law] is complied with exactly."[49]

This, for Kant, is an unproblematic stance, as, with him, one always knows the conditions under which an act must be performed so that it is the outcome of a free will. Our not-knowing affects the effective presence of such conditions, of course; to put it briefly, one shall never know whether one speaks the truth for fear of consequences or out of "love for the law." What one *does* at all times know is that, regardless of circumstance, to lie is to transgress against the moral law. *Even if there is no transparency between moral intentionality and the content of one's actions, a principle of transparency remains between moral intentionality and the form of one's actions.* One always knows *how* to act – there is no undecidability in moral praxis.[50] For Adorno, therefore, Kant's chief mistake was believing that the pure form of action, accessible to the self-thematization of the constitutive subject, could determine *a priori* its own meaning. The meaning of an action, as far as Adorno was concerned, was simply a transcendental indexing of the particularity of each case; this is what he had in view, to an extent, when stating that "the true nature of the schematism" is that it "externally coordinates the universal and the particular,

---

[48] KANT, *Critique of Practical Reason*, § 36, p. 54.
[49] *Ibid.*, § 47, p. 66.
[50] This might explain why Adorno viewed Kant's moral philosophy as an "ethics of conviction" developed on the basis of an interiority that excludes any calculation of the nature of external reality for the determination of the meaning of moral action (cf. ADORNO, *Problems of Moral Philosophy*, pp. 146-156 and *passim*).

the concept and the individual case [...]."[51] Against Kant, that is, the meaning of an action could only be established *a posteriori*, through modes of social determination.

On account of this, the term "heteronomy" carries more weight than the simple mediation through the other as a condition for the determination of the meaning of action might lead us to initially assume. It is a term whose intended sense can only be fully grasped once we accept that one's passage through the other in some sense entails a loss of self, a form of alienation from oneself in the sense of a reshaping of oneself in accordance with what one finds in an other, the perspective the latter brings dislodging and replacing one's own. This is a notion Adorno alluded to when remarking that the "identity of the self and its alienation [*Identität des Selbst und Selbstentfremdung*] are companions from the beginning [...]."[52] This reference to the other is constitutive not only in what regards the meaning of a subject's action, but also the subject's own position as an individuality, a position derived from the elevation of the ego to the condition of a privileged figure in subject constitution. Said reference, furthermore, cannot be conceived save as a form of alienation from the subject's original position, which precedes its relation with the other. Only in this way would it be permissible for us to affirm that a process of socialization capable of producing a self-identity such as the ego as a synthetic unity is in reality a process of alienation of the self in an other.

## *The drives as an indeterminacy-producing power*

If this scheme makes any sense, that is because Adorno had Freud's theory of development and maturation in view. We are aware of Freud's insistence on there being something in the subject that precedes the advent of the ego: namely, a polymorphous, libidinal body whose search for the satisfaction of partial drives (pre-ego drives, one might say) is the sole guide of its behavior; in other words, it follows urges not yet submitted to the functional hierarchy of a unity. As has been seen before, the supposed cause of the polymorphous, fragmented structure that characterizes these drives is the absence of a unifying principle (such as the ego), a principle that remains absent until a certain process of individual maturation takes place through which the subject internalizes the social representation of a coherent behavioral unity. Said unity, in its turn, allows the drives to be unified on the basis of identification with an other regarded as an ideal type.

---

[51] ADORNO & HORKHEIMER, *Dialectic of Enlightenment*, p. 65.
[52] ADORNO, *Negative Dialectics*, p. 216.

On the other hand, the polymorphous character of the drives was also seen as an outcome of the particular acceptation given to the structure of interest (in all its varied manifestations: volition, desire, etc.) by Freud, who understood it through the notion of libido, which is to say of a psychic energy entirely devoid of any *telos* – this, on account of its unimpeded circulation throughout the psychic apparatus, it being entirely un-bound by determined object representations. As has been discussed, libido was a psychic energy often characterized as "un-bound" or "free" due to how amenable it was to being transposed, inverted, deviated, repressed – endlessly displaced, in short –, a psychic energy whose actualization, furthermore, appears to be some form of "indeterminacy-producing power."

In the first Freudian topic and its distinction between sexual drives and drives of self-preservation we may find elements of great importance for the discussion at hand. We are aware that self-preservation drives, or ego-drives, are conducive to the elevation of demands for preservation of both the individual and the *principium individuationis* behind self-image unification to the condition of a behavior-guiding principle. In a tone reminiscent of Nietzsche's, Freud links the development of consciousness, of language, of memory and of judgment to demands of self-preservation mediated by the reality principle. The aim, in each one of these cases, was to find the best possible means to attain an object capable of satisfying the ego-drives and, through processes of unification, to repeat previous experiences with at least a modicum of predictability. In this sense, nothing less than such demands of self-preservation could lead to the ordering of one's experience in accordance with rules and principles. An additional corollary of this process is the abandonment of polymorphy, the purpose of which is an integration of the drives into a coherent unity of behaviors and judgments; as a consequence, one no longer identifies with certain corporeal impulses, and no longer feels directly responsible for them. This would mean giving one's *will to identity* the status of *central component of the will that founds one's position as a recognized subject*. The will to identity thus becomes the fundamental principle underlying free will, and the foundation of processes of self-preservation.

In a sense, it is as though Adorno believed the above-described will to identity to be the foundation of the social suffering produced by Kantian morality. Now, the fact that reason – understood as a guiding principle for both thinking and action – shows solidarity with demands of self-preservation is not something that should be immediately cast in a negative light – what is intended here, after all, could not be farther from an abstract defense of ego-dissolution as a model for the restoration of some sort of original freedom. Nevertheless, it should be noted that the hypostatization of the self-preservation function ends up producing its own particular type of impasse, and that the ego's inability to return to what has been left behind in the maturational process, to what has been wrecked in the course of development, is likewise and unfailingly a source of suffering. For that reason, one must bear in mind that the hypostatization of demands of self-preservation cannot but produce an ego that no longer recognizes itself in "any human utterance which has no place in the functional context of self-preservation."[53] Hence:

> The self which, after the methodical extirpation [*Ausmerzung*] of all natural traces as mythological, was no longer supposed to be either a body or blood or a soul or even a natural ego but was sublimated into a transcendental or logical subject, formed the reference point of reason, the legislating authority of action.[54]

These affirmations are extremely important; their authors are unequivocally stating that the price to be paid for the constitution of the transcendental subject as a foundation for the operations of modern rationality is the reiterated repression or systematic extermination of everything within the subject that does not submit to the general form of the logical ego. To no longer wish to be "a body or blood or a soul" means, at least in this context, for one to deliberately will oneself away from whatever may threaten an imposition of the ego as a general form for experience, as such an imposition inescapably "subordinates each impulse to logical unity. This unity is given primacy over the diffuseness of nature, indeed over all the diversity of the nonidentical [...]."[55] It is clear, then, that Adorno's strategy consists in analyzing the modes by means of which drives are integrated in an attempt to locate the regime of identity that is "sublimated" in the figure of a transcendental subject, seemingly believing such modes – whose purpose is the formation of the psychological person – to be a key for the understanding of the empirical genesis of the transcendental.

It is in reference to this process that Adorno remarked that "The dawning sense of freedom feeds upon the memory [*Erinnerung*] of the archaic impulse [*Impuls*] not yet steered by any solid I."[56] One can clearly see that what Adorno

---

[53] ADORNO & HORKHEIMER, *Dialectic of Enlightenment*, p. 22.
[54] *Ibid.*
[55] ADORNO, *Negative Dialectics*, p. 256.
[56] *Ibid.*, p. 221. This might explain Adorno's insistence on there being a paradoxical construction in Kant that stems from an articulation between "two conflicting impulses of moral philosophy, namely the idea of freedom and the idea of suppression [*Unterdrückung*]" (cf. ADORNO, *Problems of Moral Philosophy*, p. 71).

had in mind was the unification of pre-egoic drive motions. He would insist that said process be read as being correlative to a dynamic within which autonomy depends on a scheme of repressive domination over one's inner nature.[57] In this sense, both the deactivation of the dichotomy nature/freedom that Adorno conducted repeatedly since the early 1930s, beginning with the conference "The Idea of Natural History," and the subsequent critique of the metaphysics of identity he developed as a means to determine the practical dimension of reason, among other examples, involve a demonstration of how every action bears the imprint of these archaic impulses that have not been entirely subsumed by processes of socialization. Hence the following, central affirmation:

> Only if one acts as an I, not just reactively, can his action be called free in any sense. And yet, what would be equally free is that which is not tamed by the I as the principle of any determination – that which, as in Kant's moral philosophy, strikes the I as unfree and has indeed been unfree to this day.[58]

Here, let us dwell a moment longer on the question of the relation between drives and freedom in Adorno. So that the point is fully understood, let us begin by noting the importance of the notion of *impulse* (*Impuls, Trieb, Drang*) – understood as being corporeal in character – for Adorno's preparation of "a positive concept of enlightenment" meant to liberate that very concept from "its entanglement in blind domination."[59]

For instance, in his analysis of the causality of free will, Adorno criticized the idea of causality through freedom with a view towards discussing "the addendum" (*das Hinzutretende*) as an impulse required for action (*Handlung*) to occur, an impulse the transparency of consciousness cannot exhaust. This

---

[57] Adorno would employ, in addition, the Freudian conception of the genesis of moral consciousness (*Gewissen*), which is to say that said consciousness is a product of the internalization of a set of behaviors held as ideal, of an attendant need to keep drives under control, and of the ensuing production of a moral instance of supervision (the superego) in which idealized expectations and disciplinary mechanisms of drive repression converge (cf. e.g. FREUD, "On Narcissism: An Introduction," *S.E. Vol. XIV*, pp. 67-72). He will therefore insist that if, in Kant, concrete manifestations of morality invariably present general repressive traits (obedience, self-mastery, pain and humiliation, the presence of moral consciousness as a final arbiter, etc.), that is because "[the] empirical irresistibility of the super-ego, the psychologically existing conscience, is what assures him, contrary to his transcendental principle, of the factuality of the moral law [...]" (ADORNO, *Negative Dialectics*, p. 271).

[58] *Ibid.*, p. 222.

[59] ADORNO & HORKHEIMER, *Dialectic of Enlightenment*, xviii.

would allow Adorno to affirm that when it comes to processes of moral deliberation there is always a "leap" of sorts to be found between steps in a causal chain. This consideration, in turn, allowed him to hold the reduction of will to a form of rationality centered in consciousness to be nothing but an exercise in "abstraction." After all, the "addendum" in question is something corporeal that is connected to rationality while being qualitatively distinct from it. Its genesis is related to an impulse (*Impuls*) originating from an auto-erotic stage. It is into this corporeal experience that Adorno introduces that spontaneity that Kant had located in the constitutive function of the "I think." This results in the recovery of the materiality of a spontaneity that is, at bottom, a form of affective self-expression. This supplemental element points to the existence of something in every action that is not *conscious* intentionality, but rather *corporeal* intentionality[60] – the intentionality of a body that is the manifestation of a body of drives, in the Freudian mold.

Confessedly, at this point it is as yet unclear how such questions pertaining to the relations between free will and impulse can provide us with a renewed regime of reflection on moral actions; likewise, it remains unclear which model of rational deliberation can be extracted therefrom, that is, which rationality principle resides within such considerations. Are we faced here with a return to emotion-based morality? And what are we to make of this appeal to corporeity? Can the body "judge," in the sense of providing a ground for moral judgments? As "poetic" as such questions are, they appear – at least at a first glance – to lack rigor.

## A return to the origins?

Let us return, for now, to the problems that arise due to Adorno's recourse to the Freudian notion of a conflict intrinsic to processes of drive socialization. This emphasis on the disruptive potential of one's recognizing oneself in the sphere of unsocialized drives seems to invite the type of criticism Habermas indeed often raised against it. Mostly, said criticism consisted in stating that Adorno's reflection aimed to "[turn] back to the beginning in an effort to get beyond the break of culture with nature,"[61] which is to say it depended on the belief that a potential emancipation of human beings could be achieved

---

[60] Cf. MERLEAU-PONTY, Maurice; "On the Phenomenology of Language." In: *Signs*, translated by R. C. McCleary. Evanston: Northwestern University Press, 1992, p. 89.

[61] HABERMAS, *The Theory of Communicative Action, Volume 1: Reason and the Rationalization of Society*, translated by T. McCarthy. Boston: Beacon Press, 1984, p. 383.

through the resurrection of "nature." More specifically, Habermas found it odd that "the theme of an ego that turns back to nature adopts, in Adorno, the guise of a sexual utopia, as well as a certain anarchic character"[62] – a utopia that, precisely because it could never be attained by socialized subjects, inevitably led to a depressing and depressed assessment of social life as having gone entirely astray. This is a position Habermas himself articulated, writing of "the negativism of Adorno, who finds in comprehensive logic of development only the proof that it is impossible to break the spell of an instrumental reason gone mad."[63]

Axel Honneth, however, seems to be the commentator who best understood what is truly at stake in Adorno's thoughts on this matter:

> The urges withheld from consciousness represent, as it were, silent demands within the communication space opened up in the psyche, demands that perpetually force individuals to again go beyond the attained level of their compromises with the surrounding social world in order to reach a higher level of individuation in their articulation of needs.[64]

This would suggest the possibility of autonomy to depend on one's acquiring the ability to momentarily suspend the identitarian synthesis imposed by the ego so as to be able to, in a "playful fashion," integrate into the bounds of one's identity whatever said synthesis had initially kept out. Honneth, basing his perspective on psychoanalytic work conducted by Hans Loewald, even suggests there to be a need for one's temporary surrender to experiences of ego-boundary dissolution, allowing one to return to a condition that predates intrapsychic differentiations consolidated through maturational processes. The outcome of this, it is thought, is the constitution of more flexible, less stable personalities.

---

[62] "[Le] théme d'un moi qui revient à la nature prend plutôt chez Adorno les traits d'une utopie sexuelle et d'un certain anarchisme." (HABERMAS, *Profils philosophiques et politiques*, translated by F. Dastur, J.-R. Ladmiral & M. B. De Launay. Paris: Gallimard, 1980, p. 239)

[63] HABERMAS, *Moral Consciousness and Communicative Action*, translated by C. Lenhardt & S. Weber. Cambridge: Polity Press, 2007, p. 7.

[64] HONNETH, "Postmodern Identity and Object-Relations Theory: On the Seeming Obsolescence of Psychoanalysis," translated by J. Farrel and J. Köhler. In: *Philosophical Explorations: An International Journal for the Philosophy of Mind and Action*, 2 (3), 1999, pp. 232-233.

Let us reflect on the consequences of this point. It may be said that, for Adorno, there is something in moral judgment that can only be constituted once subjects grow able to recover something which maturational processes have discarded and left behind, something which developmental processes ruined. In this sense, the formative process conducive to morality is not simply a mentalist progress towards the formation of a consciousness that is, formally, more universalist when it comes to its judicative capabilities (which is what one finds in Piaget or Kohlberg). The true process of formation presupposes the capacity to recover "stages" that have been left behind, to recover modes of attachment to objects that, while seemingly obsolete, nevertheless allow for the constitution of syntheses no longer at odds with that which manifests as being radically other.

Adorno intended to go beyond this mere flexibilization of identities, however; he seems to have believed that, ultimately, it is impossible for operations of intrapsychic synthesis involving unsocialized drives to be conducted through an instance such as the ego, especially considering that, from the ego's perspective, such drives, due to their refusal to submit to the form of identity, carry the threat of potential indeterminacy and dissolution. That might explain the following statement, by Adorno:

> Men are human only where they do not act, let alone posit themselves, as persons; the diffuseness of nature, in which they are not persons, resembles the lineamentation of an intelligible creature, of that self which would be delivered from the ego [*jenes Selbst, das vom Ich erlöst wäre*]. Contemporary art innervates some of this.[65]

In other words, the recognition of "men" as subjects (and not simply as legal persons, the bearers of positive rights – it is not by chance that Adorno seems to want to operate with this distinction, which, as we have seen in the first chapter of this book, had already been advanced by Hegel) is dependent on their capacity to posit themselves as, or, better yet, to *identify* themselves with, that which no longer submits to the self-identical contours of an ego, with its protocols of individuation.

There are many consequences to be drawn from this new kind of intrapsychic synthesis for a theory of recognition and of action, starting with the fact that it compels us to reflect on actions that do not appear as the attributes of a person understood through the matrix of juridical imputability, which is to say actions whose causality does not come to an end in the free spontaneity

---

[65] ADORNO, *Negative Dialectics*, p. 277.

of an ego that places itself under the authority of a law of its own making. As Adorno suggested, such a causality would demand the existence of something corporeal at once connected to reason and qualitatively distinct from it – a something, an "addendum," linked to an impulse whose recognition would be tantamount to placing non-identity in the very heart of the subject, and lead the subject to no longer view its own actions as the actions of an ego, but as *actions arising from its tense coexistence with a corporeity not entirely subjected to the ego.*[66]

In an important text where the relation between Adorno and psychoanalysis also has pride of place, Ruy Fausto provides an interpretation that somewhat differs from the one presented here. He will focus on what he sees as the dialectical character of the ego in Adorno, simultaneously regarded as a "piece" (*Stück*) of the drive and as a representative of the reality principle within the psychic apparatus. Fausto subsequently conceives of moments in which "[the] subject 'passes' through the ego, through the Id, or, if you will, the ego 'passes' through the Id, etc. [...]."[67] This "passing through" would in turn allow us to conceive of situations where the ego can be the depositary of expectations of autonomy and freedom, and not merely a repressive, narcissistic instance responsible for psychic syntheses that are resistant to all difference.

Fausto is right, of course; this becomes clear the moment one recalls Adorno's remark, reproduced above and worth repeating, that "[o]nly if one acts as an I, not just reactively, can his action be called free in any sense." He is also right to insist that Adorno's critical stance in regards to Kantian morality did not keep him from understanding that the recourse to the transcendental was an expression – albeit an "imperfect and deformed" one – of the fact that, for human beings as they stand, coming to a true estimation of moral objectivity is impossible.[68] One could ask, however, whether this passage of

---

[66] This might explain why "[...] the sphere of moral action includes something that cannot fully be described in intellectual terms, but also that should not be turned into an absolute" (ADORNO, *Problems of Moral Philosophy*, p. 7).

[67] "O sujeito 'passa' no eu, no isso, ou, caso se queira, o eu 'passa' no isso etc. [...]." FAUSTO, Ruy; "Dialética e psicanálise" ["Dialectics and Psychoanalysis"]. In: SAFATLE (org.), *Um limite tenso: Lacan entre a filosofia e a psicanálise* ["A tense limit: Lacan between philosophy and psychoanalysis"]. São Paulo: Unesp, 2003, p. 135.

[68] This consideration allowed Schweppenhäuser, among other commentators with similar views, to go as far as stating that "Adorno thoroughly approved of Kant's refusal to subject human conscience to a genetic-psychological critique: he recognized, here, the legitimate claim of moral validity against all relativistic attempts to reduce morality to psychology. The critical and anticipatory truth content of a rationally grounded moral philosophy cannot be credited to the constantly damaged subjectivity of 'empirical character.' The latter cannot serve as a moral measure." (SCHWEPPENHÄUSER, Gerhard; "Adorno's Negative Moral Philosophy." In: HUHN, Tom (Ed.); *The Cambridge Companion to Adorno*. Cambridge:

the ego through the Id might not lead us to new modes of psychic synthesis, modes unencumbered by the principles of unity, identity, self-determination and cohesion that characterize the ego as both a psychic instance *and* as a transcendental function. That could be why Adorno would finally seek to conceive of a "self delivered from the ego," one endowed with non-violent, non-repressive models of synthesis directly derived from the generalization of reflections on *mimesis* as the formal structure underlying advanced works of art, the latter being capable of flirting with formlessness and of both implementing and suspending at once their own formal organizing principles – notions one can find in Adorno's interpretation of Berg's compositional processes, for example.

A rather symptomatic example of the consequences involved in thinking the problem of psychic synthesis through a "totalizing" critique of the ego is provided by Adorno's conception of sexual relations as a privileged space where the satisfaction of the demands of the drives and the fulfillment of intersubjective expectations of recognition overlap. He wrote:

> It's a nice bit of sexual utopia not to be yourself, and to love more in the beloved than only her: a negation of the ego-principle [*Ichprinzips*]. It shakes that invariant of bourgeois society in the widest sense, which since time immemorial has always aimed at integration: the demand for identity. At first it had to be produced, ultimately it would be necessary to abolish [*aufzuheben*] it again. What is merely identical with itself is without happiness.[69]

Much could be said concerning this love for that which, in the other, is not constituted on the basis of an ego-image, a love that flies in the face of demands for integration and, because of that, cannot be conceived as a figure of that unifying *Eros* characteristic of the Freudian life drives. On the contrary, this love is one imbued with the power to recognize and turn towards something

---

Cambridge University Press, 2004, p. 342) Evidently, I do not hold that to be the case, particularly on account of the two following reasons: first, the position in question ignores the fact that the positive content of morality is not based on a refusal of some form of "relativistic psychology," but rather on the recovery of an experience that nothing but the genetic-psychoanalytic reconstruction of ego-formation can reveal. Second, the recourse to the transcendental is eminently negative here, merely indicating the need for transcendence in what regards empirical positivity and the current state of the world; it does not ground any behavioral norms whatsoever. If the truth-content of morality cannot be attributed to the empirical personality, that is because we must appeal, instead, to that which has been repressed in the social production of personality.

[69] ADORNO, "Sexual Taboos and Law Today." In: *Critical Models: Interventions and Catchwords*, translated by H. W. Pickford. New York: Columbia University Press, 1998, p. 75.

impersonal and depersonalized in the other, something that leads desire to become attached to that which does not submit directly to the *principium individuationis*,[70] and to seek its happiness there, where the ego can no longer project its own image – there, where it must be overcome.

---

[70] I have dealt with the question extensively in "A destituição subjetiva como protocolo de amor" ["Subjective destitution as a protocol for love"], a chapter in the aforementioned *La passion du négatif: Lacan et la dialectique* (Georg Olms, 2010), p. 213, p. 238.

# CHAPTER VI

# Below zero: the "negativity deficit" in Axel Honneth

*Death is preferable to the health they offer us.*
Gilles Deleuze

*Every image of man is ideology,*
*except the negative one.*
Theodor Adorno

In the last two chapters, we saw how a reflection on the Freudian theory of drives led authors such as Lacan and Adorno to rebuild the concept of subjectivity, thus starting a movement that had major consequences for any theory of recognition that does not want to depend on the reiteration of a certain type of non-problematized normative anthropology. In my view, this perspective can serve as basis for criticizing one of the most successful attempts to recover Hegel's concept of recognition in the philosophical debate of the past twenty-five years, which was carried out by Axel Honneth. This chapter aims to show how a limited understanding of the Hegelian concept of negativity, as well as the psychoanalytic concept of drive, led Honneth to a way of understanding the problem of recognition that can only have the effect of elevating the concept of the individual to a non-problematic status, as well as raising identity demands to a pre-political basis of the regulation of social conflicts. As I intend to have demonstrated by the end of this book, the limitations of politics as a force for social change within this Frankfurtian recovery of recognition will prove evident.

We have established that theories of recognition are usually based on theories of socialization and individuation. They use a certain type of anthropology often marked by reflection on the maturation process towards an individualized person, as well as ontogenesis of practical-cognitive abilities and constitution of the autonomous Self, implying that the recognition process should necessarily be read as moving towards the affirmation of autonomy and individuality conquered. In this sense, Axel Honneth's theory of recognition, which drew heavily on the psychoanalytic anthropological approach to the theory of object relations developed by Donald Winnicott, Hans Loewald and others, is one of the best illustrative examples.

However, psychoanalysis can provide us with a radically different understanding of such processes of socialization and individuation to that presented by Honneth, if we consider Jacques Lacan's work. I would like to show how changing the psychoanalytic basis gives us a distinct view not only of the dynamics of socialization of desires and impulses, but also of the political consequences that stem from the concept of recognition. This type of view could provide an empirical and material basis for the idea that individuals seek to be recognized within a political field outside that of cultural processes of identity production. Even though Lacan does not use such formulations in a literal way, I intend to show that this is a possible consequence of their positions. In the next chapter, the political ramifications of this critical procedure will be explored in a systematic way. In this way, I aim to show the urgency of recovering, more generously, the internal potentialities of certain strands of the first attempt to rejuvenate the concept of recognition that took place during the 1930s in France.

## Being sick

This conflict surrounding the psychoanalytic matrix of reflections about recognition should be seen as a key issue. In this regard, Honneth insists that psychoanalysis provides, at its normative level, an anthropological concept of human beings that, because it recognizes the importance of the unconscious and libidinal bonds of the individual, does not risk succumbing to an idealized morality. Hence a statement such as the following: "to defend itself against the illusions of a reason morality, Critical Theory should be supplemented by a kind of moral psychology guided by psychoanalytic intuitions" (HONNETH, 2010, p. 253). Such moral illusions are present in visions of human behavior which are unable to take into account the unconscious and deeply conflicting dimensions of what motivates individuals to take action and make choices, visions that endorse anthropological normativities founded on a notion of autonomy constructed through, for example, strict divisions between free will and pathological desire for reason, affection and sensitivity.

However, we must ask whether, in fact, Honneth escapes the weight of moral assumptions which are not thematized when he resorts to psycho-analysis. His way of understanding the autonomy produced at the end of a successful process of psychic maturity is not far from the post-conventional morality of the Kantian tradition. His reasons for refusing Freud's drive theory and the traumatic nature of sexuality, as well as his way of supporting the necessarily inter-relational character of the constitution of the Self is a greater proof of the intrinsically sociable and cooperative nature of the subjects[1] and perhaps evidence of an idealized morality, linked to the perpetuation of a deeply normative view present in the elevation of communicative rationality to a privileged position as a regulator against which to construct a rational life and emancipating processes. It is possible that the real contribution of psychoanalysis is not connected to the discovery of the unconscious and of child sexuality, with a consequently more complex view of behavioral motivation. In fact, its main contribution lies not in developing a more elaborate anthropology, but a new clinical approach. Insisting on the innovative character of this psychoanalytic clinical approach is a way of asking whether we should take this dimension into account in the organization of reflections on the political sphere.

For example, one of the most innovative clinical contributions made by psychoanalysis lies in defending the idea that the experience of the pathological is the means of establishing the human condition and a privileged way to understand our formation processes, as well as traces of our behavioral structures.[2] Honneth seems to consider something along these lines by emphasizing the importance of a kind of: "back and forth between diagnosis of disease and analysis of normality, between etiology and personality theory" (2008, p 160), applicable to Freudian thought. He quotes, as examples, the proximity between mourning and melancholy or, in particular, the generalization of repression mechanisms for each and every subject, that Honneth calls "anthropologization of the potential conflict of repressed desire" (2008, p. 163). However, this back and forth movement between normal and pathological is understood by Honneth as an expression of the need for the normal personality to be able to sporadically reactivate its own psychic mechanisms of early childhood, similarly to how the pathological

---

[1] On this last point, see Joel Whitebook's critique of Honneth (2008, p. 382) regarding the relativistics and the intersubjectivists: "They believe that, by showing the self as a product of interaction, they also show that the self is intrinsically social. The postulation not assumed is that interaction is equivalent to mutuality, meaning that if the self is a product of interaction, then it is intrinsically mutualistic."

[2] It could not be otherwise for someone who believed that *the pathological behavior exposes, in a broad way, what is really at stake in the process of forming general social behavior.* One of the major metaphors used by Freud should be regarded in the same light: "If we throw a crystal to the ground, it breaks, but not arbitrarily. It breaks, according to its cleavage lines, into pieces whose boundaries, though they were invisible, were determined by the crystal structure" (1999, p. 64) Thus, the pathological is this shattered crystal that, due to its breaking, provides the intelligibility against which to measure normal behavior. For a useful review of this problem in Freud, see: VAN HAUTE, DE VLEMINCK, 2013.

was still thought of, in developmental terms, as a figure of regression to archaic states of childish behavior.

There are other ways, however, to think about Freud's reformulation of the relationship between normal and pathological. Admitting that the experience of the pathological is part of the human condition implies, among other things, accepting the irreducible character of what we call "symptoms". Wilheim Reich, for example, points out that defense mechanisms used by the self, as well as the character traits that comprise the core of the psychological personality, are made in the same way as the symptoms.[3] Such approaches open the door to transforming the experience of the pathological, as well as the act of producing symptoms, into fundamental expressions of the human condition because they are unique productions of irreplaceable constructions, and modes of desiring and acting. This could lead us to affirm, as Lacan suggests, that: "[...] the self is structured exactly like a symptom. Inside the subject is but a privileged symptom. It is the human symptom par excellence, it is the mental disorder of man" (1986b, p. 25). In this case, where the Self together with its psychic organization appears as a privileged symptom, it is not even possible to talk about distinctions between personality and disease. Ultimately, psychoanalysis is no longer seen as an additional type of psychotherapy focused on the dissolution of symptoms, as this would negate a fundamental dimension of producing the human experience.[4]

Two main consequences derive from this position. First, the idea of both the symptom and the pathological being irreducible implies the consequent recognition of the irreducibility of heteronomy, fragmentation and estrangement experiences. This feeds into current ideals of social normality, which are usually based on a belief in the emancipatory power of the concepts of autonomy, unity and authenticity, and which should be seen, primarily, as production matrixes of suffering. Because Honneth is unwilling to adopt this approach, he tends to interpret Freud's notion of "negativity" and his thematization of the dramatic relationship between individual and society as merely a distorted expression of a proto-Hobbesian view of the fragility of social bonds when confronted with the irrationality of human behavior. In doing so, he overlooks the fact that, at the end of a successful maturation process, this irrationality could be subject to the regulatory requirements of reason.

---

[3] This explains why: "The shape of the ego reactions, which differs from one character to another even when the contents of the experiments are similar, can be traced back to the infant experiences in the same way as the content of the symptoms and the fantasies" (REICH, 2001, p. 53)

[4] In this regard, see mainly LACAN, 2010.

The second consequence concerns the reconfiguration of the clinical healing process. By accepting this Lacanian perspective, we may be able to get closer to certain epistemological approaches that advocate a "dynamic nominalism"[5] in order to understand clinical categories linked to the psyche. Using such an approach, we can say that subjects do not suffer just because they have symptoms; they suffer because they perceive these symptoms as a mere expression of a way of being sick, because being sick means, in principle, assuming an identity with strong performative force. To be understood as "neurotic", "depressed" or suffering from a "borderline personality disorder", the subject names itself through a speech act capable of producing performatively new effects, and of expanding impossibilities and restrictions. A mental pathology does not describe a natural species (*natural kind*), as may be the case with an organic disease such as cancer or Parkinson's disease. As Ian Hacking reminds us, it performatively creates a new situation in which individuals find themselves inserted.[6]

If this is indeed the case, then we can say that a fundamental dimension of the analytic work consists not in dissolving the symptoms, but in dissolving the bond between the subject and the identity produced by the disease. This weakens or nullifies specific effects of the symptoms, decreasing their intensity and opening up the possibility of producing new arrangements. Nonetheless, we are still talking about symptoms, and not normativities shared intersubjectively, because the uniqueness of this process does not guarantee the enhancement of cooperative relations or the consolidation of affective understanding. It enables us, instead, to understand the fragility of interactions, especially when they are guided by the vagaries of individual demands. From a social point of view, understanding that mental disorders are not only deviations from a norm, caused neither by lack nor excess, but are also processes that create individualities, leads us to question the belief that human beings are intrinsically sociable and cooperative. Humans need the experience of the pathological, because they are beings who need to put themselves outside of the accepted norms that define a distended field of cooperation to produce something fundamental in relation to their experiences of desire, action and use of language. This may partly explain why Lacan obstinately refuses to see psychoanalysis as a

---

[5] This can be found in HACKING, 2004, p. 106. Also in this regard, see DAVIDSON, 2004.

[6] This is an important issue defended by Ian Hacking, who wrote about the classification of mental illnesses as follows: "a kind of person came into being at the same time as the kind [*as clinical category*] itself was being invented. In some cases, that is, our classifications and our classes conspire to emerge hand in hand, each egging the other on." (2004, p. 106).

"therapy"[7] or to understand the rationality that operates within psychoanalytic treatment as a therapeutic rationality; and therefore, for him, relationships of recognition will necessarily be marked by dynamics of dispossession.

Among other things, this has fundamental political consequences for demanding a thorough reconsideration of what we understand by social recognition and its limits. Therefore, if we accept that interactions are weak when they are guided by the vagaries of individual demands, we must also accept the idea that if individualities are constituted from symptoms that overlap with the structure of personality, then there are two possible outcomes: either we have to accept that the recognition of experience is structurally compromised; or that it needs to overcome a specific anthropological dimension on which the institutionalization of the concept of person is based. This second alternative could lead to an attempt to locate the experience of the political beyond the affirmation and recognition of individuality organized as personality. I will begin a discussion of this matter by showing which conceptual arrangements are necessary to support this perspective psychoanalytically.

## Honneth's mother and Winnicott's policy

Bearing this perspective in mind, it is necessary to prioritize two tasks if we want to think about the impact of psychoanalysts' reflections in shaping the political potential of the concept of recognition. The first consists in defending the notion that the psychological personality and attributes of the individual person are structured as defensive symptoms, and exploring the consequences of this position for a theory of recognition. It also implies accepting that the concept of recognition should not be focused on recognizing a person's individual attributes.

The second task involves defending the existence of an irreducibly pre-personal element in the human structure, which Lacan called "drive", an element which, due to its characteristic aversion to customization, is not

---

[7] Note that the Frankfurtian think whose approach most closely resembles this way of thinking about the problem is Adorno, as the following statement illustrates: "neuroses should, in fact, according to their form, be deducted from the structure of a society where they cannot be eliminated. Even the successful cure carries the stigma of the damaged, vain, pathetically exaggerated adaptation. The triumph of the self is the obfuscation by the particular. This is the foundation of the objective untruth of all psychotherapy, encouraging therapists to make fraudulent claims. While the cured resembles the insane, the therapist becomes sick, but without the person whom the treatment has failed becoming healthier because of it" (ADORNO, Theodor; Sociology and psychology (part II). In: *New Left Review* 1/47, January-February 1968).

organized in the form of symptoms. In fact, Lacan claims that the existence of the drive requires the establishment of a: "headless subjectivation, a subjectivation without subject" (1973, p. 169). This peculiar subjectivity without a subject (in the sense of a subjectivity that should not be understood as an expression of a substantial subject previously defined) allows us to justify the need for rethinking recognition arrangements in a way that goes beyond the institutionalized form of the person.

The most useful way to approach the first task involves criticizing the theory that a primary inter-subjectivity exists to guide the relationships of love between mother and baby; an intersubjectivity which is capable of supporting the safe construction of individuality in a way that is recognized in social spheres beyond the nuclear family. If no such inter-subjectivity exists to provide a foundation for the construction of individuality, it opens up a space in which to defend the idea that interpersonal relations are irreducibly conflictual in nature. This conflictual nature is expressed by the need of the psychological person to be structured as a defensive organization of symptoms.

The second task involves assessing Honneth's criticism of the Freudian idea that human nature can be understood by means of a theory of drives. The central issue at stake here revolves around the existence of something resembling a "death drive". The criticism of the death drive is articulated, among other things, by a refusal to define "negativity" as a comprehensive base for the structure of human desire. This critique of negativity has major consequences for Honneth's interpretation of the way in which Hegel treated the problem of recognition, especially in *Phenomenology of the Spirit*. Thus, we have one hypothesis about the general models of interpersonal relations and another about the subjective system of motivations for action.[8]

Honneth uses the thesis of primary intersubjectivity to defend the existence of a strongly cooperative and communicative tendency within the first experiences of social interaction. For this reason, it is critical to Honneth's project as well as his critique of models, which are, in his view, inadequate for the task. The German philosopher derives his thesis of primary intersubjectivity from Donald Winnicott's theory of object relations and

---

[8] In fact, the hypothesis of a primary intersubjectivity as the critical structural negativity of the death drive can already be found in the works of another Frankfurtian, namely Herbert Marcuse. For example, for Marcuse (1999, p. 199), the reality principle, based on pulsional repression, is linked initially to the internalization of the paternal symbolic Law and its principles of organization, and inside the libidinal symbiotic flow between mother and baby and traces of another means of accessing reality can be found. Marcuse talks about an "attitude not of defense and submission [as would be the case in an intersubjective interdependent relationship between mother and baby], but of full identification with the environment." There is a certain continuity between these ideas and the theses defended by Honneth.

his way of understanding the relationship of love and mutual dependence between mother and baby. He believed that these relationships constitute a solid basis for developing the ability to be oneself in another, which he explains as follows:

> [...] the inter-subjective experience of love opens the individual to this fundamental stratum of emotional security (*emotionalen Sichereit*) that allows him to not only experience, but also externalize (*Äusserung*) his own needs and feelings, thus ensuring the psychic condition of development in all other attitudes of respect to himself (HONNETH, 1992, p. 171).

In other words, from this perspective, as mature adults we bring to wider spheres of social life and personal relationships a belief in the peaceful manifestation of needs and feelings, a belief that results from the inter-subjective experience of love and self-affirmation which was initially present in the relationship between mother and baby.[9] Such a relationship can be called "inter-subjective" because it is symmetrical, at least according to Honneth, in the sense that the baby depends on its mother in the same way that the mother depends on the baby, within a relationship of "emotional identification" in which children learn to adopt the perspective of a second person. This mutual dependency can be resolved by consolidating a position of cooperative and emotional security that would allow the child to develop his "individual self-consciousness."

In this sense, it is important to evaluate how far such a view of the relationship between mother and baby is an idyllic construction designed to legitimate the philosophical hypothesis of a founding intersubjectivity of the human condition, because, for example, by adopting a perspective which Lacan takes as a starting point, we can claim that the first interpersonal relations are not symmetrical. In fact, they must be asymmetrical, since the first subjective position of the child is to be the object of the mother's fantasies, with all its attendant violent expectations and frustrations. At this point, Lacan appears to be an adherent of Melanie Klein's views about the ghostly structure of the relationship between mother and baby.[10]

---

[9] To succeed, this strategy has to reject the criticism that comes with familiarism, especially that of disciplinary (FOUCAULT, 2010) and repressive (DELEUZE and GUATTARI, 2010) apparatus whose relations do not serve as suitable grounds for thinking about situations of social emancipation. This would require a reformulation of the critique of "familiarism" as it appeared in contemporary French philosophy.

[10] Lacan (1994) developed this point extensibely, as well as the consequences of the maternal superego.

It is important to notice how the baby's physical survival depends on maternal good will and care, which means that the baby's helplessness can only be controlled to the extent of finding a place inside its mother's fantasies, while the same cannot be said of the mother, at least not to the same degree of intensity. This means that the first interpersonal relations are, in fact, relations of domination and servitude, which the child should know how to cope with, which explains why Lacan uses the structure of the Hegelian dialectic of master and slave to explain why such relationships are responsible for the formation of the Self, since the child should, to a large extent, adapt itself to the normativity embodied by maternal disciplinary requirements to survive psychologically and physically. The disciplinary requirement of adaptation explains why the child needs to mobilize, on more than one occasion, the experience of illness and the production of symptoms in order to construct its uniqueness.

One possible strategy for advancing the dispute involves considering recent studies on the nature of the first relationships of interaction and their subsequent consequences, which I intend to do more systematically at another time.[11] However, two points should be noted here. First, most of these studies expose the existence of a primary "emotional proximity" between babies and those responsible for their care. Babies know that they are objects of attention, and they identify more easily and strongly with the person who is in charge of their care than other primates. However, such affective proximity does not necessarily imply a relationship of security with respect to the sense of desire of the other. I can know that I am the object of attention, but it does not mean that I will always be so, that there will not be another subject to oust me from my position, or that I know what I must do to preserve this attention and, in particular, that I know what this attention means.[12] Therefore, the experience of being the object of desire of another, especially the maternal object of desire, is, from the outset, problematic, and not just a source of existential security. That explains why Lacan claims that there exists: "behind the paternal superego, a maternal superego even more demanding, even more oppressive, more destructive, more insistent" (1998, p. 165).

---

[11] See, for example, Bebee, Lachmann, 2002; Fonagy, and Target, Mary; 2007, n. 88, pp. 917-937, Tomasello, 2003, Braten, 2007.

[12] This is why it is claimed that: "This emotional proximity can not be characterized in terms of positive or negative valences; it involves not a cognitive judgment or a set of inferences regarding the value that others may have: on the contrary, positive attitudes, negative or even indifferent about the other depend on this affection "non epistemic" regarding the other" (GALLAGHER, VARGA, 2012, p. 255).

Moreover, it is worth remembering that even the Honnethian reading of Winnicott can be seen as relative regarding the cooperative nature of primary relationships. For example, it is worth recalling that, as the English psychoanalyst affirms: "In the development of the body, the growth factor is clearer; in the development of the psyche, in contrast, there is the possibility of failure at each moment, and it is actually impossible for growth to be distortion-free due to some degree of failure in environmental adaptability" (WINNICOTT, 1990, p. 47). If it is impossible to develop in terms of environmental adaptation without some degree of failure, one must ask whether we should really speak of a peaceful manifestation of needs and feelings, as Honneth advocates. Failures involve distortions and frustrations caused by the demands of adaptation. This could mean that we need to know how to deal with limits on expectations of cooperation with each other; in other words, it means coping with the existential insecurity that comes from the realization that the mother does not know how to fulfil fundamental dimensions of the subject of desire.[13]

It is true that Winnicott believes that, at various times: "an extreme adaptation to the baby's needs can be made by the real mother without resentment" (1990, p. 132). A successful adaptation would prevent the child from succumbing to a deep disappointment due to their recognition expectations, thus generating a pathological situation of existential insecurity. One has to ask, however, if Winnicott's insistence on the ability of maternal adaptation to provide a unique "perfect fit" could be an additional source of suffering and imbalance to the mother, especially in an era increasingly marked by the refusal of current generations to follow traditional models of motherhood and the consequent insecurity about their performance as mothers, as well as the structural susceptibility to postpartum depression.[14]

But even if Winnicott's position is not exactly what I am advocating, it is equally distant from that which Honneth ascribed to him. For example, it is worth remembering, that the consequences of the privileged manifestation of the successful character of the Inter-subjective relationship between mother and baby are the establishment of transitional states in which the child can

---

[13] Thus: "when there is difficulty, the mother and the baby may take a long time to be able to understand each other, and it often happens that the mother and the baby fail from the beginning, and so (both) suffer the consequences of failure for many years, and sometimes for ever "(WINNICOTT, 1990, p. 123)

[14] "The most appropriate analyses from most studies conclude that approximately 7.1% of women experience a major depressive episode in the first three months post-delivery. If we include smaller depressions, the rate for the same three month period increases to 19.2% "(O'HARA, p. 1265). That is, one in five mothers will undergo an experience of depression relating to the care of her child.

sustain, in the other, the illusion of having created objects in the external world. Winnicott sees in such states the source of religious and artistic phenomena. Nevertheless, art and religion are not really inter-subjective phenomena, but phenomena that fall within the boundaries of the communicational structure of language. This is what Winnicott is alluding to, in very concrete language, in the following statement:

> Someone who requires such tolerance at a later age is called crazy. In religion and the arts, we see this socialized demand, so that the individual is not called crazy and can enjoy, in exercising religion or practice and appreciation of the arts, the rest necessary to humans in their eternal task of discriminating between the facts and fantasy. (1990, p. 127)

We can interpret this assertion as meaning that the kind of social bond created from the consequences of the relationship of love between mother and baby follows a very specific order, which may not serve as a suitable basis for understanding social ties in general, something which Honneth does not seem to accept.[15] To find the foundations of a policy in this, we must remember that the circulation of fantasies in a transitional space supported by a "good enough mother" is, among other things, exclusive, as are the specific relations pertaining to religious communities and artistic experiences. If we wish to follow Winnicott's view, we have to say that only those who possess the specific behavior and character traits of the "good enough mother" can sustain this bond, which allows us to: "have the illusion of finding in reality what we create (hallucinate)" (WINNICOTT, 1990, p. 135). Since not everyone is capable of fitting this mold (of having, at best, different concrete experiences of what being a "good enough mother" means) and thus ensuring the illusion, it follows that the relationship must be exclusive, and that such reflection can only have limited political interest.

Moreover, it should be remembered here that it is not possible to make the transition from arts and religion (manifestations relating to culture) to genuinely political interpersonal relations without impunity. This explains why Winnicott stresses that, from the perspective of the interpersonal relations of ordinary life, the demands present in art and religion are unrealistic. They are only allowed as compensatory experiences rather than experiences that could

---

[15] Rather, he wants to say that: "Winnicott's fascinating observation can be expanded to include, in addition to art and religion, a group intersubjectivity as a space of experience that dissolves the boundaries between internal and external reality" (HONNETH, 2010, p. 274).

induce global changes within the shared political realm. Such changes would require a vision in which religious community ties could support social orders, or conversely, in which aesthetic experiences could reconfigure the nature of our community expectations. Honneth does not seem to be advocating either of these two possibilities.

## Fights without risk

Nonetheless, Honneth needs to create a template of a recognition process that can take the place of this one in supporting his political philosophy. Because emotional security generated by the successful character of the demands of love within the family unit forms the basis of social demands for the recognition of individual autonomy and the assertion of their particular systems of interest, they would also be found in the profound sensitivity of the subjects to experiences of contempt and injustice. Thereby, Honneth constructs a psychoanalytic anthropology designed to guide social interaction processes in which there is no place for insuperable antagonisms; an anthropology which is strongly family-focused and able to provide the moral foundations of social conflicts. However, in this case, it is a familiarism focused, largely, on just one pole of the socialization matrix of the bourgeois family, namely the mother, which ignores the conflictual nature of the father-mother relationship and its consequences for the children's development.

Honneth hopes that this psychoanalytic anthropology is consistent with aspects of reflection on social conflicts within the dialectic tradition of Hegel and Marx. For him, Hegel's fundamental idea is that: "the struggle for recognition constitutes the moral force that drives the social human vital reality towards development and progress" (HONNETH, 1992, p. 227), because the moral experience of contempt for desire and active subject dignity is at the origin of social resistance and collective uprisings. Thus, historical progress towards freedom is the story of achievement, which becomes increasingly universal, from a psychoanalytically-oriented anthropological perspective. But for Hegel, it would not be feasible to make the necessary adjustments without significant loss to his theory.

The main problem is the peculiar way in which Honneth reads the Hegelian dialectic of master and slave. Honneth recognizes in the dialectics a "transcendental fact" that appears as a prerequisite for all human sociability. But, according to his interpretation, these dialectics involve the gradual conquest of an ability for "self-restraint" by which one learns to limit the illusion of the omnipotence of one's own desire by perceiving the irreducibility of the desire of the other. Thus, the "Ego and alter ego react to each other restricting or denying their selfish desires" (HONNETH, 2010, p. 30).

This transformation of the dynamics of the master and the slave dialectic and the affirmation of a true morality is admirable, but, for such an interpretation to be possible, Honneth needs to distort what Hegel meant by "negativity in itself" (*Negativität an ihm*), reading it as a kind of self-denial through which individuals learn to restrict their own wishes. However, as I have tried to show above, this concept indicates the existence, for Hegel, of an ontological reality of the fundamental refusal to fully understand the indeterminate nature of desire. Each time Hegel claims that: "negation in itself only has one being as negation reporting to itself," (1986, p. 18) he seeks to describe a form of denial that does not fit the Kantian notion of "real opposition", as the Kantian concept may not recognize objects whose essence is not substantial, but is based on a highly negative experience. Such experiences are clearly described in statements such as the following: "The essence, while foundational, is determined as the non-determined (*Nichtbestimmte*) and it is only the overcoming (*Aufheben*) of its determined being (*Bestimmtseins*) that is your determining" (P. 81). To see this as the learning expression of the self-restraint exercise in which one discovers something not so different from platitudes such as, where my freedom ends and where does the freedom of others begin, does not seem a very consistent reading of what Hegel demands. It is worth considering, again, Hegel's famous statement, which takes the dialectic of master and slave to a certain level of resolution:

> Labour is desire restrained and checked, evanescence delayed and postponed; in other words, labour shapes and fashions the thing. The negative relation to the object passes into the form of the object, into something that is permanent and remains; because it is just for the labourer that the object has independence. This negative mediating agency, this activity giving shape and form, is at the same time the individual existence, the pure self-existence of that consciousness, which now in the work it does is externalized and passes into the condition of permanence. The consciousness that toils and serves accordingly attains by this means the direct apprehension of that independent being as its self. [...] For in shaping the thing it [the slave] only becomes aware of its own proper negativity (1992, p. 132)

Restraining the destructive impulse of desire in its object of consumption allows the self-objectification of the structure of self-consciousness in an object that is its duplicate. But we must again insist on the nature of the dialectical turn: the fact that the object has independence from the worker is not just the alienation index at work. The confrontation both with one's acting as a strange essence, while also acting to an absolute other, with the object as something that resists one's efforts, has the potential to open awareness to the character-forming experience of an internal alterity as a fundamental moment for identity creation. In saying that, in the formation process, one becomes an object of the consciousness of one's own negativity, Hegel points out how the indeterminacy of the desire for consciousness, that is, the attempt to be a pure being in itself, "takes the form of the object", and "in the work it does is externalized and passes into the condition of permanence". So, the consciousness finds in the other the same negativity, and the same indeterminacy, that constitutes its essence. Far from being an affirmation of individuals who learn to restrict themselves, and in the process learn how to negotiate their particular systems of interest, we are confronted with something totally different here. In fact, through work, the subject does not express its qualities and interests, as the Hegelian concept of work is not expressivist. We will be more closely aligned with Hegel's view if we say that, through work, the subject externalizes its negative essence, and discovers negativity in itself, by accepting that such negativity works in this way. This may help to explain why the ideas presented in the *Phenomenology of Spirit*, do not lead us towards the "institutionalization of the identity of the Self" (HABERMAS, 2007, p. 196), but instead enable us to uncover one's own negativity and the negativity that comes from the other (a Kojèvean formula that, at least on this point, is much closer to the Hegelian text than the outcome proposed by Honneth).

By seeing the conflict of individual interests as the basis of the Hegelian struggle for recognition, [16]Honneth can understand even Marxist class struggle within a framework of moral demands for individual self-fulfillment and symmetrical esteem between subjects. He relies on a trend that can be found in the political and historical writings and those of Marx's youth to assert:

> [...] The class struggle does not mean for him, primarily, a strategic confrontation for the acquisition of assets or instruments of power. It is a moral conflict whose aim is the "emancipation" of labor, an essential condition on which, at the same time, the symmetrical esteem between subjects and the individual self-consciousness depends (HONNETH, 1992, p. 233).

---

[16] As did PINKARD, 1994, and HABERMAS, 2004

However, there is a major difficulty with this strategy. So far we have seen how Honneth establishes that the suffering of injustice and contempt leads us to take political action in a pre-political terrain, marked by constitutional issues usually related to the discussion of the genesis of modern individuality: the "individual self-consciousness." That is, the very genesis of modern individuality appears as a pre-political phenomenon, as something that should be politically confirmed, and not politically deconstructed. Thus, as we shall see in a more systematic way in the next chapter, the feelings of injustice and contempt are often described as the result of blocking the possibility of social affirmation and legal recognition of traces of individual identity. Consequently, at least in this case, recognition and identity necessarily go together.

This may explain why, according to Honneth, the prime examples of struggles for recognition are struggles for affirmation of "anthropological differences"[17] related to feminist struggles, as well as those for the rights of black people and homosexuals. They are examples of this: "practical process in which individual experiences of contempt are interpreted as typical experiences of a whole group in order to motivate the collective claim of increasing recognition of relationships" (HONNETH, 1992, *p.* 260). That is, experiences of contempt about the attributes of individuals relating to their cultural differences are interpreted as forms of violence that do not only affect the individual self. However, this is not to say that we have left the sphere of individual attributes of affirmation of the person and of the social construction of identities.

This explains, for example, why the recovery of the concept of "social pathologies" is largely linked to discussions about blocking "social conditions of individual self-realization" (HONNETH, 2006, p. 35), as if the realization should be thought of as respecting individual structures or, as Honneth puts it, drawing on Freud, the structures of the "rational ego". On the other hand, it also explains why the models of suffering privileged by Honneth are the social anomie and the suffering of indeterminate identity.[18]

## Models of social pathologies

Here, we must make a distinction. Usually, discussions about anomie insist on the weakening of social norms due to the exponential development of individual demands, as the demands for individual freedom destroy the regulatory framework of social normativities. That is why Durkheim

---

[17] On the concept of "anthropological difference" see, above all, BALIBAR 2011.
[18] As can be seen in HONNETH, 2005a

repeatedly insists that: "the individual, by itself, is not a sufficient end to its activity. It is very little. Not only limited in space, it is also tightly limited in time" (2005, p 224.).

But, in fact, it is not the case that anomie exists because individuality raises specific private and identity demands that cannot be accommodated by the social order. This situation in itself does not generate anomie, but, to use a term proposed by Durkheim, "selfishness" or even political upheavals directed towards the recognition of particulars or the extension of rights about choice and decisions. On the contrary, anomie occurs when the demands are no longer determinable, and no longer have a specific form due to a weakening of standards with regard to individualization and the limitation of passions. Therefore, when Durkheim speaks of the social causes of suicide, it is important to remember that suicides motivated by anomie are distinguished from both those motivated by excessive individualization (selfish suicides) and from those motivated by insufficient individualization (altruistic suicides). In this context of anomie, we enter into a "state of indeterminacy" (DURKHEIM, 2005, p. 275) (or, to use Honneth's term, a "suffering of indeterminacy") in which no individualization is possible because society is, among other things, subjected to: "the lack of organization which is a feature of the economic state" (p 286.) with its: "thirst for new things, ignored joys and unnamed sensations, but which lose all their taste since they are known" (p. 285). Faced with the constant promises of joy produced by a growing capitalist society, all limited satisfaction is unbearable precisely because it is limited, and any identity choice is meaningless precisely because it is also a multitude of refusals. Hence Durkheim warns against: "this evil from infinity, that anomie always brings with it" (p. 304) and which can only produce anger, disappointment and lassitude, exacerbated by an over-excited sensibility.

As Durkheim uses a quantitative concept of difference between normal and pathological, [19] this means that a certain degree of anomie is necessary: "all moral progress and improvement is inseparable from a certain degree of anomie" (p. 417). However, something in the march towards progress in our society produces an abnormal and pathological situation of anomie. To counter this, Durkheim suggests a strengthening of institutional structures that can be achieved, mainly, by consolidating community bonds linked to professional groupings.

In his attempt to recover the concept of social pathology, Honneth draws on Durkheim's diagnosis, but introduces an additional element, namely the understanding of how, during the last thirty or forty years, this situation of

---

[19] As is made clear in DURKHEIM, 2004.

social anomie has been institutionalized, and has thus become a mode of managing social suffering and a driving force behind the neoliberal ideology of the current stage of capitalism. Statements such as the following help to illustrate this point:

> [...] individual self-fulfillment of expectations, which grew rapidly due to a historically unique combination of several distinct processes of individualization in Western societies of the last thirty, forty years and that, in time, became so clearly an institutionalized pattern of expectations of social reproduction, lost their inner purpose (*Zweckbestimmung*), and yet have become the system's foundation base. The result of this paradoxical inversion, in which processes that once promised a qualitative growth of freedom now become ideologies of deinstitutionalization, is the emergence of several individual symptoms of inner emptiness, the feeling of being superfluous and devoid of determination (HONNETH, 2010, pp. 207-208).

As we can see, Honneth's diagnosis sticks very closely to the framework provided by Durkheim. Requirements for individual self-fulfillment have become "ideologies of deinstitutionalization", that is, a process that undermines the cohesion and organization of social norms. As a result, it produces a deregulation of social norms with pathologies linked to depressive feelings of emptiness and inability to take action.

Like social theorists such as Luc Boltanski and Eve Chiapello (1999), Honneth clearly understand how this kind of anomie become a "productive force" within the capitalist economy in an era of the easing of restrictions and ongoing deregulation. As was shown in the previous chapter, he also understands how this social management of anomie is accompanied by the exponential development of pathologies linked to a deregulation of the ability to form identities, such as depression and its feeling of being "tired of being oneself",[20] narcissistic insecurity, and borderline personality disorders. However, I would insist that this answer does not seem to address the demand to rebuild the normative basis for institutionalities which is capable of ensuring the successful development of individuals. The problem lies not in the deinstitutionalization processes, but in the impact of other forms of social regulation linked to the mental expropriation of estrangement.

---

[20] In this regard, see Ehrenberg's influential book, 2000.

## Flexibility and fusion in a football match

This point requires further analysis. Indeed, Honneth tended to think of the forms of social pathology as coming from the generalization of the framework of anomie. Even his discussions about reification as a model of objectifying behavior based on an alleged "recognition of oblivion" did not insist on a structural critique of the restrictive nature of the identity and the individuality present in Marxist reflections about social alienation, as we shall see in the next chapter. That is, they do not explore some of the important possibilities that exist in the articulation between the Luckasian issue of reification and the Marxist problem of alienation. Nevertheless, Honneth is aware that critical theory presupposes a normative ideal of society that is incompatible with the individualist assumptions of the liberal tradition. This does not mean, in his case, understanding the decentralizing effect that the concept of recognition may have regarding a model that we might call the "egomaniac" organization of subjective experience, because it is not enough to state, for example, that to "Recognize someone means to perceive their qualities that urge us to behave not in a more egocentric way, but as the intentions, needs or desires of this other person" (HONNETH, 2006, p. 261). To insist on the central role of the recognition concept involves recognizing, in the other, something that cannot be conceived of in the form of intentions, needs or desires of a legal person with positive rights. It is not about new desires, needs and intentions that develop under the pressure of general historical transformations. It is about knowing how to recognize the malaise related to the person as a mode of subjectivity organization.

Honneth is not completely indifferent to such issues. Indeed, he is forced to consider how his concept of the individual can cope with the contemporary process of the flexibilization of fixed and rigid identities, a process that he called "intrapsychic pluralization of the subjects", for he knows that:

> [...] Concepts like "identity" and "self" mean, in the most advanced currents of sociological tradition, only operations of synthesis that the subject must make to be able to perceive a multitude of experiences, beliefs and actions pertaining to disparate temporal and social plans and consistent manifestations of the same Self (HONNETH, 2006, p. 328).

Taking this into account, and drawing on the work of the psychoanalyst Hans Loewald, Honneth speaks of the need to temporarily abandon experiences that dissolve the boundaries of the self, allowing a return to the state that existed before the intra-psychic differentiations that were consolidated through maturation processes.[21] This is how his theory accounts for the need to criticise the restrictive nature of personal identities, not by flirting with the theme of negativity and appealing to psychoanalytic concepts like the death drive.

An example of these experiences of temporary abandonments to pre-egoic undifferentiated states and fusion is: "The feeling of being part of a mass celebration, in football stadiums, at rock concerts or in isolation of a working group that lost the feeling of time and see itself as if it was playing" (HONNETH, 2010, *p.* 205). However, there is something inadequate in believing, for example, that rock concerts and football matches can constitute good examples of manifestations of a pre-egoic merger capable of realizing our discomfort with strongly consolidated identities, as we stand before such phenomena which are deeply assimilated into the normal operation of our capitalist society with all its spectacle. We may wonder whether such phenomena are in fact, on the contrary, illustrative examples of identity reification produced by the current dynamics of the consumption society. There is no more defensive, exclusive and stereotyped identity than the one that provides the link between football fans or fans of a rock group. But, those who think that it all started well in the mother's lap will have no difficulty believing that it will be even better when absorbed in a good game of football[22].

## The negativity deficit and its discontents

The speculative limitation of Honneth on this point, with its obvious political consequences, may be, however, only the result of his inability to fully engage with the Freudian theory of drives, especially the death drive. Honneth believes that critical theory should refrain from drawing on a theory

---

[21] See statements by Hans Loewald such as: "The ego mediates, unifies and integrates because it is its essence to keep the original unit in increasingly complex levels of differentiation and objectification of reality." (2000, p.11)

[22] Notice how, at this point, Winnicott is much less relationist than Honneth. Consider the consequences of passages such as: "In the life of a normal child, the rest should include relaxation and regression to non-integration. Gradually, as the self develops strength and complexity, this regression to non-integration increasingly approaches a painful state of "maddening" disintegration. So there is an intermediate state in which a baby who is cared for and allowed to fully develop can relax and not be integrated, and tolerate (but only tolerate) feeling "crazy" in non-integrated state. Next a step forward is taken, a step towards independence and the permanent loss of the ability for non-integration, except in madness or in specialized conditions provided by psychotherapy "(WINNICOTT, 1990, p. 139). Thus, Winnicott did not believe in the Rock of therapeutic strength; as soon as the Self is formed, he believed, there is no way to regularly integrate states of intrapsychic differentiation, except in its pale shadow.

of drives, reducing the subjective experience of negativity to an "inevitable result of our socialization." To see subjective negativity only as a result of socialization processes, and not as an essential determinant of the human condition, effectively reduces it to the expression of aggressive, antisocial or self-destructive tendencies which need to be overcome. This leads him to ponder the following question: "Why a critical theory of society could only be considered 'critical' to their theoretical assumptions about socialization by accepting the existence of a structural conflict, expressed through the 'negativity' of the subject, between the individual and the social order?" (HONNETH, 2010, p. 210).

Initially, we can see that this way of framing the problem is already fraught with assumptions. Freud's notion of structural conflict is not just something that occurs between the individual and the social order. In fact, it is internal to the individual, and thus is between the individual and what, in itself, does not conform to the shape of the individual. Since it cannot be a unitary instance, the individual will eventually reconfigure their internal conflict, turning it into an external difference between themselves and the social order.

On the other hand, if the subject turns to negativity as a fundamental means of subjective expression, it is because there is something deeply alienating about the models of identity determination provided by the current social order, which leads individuals to seek the experience of negativity as a manifestation of that which still does not have an image within our ways of life and within the available anthropological differences.

But it is true that the Freudian appeal to a death drive seems to transform negativity into an "almost natural force" that leads to a "pre-social constitution of the subject." We know that, at least according to Freud, the idea of an instinctual tendency towards death was not only a hypothesis related to human behavior, but a fundamental biological hypothesis for each and every organism (as can be seen in *Beyond the Pleasure Principle*). However, discussions about the Freudian concept should start by questioning the relevance of the biological hypothesis. In this sense, it is interesting to consider how philosophers such as Georges Canguilhem (1990) approached reflections about biology, claiming not see what should be refuted in the Freudian theory. Recent work in the field of biology, such as that of Henri Atlan (1979; 2006) and Jean Claude Ameisen (2003), could support the hypothesis. This implies that a significant part of the discussion will involve evaluating the plausibility of the defense of the death drive as a biological hypothesis, which Honneth does not do.

In fact, Honneth is content to say that aggression is not the expression of an endogenous drive. Following Winnicott, he prefers to see it as an:

"expression of a kind of ontological experiment to test the independence of the world" (HONNETH, 2010, p. 220)[23] and its resistance to one's capacity for aggression. Similarly, antisocial tendencies would not need to be attributed to a drive, but could be regarded as the result of a constant impulse to deny intersubjectivity, regressing to a state of fusion with primary objects. Through this interpretation, Honneth can claim to treat episodes of fusion as something produced by a mature Self, and not phases. Therefore, this leads him to wonder: "Why the idea of a provision in the merger contradicts the concept of recognition?" (p. 223); despite the fact that, from a Freudian perspective, the drive responsible for the formation of mergers and units is the drive for life, not the death drive.

It is not entirely accurate to see in the death drive only images of aggression and antisocial tendencies. While this is one of its possible social configurations, it is far from the only one[24]. It can also appear, for example, in the form of polymorphs and fragmentary sexuality[25]. By immediately understanding the death drive purely as an instinct of destruction, we end up not appropriately thematizing psychoanalytic discussions about productive experiences of uncertainty, negativity and depersonalization (or even of subjective destitution). If we follow Honneth's line of reasoning, such experiences will eventually become transformed into compensatory experiences designed to create a concept of individuality still strongly characterized by its need to preserve fundamental identity structures of the modern individual.

A perspective based on the refusal to accept the concept of the death drive still has a major impact on discussions of social pathologies, because it prevents us from realizing the specific category of malaise (*Unbehagen*) as understood by Freud. This is a key concept which describes the existence of a higher form of social suffering that concerns not the deregulation of social norms, but the very normativity of the processes of individualization and personalization, as developed in dynamic, modern Western civilizations. If we look for a point of entry to addressing the problem of malaise, we can say that it shows how the model of hegemonic social norms used in our way of life is inseparable from: "the existential feeling of loss of place, of the actual experience of being out of place"[26]. In other words, this type of experience is not the result of deregulating the planning capacity of social norms, but

---

[23] On the problem of the anti-social tendency, see WINNICOTT, 2000, p. 406-417

[24] This is, in fact, the most current reading, as can be seen, for example, in Kernberg, 2009.

[25] As can be seen in LAPLANCHE, 1997. Laplanche demonstrated how the disruptive nature of the sexual impulse in Freud's first topic eventually ended up embedded in discussions about the death drive in the second topic.

[26] DUNKER, Christian; *Mal-estar, sofrimento, sintoma*, Boitempo: São Paulo, 2015, p. 196

is deeply linked to the dysfunctionality implied by own instinctual life. The instincutal life can only be socialized for something as non-functional standard systems, that is, those which are not designed to determine general and stable models of individuality; systems that do not incite the transformation of wholly inadequatemodels as aggression to be further repressed, introverted and neurotized as guilt through the establishment of the superego as psychic instance. In this sense, Freud claims that guilt as the fundamental problem of civilization is, among other things, produced by the consciousness of guilt (*Schuldbewusstsein*) linked to the understanding of the social genesis of the feeling that remains largely unconscious, manifesting as malaise, and not necessarily as a symptom. The consciousness of guilt could help us to understand how: "Not only is civilization founded on a detour of libido in its favor, but it should also seek to control the different forms of revolt against its libido domination" (RENAULT, 2008, p. 276). In other words, it could lead us to regard guilt as inseparable from the disciplinary production of hegemonic modes of socialization.

In this sense, the Freudian notion of malaise can provide an evaluative view of different social pathologies which differs from that based on the hegemony of the diagnosis of anomie. The Freudian concept reminds us how: "man becomes neurotic because he can not bear the amplitude of deprivation that society imposes, for the sake of its cultural ideals" (FREUD, 2010, p. 45). It should be noted, however, that the deprivation of libidinal satisfaction is not simply linked to a fantasy refusal of the desire for omnipotence. The instinctual renunciation also refuses the polymorphy and fragmentation of a structurally dispersive sexuality and an instinctual structure which does not define them without a natural object, a refusal aimed at ensuring order and the hierarchy of pleasures linked to the reiteration of identity boundaries of the Self. That explains why Lacan ties malaise to the problem of enjoyment of the destination, or more precisely, the pathological description of what does not conform to superegomaniac imperatives of enjoyment or, even that which does not conform to the submission of enjoyment to an imperative. This prompt us to recall Dunker's happy formula: "Superego is what remains real, as a source of unease and enjoyment condition, after the paternal metaphor"[27]. Thus, it is what remains when the function of the paternal metaphor, in its susceptibility to a certain lack of predictability of enjoyment, cannot impose its hegemony[28].

---

[27] DUNKER, Christian, op. cit., p. 212

[28] On another occasion, I demonstrated how the law brought by the paternal metaphor was a transcendent law that provides an empirical and imaginary object to desire. From the articulation point of view of the objects that would be in accordance, *such law is empty.* This may

On the other hand, we could say that it is very likely that the Freudian notion of malaise connected to modern individuality is not going to be resolved through controlled fusion experiments in disciplinary figures appropriate to our societies of the spectacle. In fact, as we will see in the next chapter, he advocates the invention of a genuinely political space in which it would be possible to reference processes to themselves in a radically antipredicative way, that is, a space in which recognition demands could not be presented as predicates of the individual person.

It is possible to uncover important foundations for what we might call "antipredicative recognition" if we pay attention to the productive experience of indeterminacy that enabled Lacan to state that the subjectivity of the death drive is a fundamental process in analytic treatment because it can lead us to a "creationist sublimation" (1986a, p. 251). By understanding the Self as a narcissistic unit that develops interpersonally, projectively and is marked by relations of aggression, as well as understanding the psychological personality as a construction of defensive symptoms, Lacan needs to insist on the need for analytic treatment to appeal to a dimension which is not egomaniac of the subjectivity. His way of constructing distinctions between subject and Self is based on the defense of modes of synthesis which are not copies of the Self's own unit model.

In Lacan's case, this strategy passes, largely, through the reconstruction of the concept of the death drive and comes from an impulse provided by his reading of Hegelian *Begierde*. Such a desire is linked to a deep sense of uncertainty that cannot be understood only as a source of suffering, but also as a fundamental stage of self-affirmation. Furthermore, this uncertainty is never a fully-structured space, of the kind that I would like to defend, but it appears as a fundamental dimension of the negative experience of freedom. We will see, by the end of the book, how such experiences of indetermination may act as an important political force, because they resolve the conflicts found in the land of cultural differences, with its construction processes and affirmation of identities as attributes of the person, opening up the possibility of establishing a genuinely ontologically political zone of recognition, that lies beyond cultural conflicts about identity.

---

explain why Lacan estabilishes a clear contrast between the effects of the paternal metaphor and the effects of the superego (see SAFATLE, Vladimir; *A paixão do negativo: Lacan e a dialética*, São Paulo: Unesp, 2006)

# III.
# Action

# CHAPTER VII

# Our time unlocks a multiplicity in each desire

*By repetition that which at first appeared*
*merely a matter of chance and contingency*
*becomes a real and ratified existence.*
Hegel

*He thought in other heads;*
*and in his own, others besides himself thought.*
*This is true thinking.*
Bertolt Brecht

While the foregoing discussion of psychoanalytic drive theory has brought us to a renewed understanding of the problem of negativity, and allowed us to conceive of an individuality no longer subjugated to what we have termed the egological reduction of the subject, we have yet to examine how the restructuring of psychic activity is to be conducted; in particular, how psychic syntheses – understood here as being no longer exclusively dependent on ego-derived modes of synthesis – operate.

In Chapter III, we have seen how a proper conception of negativity demanded that any syntheses conducted within time be conceived in terms of a model of determination founded on a dialectical relation between finitude and infinity. This model gave us the means to more fully understand the transformative process involved in the constitution of a historical subject. Properly conceived, a historical subject is merely a medium for the conveyance of a particular sort of action, namely one consisting in the actualization of a trans-individual multiplicity of actions, in a reoccurrence of past events and their concomitant redimensioning. Therefore, historical subjects require nothing less than history as their proper object, or in other words the aforementioned trans-individuality, condensed into the form of an object.

The present chapter also addresses the question of syntheses in time, but in a different context: here, we inquire into the possibility of employing the previously-described dynamic to explain not only syntheses taking place within historical time, but psychic syntheses as well. One way of approaching the issue is through an articulation between fantasy and memory in a Freudian vein. Given the need for processes of determination to be conceived anew, I would like to demonstrate what the Freudian conception of fantasy can add to the matter. After all, an aspect of fantasy entails the actualization of multiple series of virtual, trans-individual desires. Fantasies, in this sense, may be regarded as fundamental dimensions of a historicity whose actualization is the outcome of the systematic weakening of finite determinations. Thus, fantasies establish a facet of psychic life in which a kind of social memory may be found, one indelibly marked by desire.

A useful way of considering this matter is one that encompasses both Freud's notion of remembering and an understanding of fantasy as a subset of the modes of synthesis with which memory operates. While the concept of drive was emphasized in the preceding two chapters, there is still a need to explain how the drive experience, as characterized above, impacts on the constitution of objects. We have seen how certain anxiety-related experiences can lead drive-objects to manifest. These moments of great anxiety should function as no more than momentary situations for the reconfiguration of one's capacity for determination; however; to allow such a state of anxiety to persist beyond that would be dangerous. In this regard, an appeal to the synthetic power of the concepts of fantasy and memory should prove beneficial. For, if fantasy is usually understood as a defense against anxiety, it would be logical to suppose that there are some situations in which this defense involves more than a simple negation. To that end, we must reacquaint ourselves with Freud's use of remembering as a clinical tool.

## Healing through remembering

Remembering (*Erinnerung*) constitutes one of the central devices at work in the Freudian school's declared processes of healing (*Erinnerung*). Be that as it may, the question arises of in what sense are we to understand memory and the act of remembering as fundamental elements in the attainment of a cure for so-called mental illnesses? Under what conditions would it be permissible to view the painstaking rituals of an obsessive-compulsive disorder sufferer, or the self-defensive destruction of one's own desire, or even the serious deficits in motor and sensory function experienced by those afflicted with conversion disorder (among other equally distressing conditions), as no more than symptoms of one's *inability to remember* those processes through which one's subjectivity was constituted? These are questions that may help us achieve a fuller understanding of central aspects of the Freudian school of thought, and that lead us to pose an additional question whose apparent simplicity is deceptive: what exactly does Freud mean by the term "remembering"?

Answering this question implies a need to explore not only the clinical uses of the act of remembering, but also to investigate the relation that exists between memory and fantasy. Such an exploration seems likely to reveal a rather peculiar application of remembering that sets Freudian reflection firmly outside the bounds of any philosophical traditions that believe mnemonic processes to be fundamental in unifying the temporal experiences of individual consciousness into a cohesive whole. In other words, Freud's interpretation of mnemonic processes may be said to exceed the limits commonly established for philosophies of consciousness.

Let us begin by attempting to more fully understand the clinical uses of the act of remembering. In order to do so, we need to examine specific articulations linking remembering and transference in the Freudian corpus. In "On Psychotherapy," a text that focuses specifically on the therapeutic applications of psychoanalysis, Freud described what he saw as the core of his psychoanalytic practice as follows:

> It is not a modern dictum but an old saying of physicians that these diseases [*i.e. psychoneuroses*] are not cured by the drug, but by the physician, that is, by the personality of the physician, inasmuch as through it he exerts a mental influence. I am well aware that you favour the view which Vischer, the professor of aesthetics, expressed so well in his parody of Faust: *"Ich weiss, das Physikalische / Wirkt öfters aufs Moralische"* ["I know that the physical / Often influences the moral"]. But would it not be more appropriate [*adäquater*] to say – and is it not more often the case – that moral (that is, mental) means can influence a man's moral side?[1]

Taking a firm stance in the debate that raged throughout the nineteenth century about the nature of, and relationship between, the physical and the moral, Freud upheld a view dating back to Pinel, which involved grounding the effectiveness and adequacy of clinical practices in the physician-patient relationship. While his remarks echoed widely accepted "moral" notions regarding therapy, Freud went as far as characterizing psychoanalytic treatment as a form of "re-education [*Nacherziehung*] in overcoming [*Überwindung*]

---

[1] FREUD, "On Psychotherapy," *S.E. Vol. VII*, p. 259.

internal resistances"[2], ample evidence that, for him, there was no question that the power of suggestion affects the relationship between physician and patient. Such power, in this case, was seen as facilitating the patient's attainment of a condition of "final independence" (*endliche Selbständigkeit*) – contingent on a concurrent liquidation of the transference – seen as necessary for "the *practical* recovery of the patient, the restoration of his ability to lead an active life and of his capacity for enjoyment [*Genuss*]."[3]

The vocabulary employed in such passages seems strikingly familiar; one could, for example, follow Foucault's lead and claim that we are confronted with a process of "re-education" aimed at reconstructing individual autonomy, or achieving a state of "final independence," which could only be the outcome of one's internalization of disciplinary practices and procedures, the latter being dependent on the transformation of the physician into an ideal type.[4] The point, here, is that the clinical implementation of a device is seen as inseparable from the logic of disciplinary power. To show that this is not the case seems to require a careful analysis of the constitution of Freudian clinical practices, conducted mainly through one of its two central axes, *transference* (the other axis being *interpretation*, a procedure closely connected to processes of recollection and construction).

The first step towards the thematization of transference was Freud's notorious use of what he and Breuer termed "the cathartic method." Nineteenth-century discussions on the notion of catharsis signaled an important shift in the way the "therapeutic" function of tragedy was understood. In this context, the importance of the work of philologist and philosopher Jacob Bernays – an uncle of Freud's wife Martha, as well as a significant influence on Nietzsche – should not be overlooked.[5]

Bernays had sought to highlight the fact that, contrary to popular belief based on the popularity of Lessing's interpretation, the notion of catharsis often employed in accounts of the effect produced by theatrical tragedy was in reality not connected to a form of "moral purification" and the consequent desire of an individual to strive to act compassionately. Rather, it was linked to "purgation" in its medical sense, meaning the ejection of a pathogenic element from the body, and thus, in this context, an affect over which the subject lacks conscious control.

---

[2]  *Ibid*, p. 267.
[3]  FREUD, "Freud's Psycho-Analytic Procedure," *S.E. Vol. VII*, p. 253.
[4]  Ideas amply explored in Foucault's aforementioned *Psychiatric Power: Lectures at the Collège de France 1973-74*.
[5]  Cf. in particular, BERNAYS, J.; *Zwei Abhandlungen über die aristotelische Theorie des Drama*. Darmstadt: Wissenschaftliche Buchgesellschaft, 1968.

Nonetheless, it is worth noticing, that what concerns us here is a process that arises when there is identification between subject and dramatic scene, when one is confronted with a theatrical situation that one feels part of. One of the chief characteristics of this process is its eminently visual nature; the subject is led to identify with an image whose power is sufficient to unleash repressed affects. Similar kinds of conceptions even seem to have underlain the nineteenth-century psychiatric practice of reenacting delirious states.

Following this scheme, the cathartic method employed hypnosis in an attempt to bring a patient diagnosed as hysterical to the particular psychological state in which his or her symptoms were first experienced. Memories, thoughts and impulses, endowed with great emotional expression (*Affektäusserung*), would then arise and, once the relevant affect was identified, it would be sublated (*aufgehoben*). In most cases Freud wrote of an affect as having been "abreacted," that is, as having undergone a process of "release" (*Abfuhr*). Thus, the attainment of a cure for the condition was associated with an almost physical process of emotional discharge, involving the manifestation of deferred reactions to past trauma. This explains why Freud claimed that "hysterical patients suffer from reminiscences": these patients, invariably female, were seen as being tortured by traumatic memories (normally related to sexuality) that had not been sufficiently abreacted. In this regard, Jean Starobinski's remarks are illuminating:

> The characteristic disturbance in hysteria consists of a perturbation of the motor response, which, when delayed or deviated, cannot function properly. In adopting this conception of hysterical behavior, Freud subscribed to the widespread theory that explained cerebral functions according to a model based on physiological experiments involving the sensory-motor spinal reflex. At the time, the reflex notion was a guarantee of scientificity.[6]

The end of the nineteenth century witnessed a resurgence in the use of hypnosis as a recognized therapeutic practice, precipitated, on one hand, by Jean-Marie Charcot, and, on the other, by the Nancy School (including, among others, Ambroise-August Liébeault and Hippolyte Bernheim). Freud was well acquainted with both camps, having been a student of Charcot's as well as having personally translated works by Bernheim. The latter clearly regarded hypnosis as a technique of suggestion, which is why, as Ellenberger put it, "Bernheim taught that hypnosis was easier to induce in people accustomed

---

[6] STAROBINSKI, *Action and Reaction*, p. 185.

to passive obedience such as old soldiers or factory workers, among whom he had his best therapeutic successes. He had poor results with people of the higher and wealthier classes."[7] Indeed, it was precisely this suggestive character of hypnosis that would ultimately make it inadequate for the purposes Freud had in mind, namely the possibility of a reflexive understanding of the causal processes responsible for the traumatic situation. This is not to say that he sought the imaginary reenactment of trauma, per se, but rather a reflexive appropriation of its causal structure; not repetition, then, but self-reflection.

In this regard, Freud's most significant innovation was methodological in nature, and involved the recognition of the *subjectivity of meaning*. The method he used consisted in employing an interpretive principle built on a recognition of the uniqueness of each signifying context. Subsequently, interpretation could no longer depend on any sort of *a priori* schematic symbology (although Freud nevertheless acknowledged that dreams often evinced symbological aspects), but should instead allow for processes of contextual reconstruction in which the subject must play an active role. This was a radical departure; as Georges Politzer put it, "the idea that there could be a purely individual dialectic, to which individual acts would lend a purely individual meaning, [*while central to psychoanalysis,*] is one that is entirely foreign to classic psychology [...]."[8]

Freud would consequently abandon hypnosis in favor of free association. In the final analysis, free association may be regarded as a method for facilitating the reconstitution of signifying contexts. It is founded on an association theory whose roots belong to British empiricism (which deeply influenced Cabanis and Pinel, among others), as evidenced by the following remarks from Scottish philosopher David Hume:

> [Even] in our wildest and most wandering reveries, nay in our very dreams, we shall find, if we reflect, that the imagination ran not altogether at adventures, but that there was still a connexion upheld among the different ideas, which succeeded each other. Were the loosest and freest conversation to be transcribed, there would immediately be observed something, which connected it in all its transitions.[9]

---

[7]  ELLENBERGER, Henri; *The Discovery of the Unconscious: The History and Evolution of Dynamic Psychiatry*. London: Fontana Press, 1994, p. 87.

[8]  "[L'idée] qu'il pouvait y avoir une dialectique purement individuelle, à laquelle les actes individuels empruntent une signification purement individuelle, est totalement étrangère à la psychologie classique [...]." (POLITZER, Georges; *Critiques des fondements de la psychologie*. Paris: PUF, 2000, p. 102)

[9]  HUME, David; *An Inquiry Concerning Human Understanding*. New York: Oxford University Press, 2007, *p.* 23.

What the association of ideas demonstrates is that ultimately there is no such thing as a neurotic narrative devoid of some form of amnesia, repressed content or structured resistance to consciousness. Consequently, analysis may be construed as an interpretive art whose aim is the reconstruction of a causal structure previously ejected from the patient's consciousness. Hypnosis, conversely, cannot fail to conceal resistance, and is therefore incapable of uncovering what lies behind the operations of distortion which characterize symptoms.

Therefore, this context needs to be taken into account, if the development of transference as a concept is to be fully understood. The notion of reflexive symbolization had already provided Freud with sufficient material for the development of an initial form of psychotherapy; nevertheless, frequent use of the cathartic method led him to recognize the fundamental power inherent in imitation, or in bringing back past content to center stage for reenactment. Unsurprisingly, then, these notions jointly contributed to constituting the concept of transference.

Consequently, one aspect of transference can be inextricably linked to this foregrounding of past content which formed part of the cathartic method. In this regard it is helpful to recall Freud's remarks in "The Dynamics of Transference" (1912), where he reminds us that, due to a combination of natural constitution and early childhood experiences, the love life of each individual is determined in its own inimitable way, and so is the manner in which his or her drives are satisfied. Later, in "Observations on Transference-Love" (1915), Freud even metaphorically employed the photographic term *Abklatschen* (meaning "copies," or "simulacra") to describe transferential instances in which affective behavior is shaped by these elements.

These "copies" are ultimately the manifestation of a set of *fundamental relational structures* developed in the context of the first nucleus of socialization to which a subject is exposed, namely the family. They are formative images, in which there is significant libidinal investment, and they reflect the subject's relationship to maternal, paternal and fraternal figures. Beyond that, however, such images may also represent the "mixture in the patient's phantasy of the parents as one figure," as Melanie Klein reminds us.[10] Indeed, these *imagos* – to use a term favored by Freud which would go on to acquire great importance in the work of both Jung and Lacan – are fundamental modes of socialization and subjective organization whose characteristics determine the constitution of subjects.

---

[10] KLEIN, Melanie; "The Origins of Transference." In: *The International Journal of Psychoanalysis*, 33, 1952, p. 437.

Thus, transference simply consists in the process of bringing these formative images to center stage. This is feasible insofar as the therapeutic power exerted by the physician's personality derives precisely from his or her position as a blank canvas for the projection of images produced by the patient; images that actualize structures that are fundamental to the constitution of modes of relation. Thus, when Freud introduces the notion of "transference-love," a form of libidinal investment occasioned by a situation of transference between analysand and analyst, he stresses that the amorous condition is in reality *the reenactment of past occurrences* by the patient, a repetition of childhood reactions and fantasies that posits transference as a path leading to the infantile foundations of love.

Satisfactory analytic progress requires that this love that arises from transference must not be satisfied or reciprocated, but rather de-actualized, which means that the analyst must adopt a largely unresponsive position. This strategic silence, or ambiguous indifference, was intended to force the analysand to project with increasing intensity the infantile foundations of that love by means of which he or she seeks the total colonization of the other. Hence Freud's admonition:

> [The analyst] must keep firm hold of the transference-love, but treat it as something unreal, as a situation which has to be gone through in the treatment and traced back to its unconscious origins and which must assist in bringing all that is most deeply hidden in the patient's erotic life into her consciousness and therefore under her control [*Beherrschung*].[11]

And yet, analytic technique cannot entirely consist in the transferential projection of these images within the physician-patient relation, as though its single purpose were to reform malfunctioning socialization schemes in the affective life of certain neurotic subjects. In reality, familial authority figures must be actualized in the process of transference with a view to unveiling the source of their "power," namely the libidinal mechanisms which underpin them. That explains why transference must play this contradictory, dual role as both a necessary condition for, and a significant obstacle to, a cure. It is a necessary condition, on one hand, because it allows the structures that determine a subject's behavior and modes of desiring to receive undivided attention within the physician-patient relation. In this regard, Freud remarked that an important step in the analytic process is the transformation of neurosis

---

[11] FREUD, "Observations on Transference-Love," *S.E. Vol. XII*, p. 314.

into "transference-neurosis." And yet, on the other hand, transference is also undeniably a form of *resistance to analysis*, in the sense that the mere projection of those relational forms that cause the subject to experience suffering does not entail their deactivation; hence the need for an articulation between transference and an additional clinical process which, as we shall see, serves a largely complementary function.

## *Remembering, in a Freudian vein: bound to a philosophy of consciousness?*

An account of the complementary process in question may be found in one of Freud's major texts, *Remembering, Repeating and Working-through* (1914). In this work, Freud establishes that *remembering* and *repeating* are fundamentally dichotomous processes. While these notions may not initially appear dichotomous, Freud justifies his position through the fact that, in this particular context, repeating is essentially one of several forms of *forgetting* (alongside parapraxes, lapses, screen memories, etc.). The type of forgetting that is characteristic of repetition was seen as being deeply connected to transference, as if these images that colonize the doctor-patient relationship ultimately camouflaged some element essential for an adequate understanding of the patient's condition. Thus, in situations of this nature, instead of remembering relevant pathogenic complexes or pathological traces, subjects repeatedly act them out: the analysand reproduces such a fragment "not as a memory [*Erinnerung*] but as an action; he *repeats* it, without, of course, knowing that he is repeating it"[12], as though, to paraphrase Marx, patients knew not what they did.

Freud then makes recourse to the transformation of repeating into remembering wrought by the liquidation of transference. At the heart of this transformation lies the idea that, while transferential repetition is an important process, it is nevertheless reliant on a supplementary reflexive elaboration whose validity can be ensured solely by the notion of remembering. This elaboration fulfills Freud's stated desire for an "intelligible, consistent and unbroken case history." After all, "[whereas] the practical aim of the treatment is to remove all possible symptoms and to replace them by conscious thoughts, we may regard it as a second and theoretical aim to repair all the damage to the patient's memory [*Gedächtnisschäden*]"[13], a theoretical aim that brings to

---

[12] FREUD, "Remembering, Repeating and Working-Through," *S.E. Vol. XII*, p. 150.
[13] FREUD, "Fragment of an Analysis of a Case of Hysteria," *S.E. Vol. VII*, p. 18.

mind Derrida's assertion that memory "is not a psychical property among others; it is the very essence of the psyche [...]."[14]

This seems to suggest that Freud would agree with Deleuze's critical statement that "the less one remembers, the less one is conscious of remembering one's past, the more one repeats it – remember and work through the memory in order not to repeat it."[15] It is one of the reasons why Freud encouraged his patients not to make any important, life-altering decisions – in essence, not to act – while undergoing analysis; according to this argument, every action by an individual in a situation of analysis is an instance of transferential repetition (whether it takes place within the analytic setting or outside of it). In this sense, the handling of transference is intimately connected to an analysis of the patient's resistance to remembering, leading more than one psychoanalyst to conclude that, as Otto Fenichel memorably expressed it, resistance "distorts the true connections. The patient misunderstands the present in terms of the past; and then instead of remembering the past, he strives, without recognizing the nature of his action, to relive the past and to live it more satisfactorily than he did in childhood."[16]

So far, however, the reason why the constitution of a narrative should have the power to trigger curative processes remains elusive. We must refrain from relativizing the fact that, for Freud, remembering is a central mechanism within the paradigm that organizes the rationality of the psychoanalytic cure, and one of the most significant causes of its non-medicalized character. And yet the question needs to be asked, *is remembering simply a process of reorganization by an individual consciousness of previously-experienced events in the form of causal links in a narrative chain*, as effectively suggested by Freud's own clinical accounts? If that is the case, we need to ask ourselves too, whether remembering, as conceived by Freud, can consist in more than simply broadening the understanding of a consciousness; and whether remembering should be regarded, consequently, as a strategy to cure dissociations of consciousness through protocols of self-reflection. Cured of these dissociations, subjects would then be able to reorient their actions on the basis of a more complete apprehension of the motivations underpinning them, and of the true objects of their desires.

---

[14] DERRIDA, *Writing and Difference*, p. 252.
[15] DELEUZE, *Difference and Repetition*, p. 15.
[16] FENICHEL, Otto; *The Psychoanalytic Theory of Neurosis*. New York: Routledge, 2005, p. 26.

It is worth recalling how Freud unequivocally stated that, in the analytic process, "[what] we are in search of is a picture [*Bild*] of the patient's forgotten years that shall be both trustworthy and in all essential respects complete."[17] The importance of such a "trustworthy picture" does not derive, at least not exclusively, from the fact it allows for a totalization of the individual's subjective history, but from its ability to unveil the causal links responsible for turning seemingly banal occurrences into traumatic experiences that cannot be symbolized, or integrated into the individual's consciousness. In this context, the understanding of the causal chain to which a symptom belongs (in the sense of its integration into consciousness, its internalization – a meaning present in the German term *Erinnerung*) is seen as the very condition for its ceasing to manifest.

Describing these traumatic occurrences, Freud frequently employs physicalist language to describe the quanta of excitation or libidinal energy which, under these circumstances, the subject cannot tame through representational binding, and therefore is unable to master. We are familiar with Freud's account of traumatic events in connection with, for example, one of his most notorious cases, that of the "Wolf Man." This involved a case of obsessive neurosis, whereby Freud believed he had identified a primal scene (*Urszene*), witnessed by the patient at the age of eighteen months: the thrice repeated coupling of his parents in the manner of wolves, with his mother on all fours, *more ferarum*. This is a scene which would have been impossible to symbolize properly, on account of its incomprehensibility to a child of that age; however, because of the particular characteristics it involves (heavy breathing, moaning, seemingly violent motion, and so on), it mobilizes a quanta of libidinal energy that is not restrained by any form of representation, and which cannot be integrated except *a posteriori*. Fragmentary mnemonic traces are all that remain of the experience; shards to be reinscribed by a later context.

As we have established, the traumatic character of the scene is in reality an *a posteriori* construction. It was only through the subsequent association of the scene with later occurrences in the patient's life (his exposure to fairy tales in which children are devoured by wolves, the threat of castration that insinuated itself when he became sexually aroused from watching a maid clean the floor on her knees, etc.) that its traumatic sense was constructed, the specific turning point being a distressing dream at the age of four, in which wolves, crouching in a tree, watched him intently as he lay in bed. As Freud reminds us, in this particular case the primal scene was activated

---

[17] FREUD, "Constructions in Analysis," *S.E. Vol. XXIII*, p. 258.

(*Aktivierung*), rather than remembered,[18] and its activation could therefore be said to be associated with the establishing of a connection between the primal scene and the threat of castration. In this sense, the fantasy of the primal scene evinces, in the present as well as retroactively, "the child's introjection of adult erotism."[19]

In fact, strictly speaking, the act of remembering does not take place until the patient, under analysis and in a situation of transference, narrates his dream. Thus, we can discern three distinct stages: the fact as apprehended by the infant at the age of eighteen months, with its fragmentary inscription; the activation of the trauma following a dream at the age of four, which provided an *a posteriori* signifying context; and the patient's act of remembering under analysis at the age of twenty-nine. This retroactive temporality is fundamental in demonstrating how the trauma occurs when the event manifests for a second time; in other words, the construction of the traumatic incident is actually a two-stage process. The reoccurrence of the event takes place not in reality but in dreams, however, thus revealing its eminently phantasmal character.

Freud was keenly aware of the paradox involved in stating that the meaning of the traumatic occurrence cannot be established until it is remembered as part of the analytic process. It is almost as if the significant chronological distance separating the second and third stages of the constitution of the trauma could be regarded as negligible. However, this apparent negligibility is a direct result of one of Freud's central notions, which is that memory and the act of remembering are not the unveiling of formative, primal experiences, but rather the reinscription of past processes in light of the pressures exerted by a current situation. Indeed, remembering is in itself a curative process, as it provides the means for a reorganization of the present by integrating the opacities of the past (and much remains to be said regarding the precise meaning of the term "integration" in this context).

---

[18] Here, it is well worth recalling what Laplanche and Pontalis have written on the topic: "On the one hand, in the first stage, sexuality literally breaks in from outside, intruding forcibly into the world of childhood, presumed to be innocent, where it is encysted as a simple happening without provoking any defence reaction – not in itself a pathogenic event. On the other hand, in the second stage, the pressure of puberty having stimulated the physiological awakening of sexuality, there is a sense of unpleasure, and the origin of this unpleasure is traced to the recollection of the first event, an external event which has become an inner event, an inner 'foreign body', which now breaks out from within the subject." (LAPLANCHE, Jean & PONTALIS, J.-B.; "Fantasy and the Origins of Sexuality." In: BIRKSTED-BREEN, D., FLANDERS, S., and GIBEAULT, A. (eds.); *Reading French Psychoanalysis*. New York: Routledge, 2010, p. 316)

[19] LAPLANCHE & PONTALIS, *op. cit.*, p. 317.

## Memory and fantasy

Concerning the nature of the aforementioned opacity, let us first address a few supplementary points, beyond any issues related to excitation quanta. One of the sources of the opacity that is characteristic of traumatic events is the fact they have never been completely present. The fact that the primal scene is activated by purely phantasmal means already implies that we are no longer dealing with the dimension of facts as presented to an individual consciousness. For Freud, fantasizing is a process that is directly related to phylogeny. The fact that fantasies with remarkably similar content are experienced by a large number of unrelated individuals – in other words the dimension of fantasy is not one of irreplaceable singularity, but one of constant, schematic repetition – convincingly demonstrates, in Freud's view, that fantasies are essentially representations of past occurrences transmitted down through generations. Hence, it may even be said that no such thing as an individual fantasy exists, or perhaps that *within fantasies there is no such thing as an individual.* All fantasies are "social fantasies," trans-individual and supra-temporal processes that reemerge within individuals. Through fantasy, subjects encounter temporal layers whose scope transcends that of mere individual experience. Fantasy is thus a fundamental dimension of one's experience of historicity, as it is a space in which the promises of happiness that mobilized one's forebears – that mobilized the history of desires – can aspire to actualization. Therefore, fantasies may be understood as temporal layers condemned to retain their relative opacity, in that they present us with the problem of how to signify a desire that is not entirely our own (having originated with those who preceded us), yet which remains a significant part of our very constitutions.[20] As Deleuze observed, "even our childhood love for the mother repeats other adult loves with regard to other women, rather like the way in which the hero of *In Search of Lost Time* replays his mother Swann's passion for Odette."[21] Hence, the fact that the act of remembering fundamentally consists in the recollection of mnemonic traces reinscribed within fantasies is something that we cannot ignore.

At this point, it is useful to elaborate further on the "reality" of the primal scene. Freud openly resisted a definitive characterization of primal scenes as fully phantasmal in nature, furthermore insisting that the fact that such scenes manifest as dreams, and give rise to strong feelings of "conviction"

---

[20] It was no coincidence, then, that Lacan would find clear correspondences between the time of fantasy and the time of myth; on this notion, cf. LACAN, "The Neurotic's Individual Myth," translated by M. N. Evans. In: *Psychoanalytic Quarterly*, XLVIII (3), 1979, pp. 405-425.

[21] DELEUZE, *Difference and Repetition*, p. 17.

(*Überzeugung*) in the patient when presented by the analyst should suffice as evidence of their "utmost value." Taking the case of the "Wolf Man" as an example, Freud also stressed that the existence of an infantile neurosis accompanied by the constitution of a phobic object between the ages of four and five is a clear indication that an actual incident must have taken place in early infancy. Nevertheless, such an incident may turn out to have been no more than, say, the patient's chance encounter with copulating dogs as a child (and not necessarily a child of the age suggested by Freud, either), representing a first confrontation with sexual intercourse that would subsequently be projected onto the child's parents. The high regard in which he held that hypothesis led him to remark that he would rather "close the discussion of the reality [*Realwert*] of the primal scene with a *non liquet*."[22]

Nonetheless, a "question of method" remains: at the core of the phantasmal construction there must be an empirical fact of sufficient power to provoke a superlative degree of excitation, of which mnemonic fragments persist. Freud had a similar view of fantasies related to the threat of castration: actual events of this nature must have taken place at some point in humanity's historical past, leaving traces in the phylogenetic heritage of the entire species. However, at least in the former situation, the empirical fact cannot provide us with any sort of positive signifying principle, but merely with *an open question* produced by uncovering the contingent character of certain occurrences, an open question which will eventually have to be integrated into the subject's symbolic constructs. In other words, "traumatic events" ultimately appear to be bereft of any semblance of deterministic weight – they merely serve to prise open certain issues, nothing more.

This becomes abundantly clear when one recalls that such a reduction of past occurrences to the condition of traces to be reconstituted by fantasies – fantasies in which the weight of social dramas makes itself distinctly felt – is something that paves the way for Freud to insist on a unique method, peculiar to psychoanalysis, through which to gain mastery over the past. Freud began his argument by acknowledging the existence of certain limitations intrinsic to the process of remembering which are related to limitations inherent in memory itself as a record-keeping mechanism. Consequently, according to Freud, the patient can never recall his or her repressed content in its entirety; there is even a chance that precisely what is most essential for treatment is something that lies beyond the patient's powers of recollection. To clarify the matter further, he suggested that, in the course of analysis, primal scenes are not reproduced under the guise of recollecting a past occurrence; rather, they

---

[22] FREUD, "From the History of an Infantile Neurosis," *S.E. Vol. XVII*, p. 60.

result from a process of "construction," a consideration that illuminates the true character of remembering as conceived by Freud. In other words, with regard to the analyst's role in constructing memories, Freud makes it clear that remembering must be understood as a productive compositional process. In this context, the thoughts of scientific historian Israel Rosenfield on the nature of memories are highly relevant:

> Memories are not fixed but are constantly evolving generalizations – re-creations – of the past, that give us a sense of continuity, a sense of being, with a past, a present and a future.[23]

This is an aspect of Freud's clinical approach of which Lacan was in full command, as the following excerpt illustrates:

> History is not the past. History is the past in so far as it is historicised in the present – historicised in the present because it was lived in the past. [...] [The] fact that the subject relives, comes to remember, in the intuitive sense of the word, the formative events of his existence, is not in itself so very important. What matters is what he reconstructs of it. [...] I would say – when all is said and done, it is less a matter of remembering than of rewriting history.[24]

Such statements fully support Freud's perspective (and even the history-related problems discussed in Chapter III might usefully be approached in this vein). Indeed, Israel Rosenfield argued convincingly that Freud had been fully cognizant of the fragmentary and ambiguous character of mnemonic images. In any case, these images are not stored away as impressions of things, and the processes of displacement and condensation that are so characteristic of oneiric formations may be said to derive precisely from their fragmentary character. Thus, it is not a lack of context that causes dreams to rework and over-determine memories, but the fact that memories are stored as fragments. In this sense, the actualization of a memory could never be the direct manifestation of fully-formed stored content. Instead, it is a process of meaning construction which aims to meet demands imposed by a current situation. In one of the most significant texts ever written on the Freudian conception of memory, Derrida alludes to and clarifies this notion in the following passage:

---

[23] ROSENFIELD, Israel; *The Invention of Memory: A New View of the Brain*. New York: Basic Books, 1988, p. 76.
[24] LACAN, *Seminar I*, pp. 12-14.

The conscious text is [...] not a transcription, because there is no text *present elsewhere* as an unconscious one to be transposed or transported. [...] There is then no unconscious truth to be rediscovered by virtue of having been written elsewhere. There is no text written and present elsewhere which would then be subjected, without being changed in the process, to an operation and a temporalization (the latter belonging to consciousness if we follow Freud literally) which would be external to it, floating on its surface.[25]

If there is no text present elsewhere, that is because memory is not a filing system, but a ceaseless process of interpretation; and memories, previously thought immutable, are actually continuously-rearranged reconstitutions of the past. Memories, in other words, are not discrete mnemonic units that endure throughout time; instead, what we have is a dynamic system that integrates mnemonic traces into relations established *a posteriori*, in accordance with current perspectives.[26] In view of this, it becomes clear that the past was never a "present that has passed." The past is a dimension within which we have the experience of being inhabited by open questions that emerge from a virtual temporality. According to Freud, humankind never lives entirely in the present, and the history of a subject's desire shows this assertion to be valid for the past as well ("the past was never completely present").

An important question arises here, however, which concerns the apparent proximity between the clinical processes of remembering and fantasy production: could the process of construction itself be regarded as a product of the analyst's fantasy, at least to some extent? And would it not be fair to say that this reconstructive character of remembering provides strong evidence to support the view that the curative power of analysis, even as Freud understood it, is essentially one of suggestion? In his text "Constructions in Analysis" (1937), Freud reminds us that even constructions of a delusional or hallucinatory character contain some "historical truth" derived from the subject's past experiences. Can the same be said of analytic constructions?

The general role played by construction in articulating the history of desire indicates that individual history is itself a mode of participation in a symbolic social universe from which experiences of meaning can be derived, as if the

---

[25] DERRIDA, *Writing and Difference*, p. 265.

[26] Considerations that led Rosenfield to remark, following Freud, that, in reality, "we are all 'redoing' the past, and an act of repetition must be understood not as an act symbolizing a specific past event but rather as a whole history of attempts at recapturing the past, a history that is being put into a specific context at a given moment when the repetition is occurring [...]." (ROSENFIELD, *op. cit.*, p. 80)

history of the individual repeated, in its own way, the general history of the symbol. In this sense, the specificity of Freud's perspective derives from his insistence that the general history can only be correctly read as a modulation of the Oedipus complex and of the theories of infantile sexuality. This could easily lead us to understand the Freudian clinic as a process for the disciplinary reorganization, based on the Oedipus complex, of the subject's relation to his or her own body and desire.

Freud maintained that constructions in analysis were more than mere suggestions, and that they had what could be termed objective truth insofar as they could lead a subject to new, construction-engendering processes of remembering. This argumentative strategy, which essentially depends on the effectiveness of the process by means of which associations between ideas are developed for its validity, may seem rather flimsy. After all, analytic constructions are not the only kind which have proved advantageous in the development of associations between ideas. Their apparent effectiveness might be connected to nothing more than their ability to reinforce existing schemes for desire socialization that underlie the constitution of subjects, unless it is possible to show that, within the conceptual framework developed by Freud, one can find the idea that the act of remembering, in actualizing fantasies and complexes, creates a space wherein singular reinscriptions of something formerly inscribed as no more than a mnemonic trace may occur. Such reinscriptions may be qualified as "singular" because they lead the subject to confront the radically unstable character of the significations present in fantasies and complexes, an instability which, while not powerful enough to dissolve them, is more than sufficient to destabilize their effects. In this sense, the notion of remembering is freed from its assumed character as the unveiling of formerly-established and still fully-operational causal structures. Instead, it should be regarded as something closer to a means of dissolving closed causalities through repeated reinscriptions. In other words, *there is a performativity inherent to every act of remembering.*

Thus, in remembering, the "Wolf Man" can do more than simply uncover the existence of a neurotic bond between the sex act, castration anxiety, and a phantasmal identification with the father figure (and which stems from a process of association which has the signifier "wolf" at its core). He was also able to fully comprehend how the manner in which he brought his phantasmal identification with the father and the signifier "wolf" to bear on one another at a deep level represented an attempt to inscribe his familial problems within the trans-individual experience that the historically-laden polysemy of the signifier "wolf" was able to provide. It could be argued that the aim of such an attempt was to create a breach in subjective time which allowed an otherwise inaccessible – on account of its being mostly opaque to the form of experience typical of an individual – trans-individual memory to be made manifest. Deleuze and Guattari emphasized this particular aspect of the case when they wrote about Freud's patient's unsuccessful attempts to heed the call to "become-wolf"[27], as if the subject's identification with the perpetually-roaming wolf pack encompassed, among other things, the aforementioned attempt to inscribe familial conflicts peculiar to the formation of the personality into depersonalized processes. This is especially so in view of the fact that, if we accept Freud's interpretation that the wolves are representations of the father, we would have to admit that it involves a distortion of not only the usual signification of "wolves" but also of "father" as well. An exploration of the meaning behind an attempt of this nature might have been a more fruitful strategy for the analysis in question, which, sadly, instead became a prime example of what an unsuccessful, interminable analysis looks like – the embodiment of "bad infinity" at its most characteristic.

Freud often compared the analytic work of construction to an archeological process. Yet ruins, according to Hegel, were not merely remnants of a present that has passed, of a time that once existed yet of which only traces now remain, but proof that time was always inhabited by a certain restlessness which undermines the possibility of full presence. This intuition of Hegel's finds a parallel in certain uses of remembering authorized by Freud's theoretical constructions. It leads us to a rather peculiar use of the notion of remembering that places Freud's reflections entirely outside the boundaries of any philosophy for which memory is the fundamental process through which individual consciousness unifies its temporal experience. In other words, if psychoanalysis tends to be separate from any form of philosophy of consciousness, it may be said to be a direct consequence of the particular use of remembering by Freud discussed above.

## Lenin's fantasy and the arduous production of a dress

We can now attempt to provide an answer for the question posed at the beginning of this chapter, namely: under what conditions would it be permissible to perceive the rituals of the obsessive-compulsive individual, or the self-defensive destruction of one's own desire, or the symptoms that

---

[27] Cf. DELEUZE, Gilles & GUATTARI, Felix; *A Thousand Plateaus: Capitalism and Schizophrenia*, translated by B. Massumi. Minneapolis: University of Minnesota Press, 1987, pp. 28-29.

characterize conversion disorder, and so on, as symptoms of one's *inability to remember* those processes by means of which one's subjectivity was constituted? As has become clear, the problem does not concern pressure exerted by repressed mental contents and intentional dispositions "present elsewhere," outside the sphere of consciousness, which are supposedly constitutive of action nuclei no longer recognizable by the ego. In reality, these symptoms, inhibitions and anxieties must be taken as signs of the patient's inability to see the dimension of fantasy as anything other than a defense mechanism against impasses that result from the very structures that determine his or her desires and constitute his or her individuality.

The classic psychoanalytic definition of fantasy is that it represents a form of defense against anxiety: when an anxious state develops as a result of an inability to determine the object of one's desire, fantasy manifests as the process that produces the necessary determination. In this sense, its temporality is the temporality of the repetition of that very process. Fantasies may uncover a different temporality, however, which as far as consciousness is concerned, is as yet formless. Determining the object of desire thus remains an impossible task, unless one learns to recognize its negative character.

Donald Winnicott described a clinical case that helps to illuminate this point more clearly. It concerned a woman in her fifties who came to the sudden realization that the life she had built for herself was one in which "nothing that was really happening was fully significant to her." Winnicott described her as having become "one of the many who do not feel that they exist in their own right as whole human beings," on account of a dissociation from what was actually "the main part of her," and which lived a separate, phantasmal existence.[28]

Within her rich fantasy life, an existence shielded from any sort of confrontations with concrete situations, she was able to maintain her delusions of omnipotence; and yet, as she eventually came to realize, whenever she fantasized she was not really herself, but an other. Winnicott ascribed the etiology of this dissociative condition to situations experienced in early childhood, in which the patient – who was the youngest in the family and had many older siblings – had to internalize "a world that was already organized before she came into the nursery," in order to relate to the other children[29] Thus, when she played with her siblings, she was playing "other people's games," activities she performed while engaged in the act of fantasizing. In this dissociative state, she could "watch herself playing the other children's

---

[28] WINNICOTT, D. W.; *Playing and Reality*. New York: Routledge, 2009, pp. 39-40.
[29] *Ibid.*, p. 38.

games as if watching someone else in the nursery group,"[30] meaning that the patient, trapped by the gaze of the Other, was constrained to play a game whose rules had no relevance to her personally. Fantasizing, in this case, could be regarded as a defense mechanism against something in her desire that was struggling to be released from the game.

However, at some point when she was in an ambiguous state between dreaming and fantasizing, the patient produced a scenario that would prove essential for the progression of her analysis; in it, she saw herself desperately struggling with the arranging and cutting out of a length of fabric she had been trying to shape into a dress. She found the activity exasperating. Winnicott's interpretation of this revolved around the notion of "formlessness": viewed as a dream, the scenario suggested to him that "[her] childhood environment did not allow her to be formless but instead, as she experienced it, patterned and shaped her into forms conceived by other people."[31] After hearing this interpretation, the patient experienced intense feelings relating to the notion that, from her perspective, there had been no one in her childhood able to understand that "she had to begin in formlessness." As her analysis progressed, this mediation through formlessness was recognized as the means through which she could stop the dissociative fantasizing that alienated her from her own existence. In other words, it gave her the means to overcome a situation of anxiety in which (as Lacan once put it) "the lack is lacking."

By the end of the last session recounted by Winnicott, the patient appeared to be divided. On one hand, she felt that finally she could "be in charge" of herself, that is, to undo the primary diremption between her empty external life and the omnipotence she felt while fantasizing. On the other, she seemed nostalgic for the certainty provided by her illness; the sense of security that, while there was nothing to look forward to (as her fantasizing was not really her own and did not bear any relation to her actual life, which consequently grew emptier by the day), the omnipotent character of her phantasmal productions made this emptiness completely bearable. Her awareness of this new situation precipitated a state of deep anxiety, she had now reached a point at which entirely new games, whose rules were still unclear, would have to be played. Hers was the anxiety of one suddenly tasked with producing dresses tailored to fit nothing less than formlessness itself.

What can this particular case tell us in light of the elaborations on fantasy presented above? Let us attempt to contextualize these elaborations with reference to one of the fundamental principles of Freudian metapsychology,

---

[30] *Ibid.*, p. 39.
[31] *Ibid.*, pp. 45-46.

namely that psychic life finds its structure in repetition. "Repetition," here, entails more than just habitual, regularly reoccurring behavior; indeed, it is in the dimension of fantasy that the fundamental core of those repetitions that constitute psychic life may be found. Fantasy is thus directly responsible for a means of temporal synthesis. And yet, precisely because of that, it is through fantasy that the true character of individual actions is revealed, allowing them to unfold into series of past actions that transcend the individual and become a mode of actualization for social histories. The desire for the destruction of desire that torments certain obsessive individuals, for instance, may be seen as the actualization of conflicts that have subsisted throughout whole series of individualities. Lacan had this in mind when he suggested that at least two generations are required for the production of a psychotic individual; a dramatic way of reminding us that there is nothing more effective than our fantasies in demonstrating how every action cannot help but be trans-individual, and how every single desire conceals a multiplicity of desires.

However, to reductively regard actions as no more than the sheer repetition of fantasies is essentially to submit them to the rules of "the other people's game," a game repeatable *ad infinitum*. We know that memory is not a filing system, but a ceaseless process of reinscription and reorganization of fragments of the past. Could the same be said of fantasies? Do subjects possess the power to turn fantasies into the actualization of a multiplicity no longer subjected to alienating repetition? If so, that might explain why Lacan insisted that fantasy was the only means of accessing the reality of the drive which, through fantasy, seems capable of causing an individual's entire organizational structure to unravel.[32] It could perhaps be argued that this access results from an alteration in the nature of fantasy: once merely a narcissistic defense against anxiety, fantasy becomes the means for opening up individuality to the experience of un-identity. Furthermore, the ensuing production of an *unheimliche* position might suffice to deactivate the narcissistic structure that fantasy sustains.

We could say that, in this particular case, it is through recourse to fantasy that past conflicts could once again be made present, every action therefore being imbued with potential historical density. Fantasies are our history. Yet what if history has always been unstable in regards to its meaning; what if "other people's games" have always been haunted by a dimension of unclear rules, a dimension wherein one therefore has to *make* one's own rules? At this point, it seems pertinent to ask what led Winnicott's patient to grow so attached to "other people's games" in the first place; what was it about others that struck her as essential for the sustenance of her own desire. Could it be

---

[32] Cf. LACAN, *Autres écrits*. Paris: Editions du Seuil, 2001, p. 326.

that behind alienation a hope for *separation* lay hidden, because this separation would allow her to uncover in the other the very formlessness underlying her own constitution? What if "other people's games" were so constituted as to furnish moments of wide openness, moments in which neither she nor the other knew the rules governing the movements to come? What if it were in the nature of every fantasy to be on the brink of losing itself, or changing its polarity, and abandoning all of its narcissistic traces to allow a multiplicity of voices to be heard, and to create a composite temporality from inextricably-linked layers of time?[33] Fantasy, in that case, could be viewed as a mode of repetition whose function is to allow one to hear the instability of the voices of others within one's own voice – similarly to Lenin, who distinctly heard the French Jacobins while toasting the Russian revolution.

---

[33] This is a hypothesis I had not been aware of at the time of writing *A paixão do negativo: Lacan e a dialética* (Unesp, 2006); hence, the problem of fantasy is revisited here from a different perspective, one which, while not invalidating what I wrote many years ago, unveils degrees of complexity inherent in the notion of fantasy that were beyond my grasp at the time.

CHAPTER VIII

# On the political power of the inhuman

*Man is that which is in relation to his end,*
*in the fundamentally equivocal sense of the word.*
Jacques Derrida

*When the founders of the Humanist Union invited me*
*to become a member, I replied that "I might possibly be willing to join*
*if your club had been called an inhuman union, but I could not join one*
*that calls itself 'humanist.'"*
Theodor Adorno

If we accept: (a) the general consequences that follow from the mode of reflection on the nature of the subject presented in the first two parts of this book; as well as (b) the demands that recognition theory must consequently be able to meet, how are we to conceive of the practical dimension of rationality? Or, more specifically: once the rational normativity dependent on transcendental determinations of free will is removed as a reference point, for instance, what grounds remain for reflections on the morality of an action? Once we accept the proposed articulation between modes of psychic synthesis and historical trans-individuality, and thereby the proposed limitation to the modern conception of individual, how are we to understand the motive forces that drive rational deliberation?

These questions as yet remain unanswered. Trying to do so exclusively through recourse to Lacan and Adorno would be undeniably complex, especially because the historically-rooted diagnosis common to both theorists prevents them from appealing to supplementary strategies such as, for example, a defense of the existence of socially-shared rational practices to guide life's processes of material reproduction. The theory they both espouse concerning the alienating character of subjectivities, centers on the figure of the ego as the fundamental principle underlying psychic synthesis. This in turn prevents them from appealing to some form of moral development theory (as is the case with Habermas' recourse to Lawrence Kohlberg and Jean Piaget) or to the notion that social recognition could be attained through individual maturational processes (as Honneth did, based on Donald Winnicott's work), theoretical models capable of providing morality with an ontogenetic foundation.

The present segment of this book aims to show that, regardless of these limitations, and contrary to long held belief, neither Lacan nor Adorno leads us to some form of moral nihilism or irreducible aporia in regard to the practical dimension. Rather, they provide useful models for the construction of a theory of action which, being no longer dependent on what we have termed the "egological reduction of the subject," possesses great significance for both moral and social philosophy.

Thus, such questions will be addressed in the following chapters. The strategy employed differs slightly from the one relied on in the preceding pages, however. Additional questions will also be considered which, while undeniably autonomous, are nonetheless closely connected with the problems unearthed by the investigation conducted thus far. In this chapter, general considerations on certain aspects of the critique of humanism will be put forward, which should allow us to reach a better understanding of what was truly at stake in Lacan's attempts to reflect on moral action through the figure of Antigone and her conflict-ridden relationship with Theban law. Subsequently, in chapter IX, the contemporary discussion about the political uses of he category of recognition will be contextualized in detail. A discussion of this assessment should provide us with the necessary conditions for understanding possible political uses of a concept of recognition reconstructed by a articulation between psychoanalysis and adornian critical theory. Thus, let us begin by tracing the path that leads from a discussion of the inhuman to Antigone.

Before this chapter begins in earnest, it may prove beneficial to recall what was stated in the introduction to this book, primarily to illuminate its central strategy more clearly. One of the fundamental presuppositions of this work is that problems unearthed by the critique of humanism may give rise to an increase in the number of potential political applications of the concept of recognition, a feat accomplished by freeing it from the shackles of the communicational paradigm. Indeed, this unshackling is sorely needed, as the aforementioned paradigm, precisely because of its excessive reliance on the entification of the limits imposed by the grammar of common sense, has become dependent on the normative horizon present in our forms of life (and against which, therefore, our critical efforts ought to be directed), a horizon which is in turn excessively dependent on the limits of an anthropology we can only qualify as "humanist". Hence, the present chapter examines what is to be understood by this overused yet under-defined term.

For that reason, the focus of the problem of recognition must gradually shift away from the *recognition of alterity* towards the *recognition of that which suspends the regime of social normativity that makes us completely dependent on a ceaseless reproduction of the current figure of "man."* The aforementioned shift, which is simply the transition from alterity to abnormativity, should provide us with the means of reconstructing the notion of freedom that extricates it from the juridical-normative paradigm (a paradigm which favors a conception of freedom based on the predication of positive rights, the latter being dependent on juridical ordering for their potential ratification). Reconceived in this fashion, freedom becomes that which connects us to the unconditionality of a non-substantial universality. In other words, *freedom may be conceived as a form of reconciliation through which an individual's actions, and any attendant pathos, become expressions of a need whose universal validity can now attain full recognition.*

It is clear we have come a long way from the autarchic conception of freedom as equivalent to some form of individual free will. To conceive it instead as the mere acceptance of modes of conduct determined by normativities that aspire to universal validity, however, is not the point. Freedom is an individual decision which enables one to determine, by means of an action carried out within the social fabric, the mode of application of such normativities. As the action in question is above all a *social* action, its sense and significance can only be ascertained *a posteriori*, through the unfolding of its consequences within the life of society. One cannot tell whether a decision, or a chosen mode of application, has been truly "successful" until its impact upon social life has been properly gauged, or to put it more simply, one can only tell whether or not one has acted freely *a posteriori*, just as it is only possible to know *a posteriori* whether or not one's actions have been moral. While the absence of conscious intentionality more than suffices as a criterion by which to qualify an action as neither moral nor free, it must be stressed that the presence of conscious intentionality alone is not enough to determine whether one's actions are free or otherwise. From this chapter onwards, we shall have occasion to dwell on what such considerations entail.

## A humanity freed from the figure of "man"

By now it has probably become obvious that this book's recourse to Hegel, Lacan and Adorno is chiefly intended to delineate the general contours of a new type of subject with characteristics derived from this as yet underexplored dialectic tradition. This is a strategy that could be criticized on the grounds that, in its insistence on indeterminacy, depersonalization, and a critique of the ego and of egological reduction, it seems to do little more than underscore the common diagnosis that the present age is one in which the *humanity* of human beings has been examined to exhaustion. One of the fundamental components of the philosophical project of modernity is the specific image of humanity it has forged, an image perceived as the essential quality underlying all that is properly human. This is seen as its fundamental legacy, especially considering how possibilities for the social actualization of the humanity of human beings are tasked with providing a stable horizon with which to regulate what is to be understood as a free and just society. Such a society would be capable of providing the institutional conditions required for carrying out a project that humankind has set itself, whose aim is to allow the self to manifest through fundamental attributes and, in doing so, render viable the implementation of a fully-determined human essence. We have grown to expect these attributes to be given the juridical form of general rights, and have therefore become accustomed to seeing any perceived hindrances to this process as the very foundation of our political struggles, our moral demands, and even of the critical strategies we employ when dealing with what exists. Indeed, in what may be regarded as the founding moment of political modernity, namely the adoption of the Declaration of the Rights of Man and Citizen in August of 1789 – a document whose opening paragraph unequivocally states the main objective of social life to be the maintenance of general happiness – one already finds complete social implementation of the attributes that define the humanity of human beings as the ultimate aim of political action, and its proper evaluative criterion.

Nevertheless, the present era seems to be inching closer, instead, to the kind of dissolution described by Michel Foucault: "As the archaeology of our thought easily shows, man is an invention of recent date. And one perhaps nearing its end. If those arrangements were to disappear as they appeared [...], then one can certainly wager that man would be erased, like a face drawn in sand at the edge of the sea"[1] – in other words, the complete erosion of the humanity of humankind and all of its lofty aspirations to social rationalization. With these words, written nearly fifty years ago, Foucault seemed to be hinting

---

[1] FOUCAULT, *The Order of Things*, p. 422.

at a potential liberation, whose attainment depended on our accepting the inexorable disappearance of "man" as resignedly as we accept the breaking of the waves. However, rather than a form of *liberation*, we tend to regard the death of "man" as the utter *liquidation* of the potentialities of the political, a liquidation which favors the entification of what Foucault termed "modern technologies of power that take life as their objective," processes of societal control which have at their foundation the biopolitical management of bodies, and the colonization of desire through sexuality-management apparatus. Still, is this reason enough to resurrect that "edifying discourse" which presents humanism as conducive to the practical attainment of the conditions required so that the humanity of humankind may be asserted? Is it really true that only two paths lead to our intended destination, namely a defense of humanism or, failing that, a passive acceptance of biopolitical management (which, thanks to contemporary technological advances, has attained prodigious dimensions)? What if it could be shown that these two seemingly disparate positions are not only closely allied, but equally deserving of criticism?

This is precisely what will be attempted here, in light of what has been discussed above regarding subject theory. In order to do so, we need to rethink the notion of subject using fundamental aspects of a critique of humanism common to French intellectual circles in the 1960s, a mode of thought particularly significant to the work of Derrida, Foucault and Deleuze (albeit for different reasons, and therefore eliciting very different results). All three authors chose to examine the same problem, one whose lucid articulation by Derrida carried echoes of a perspective common to both Nietzsche and Heidegger: "[The] history of the concept of man is never examined. Everything occurs as if the sign 'man' had no origin, no historical, cultural, or linguistic limit"[2], nor, it could be added, a metaphysical limit. And yet, ignoring whatever restrictions prevented the aforementioned examination, these authors announced that the subject, as a regulative category, had finally collapsed.

Conversely, authors more closely aligned with the dialectical tradition such as Lacan and Adorno would see this conundrum as a *moment* to be sublated (in the sense of being subjected to a process of negation that nevertheless preserves that which has been negated) through a renewal of the theory of the subject. This is evident in the fact that neither Lacan nor Adorno abandoned the figure of the acting subject at any point, although they also refused any attempts at regulating this agency on the basis of concepts engendered so as

---

[2] DERRIDA, "The Ends of Man," in *Margins of Philosophy*, p. 116. Much remains to be said, of course, regarding the fact that discussions about the notion of subject that feature transcendental resolutions seem dependent on a particular form of anthropology.

to portray the humanity of humankind as having already been actualized. Ultimately, their purpose was to free human agency from the bonds of a "philosophy of consciousness", which might explain why Lacan developed the seemingly contradictory category of a "subject of the unconscious".

The central point here is that it is precisely because these authors did not believe that the humanity of humankind had already come to be actualized that we can find in every single one of them (for different reasons, it bears repeating) a *defense of the inhuman*. What is meant by this is a defense of the idea that one's capacity to confront the inhuman, in other words that which lies within the subject, yet does not possess a human form, is the ultimate requirement for the regulation of any and all political action whose aim is to meet general demands for emancipation. However, it is undeniable that we have learned to associate the notion of the inhuman with the sphere of historical catastrophes, to the point where it seems as though the gates of destructive violence or normative dissolution could be thrown wide open as soon as one forgets what humankind is supposed to be, what its essential attributes are, and what predicates determine it. Under those circumstances, to once again encounter the identitarian image of "man" as a recognizable human face is reassuring, inclining one to believe that, if the image was absent, nothing could ensue but utter chaos, and the irrevocable ruin of all projects of social rationalization. It could hardly be otherwise, considering that reason is more than simply that which orients one's judgment, but rather a normativity whose aim is to produce a *form of life* within which the complete determination of the humanity of humankind may be attained. Nonetheless, it must be agreed that this is a rather limited way of thinking; after all, it is precisely in one's capacity to recognize oneself in that which is devoid of human identity that the basis for a non-normative, renewed determination of reason may be found. To bring about the actualization of a *humanity freed from the image of "man"* could potentially provide a new outlook for our political struggles as well as for the critical strategies we direct at what exists.

## Autonomy, authenticity and unity

So that there remains no doubt as to why a critique of humanism is necessary, we must first acquaint ourselves with exactly who this "man" is who is being dissolved into nothingness, and what one can actually expect from this irreversible historical process.

It could be said that this "man" – this human figure being eroded away on the sea shore – is above all a locus wherein one finds three attributes traditionally used to define the humanity of humankind, the meaning and significance of which are inextricable from the very development of modern thought. The first of these is individual *autonomy* in both will and behavior. Autonomy is understood here as being directly related to the ability of subjects to establish their own moral law, and thus to become moral agents capable of self-rule.

Subjects that have become their own legislators are, on one hand, subjects capable of *self-determination*. This is a crucial notion, in that it brings to that which is human a movement characteristic of what is often termed the "first substance" (*substantia prima*), namely that of being its own cause, *causa sui*. Autonomous subjects are capable of self-determination because that which causes their actions is immanent to them – a product of their freedom - rather than something extrinsic to their constitution. And yet, precisely because they are autonomous, subjects are on the other hand capable of rational deliberation within the safety of their own *interiority*, a "tribunal of the mind" wherein it is possible for one to transcend one's own inclinations and desires and maintain sufficient distance from one's own actions – whether these are actualized or merely potential – to judge them on the basis of the same self-imposed law that makes one a subject.

Furthermore, because they are capable of self-judgment and rational deliberation, and thus of rejecting desires that they regard as irrational or immoral, it is always possible for subjects to have acted differently to how they actually acted; they may therefore be said to be *imputable*, and thus be held morally responsible for everything they do or desire. This explains why individuals who lack autonomy (for example due to insanity, or to not having yet developed the psychological faculties required for autonomous thought and behavior, as is the case with children) are not considered legally responsible for their actions.

If the first attribute without which humankind is less than human is autonomy, the second is *authenticity*, a category underlying subjective expectations in regard to the expression of one's autonomous *individuality* within the social spheres of labor and language. Traditionally, it is authenticity that allows a subject to recognize him or herself in, and be recognized by, exteriority as an irreplaceable individuality capable of self-production and self-expression in his or her own particular *style*. What is meant here by "style" is, in the words of Granger, a "mode of integration of the individual into a concrete process, which is labor, and which is necessarily present in all forms of practice."[3] Such individualities are believed to be able to give form, through the singularity of their style, to something whose reality has been exclusively linked to that intentionality found in the irreducibility of pure interiority. In this sense, authenticity is the attribute that ensures that a *principle of expressibility* legitimately exists between the potentialities of one's singular individuality and the intersubjective exteriority of the spheres of labor and language.

It is clear that the aforementioned attributes taken together produce a tense state of affairs, whose eventual resolution must be sought precisely within the humanity of humankind. Once this tension is dissociated, it engenders two separate models of freedom: one based on moral autonomy; the other on individual authenticity. To conceive of a way to overcome this diremption is perhaps the most significant challenge currently facing moral philosophy, to the extent where the effort involved in overcoming it underlies much of its current development.[4]

Having accepted the importance of this undertaking, our attention should now turn to the third and final attribute on which the determination of the humanity of humankind depends: the *reflexive unity* of that which is self-aware. This reflexive unity, which places subjects on the firm ground of *self-identity*, ensures not only that all of one's mental representations can be recognized as being *one's own*, but also provides a foundation for the coherence of one's personality, a characteristic without which psychological development as we understand it – a process in which each singular moment is a stage in the unfolding of one and the same identity – would not be possible. Several factors can undo this unity, including a number of symptoms, for example machinelike automatism, which render one incapable of recognizing one's own inner self. What remains, in such cases, is something along the lines of an authenticity which can no longer assert itself. In this regard, it is helpful to recall how, in Freud's work, the unconscious is chiefly the domain of *das Es* – of the *id*, to use Strachey's Latinized translation – a psychic instance invariably apprehended as a foreign body within the self, as something that stubbornly refuses to submit to the determinations of the first person singular, and remains ensconced within the indeterminate third person. Nevertheless, it initially appears that ruptures of this nature are pathological situations, and that these could be overcome through the constitution of more flexible unities, provided that the latter are no less effective in their capacity for synthesis.

---

[3] GRANGER, Gilles-Gaston; *Essai d'une philosophie du style*. Paris: Éditions Odile Jacob, 2de. éd., 1988, p. 8.

[4] We have already encountered a few examples of what the hypostatization of these two models of freedom might entail in the discussions of Hegel's philosophy of right that appear in Chapter II. Cf. also HONNETH, *Suffering from Indeterminacy*, p. 45.

The fact that autonomy, authenticity, and unity – along with all the other concepts that can be derived from these, such as imputability, self-determination, individuality, style, interiority, and self-identity – are regarded as the cardinal attributes of the humanity of humankind, largely explains why these very terms constitute elements in the regulating criteria for the various fields of reflection that have human action as their chosen object. It is no coincidence that "autonomy," for example (and this is of course also true of its direct opposite, "alienation"), is an unavoidable term for both moral and political philosophy, for clinical psychology and psychiatry,[5] and for aesthetics (whose very inception as a field of reflection is inextricable from discussions about the autonomy of works of art and the subsequent advent of the notion of autonomous form).

The same can be said for "authenticity," a key value in regards to both aesthetic reflection and the formulation of a critique of the stereotyped representation of the sphere of labor put into circulation by the type of social critique that arose in the wake of the events of May 1968. This critique is characterized – as sociologists Luc Boltanski and Eve Chiapello have aptly demonstrated[6] – by demands for a reinvention of social practices on the basis of values such as creativity, pleasure and the power of the imagination, as well as for an unqualified end to uniformity. The notion of authenticity also makes its presence felt in the political arena, when the so-called "spontaneity" of the masses and of social movements is referred to as though it were a regulative value. Likewise, clinical attempts to deal with and describe psychic distress often make use of what might be termed hindrances to authenticity, as is the case with the notion of "empty speech" favored by Lacan.[7] Finally, the polysemy of the term "unity" is self-evident, and points to the same factor that causes these terms to reappear within different,

---

[5] An essential dimension Michel Foucault's work is his exploration of the fundamental tenets of modern psychiatry through the thinking of its founders, Philippe Pinel and William Tuke. As Foucault demonstrated, psychiatric practices are oriented by diagnostic analyses having at their core regulative notions such as "autonomous will" (as opposed to an "alienated will"). On these questions, cf. FOUCAULT, *Psychiatric Power* (Macmillan, 2006).

[6] Cf. BOLTANSKI & CHIAPELLO, *The New Spirit of Capitalism* (Verso, 2007), an important work which includes a convincing demonstration that the deregulation of the sphere of labor and the transformation of notions like "flexibility," "risk," and "continual improvement" into justification mechanisms for the capitalist *ethos* are intimately connected to the absorption by capitalism of a critique developed on the basis of demands for authenticity which gained momentum as a result of the events of May 1968 in France. The authors refer to it as the "artistic critique," because it was connected to attempts to actualize a bohemian way of life through articulations of the general disenchantment felt in relation to the sphere of labor and denunciations of its perceived inauthenticity.

[7] On the role of demands for authenticity in the relation between subject and language in Lacanian psychoanalysis, cf. DEWS, Peter; "The Truth of the Subject: Language, Validity and Transcendence in Lacan and Habermas," in DEWS, P. & CRITCHLEY, S. (eds.), *Deconstructive Subjectivities*. Albany: State University of New York Press, 1996, pp. 149-168.

seemingly autonomous, fields of knowledge and practices: regardless of context, whenever the question at stake involves the notion of "man" we are invariably faced with the same horizon of validation and judgment.

It is nevertheless appropriate that autonomy, authenticity and unity should be the fundamental attributes of the humanity of "man," as they are attributes that humankind shares, in a sense, with the divine being, as traditionally conceived: "man", that very figure of the human that is a product of the philosophical project of disenchanted modernity, was supposedly made in the image and likeness of God. Unsurprisingly, the traits shared by these very different beings are precisely those that provide regulative criteria: being *causa sui* (autonomy); denying any irreducible difference between potency and act (authenticity); and remaining self-identical throughout myriad potential actions (unity). As Deleuze observed, "[h]uman or divine [...], the predicates are the same whether they belong analytically to the divine being, or whether they are synthetically bound to the human form."[8] This is a decisive remark, not least because of its insistence that what provides humans with their characteristic form is essentially indistinguishable from what constitutes the theological-political project that characterizes the Western world's particular brand of self-consciousness. Inevitably, then, one must ask whether attempts to preserve the humanity of humankind are ultimately just clever strategies designed to keep Western thought within the grip of a type of theology that dare not speak its name. In other words, *it is as if "man" ultimately consisted in nothing more than a shrewd theological-political project*, one with far-reaching sociopolitical consequences. Thus, although it may seem counterintuitive, in the end, the critique of humanism is a critique of the circumscription of the field of potential experience by modes of thinking inherited from theological constructions, which goes to show that humanism has always been *the continuation of theology by other means*.

## A therapeutic project

However, this does not go far enough; to claim that a certain way of thinking employs schemes inherited from mythico-religious traditions is to raise, in the final analysis, a trivial point. After all, to locate a way of thinking that does not make use of structures inherited from such traditions in some form or other would be difficult. This is especially true in view of the fact that these structures

---

[8]    DELEUZE, *The Logic of Sense*, trans. by M. Lester & C. Stivale. London: The Athlone Press, 1990, p. 122.

consist, as Hegel often pointed out, in social elaborations designed to allow subjects to reflect, albeit in a simplified manner, on that which is unconditional and aspires to universal validity. In this sense, although such elaborations are incomplete, they may be understood as significant moments for any form of reflection which has as its object universality and unconditionality.

Nonetheless, one might feel inclined to wonder which form of life this theological-political project, connected as it is to the ultimate fate of the category "man", presupposes. Which experiences fall within the grasp of "man," and which are for him entirely impossible? It should perhaps be clarified here that "impossible" does not mean "inexistent," but "inconceivable," in the sense of something that cannot be conceived on account of its being a contradictory object; for instance, for Socrates to be both *man* and *not-man* at the same time is commonly regarded as *inconceivable*. To put the question in another way: which experiences cannot even be conceived, let alone integrated into life, as a direct result of the very constitution of the category "man"? Every theological project imposes a separation of some sort, and one cannot help but wonder just how much has been excluded from subjective experience by the coming of "man."

The above considerations are a more widely-applicable outcome of a critical strategy first employed in the fifth chapter of this book. Its application here would be very pertinent, as it would allow us to ask whether the set of values described above – autonomy, authenticity, unity, identity – ultimately produce a "damaged life," a mutilated form of living into which certain experiences cannot be integrated, and which prevents these experiences from even being conceived of by subjects, who must instead make strenuous efforts to repress them, deny them, or expel them from themselves. Clearly, these are experiences that cannot be conceived at all, except where the image of "man," like a "face drawn in sand at the edge of the sea," is dissolved. It is worth stressing the point here that "man" fundamentally consists in a *way of thinking*. This should become self-evident once we recall that the *unity* of "man" is a notion which depends on our elevating the principles of identity and non-contradiction from the status of logical principles to that of ontological postulates. Similarly, the *autonomy* of "man" presupposes unconditional assent to a model of transcendental constitution of objects of experience, while his *authenticity* in turn presupposes the reality of true uniqueness. These three procedures combined, generate what Gilles Deleuze once termed an *image of thought*, essentially, the particular mode of constitution by thought of objects and processes that results in their blindly reiterating a set of grammatical rules presented as natural, unquestionable presuppositions. This naturalization of the grammar in question as *the* grammar ultimately and inescapably leads to the entification of a *sensus communis*.[9]

In this sense, I would like to advance the following hypothesis: "man," as the entification of a particular regime of thought, consists in a project whose nature, rather than exclusively theological-political, is above all *therapeutic*. Therapy, here, is understood to be a set of procedures whose aim is to impose a specific conception of normality as a normative standard for life, as well as to strengthen this normalized life against anything that might threaten it, in the sense of anything that might make it deviate from the norm.

Therapy is commonly understood as an attempt to liberate oneself from a state of suffering. Indeed, "man" as modernity's fundamental regulative project appears as a defense mechanism against a state of suffering that might be termed, following Axel Honneth, "suffering from indeterminacy."

In the first chapter we saw how, beginning with Hegel, modernity is often characterized as a period in which subjective feelings of indeterminacy and anomie abound, which result from the loss of stable socialization horizons. Once this state of affairs becomes sufficiently pervasive, the individual becomes characterized in the following way:

> that night, that empty Nothingness, which contains everything in its undivided simplicity [...]. That is the night that one perceives if one looks a man in the eyes: then one is delving into a night which becomes terrible; it is the night of the world which then presents itself to us.[10]

Furthermore, it may be said that the falling of this "night of the world" is the very threat that "man," as a therapeutic project, was meant to defend us from. Hegel, as we have seen, rejected this perspective, regarding the unfolding

---

9   What is meant here by the term "image" is that element which determines the regime of visibility of thought, which determines what it is that thought can "see," avail itself of, and determine (much like one determines and differentiates things in space). This condition of the "visibility" of thought is inseparable from tacit presuppositions that direct thought to that which is "natural." What such considerations entail, then, is the need for the question of the relation between philosophical language and pre-philosophical language to be given the unequivocal status of a major philosophical problem. It is the pre-philosophical, "ordinary", *commonsense* use of language that provides philosophical thought with its set of unspoken, unproblematized presuppositions. Deleuze expresses it as follows: "Postulates in philosophy are not propositions the acceptance of which the philosopher demands; but, on the contrary, propositional themes which remain implicit and are understood in a pre-philosophical manner. In this sense, conceptual philosophical thought has as its implicit presupposition a pre-philosophical and natural Image of thought, borrowed from the pure element of common sense." (DELEUZE, *Difference and Repetition*, p. 131)

10  HEGEL, *Jenenser Realphilosophie II*, pp. 180-181, *apud* KEENAN, *Hegel and Contemporary Continental Philosophy*, p. 187.

darkness as the manifestation of a *power of indeterminacy and depersonalization* possessed by every subject, which is nothing but Hegelian infinity by another name, given how the term denotes precisely that which reveals the instability of all finite determinations; the collapse of the analytic of finitude. This is what made it permissible for us to maintain that "subject" is, for Hegel, a term denoting that process by means of which infinity is inscribed into the fabric of the existent. It also explains why the two terms Hegel employs most frequently to characterize subjects understood in this way are "fluidity" (*Flüssigkeit*) and "restlessness" (*Unruhe*), – the fluidity and restlessness of that which reveals the instability of all finite determinations. This feature underscores Hegel's evident lack of commitment to any normativity derived from the anthropological figure of "man". If anything, his position is essentially the opposite: if humankind is the "night of the world," that is so because the human animal can only be fully constituted precisely when it is able to accept its own disappearance, when it is capable of conducting operations of synthesis with precisely that which negates it.

Despite Hegel's admonitions, the latter remark becomes particularly significant in light of our having collectively grown accustomed to exorcizing indeterminacy through the belief that a proper articulation of autonomy, authenticity, and ego-derived procedures of synthetic unification should allow us to engender normativities capable of safely and accurately orienting our actions and judgments. The point must be insisted on: within this mode of belief, the humanity of humankind and its attributes appear as a promise of a "cure" for indeterminacy. It is as if until the present day we could not regard the figure of "man" without uttering those ominous words: "Without this Being or this Form, you will only have chaos …"[11] More specifically, it is the promise of eventual separation from our inner potency of indeterminacy, which, having made us grow unaccustomed to finitude, consequently seems to be leading us towards self-dissolution. Against this therapeutic project whose aim is the perpetuation of "man", we should perhaps consider the words of Deleuze:

> If one asks why health does not suffice, why the crack is desirable, it is perhaps because thought never occurs save through it and upon its edges, and everything that has ever been good and great in humanity enters and exits through it, in people ready to destroy themselves, and because death is preferable to the health that we are offered.[12]

---

[11] DELEUZE, *Logic of Sense*, p. 106.
[12] *Ibid.*, p. 160.

If even death seems preferable, that is because, as we have seen in the previous chapter, it is extremely likely that the most excruciating suffering we are capable of is not directly related to feelings of indeterminacy ensuing from the loss of substantially-rooted social relations; rather, *our most excruciating suffering is that which results from the repressive character of identity*.

It is as if contemporary thought suddenly recognized that for all the emancipatory expectations associated with rationality – expectations that humankind would emerge from its "self-incurred minority" to become, as Descartes put it, the "lords and masters of nature" – what it actually brought about was the very opposite: a reversal of emancipation in a form of self-domination ultimately connected to the fate of the foundational concept of modern rationality, namely "man." Indeed, many have asked questions that reveal this growing awareness: what price would we have to pay if human unity, autonomy, transparency and identity were imposed upon us as blueprints for reality? In what ways must our experience of ourselves be altered so as to conform to these categories? Lastly, what happens to our experience of the world when it is grounded on the imposition of boundaries to the constitution of subjects based on these attributes?

## What is the inhuman?

One way of answering these questions involves attempting to define what exactly a subject might consist in once it is no longer conceived through these attributes that ground the humanity of humankind, in other words, once it becomes inhuman.

Firstly, it should be said that it would be a mistake to conceive the inhuman as a heteroclite set encompassing anything and everything that does not accord with the current image of that which is human, for this would entail a definition of both "human" and "inhuman" based on a relation of indifferent externality, when, in reality, the relation between the two terms is one of profound yet complementary opposition. When it is said that "living conditions verge on the inhuman," for instance, the meaning assigned to the term "inhuman" excludes everything which is considered "human." The inhuman is what that which is human must negate in order to affirm itself as such; in other words, if it wishes to recognize what is left of itself in a human image. This is a particularly strong negation, as the inhuman is an inner potentiality to which the human can always return – it is *the internal limit borne by whatever is human*. And yet, if it is by means of a joint articulation of the attributes of autonomy, authenticity and unity that the humanity of humankind is defined, then it follows that, conversely, the three fundamental features of the inhuman consist precisely in disarticulations of these same three attributes.

Rather than autonomy, the inhuman appears as a sphere characterized by the animality latent within human beings. What we have arrived at, therefore, is a reiteration of the classical distinction between *humanitas* and *animalitas*; "animality" suggests blind behavioral submission to the mechanistic causality of nature, with the latter being necessarily understood as freedom's other. It is as if, in other words, nature must be a dimension from which human freedom is entirely absent. Still, it is important to ask ourselves, given what we currently know about nature, whether this is a dichotomy worth revising.

Indeed, to claim that what is human must by definition eschew the experience of animality and hence must radically differentiate itself from whatever is animalistic in nature, is tantamount to denying that which exists within ourselves yet nonetheless bears a mimetic affinity with what is not immediately recognizable as human. The force of this denial is easily diverted into acts of domination and violence directed against that aspect of ourselves that sees its own reflection in the opaque eyes of an animal. Consequently, the peremptory assertion of the humanity of humankind is ultimately and ironically converted into a form of savagery against everything within ourselves that still possesses identifiable traces of a former animality (namely our instinctual impulses, our drives, our so-called "pathological" desires, and so on). This "humanity" is actualized in the inverted form of distorted animality, of sheer animalistic brutality against that which is animal in nature, whose deactivation depends, therefore, on a recovery of the dimension of the inhuman.[13]

The inhuman may also be regarded as standing in opposition to authenticity, on account of its being the dimension *par excellence* of the radically impersonal. It should be stressed here that the term "impersonal" denotes that which can no longer be individuated through the institutionally-recognized reality of the person, nor through the ego as a psychological personality. The wording here is deliberate, and intended to designate a precise temporality: this *can no longer* be done because what is under discussion is something within ourselves which refuses any further subjection to egoic forms. If: (a) we accept that the ego is, as Lacan has clearly demonstrated, the final outcome of a process of alienation that is itself the fruit of processes of socialization that fundamentally operate through identifications in which one internalizes the modes of synthesis and personal qualities of an other; and if (b) we recall that "person" is a category

---

[13] For a detailed description of this process, cf. HORKHEIMER, Max; "The Revolt of Nature," in *Eclipse of Reason*. London: Continuum, 2004, pp. 63-86.

historically derived from Roman property law which, because it retains traces of the absolutization of property relations and thus possesses a merely abstract and formal nature, was seen by Hegel as an "expression of contempt"[14] when applied to an individual, then we can see how the impersonal is a corrosive form which allows us to conceive of the self in a way that transcends those modes of individuation characteristic of the rights-bearing legal person and of the psychological ego. For Hegel, the absolutization of the person led to falsehoods and little else, among these the egregious error of conceiving every intersubjective relation as a *contract* between property owners. A striking example of this mindset, which the German philosopher condemned as a "barbarism", has already been discussed above: Kant's conception of marriage as a contract between "two persons of different sexes" with a view to mutual and lifelong possession of one another's "sexual attributes."

Admittedly, linking the self to the dimension of the impersonal may seem counterintuitive; for instance, there is no question that the intended meaning of a sentence such as, "this is an impersonal text," is that the text is devoid of any personal style, and employs a "language of no one" which is incapable of expressing any personal quirks. Still, it is no coincidence that decisive moments in contemporary art were animated by the struggle against expression and style (a recurring theme in modernist thought).[15] In this context, style and subjective expression were seen and duly denounced as, respectively, the depositary of a reified grammar of forms and an attempt to fetishize a "second nature." The fact that Franz Kafka, one of the greatest writers of the twentieth century, wrote his work in a disaffected tone that mimicked the dry impersonality of this bureaucratic "language of no one" bolsters the argument that "[a]uthentic art knows the expression of the expressionless, a kind of weeping without tears."[16] In other words, and as Samuel Beckett has repeatedly demonstrated, any art that is loyal to its truth content is deeply distrustful of the first person pronoun.

Finally, as opposed to unity, the inhuman can be seen as the sphere of *monstrosity*, meaning that which is anomalous to a superlative degree, as Georges Canguilhem explains:

---

[14] HEGEL, *Phenomenology of Spirit*, § 480, p. 292. For a detailed reconstruction of the development of the notion of "person," cf. MAUSS, Marcel; "A category of the human mind: the notion of person; the notion of self," translated by W. D. Halls. In: *The category of the person: Anthropology, philosophy, history*. Cambridge: Cambridge University Press, 1985, pp. 1-25.

[15] On this, cf. ALMEIDA, Jorge; "Estilo." In: *Crítica dialética em Theodor Adorno: música e verdade nos anos vinte*. São Paulo: Ateliê Editorial, 2007, pp. 79-100.

[16] ADORNO, *Aesthetic Theory*, translated by R. Hullot-Kentor. New York: Continuum, 2002, p. 117.

'Anomaly' comes from the Greek *anomalia* which means unevenness, asperity; *omalos* in Greek means that which is level, even, smooth, hence 'anomaly' is, etymologically, *an-omalos*, that which is uneven, rough, irregular, in the sense conveyed by these words when speaking of a terrain.[17]

In this sense, the monstrosity of the inhuman is such a tremendous irregularity that it would no longer be possible to conceive it through the normative human form, at least not without imposing upon it some other, fully-actualized form. Hence, some degree of formlessness must always be present in that which is truly monstrous.

At this juncture, Canguilhem's question on the nature of the monstrous seems especially relevant: "To the extent that living beings diverge from the specific type, are they abnormal in that they endanger the specific form or are they inventors on the road to new forms?"[18] Consequently, the presence of the inhuman, as a power capable of corroding away the determined form of the human, could be seen as representing the very condition that could signal an end to the enslavement of subjects to that normative human form which is inextricable from the *currently actualized* figure of "man". If we take into account the fact that every actual historical experience, meaning every experience that has produced a break with the redundant repetition of past conventions, consisted in an action which had a problematization of the then-current figure of the human at its core, then we might wonder whether our inability to properly conceive of the inhuman and to integrate it into our lives is not a symptom of a *fear of history* and, perhaps more profoundly, of a *fear of the political*, especially since it may be argued – against Aristotle's assertions of the human being as a *zoon politikon* – that politics is not the chief attribute of the human animal. On the contrary, the political sphere is a space within which human beings incessantly seek to create, through that which is inhuman, modes of self-recognition which urge us to venture far beyond the boundaries of the image we give ourselves.

---

[17] CANGUILHEM, *The Normal and the Pathological*, translated by C. R. Fawcett in collaboration with R. S. Cohen. New York: Zone Books, 1991, p. 131.

[18] *Ibid.*, p. 141. A characteristic of Judith Butler's queer theory that has great emancipatory potential is precisely its understanding of the monstrous – a notion that, in the sense employed here, is not too dissimilar to the notion of inherent queerness – as the initial, preliminary figuration assigned to several new modes of living in the sphere of sexuality. For further developments of this notion, cf. BUTLER, *Gender Trouble: Feminism and the Subversion of Identity*. New York: Routledge, 1999.

## The true catastrophe

The point made above seems worthy of greater elucidation, to which end recourse to Sophocles' tragedy *Antigone* may prove beneficial. The reason for this may be expressed as follows: we have grown accustomed to assigning a common cause to our sociohistorical catastrophes and our subjective impasses, namely neglect, whether collective or personal, of the essential attributes of the humanity of humankind, and yet, the reverse appears to be true: such catastrophes appear to result from our inability to recognize ourselves in that which no longer takes a human form. Ironically, this is something we should have known all along, as it was made abundantly clear in *Antigone*.

Much has been written about this tragedy which, at least since the era of German Idealism, has consistently been alluded to in the context of reflections concerning the tension between demands for subjective recognition and the structures of social normativity; yet much remains to be said, particularly regarding the many transformations the interpretative slant given to this play has undergone throughout the years. An in-depth discussion would likewise be beneficial on how certain ancient texts, including *Antigone* and *Oedipus Rex*, jointly constitute a kind of *prehistory of subjectivity* whose impact on our understanding of the tensions that operate within the modern category of subject should not be underestimated (a position Adorno and Horkheimer have defended in relation to *The Odyssey*). Such a discussion should take into account the fact that renewed interest in *Antigone* was significantly connected to the advent of the French Revolution and the attendant awareness that it was possible for something possessing universal validity to withdraw from the sphere of juridical ordering and find a home in the principle of subjectivity, an idea in favor of which George Steiner has convincingly argued.[19]

Here, however, our discussion will be confined to a single aspect (albeit a fundamental one) of an interpretation advanced in the second half of the twentieth century, which would prove highly influential to everything that followed: that of Jacques Lacan. The point, then, is not to exhaustively analyze Lacan's reading of the tragedy in question, but merely to shed light on the fact that the psychoanalyst saw the question of the confrontation with the inhuman as occupying pride of place within that narrative. In Lacan's words, "[this] then is how the enigma of Antigone is presented to us: she is inhuman," she appears to our eyes as someone who has gone "beyond the limits of the

---

[19] Cf. especially the first chapter of STEINER, George; *Antigones: The Antigone Myth in Western Literature, Art and Thought*. Oxford: Oxford University Press, 1984.

human."[20] It was little wonder, therefore, that Sophocles should have been the author appealed to when Lacan defended his ostensive position, which he described thus: "As for us, we consider ourselves to be at the end of the vein of humanist thought. From our point of view man is in the process of splitting apart [...]."[21]

In addition to all this, it is worth recalling that *Antigone* is the oldest extant Greek text in which the word αὐτόνομος appears, in line 821, where the chorus employs the word to qualify Antigone's descent into Hades (a metaphor euphemistically describing her live entombment) as taking place in accordance with her own free will: "[You] / are the only mortal who / Will go down alive into Hades," they tell her, "answering only / To the law of yourself."[22] In this context, autonomy appears as the expression of a will whose fulfillment takes precedence over even the physical integrity of its agent. What confronts us, then, is the inauguration of something akin to a "moral integrity", a *subjective* assessment of the necessity of certain actions that can lead, under certain circumstances, to no less than the relativization of those demands that are characteristic of the hypostatization of the principle of self-preservation.

Let us return, however, to the main topic of discussion: Lacan's interpretation of the play. Initially, the French psychoanalyst stressed the inhuman character of Antigone and her actions: going beyond simple utilitarian calculations of pleasure and displeasure, she would ultimately refuse all that might have individualized her as a person endowed with particular interests. In this regard, Lacan seemed to be alluding in particular to Antigone's awareness that, once she had buried Polynices' corpse, she would be forever barred from performing those social roles that impressed upon Theban women their socially-recognized identities as wives and mothers. Thus exiled from the symbolic universe that structured the polis, she would die not once, but twice: a symbolic death would befall her, in addition to the physical one. Despite this recognition, she nonetheless chooses to act, not just once, but repeatedly.

It is important for Lacan's argument to draw attention to the *uncalculating nature* of these actions, as this characteristic supported his idea that Antigone had originated an ethical standard that lay beyond the pleasure principle. However, to assert that actions are sometimes carried out with no regard for utilitarian calculations relative to the maximization of pleasure and the avoidance of displeasure does not necessarily mean that a distinction should be made between particularized desires – desires predominantly attached to

---

[20] LACAN, *Seminar VII*, p. 263.
[21] *Ibid.*, pp. 273-274.
[22] SOPHOCLES; *Antigone*, trans. by R. Gibbons & C. Segal. New York: Oxford University Press, 2003, lines 821-822, p. 90.

"pathological" objects – and a pure autonomous will capable of fulfilling aspirations to universality. In this sense, Antigone's choice cannot be said to follow that model which comprises the self-imposition of a moral law by an autonomous subject. It is as if Lacan were trying, through the figure of Antigone, to conceive a model of rational deliberation within which the "heteronomy" of a pathological object-attachment could *express* demands for universal validity.

This point is easily overlooked when one attempts to understand in a particularistic vein the reasons that moved Antigone to bury her brother in defiance of Theban law. Lacan was aware of this, and thus warned his readers not to forget that, from Antigone's perspective, what her provision of funeral honors to her socially-reviled brother actually revealed was the particularized character of Theban law as expressed through the contingent nature of a single man, Creon. The following verses illustrate this point:

> It was not Zeus who made that proclamation / To me; nor was it Justice, who resides / In the same house with the gods below the earth, / Who put in place for men such laws as yours. / Nor did I think your proclamation so strong / That you, a mortal, could overrule the laws / Of the gods, that are unwritten and unfailing. / For these laws live not now or yesterday / But always, and no one knows how long ago / They appeared.[23]

The above excerpt has at its core the notion that the legitimacy of Antigone's actions does not merely derive from the natural bond that exists between blood relations, or from the irreplaceability of a lost sibling, but first and foremost from the fact that divine law bestows upon family members the sacred duty to *recognize the unconditionality of the positing of subjects*, regardless of any and all additional determinations that particular contexts may confer upon one's actions, an unconditionality expressed in the fact that the performance of funeral rites is not a choice, but a duty. As Lacan put it: "Antigone's position represents the radical limit that affirms the unique value of [Polynices'] being without reference to any content, to whatever good or evil Polynices may have done, or to whatever he may be subjected to."[24]

On this particular point, Lacan revealed himself to be a faithful follower of Hegel's take on Antigone: the German philosopher rejected the view that the ethical connection between members of a family is based on "feeling," or

---

[23] SOPHOCLES, *Antigone*, lines 495-504, p. 73.
[24] LACAN, *Seminar VII*, p. 279.

on the exclusivity of "the relationship of love." Instead, he believed that "[this] determination does not fall within the Family itself, but bears on what is truly universal, the community; it has, rather, a negative relation to the Family, and consists in expelling the individual from the Family, subduing [*unterjochen*] the natural aspect and separateness of his existence, and training him to be virtuous, to lead a life within and for the universal."[25] It is nevertheless symptomatic that Hegel should single out the execution of funeral rites – the care rendered to a member of the community who has died – as the most complete expression of this formation of the individual towards a universalized existence. The deceased, after all, is "the individual who, after a long succession of separate disconnected experiences [*that is, his Dasein*], concentrates himself into a single completed shape [*that venerable figure memory alone preserves*], and raises himself out of the unrest of the accidents of life into the calm of simple universality."[26] The notion that there are actions whose intrinsic value must be regarded as unconditional, and which must therefore be unconditionally preserved, is the essence of the divine law which drives Antigone, a law whose power lies in "the abstract, pure universal, the *elemental* individual which equally draws back into the pure abstraction which is its essence [*Grund*] the individuality that breaks loose from the element [...]."[27] Thus, divine law is the first positing of individuality as unconditionality, or, at least momentarily, as abstraction. Hegel would undoubtedly remind us, however, that this is the basis of individuality itself, and that something of this foundation must inevitably appear in that which is founded.

Hence, it may be concluded that the fact that positing this basis would be a complete impossibility within the polis reveals the unrealized status of the notion of ethicity in the Greek world, a deduction that Hegel had already made. In this regard, let us recall Hegel's insistence that the polis had to uphold a double law: the law in its divine character, whose proper sphere was the family; and the law of the community. Compelled to follow the dictates of this double law, citizens of the polis had to walk the tightrope between avoiding transgressions against either facet. This was clearly an impossible task, as the positing of one implied the reduction of the other to the level of the particular. The task would have been impossible for any collectivity which did not have as its organizing principle demands for the recognition of a general universality capable of serving both as the basis for singular consciousness and as the essence of family law, and it was certainly the case for the Greek polis,

---

[25] HEGEL, *Phenomenology of Spirit*, § 451, p. 269.
[26] *Ibid.*, § 451, p. 270.
[27] *Ibid.*, § 453, pp. 271-272.

unfamiliar as Ancient Greek culture was with the notion that the subject can find actualization in a state bereft of all communitarian and identitarian traits. In other words, that which is strongly embedded within the private world of the family should not be repressed but recognized for what it is, something which insistently if imperfectly makes demands for an unconditionality that the polis cannot quite meet. This is a fact historically underscored by the efforts of womankind itself, to which the epithet of "everlasting irony of the community" has been applied.

By taking up arms against a force it will not recognize, the community brings about its own ruination. Ultimately, what the government disapprovingly regards as a particularized interest is precisely that which ends up revealing the particularity of governmental interests, and the absence of any immediacy in their connection with the law. Once that situation occurs, the ethical substance becomes nothing but a formal universality, and any ensuing collectivity will have that soulless character found in the communities that flourished under the Roman rule of law. Therefore, and contrary to what Lacan believed, Hegel's reading of *Antigone* prevents us from harboring any hopes of an ultimate reconciliation.

## *The humanity of those who recognize the inhuman*

Keeping the foregoing discussion in mind, let us return to Lacan's interpretation so as to identify some of its main characteristics. Many have read *Antigone* as an insoluble conflict between the law of the family and the law of the polis, represented by Antigone and Creon, respectively. However, Lacan markedly dissents from that tradition, whose chief representative and strongest proponent is Hegel, by asserting the ethical significance of Antigone's defiance of Creon's edict. More specifically, Lacan does not see Creon as the mouthpiece of a lawful principle in direct confrontation with another, equally lawful, principle, but as an individual who wishes to inflict a *second death* upon his enemy, the traitorous Polynices. According to Lacan, this private desire to kill his opponent again is cleverly couched in a "language of practical reason," which means that what we are faced with here is an attempt to transform "the good of all" into a "law without limits" whose aim is to annihilate any and all points of excess; anyone or anything who resists that specific enunciation of the law.

Lacan's interpretation of this is very characteristic of its age, in that it betrays a complete lack of belief in the possibility that the law underpinning social relations might meet subjective demands for recognition. It may even be said that in such situations wherein ethicity has all but collapsed, resorting to the irreducibility of subjectivity appears to be the only alternative. That explains why Lacan must insist that the law upheld by Creon had long since lost all substantiality. That this is a most cunning position to adopt becomes clear once he asserts that, if the law of the polis can no longer encompass imperatives of universality, then this may be taken as evidence of the aforementioned loss of substance, especially when one recalls that *these imperatives of universality were enunciated from a position that from the perspective of the polis appears completely particularized.*

The above considerations may help us to reconcile with that curious ethical imperative advanced by Lacan, namely that, "the only thing of which one can be guilty is of having given ground relative to one's desire."[28] Contrary to initial appearances, this is definitely not a particularistic profession of faith; rather, it is essentially a statement to the effect that whenever desire produces a singular attachment to the condition of a universal – whenever, that is, desire yearns to establish a universal on the basis of a singular situation – conceding ground is not ethically admissible. To give ground when faced with such a situation would be tantamount to denying even the possibility that the universal might attain actualization. In this sense, what Lacan is proposing might be rearticulated as follows: *there are situations in which a pathological attachment to singular objects is precisely the means through which the universal attains actualization.* In situations of this nature, it would be inconceivable to yield.

This point bears more thorough investigation. One possible reading of Lacan's seventh *Seminar* is that what Lacan sought to accomplish by means of his reflections on the nature of moral action was primarily a critical assessment of the model of rational deliberation which had as its foundation a supposed autonomy of the will. Consequently, it would be wrong to conceive of psychoanalysis as a clinical process directed at reconstructing the subjective conditions required for autonomy, or, by the same token, for a recovery of authenticity or unity. This would explain why, for the duration of the seminar, Lacan insists on connecting the notion of moral action to a subject's capacity to recognize him- or herself in something that disarticulates his or her own unity and identity; the capacity, that is, to recognize him- or herself in something to be unavoidably acted upon, not in the kind of carefully-developed project one deliberately embarks upon as a supposed exercise in free will, but in an irresistible enjoyment which, from the perspective of the system of interests inextricable from the self-preservation mechanisms of *homo psychologicus*, appears entirely heteronomous. In this case,

---

[28] LACAN, *Seminar VII*, p. 321.

then, the "free will" associated with a personal project gives way entirely to the *pathos* of an enjoyment whose very nature reaffirms the notion that "[it] is just the strength of the great characters that they do not choose but throughout, from start to finish, *are* what they will and accomplish."[29]

It should be borne in mind, however, that, for Lacan, this experience of enjoyment is closely related to the recovery of something from which the subject forcibly extricates itself on the road to becoming an autonomous, self-identical "I". Consequently, this "something" must appear as radically foreign to this unified subjective image, or, in Lacan's words, is "the absolute Other of the subject."[30] Interestingly, the significance that psychoanalysis confers on experiences of this sort is precisely what caused its rupture with linear evolutionist perspectives: from a psychoanalytic perspective, the subject undergoing a process of development and maturation cannot simply progress from one stage to the next, but must learn to recover aspirations intrinsic to what is left behind in the transition; to internalize that which still pulsates beneath the wreckage of the past. It is precisely this capacity to heed the voice of something demolished on the way to individuation that will enable a subject to constitute non-narcissistic relations, both with itself and with others.

This capacity to recognize mimetic affinities with what has been rejected and destroyed in the ego's constitution of self-identity is, from a Lacanian perspective, moral in nature: it provides us with a behavioral model whose chief characteristic is the establishing of broad demands for social recognition as a horizon for social action. According to this model, the fitness of an action must no longer be judged in respect to whether or not it allows for the recognition of a different system of individual desires and aspirations, but rather in respect to whether or not it permits the recognition of an otherness of a degree such that it cannot be conceived through the figure of another individual, or of some other distinct identity with its own system of interests. For this reason, Lacan deliberately employs the term *das Ding* to denote this "Other", thereby reminding us that what is being referenced is something that evades immediate submission to the figure of the individual; an alterity that consists not exactly in the *presence of the other*, but in an *abnormativity* of sorts, a form of resistance against submission to a normative grammar.

In this sense, Antigone's actions are exemplary for Lacan, in that they reveal how an insistent attachment to that which has been banished from the sphere of the named can reignite the libidinal dynamic of a desire left unfulfilled by

---

[29] HEGEL, *Aesthetics: Lectures on Fine Art, Vol. II*, translated by T. M. Knox. London: Oxford University Press, 1975, p. 1214.

[30] LACAN, *Seminar VII*, p. 52.

whatever pleasure may be derived from the consumption of objects that are just imaginary loci onto which the ego has narcissistically projected itself. This libidinal dynamic can only find fulfillment through the constitution of an object entirely foreign to the sphere of social representations, which is a sphere connected to limitations intrinsic to the current figure of the human. It could even be said that recognition of this dynamic – a ceaseless dynamic of indeterminacy – would allow for the establishment of social bonds characteristic of a substantive conception of democracy, amenable to dynamics of this sort.

The position described above could be criticized on the grounds that it avoids addressing so-called "controversial" statements that appear in the same seminar, such as the following:

> [Antigone] pushes to the limit the realization of something that might be called the pure and simple desire of death as such. She incarnates that desire. [...] No mediation is possible here except that of this desire with its radically destructive character.[31]

This passage has been interpreted as implying that Antigone should be seen as a figure hopelessly entranced by the purity of a desire characterized as pure negativity, and therefore only capable of being realized in the form of crude, destructive impulses.

This point could be discussed at greater length; here, however, it should suffice to point out that statements of this nature should be read in the context of Lacan's efforts to integrate the death drive into psychoanalytic thought as the motive force driving clinical progress. As Richard Boothby pointedly reminds us, "[for] Lacan, the disintegrating force of the death drive is aimed not at the integrity of the biological organism, as Freud had concluded, but rather at the imaginary coherence of the ego."[32] As we have seen, Freud believed that the ultimate fulfillment of the death drive was characterized by the self-destruction of the person; while it is true that for Lacan the death sought by this drive is indeed the "self-destruction of the person," it should not be forgotten that what he meant by "person" is merely the subject's identity within particular legal orders. In this sense, it can be said that the death drive does not *necessarily* appear in the context of social relations as a violent, destructive force; it may also appear as a force leading an individual to act beyond his or her own system of interests as an individualized person.

---

[31] LACAN, *Seminar VII*, pp. 282-283.
[32] BOOTHBY, *Freud as Philosopher*, p. 151.

Some have suggested that the destructive character of Antigone's desire should be understood as a complete suspension of the symbolic order, and thus as something leading inexorably to the destruction of the city-state, which equates to a refusal of the symbolic pact. However, a very different interpretation is possible: Antigone, we would suggest, is not responsible for the destruction of the polis; rather, Creon is the person who has to bear that responsibility: the fate of the polis was sealed the moment he decided he would no longer submit to divine law, as laid down by the gods, through which the unconditionality of funeral rites is established as a precondition for a society at least minimally reconciled. For Sophocles, the fact that the carrying out of funeral rites was mandatory in character – an injunction which did not exclude even enemies of the state – was a central question, which also featured prominently in his *Ajax*. Given this context, it is clear that Antigone's actions did no more than expose the fact that the polis had become an unlawful state, which had already been destroyed at its most substantial level by the very power that was meant to preserve it.[33] This means that our assertion regarding the uncalculating nature of Antigone's actions must be qualified: while it may be said to be true, it is *only* true in respect of utilitarian calculations aimed at maximizing pleasure and avoiding displeasure. Antigone's actions are in fact fundamentally calculating; she understood, that no true life is possible within a society unable to ensure the existence of conditions which allow at least the most fundamental processes of reconciliation, as well as of recognition of the inalienable character of the condition of subject, to take place. Thus, the calculation in question consisted precisely in realizing that in situations of this nature the only possible course of action is to expose their completely unsustainable character.

Finally, it is worth recalling that certain commentators have very accurately and skillfully criticized Lacan's interpretation on the grounds that it fails to even entertain the possibility that the one character in the play to whom a psychoanalytic approach is most suited is Creon, the ruler of Thebes, being the only character who undergoes any significant change throughout the narrative, who learns from his mistakes and alters his subjective position by the narrative's end. As Philippe Van Haute put it:

---

[33] On the notion of an "unlawful state," cf. SAFATLE, "Do uso da violência contra o estado ilegal" ["On the resorting to violence against an unlawful state"], in SAFATLE, Vladimir, & TELES, Edson; *O que resta da ditadura* ["What remains of the dictatorship"]. São Paulo: Boitempo Editorial, 2010, pp. 237-252.

Creon recognizes his own guilt, and adjusts his story accordingly. He and he alone is to blame for what transpired. Having thus accepted his responsibility, Creon is given a *human dimension* lacking in Antigone.[34]

This is a perspective Van Haute shares with Patrick Guyomard, as may be gathered from the following extract from Guyomard's classic book *La jouissance du tragique*:

> In the case of Antigone, the appeal of the absolute leads her to suicide. Estranged from Antigone, and faced with the question of what he regards as her "madness," Creon, moving beyond his own sorrow, sets upon a new path: the path of one who, no longer seeing in "madness" an absolute or in loneliness the final stronghold of [Antigone's] pride, can tell us precisely *how* he has come to that place in which he now stands.[35]

In other words, it is through a process of critical self-reflection that Creon comes to understand the nature of his own fate.

However, it is possible to regard the situation differently and state that, if Lacan insists on the neutrality of Antigone's actions, it is because he wants to remind us that Creon is the one who upheld a false law, a law marked by a triple interdiction against the recognition of that which manifests as inhuman. First, the polis consents to the banishment of Oedipus, who is regarded as *monstrous* on account of his essential placelessness; of his having moved into the sphere of the unnamable as a result of his disarticulation of the most elementary structures of kinship. Secondly, the polis relegates Polynices to the sphere of *animality* – the sphere of those too lacking in dignity to deserve proper burial, and who thus must be left to rot like beasts – on account of his purported disregard for the rules of succession and subsequent attempt to regain power over the state by forging an alliance with a foreign power. Finally, the polis sentences Antigone to live entombment as punishment for having exposed the particularistic nature of its laws, thus fulfilling her destiny as a fully *depersonalized* individual, an individual incapable of finding actualization as a person. And, of course, *those who bind themselves to any law whose maintenance depends on the reiterated rejection of the inhuman can only attain humanity once it is far too late*; those who turn monstrousness, animality, and depersonalization into the no-place of the

---

[34] VAN HAUTE, Philippe; "Antígona: heroína da psicanálise?" ["Antigone: Heroine of Psychoanalysis?"]. In: *Revista Discurso*, n. 36, 2006, p. 308.

[35] GUYOMARD, Patrick; *La jouissance du tragique. Antigone, Lacan et le désir de l'analyste*. Paris: Flammarion, 1998, p. 115.

unnamable, which must have no contact with the human dimension, can only attain humanity once it is far too late.

It should be noted, however, that Antigone's inhumanity is in a sense already a form of humanity, as it has that liberal character found in those who are able to accept that which is to them entirely dissimilar. This dissimilarity is more than simply the alterity inherent in an encounter with a separate consciousness, but the abnormativity of that which questions the ordering that structures one's form of life. Hence, we may regard Antigone as representing *a humanity that no longer needs to have recourse to a human image*; she is the promise of a *coming humanity* – one that, from our current perspective, can only manifest as "inhumanity." Only an individual such as Antigone is capable of denouncing the state's inexorable march towards its own ruin, a consequence of its absolute attachment to the current figure of "man". To frame the question in more contemporary terms, it may be said that this particular conformation of the state is none other than the state of fear, or the state of exception; and that what turns its politics into "a frightening rallying of frightened men"[36] is precisely this fear, the fear that overtakes all those who lose their ability to utter the words Theseus addressed to that great *inhuman*, Oedipus:

> [In] pity I'd / ask you, ill-fated Oedipus, what you want / of my city and me – you and your ill-fated guide. / Teach me that. For I know / it would have to be some act beyond telling / to make me want to turn away. Like you, / I was raised an exile, far from home, / and often, on my own, I had to face / mortal danger. So I could never turn aside / and not try to save any stranger / in the state I find you in now.[37]

Such is the state we call our own.

## *Pathologies of humanism*

In order to unequivocally present the assumptions at work in this chapter, as well as respond to certain objections that were raised during a public presentation of some of the ideas discussed herein, a few sentences of clarification regarding contemporary attempts to restore humanism are necessary. What is being defended here is, essentially, the idea that the likely

---

[36] ZIZEK, "Introduction," in ROBESPIERRE, *Virtue and Terror*, p. xxvi.
[37] SOPHOCLES, *Oedipus at Colonus*, trans. by E. Grennan & R. Kitzinger. New York: Oxford University Press, 2005, lines 617-627, p. 59.

cause of our suffering is not our having lost all reference points leading to our humanity, but rather our being too strongly attached to the current figure of "man" and therefore not knowing how to deal with experiences that fall beyond the scope of that figure. In this sense, any discourses that seek to prevent us from deconstructing the current figure of the human, or that of the contemporary individual – discourses that may be subsumed under the rubric of "humanism" – are responsible for a very important type of social suffering which manifests in both the clinical and political spheres, where the term "political" denotes the sphere of actions aimed at the creation of institutional conditions conducive to subject recognition.

Hence, we should not regard with indifference the existence of words that can only be heard when shouted. Shouting requires a great deal of force, however, and even words themselves can sometimes grow too feeble to be shouted; when this happens, all one can do is hope that once all that opposes them has been reduced to silence – to that condition of emptiness peculiar to whatever has been radically expelled from the *polis* – such words may once again grow audible. Precisely because of this we should also not be indifferent to the fact that, currently, every time the word "humanism" is uttered, it is accompanied by a bizarre procession of what may be termed "unpronounceable designations". The purpose of such designations is to banish whatever is other into irreversible isolation, to cast alterity into oblivion with the rest of the unnameables. While these terms are in themselves devoid of meaning, if repeated insistently and desperately enough, they seem to become endowed with sufficient power to exorcize alterity, or else grind it to dust.

Let us see with the attentive gaze of one first uncovering a revealing symptom that those who cast anchor in the port of humanism are the very same ones who tirelessly and disapprovingly look upon other seas while loudly denouncing those who sail there as "nihilists," "irrationalists", even "terrorists", if there is something to be gained by it. Their strategy is clear: from the moment the designation is imposed upon its intended object, that object shall no longer be spoken of or to; to do so would thenceforth bear the stamp of impossibility. They argue that the object in question cannot be truly engaged for it cannot speak: these disjointed sounds it calls its speech, these simulacra of arguments it attempts to advance, are the fruit of sheer "fanaticism". There is far too much "resentment" underpinning its intentions; its actions are too greatly imbued with "nihilism". One finds, in other words, too great an abundance of *nothing* there.

When confronted with situations of this nature, it pleased Bento Prado Júnior (who knew better than most what hides behind such furious exorcisms) to point out that "one is always someone else's irrationalist." Sadly, all evidence suggests we are approaching a time when we shall be forced to add that "one is always someone else's nihilist" and, worst of all, that "one is always someone else's terrorist." In other words, there will always be someone who wants nothing less than to exile us from rationality, or from the act of creation, or from politics. Against that, it should perhaps be remembered that among the ranks of philosophers one would be hard-pressed to find an irrationalist or a nihilist, not to mention a terrorist. Accusations of this kind are merely the last, desperate resort of those who fear that critical endeavors will be "taken too far" and call into question that which, for some, should never be questioned; those who are fearful that critical thinking may evolve beyond the comparisons of principles and cases into a tool by means of which our most fundamental values will be interrogated. Spinoza, Schelling, Rousseau, Heidegger, Nietzsche, Derrida, Adorno, Foucault, Bataille, Benjamin, even Hegel (held in contempt by, among others, Karl Popper), were all forced to endure assaults of this nature at some point.

That only goes to show that if, on one hand, no philosopher has ever been a nihilist or an irrationalist, on the other, regrettably, several have voluntarily traversed the broad and safe paths of oversimplification, of reductive interpretation, too petty to attempt to oppose their philosophical antagonists by engaging with their best arguments (rather than simply their mistakes – and what philosophy that can be considered truly great has not incurred some error of similar dimensions?). Even the gospels side with us in this regard, because they also believe those who choose the narrow road over the broad one to be wise; after all, those who pick the rigors of the former are those willing to think without fear.

In this sense, the fact that humanist perspectives cannot currently be expressed except through these unpronounceable designations – the fact, that is, that their enunciation can only occur in tandem with the opening of a void to which all that falls beyond the scope of the current figure of "man" must be exiled – is something that betrays the deeply segregational and totalitarian nature of humanism. This is unsurprising, given that humanism has invariably preached a gated-community variation on the gospel of tolerance lately, promulgating the rationalism of those who believe that the ultimate expression of justice is the waging of preventive wars against whatever may lie to the east of Turkey, which is to say the rationalism of those who are ostensibly willing to communicate with everyone, provided that "everyone" holds the same values and principles that they do, naturally.

Above all, "humanism" is a byword for those who want to chain us to the present. One of the defining characteristics of the twentieth century was the proliferation of struggles aimed at finding an opening to that which still lacked a figure, to bring about something which the mindless repetition of the current figure of the human and the modes associated with it could not fully exhaust. Such struggles, which are prevalent in discussions pertaining to aesthetics as well as to politics, to clinical psychotherapy as well as to philosophy, have at several points in our recent history shown themselves more than capable of affecting historical processes, and engaging subjects in modes of living that transcend their immediate present. Currently, however, significant effort has been expended in erasing or criminalizing this history, as though descriptions of these past attempts at escaping the limitations of the human figure were all to be understood as descriptions of processes whose full actualization would result in nothing less than catastrophe; as though it were no longer permissible to look back and reflect on new ways to recover such moments, in which time stood still and the possibilities for the transformation of the human seemed endless. Indeed, humanism seems intent on preaching that the past reeks of the smell of catastrophe, and that the future is unlikely to be too dissimilar from our present reality. It might be the case, then, that the most its defenders can achieve, be they mild or radical, is to hinder our capacity to act inspired by notions of a coming humanity, and model, in the attempt to accustom us to a present that no one really believes in anymore, and of which many have grown weary. In other words, the best they can do is elevate fear to the condition of central political affection – nothing more.

Ultimately, what is needed is a name from which no normativization ensues. In order to find it, however, we shall have to resort to an expedient often employed in the history of philosophy: to recover that which has at some point been excluded, expelled, repressed, and locate its truth content. To that end, something more encompassing than humanism and its macabre procession of unpronounceable designations is required. Only something with a scope far broader than the current strain of humanism can truly do justice to the sole form of humanism worth preserving, the infinite humanism that Lévi-Strauss announced by remarking that "nothing human can be alien to humankind." To that, it may be added: even that which has been consigned to the pit of inhumanity has much to teach us about being human.

# CHAPTER IX

# Towards an anti-predicative concept of recognition

*'Nobody, friends' – Polyphemus bellowed back
from his cave – 'Nobody's killing me now
by fraud and not by force!'*
Homer

*No more has any estate [...] that revolutionary daring
which flings at the adversary the defiant words:
I am nothing but I must be everything.*
Karl Marx

As has been suggested above, the concept of *recognition* has attained almost hegemonic status within the philosophical and social debates of the past two decades, as the central operator through which the rationality of political demands is understood. First recovered in the 1930s, the political dimension of the concept would not be systematically explored until the early 1990s, with the publication of third-generation Frankfurt School theorist Axel Honneth's *The Struggle for Recognition: The Moral Grammar of Social Conflicts* (1992), and of Hegel-influenced philosopher Charles Taylor's *Multiculturalism: Examining the Politics of Recognition* (1992). Hence, if we are to adequately reflect on the contemporary uses of the concept of recognition, we must take into account the sociohistorical context of its recovery in the late twentieth century, a context which, in the final analysis, cannot be dissociated from the diminishing importance ascribed, over the past few decades, to the discourse of class struggle as a key to interpreting social conflicts.

This discourse seemed to reduce social conflicts to general problems related to an *egalitarian redistribution* of wealth, or lack thereof (problems that, as we are well aware, are more than mere expressions of a theory of redistributive justice), thus overlooking moral and cultural aspects of these conflicts that would ultimately prove impossible to understand as purely reflections of class structures. That being the case, from one perspective it may be said that an accumulation of independent changes was responsible for creating a particular

271

set of conditions that have, in turn, brought the question of recognition to a position of centrality as a political problem. Among such changes, three appear to have been fundamental.

The first is the disempowerment of the proletariat as a historical agent for revolutionary social transformation, an issue that has been thematized by the Frankfurt School since at least the 1930s, with its research work on the political regression of the working classes that would lead to their becoming supporters of Nazism.[1] The assimilation of the working classes, starting in the 1950s, into the social security programs and corrective policies of the so-called welfare states doubtlessly consolidated this process. Of particular note is the way Habermas noticed the scarcity of candidates willing to operate as global agents for revolutionary change after the working classes became coopted by the welfare state and the subsequent decline of the welfare state model itself, and insisted on reading the situation as an expression of the exhaustion of "a particular utopia that in the past crystallized around the potential of a society based on social labour."[2] This was a historical exhaustion of such mammoth proportions that it prompted Axel Honneth to remark that the belief that the proletariat played a privileged role in revolutionary politics was nothing but a "philosophical-historical dogma."[3] Once this position is accepted, any investment in the discourse of class struggle as a central axis for the organization and constitution of identities within political struggles is perforce sapped of its strength, and, consequently, space opens up for new candidates willing to perform this function.

On the other hand, once the proletariat leaves the stage as the representative of political subjectivity *par excellence*, the twentieth-century's most important device for the generic determination of social struggles is lost. The expression is deliberate: it was a device for "generic determination" in the sense that the proletariat played the part of "universal subject," unifying a great multiplicity of social manifestations that had political emancipation as a common aim. This largely explains why the first attempt to recover the concept of recognition by French intellectual circles privileged spaces concerned with singularity, such as clinical psychoanalysis and reflections on ethics. As the political debates

[1] Cf. e.g. FROMM, Erich; "Arbeiter und Angestellte am Vorabend des Dritten Reiches. Eine sozialpsychologische Untersuchung," in *Gesamtausgabe*, vol. 3. Stuttgart: Deutsche Verlag-Anstalt, 1981, pp. 1-224.

[2] HABERMAS, "The New Obscurity: The Crisis of the Welfare State and the Exhaustion of Utopian Energies," in *The New Conservatism: Cultural Criticism and the Historians' Debate*, trans. by S. W. Nicholsen. Cambridge: Polity Press, 1989, p. 52.

[3] HONNETH, "Redistribution as Recognition: a Response to Nancy Fraser," in FRASER, Nancy & HONNETH, Axel; *Redistribution or Recognition?: A Political-Philosophical Exchange*, trans. by J. Golb, J. Ingram & C. Wilke. New York: Verso, 2003, p. 116.

of the period still revolved around the proletariat's generic determination, discussions relating to recognition in the political sphere were unnecessary. Only after belief in the concrete universality of the proletariat comes to be gradually abandoned does the question arise of how such multiplicities can attain the recognition due to them within social struggles.

Yet before the current centrality of the concept of recognition could be consolidated, the aforementioned loss of faith in the proletariat's revolutionary role had to be supplemented by a phenomenon related to the transformation of expectations regarding the dimension of labor, which had been central to the advancement of political struggle. Luc Boltanski and Eve Chiapello explained this transformation as follows: in the aftermath of the political uprisings of May 1968, they suggested, a new capitalist ethos started to take shape.

The social critique that developed in this period took as its most significant object the sphere of labor and its inability to meet authentic social demands. Seen as a dimension of pure rigidity, of imposed schedules and controlled time, stereotypical entrepreneurial hierarchies and Taylorist alienation, the purported value of labor was regarded by the youth of '68 with increasing suspicion. Studies dating from the early 1970s describe the increasing disaffection displayed by young people for the system of labor as it had existed until then, and the way in which they appeared to favor more flexible activities even if these were less well paid. This critique is understood as having triggered the reconfiguration of the ideological core of capitalist society, and the attendant transformation of the ethos of labor. Values such as safety, stability, and respect for functional hierarchy and specialization, which had once made labor a fundamental realm for the imposition of rigidly fixed identities, gave way to a different set of values, derived directly from the critique of labor. Risk-taking ability, malleability, and the deterritorialization that results from infinite processes of reconfiguration: these values jointly comprised labor's new ideological nucleus. Through this change the realm of labor as it exists within capitalist societies became more adept at acknowledging and meeting demands for the recognition of individuality and altering the matrix of the experience of alienation, effectively detaching this matrix from the theme of economic spoliation and repositioning it nearer to the theme of imposing an inauthentic mode of existence, that is, a life where no space exists for the development of individual requirements for self-actualization. This transition from spoliation to inauthenticity that lay at the heart of the critique of labor was an additional cause for the decline in importance of the concept of class struggle, as well as for the increasing centrality of the problem of recognition as a political device.

Finally, it is worth recalling that this change converged with an additional series of changes that have taken place from the 1970s onward, resulting from a growing awareness of the fact that the struggles of historically vulnerable social groups, such as women or racial and sexual minorities who were often deprived of fundamental rights, were ultimately concerned with the cultural affirmation of differences. In other words, these struggles came to be seen as more than mere subsets of a broader struggle aimed at extending universal rights to groups that had previously been excluded; they were seen as processes engaged at a deep level in the affirmation of differences against a framework that, while supposedly universalist, was actually committed to the perpetuation of norms and forms of life peculiar to culturally hegemonic groups. This new perspective owed its existence, to a significant degree, to the development of themes connected to multiculturalism.

The term "multiculturalism" had been employed to describe the multi-linguistic character of the Swiss Federation as early as 1957; Canada would be the first region to raise multiculturalism to the status of state policy, however. A country culturally marked by conflicts between its Francophone and Anglophone communities as well as by high immigration rates, Canada, under the social-democratic government of Pierre Elliott Trudeau, officially implemented its multiculturalism policy in 1971, a historic occasion marked by the publication of Trudeau's *Announcement of Implementation of Policy of Multiculturalism within a Bilingual Framework*.[4] The introduction of this policy enabled Canada to define itself as a multicultural society, one that among other things acknowledged the pressing need for additional, state-financed policies aimed at preserving this multiplicity. In 1988, these policies were reinforced by the enactment of the *Canadian Multiculturalism Act*. Several countries followed suit, although they were almost exclusively countries of Anglo-Saxon origin (the Netherlands being the only exception). It is unsurprising, therefore, that the Canadian philosopher Charles Taylor

---

[4]  The nature of the policy in question was made clear by the words of then-Prime Minister Trudeau: "A policy of multiculturalism within a bilingual framework commends itself to the government as the most suitable means of assuring the cultural freedom of Canadians. Such a policy should help break down discriminatory attitudes and cultural jealousies. National unity, if it is to mean anything in the deeply personal sense, must be founded on confidence in one's own individual identity; out of this can grow respect for that of others and a willing-ness to share ideas, attitudes and assumptions. A vigorous policy of multiculturalism will help create this initial confidence. It can form the base of a society which is based on fair play for all. The government will support and encourage the various cultures and ethnic groups that give structure and vitality to our society. They will be encouraged to share their cultural expression and values with other Canadians and so contribute to a richer life for us all." (TRUDEAU, Pierre Elliot; "Statement on Multiculturalism," in FORBES, Hugh Donald (ed.); *Canadian Political Thought*. Toronto: Oxford University Press, 1985, p. 350)

should be among the first to try to recover the concept of recognition, and that his efforts should take place in the context of a debate on multiculturalism.

This multicultural tendency played a predominant role in the orientation of the political left from the 1980s onward, mostly because of its being potentially useful in the defense of ethnic-cultural minorities as well as conducive to practices of the institutionalization of diversity in regards to sexual orientation. At the same time, the development of philosophical reflections sensitive to the disciplinary nature of structures of power, whose sole purpose is the imposition of normativity upon the spheres of sexuality, desire, psychic normality, family structure, and the constitution of social roles, provided a useful conceptual framework within which the consequences of such struggles could unfold.[5] If the reemergence of the theory of recognition cannot be ascribed to the efforts of authors like Michel Foucault, Gilles Deleuze and Jacques Derrida (and it could hardly be otherwise, given the strict anti-Hegelianism of the first two, and the attenuated form of the same in the latter), it is nonetheless undeniable that their critique of the traditional Marxist perspective in regards to political struggles, as well as their ethical defense of the primacy of difference, contributed significantly to the consolidation of a philosophical framework more amenable to the promotion of the question of alterity recognition to a central political problem. General conditions were thus established for the philosophical understanding of political struggles to shift from an approach centered on the distribution of wealth to a more encompassing approach, one based on multiple forms of recognition in the spheres of culture, sexuality, and ethnicity, as well as on the development of individual potentialities – a multiplicity of spheres that occupied a central role within the political scene after it was generally, though tacitly, accepted that a revolutionary politics built around the instrumentalization of class struggles was a simply unattainable proposition.

In this case, we would be forced to admit, at least within the parameters of this particular reading, that the concept of recognition is geographically limited to the description of social struggles in so-called First World countries; countries whose proletariat has already been integrated into the middle classes and who have already recognized the need for their cultural matrices to be decentralized through a general acceptance of the tolerant affirmation of ever-changing forms of life. Therefore, it must be insisted that one of the first uses to which the concept of recognition was put, following its second recovery, was

---

[5]  Cf. e.g. DELEUZE & GUATTARI, *Anti-Oedipus: Capitalism and Schizophrenia* (University of Minnesota Press, 1983), and FOUCAULT, *The History of Sexuality, Vol. 1: An Introduction* (New York: Pantheon Books, 1978).

one precisely connected to reflections on the social dynamics of multicultural societies, such as those found in Charles Taylor's aforementioned work.

However, this particular reading does not correspond to the historical reality of the resurgence of the concept within social philosophy, which took place, as we have seen, in the early 1990s, and which was thus concomitant with the beginning of the slow process of disintegration of the economic achievements of the so-called welfare states, the progressive dismantling of workers' rights, the partial or complete privatization of social security, and the deterioration of education, health and other public services. This process of disintegration took place at a time when several theorists stated that we were about to enter a "post-ideological" era, that is, one marked by the demise of the belief in revolutionary social transformation and the subsequent acceptance of the normative horizon of liberal democracies as the endpoint of social struggle.

That may explain why commentators who criticize the importance accorded to the concept of recognition – predominantly, though not exclusively, those of a Marxist orientation – have often insisted that what we are faced with here is merely a *compensatory* concept. For them, the situation is one where, given the impossibility of implementing effective policies related to wealth redistribution, or of attacking inequality in a radical, decisive manner, discussions about the implementation of compensatory policies of recognition is simply all that remains.[6] Likewise, given the now unquestionable status of Capital as the only thing capable of universal reach within the liberalism of multicultural societies, there is little left to do, they contend, apart from reinventing demands for the recognition of communal identities in their various forms, in the attempt to bestow a greater meaning on

---

[6]  This appears to be the intended sense of the following remarks: "It is effectively as if, since the horizon of social imagination no longer allows us to entertain the idea of an eventual demise of capitalism – since, as we might put it, everybody silently accepts that *capitalism is here to stay* – critical energy has found an alternative outlet in fighting for cultural differences which leave the basic homogeneity of the capitalist world-system intact." (ZIZEK, "Multiculturalism, or, the Cultural Logic of Multinational Capitalism," in *New Left Review* II/225, September-October 1997, p. 46) Let us also recall, here, the words of left-wing liberal Richard Rorty, who wrote: "So we still need an explanation of why cultural recognition is thought so important. I think one reason it has become so important in the discourse of the American academic left may be the result of a specifically academic set of circumstances. The only thing we academics can do, in our specifically professional capacities, to eliminate prejudice is to write women's history, celebrate black artistic achievements, and the like. This is what academics who work in such programs as Women's Studies, African-American Studies, and Gay Studies do best. These programs are the academic arms of the new social movements – the movements which, as Judith Butler rightly says, have kept the left alive in the United States in recent years, years during which the rich have consistently had the best of it in the class struggle." (RORTY, Richard; "Is 'Cultural Recognition' a Useful Concept for Leftist Politics?," in *Critical Horizons*, 1 (1), 2000, p. 11)

our communities than merely that of being a delimited space; little remains, ultimately, apart from discussing the moral nature of our social demands in light of the impossibility of large-scale social transformation.

## *The economy of individual identity*

To demonstrate that the device in question was not merely compensatory in nature, but in fact endowed with significant transformative potential in regards to social structures, was a task to which several defenders of the political application of the concept of recognition devoted themselves over the past twenty years. Accomplishing this task involved shedding light on the fact that, in the context of concrete political processes, the emancipatory power of recognition was closely related to discussions about the egalitarian redistribution of wealth; it also involved reminding critics that discussions about cultural differences and social identities did not necessarily mask structural problems connected to the struggle between classes for the redistribution of wealth. It is this project Axel Honneth appears to have had in mind when he wrote that "even distributional injustices must be understood as the institutional expression of social disrespect – or, in other words, of unjustified relations of recognition," a position that several commentators have echoed since[7] This realization in turn led him to defend the proposition that even the workers' movement "essentially aimed at finding recognition for its traditions and forms of life within a capitalist value horizon."[8]

It is clear, then, that one of the main aspects of Honneth's strategy involved attempting to assimilate the problem of wealth redistribution into the broader framework of discussions pertaining to recognition. To that end, the social sentiment of economic injustice had to be understood as potentially an expression of the "motivational sources of social discontent and resistance,"[9] clearing the way, at least as far as Honneth was concerned, for the possible establishment of a unified motivational framework, centered on the idea that "what subjects expect of society is above all recognition of their identity claims."[10] Coming from the same author who wrote that "subjects perceive institutional procedures as social injustice when they see aspects of their personality being disrespected which they believe have a right

---

[7]  HONNETH, "Redistribution as Recognition," p. 114.
[8]  *Ibid.*, p. 123.
[9]  *Ibid.*, p. 125.
[10]  *Ibid.*, p. 131.

to recognition,"[11] the aforementioned proposition seems unsurprising. This is a conceptual movement that introduces the notion of "personal integrity" into the regulating mechanisms of processes of recognition, a notion whose fundamental presupposition is the *de facto* naturalization of the structures of the psychological concepts of "individual" and "personality." According to Honneth, political struggles, even those founded on demands for economic redistribution, ultimately aim to ensure the existence of concrete conditions for "personal identity-formation." [12] In other words, and as suggested elsewhere in this book, the very genesis of modern individuality is seen as a pre-political foundation for the political sphere; something to be politically confirmed, rather than politically deconstructed. Hence the following, decisive statement: "I proceed from the premise that the purpose of social equality is to enable the personal identity-formation of all members of society."[13]

Once he has effected this naturalization, Honneth draws on studies by historians such as E. P. Thompson and Barrington Moore, among others, to strengthen his arguments in favor of the view that the motivational structure of working-class struggles was primarily based on "the experience of the violation of locally transmitted claims to honor,"[14] because, it was argued, feelings of disrespect stemming from the refusal of individuals' demands for recognition far outweighed in relative importance the satisfaction of material needs. By insisting that the moral experience of feelings of "disrespect" is the main driver of political struggle, and thus raising this particular emotion to the status of motivational grounds for all human conflict, Honneth is able to inscribe problems relative to redistribution into the more general framework of moral demands. Hence, and in view of the fact that social vulnerability is connected to impoverishment, which is understood here essentially as the material expression of the impossibility of one's moral demands for respect being met, and that struggles for redistribution are understood as inextricable from experiences of social disrespect, Honneth can reasonably claim that "the distinction between economic disadvantage and cultural degradation is phenomenologically secondary."[15]

---

[11] *Ibid.*, p. 132.

[12] *Ibid.*, p. 174.

[13] *Ibid.*, p. 177.

[14] *Ibid.*, p. 131. Defending this long-held perspective, Honneth even states that (as has been suggested above) Marx initially "conceives of class struggle not as a strategic battle over the acquisition of material goods or instruments of power but rather as a moral conflict in which what is at issue is the 'emancipation' of labour as the crucial condition for both symmetrical esteem and basic self-confidence." (HONNETH, *The Struggle for Recognition*, p. 147)

[15] HONNETH, "Redistribution as Recognition," p. 170.

Among the many problems that result from this perspective, special consideration should be given to at least three. Firstly, a theory that regards distinctions between economic and cultural degradation as being of secondary importance, and that substantiates this perspective by recourse to a form of "moral monism," is a theory that leaves no room for reflection on the specificity and the irreplaceability of a politics of redistribution. If what we are faced with here are the myriad forms under which the impossibility of demands for respect being met appears, it is unclear why problems relating to economic inequality would not find some degree of compensation and mitigation through, for instance, a politics of cultural affirmation. The fact that struggles for redistribution are defined as processes of affirmation of the material conditions required for personal identity formation should make it possible for us to believe that the development of additional processes capable of ensuring the viability of this identity formation would have a compensatory impact on, and thus strengthen, demands for economic equality. Once we allow a single social-ontological matrix for every form of social suffering, however, reflecting on the irreducibility of a politics of redistribution becomes completely impossible.

Secondly, once demands for redistribution are classified as demands of a moral nature, their "psychologization", that is, their being treated as problems that follow from the imposition of restrictions on the development of psychological individuality, can no longer be prevented. This is a scenario in which, ultimately, complaints of a psychological nature would overtake political discourse; worst of all, however, is the fact that every attempted response to demands for redistribution would become a "therapeutic" action guided by public policies developed on the basis of a conception of political subjects as something akin to proto-subjects. As such, proto-subjects are psychologically vulnerable in terms of their identities, and their appearance in the public sphere is accompanied by the sort of discourse that characterizes those who expect to be supported and cared for.[16] Thus, demands for social

---

[16] Regarding this, cf. the uses of the concept of *care* within political debate in general and, more specifically, with a view to defining the nature of welfare policies, particularly as discussed in VASSET, Philippe, & VIANNAY, Clotilde; "Abécédaire de la crise. Politiques du care. Micropolitique de l'habitat non-ordinaire," in *Revue Multitudes*, 37, 38, 2009, and in FASSIN, Didier, & RECHTMANN, Richard; *L'empire du traumatisme. Enquête sur la condition de victime*. Paris: Editions Flammarion, 2007. In his way, Alain Badiou had already pointed out the risks inherent in this psychologization of social suffering; cf. BADIOU, *Ethics: An Essay on the Understanding of Evil*, trans. by P. Hallward. New York: Verso, 2001. On other aspects of the same problem, cf. also KEHL, Maria Rita; *Ressentimento* ["Resentment"]. São Paulo: Casa do Psicólogo, 2005.

change would eventually become demands for social care. And yet, demands for care, if they are to be adequately met, must by definition recognize the legitimacy of the other's position as someone under whose care one may be placed. These cannot be regarded as political demands for transformation, then, but as therapeutic demands for protection and assistance. An individual who demands to be cared for reinforces the position of those who are to provide such care.

Honneth's perspective has yet another negative consequence worth mentioning. Through its reduction of the totality of social struggle to demands for the affirmation of the conditions allowing for personal identity-formation, it obliterates a dimension historically regarded as fundamental for a genuine understanding of class struggle: namely, that power of *nonidentity* that is peculiar to the proletariat as conceived by Marx. By seeing the revolutionary potential of the proletariat as nothing but a historical-philosophical dogma, Honneth jettisons what could be termed the "ontological function" served by the proletariat in Marx's thought. It is this ontological function that makes the proletariat, thus conceived, into the social manifestation of a principle of un-identity and un-differentiation; in other words, a sort of "proletarian condition" can be found in Marx's writing that operates as a regulatory criterion for his radical brand of egalitarianism. This condition is one that contemporary political reflection would gain much by revisiting.

### *The social indeterminacy of the proletariat*

According to Marx, revolution can only be accomplished by the class comprised of those that are without predicates, those deeply bereft of any identity; a class composed of "*world-historical,* empirically universal individuals in place of local ones."[17] This is something that diverges significantly from the traditional conception of workers struggling for recognition of their customs and modes of living. A fundamental requirement for the appearance of world-historical individuals is a certain experience of negativity that has, since Hegel, been the condition without which true universality is impossible; an experience the proletariat undergoes in the form of the complete self-dispossession described by Marx in the following terms:

---

[17] MARX, Karl, & ENGELS, Friedrich; *The German Ideology, including Theses on Feuerbach and the Introduction to the Critique of Political Economy.* Amherst: Prometheus Books, 1998, p. 57.

> The proletarian is without property [*eigentumslos*]; his relation to his wife and children has no longer anything in common with the bourgeois family relations; modern industry labour, modern subjection to capital, the same in England as in France, in America as in Germany, has stripped him of every trace of national character. Law, morality, religion, are to him so many bourgeois prejudices, behind which lurk in ambush just as many bourgeois interests.[18]

As we can see, poverty is not the sole characteristic that defines the proletariat; equal weight is given to a complete annulment of any attachment to traditional forms of life. Once these attachments are severed, they cannot be restored through political processes of self-reaffirmation. The question here is not about allowing proletarians their own nation, or their own bourgeois families and morality and religion. The process of negation which renders such normativities null is one from which no return is possible. It must be added, however, that the negation in question does not cast the proletariat as that "indefinite, disintegrated mass, thrown hither and thither, which the French term *la bohème*"[19], and which Marx called the "lumpenproletariat."[20] In fact, the anomie and lack of structure that characterize the lumpenproletariat is typical of those who still hope for a return to order, and are unable to conceive of anything outside an ordered structure they themselves know to be damaged beyond salvation. This is precisely what turns their political actions into a mere "parody" of transformative action, a "comedy," or a "masquerade", all of which terms are employed by Marx in the *Eighteenth Brumaire* to describe purportedly revolutionary actions that amount to nothing more than attempts at stabilizing chaos.

The actual proletariat, then, may be said to be distinguished by the total absence of any hope for a return. Being thus entirely devoid of property, nationality, attachment to traditional modes of living, or trust in established social normativities, the proletariat can turn its destitution into a political force to radically transform existing forms of life, as Marx emphasized in his yearning for:

---

[18] MARX & ENGELS, *Manifesto of the Communist Party*, trans. by S. Moore. New York: Verso, 1998, p. 48.

[19] MARX, *The Eighteenth Brumaire of Louis Bonaparte*. Moscow: Progress Publishers, 1972, p. 63.

[20] On this notion, cf. e.g. THOBURN, Nicholas; "Difference in Marx: the lumpenproletariat and the proletarian unnamable," in *Economy and Society*, Volume 31, 3, August 2002: 434–460.

a *universal* intercourse between men established, which produces in all nations simultaneously the phenomenon of the "propertyless" mass (universal competition), makes each nation dependent on the revolutions of the others, and finally has put *world-historical*, empirically universal individuals in place of local ones.[21]

To that end, we must understand that the affirmation of the proletarian condition is an entirely distinct phenomenon from demands for recognition of forms of life clearly organized in relation to their particularities but that have yet to receive the respect they are due. Quite the contrary: the affirmation of the proletarian condition gives rise to that class of subjects without predicates that, as stated in *The German Ideology*, can find fulfillment in whatever activity they may apply themselves to; subjects that can "hunt in the morning, fish in the afternoon, rear cattle in the evening, criticise after dinner" without, importantly, "ever becoming hunter, fisherman, shepherd or critic,"[22] in other words, without being entirely determined by its predicates. What this means is that any activity performed by a subject, whether it be hunting or fishing, shepherding or criticizing, must not play any part in its identification.

As Hegel believed, the positing of the subject, its exteriorization, reveals that what drives the movement of essence is something whose nature is radically anti-predicative.[23] It could not be otherwise, not if we conceive the proletariat as a class that is "itself the expression of the dissolution of all classes, nationalities, etc., within present society,"[24] a class composed of that which dissolves all classes, that which represents "the complete loss of humanity,"[25] and, finally, for which no figure remains in the contemporary image of "man." In this sense, by adopting a broadly Hegelian view of the subject (although Marx would be the first to challenge this appropriation, seeing in Hegel nothing but an abstract elaboration of the problem), it may be said that the proletariat can

---

[21] MARX & ENGELS, *The German Ideology*, pp. 54-57.

[22] *Ibid.*, p. 53.

[23] In the words of Alain Badiou, "Marx had already underscored that the universal singularity of the proletariat derives from its bearing no predicate, possessing nothing, and in particular not having, in the strong sense of the term, any 'fatherland.' This anti-predicative, negative and universal conception of the new man traverses the century." (BADIOU, *The Century*, trans. by A. Toscano. Cambridge: Polity Press, 2007, p. 66) Let us also recall that "[in] Latin, *proletarii* meant 'prolific' people – people who make children, who merely live and reproduce without a name, without being counted as part of the symbolic order of the city" (RANCIÈRE, Jacques; "Politics, Identification and Subjectivization," in RAJCHMAN, John (ed.); *The Identity in Question*. New York: Routledge, 1995, pp. 66-67).

[24] MARX & ENGELS, *The German Ideology*, p. 60.

[25] MARX, *Critique of Hegel's 'Philosophy of Right,'* pp. 141-142.

only overcome its alienation by confronting the deep indeterminateness in which it is rooted and subsequently retaining something of its indeterminate character. Its role in attaining *redemption* (*Erlösung*) cannot be performed unless it accepts that its essential nature is *dissolution* (*Auflösung*). As Balibar wrote, the advent of the proletarian as a political subject is the advent of an "empty subject," which is to say of a "subject as emptiness,"[26] one that is by no means bereft of practical determinations, however. This manifestation of a void where current identitarian determinations would normally be can help us to see that self-recognition only becomes an attainable goal once we have subjected any and all attempts to reinstate immediate identities between the subject and its predicates to a deep and thorough critique.

If that is indeed the case, it may be said that Marx saw class struggle as more than just a moral conflict motivated by a defense of the material conditions required for the symmetrical valuation of subjects that wish to attain recognition for every aspect of their personalities. The abolition of private property must necessarily be accompanied by the abolition of a psychic economy founded on the affirmation of individual personality as an identitarian category. In this sense, Marx's perception of class struggle must not be understood merely as a struggle against economic injustice, but as a critique directed at attempts to establish individuality as the ultimate criterion for any and all processes of social recognition. It would be very difficult to regard it any differently, especially in light of the fact that "person," as discussed above, is a category historically derived from Roman property law, one that Hegel regarded as an "expression of contempt" on account of its merely abstract and formal nature (a feature derived, it bears repeating, from the absolutization of property relations).[27] Marx would later echo this position, insisting that

---

[26] BALIBAR, Etienne; *Citoyen sujet et autres essais d'anthropologie philosophique*. Paris: PUF, 2011, p. 260. This is an idea also present in the works of Jacques Rancière, who wrote: "The proletariat are neither manual workers nor the labor classes. They are the class of the uncounted that only exists in the very declaration in which they are counted as those of no account." (RANCIÈRE, *Disagreement: Politics and Philosophy*, trans. by J. Rose. Minneapolis: University of Minnesota Press, 1999, p. 38)

[27] Here, it is worth recalling Locke's canonical statement: "Though the Earth and all inferior Creatures be common to all Men, yet every Man has a *Property* in his own *Person*. This no Body has any Right to but himself." (LOCKE, John; *Two Treatises of Government*. Cambridge: Cambridge University Press, 2005, p. 287) This articulation between "person" and "property" was the foundation for a broad tradition of thought whose influence may be felt in recent discussions on the notion of "self-ownership" as a fundamental attribute of the person (which one finds in among others COHEN, G. A.; *Self-Ownership, Freedom and Equality*. Cambridge: Cambridge University Press, 1995). While this is a debate to which numerous slants have been and are given, the dialectical tradition stemming from Hegel and Marx tends to interpret it as described above.

the notion of freedom that appears in the *Declaration of the Rights of Man and of the Citizen* of 1793 was one that presupposed an absolutization of the property-owning individual. In his words:

> The limits within which each individual can act *without harming others* are determined by law, just as the boundary between two fields is marked by a stake. It is a question of the liberty of man regarded as an isolated monad, withdrawn into himself. [...] The practical application of the right of liberty is the right of *private property.*[28]

Freedom, for Marx, must necessarily encompass the unshackling of the subject from its condition as an individual whose relationship to other individuals mirrors that of a fenced-off piece of land with the surrounding terrain. Thus, to perceive class struggle as the means through which a post-identitarian social experience can take place is to stick closely to the spirit of Marx's words.

It may even be said that *"proletariat" is simply the political name given to a social force of identitarian un-differentiation the recognition of which could lead to a complete dismantling of any societies organized on the basis of the hypostatization of general property relations.*[29] The great ingenuity involved in Marx's creation of this concept was nowhere more evident than in its capacity to articulate political logic and sociological description, with the ensuing establishment of a profound interrelatedness between actual, existing laborers (who together composed a significant social majority) and proletarians.[30] However, it is not essential for this interrelatedness to be preserved in order for the Marxist conception of proletariat to retain its operational effectiveness. In fact, the current historical scenario, wherein attempts have been made to reconfigure the system of work, seems conducive to a rethinking of this relation, especially in terms of opening up new spaces for the manifestation of those demands

---

[28] MARX, "On the Jewish Question," in TUCKER, Robert C. (ed.); *The Marx-Engels Reader*. New York: W. W. Norton & Company, 1978, p. 42.

[29] The fact that this power of un-differentiation peculiar to the notion of proletariat became prominent due to the work of French Marxists such as Badiou, Balibar and Rancière suggests that something of the decentralization that characterizes the Lacanian conception of subject reached the political arena through former students of Louis Althusser. The matrix of this decentralization, however, is the notion of "negativity" that characterizes the Hegelian subject; which means that, as history with its supreme sense of irony would have it, something of the Hegelian concept of subject ended up being brought back to the contemporary political and philosophical stage as a result of the tacit influence it exerted over the textual production of former students of Althusser, the anti-Hegelian *par excellence.*

[30] As Ernesto Laclau dutifully reminds us in LACLAU, Ernesto; *La razón populista*, trans. by S. Laclau. Buenos Aires: Fondo de Cultura Económica, 2005, p. 308.

that characterize the ontology of the subject presupposed by the Marxist construction.[31]

## Beyond the cultural difference principle

Once we accept this hypothesis and the post-identitarian landscape it suggests, we can make use of some recently-advanced alternatives to reflect on the possibility of a theory of recognition that resists being reductively portrayed as a politics of compensation. In the context of a debate with Axel Honneth, Nancy Fraser attempted to resolve this conundrum by defending a type of dualism which was capable of acknowledging that, regardless of the mutual overlapping of the two spheres, solutions must exist to problems related to redistribution and recognition that take account of the fact that economy is both inextricable from, and irreducible to, culture. It is in light of this that remarks such as the following should be interpreted:

> [J]ustice today requires both redistribution and recognition. And I propose to examine the relation between them. In part, this means figuring out how to conceptualize cultural recognition and social equality in forms that support rather than undermine one another. [...] [Especially considering that], far from occupying two airtight separate spheres, economic injustice and cultural injustice are usually interimbricated so as to reinforce one another dialectically.[32]

Indeed, it is unlikely that what Marx once termed the "the practical overthrow of the actual social relations"[33] would be attainable through any kind of alterations, concrete or otherwise, to established relations of economic exploitation, especially considering that there is no guarantee that the struggle

---

[31] It is perhaps in this light that statements such as the following should be understood: "It would be too easy if there were just the calamity of the struggle between rich and poor. The solution to the problem would have been found pretty quickly. All you have to do is get rid of the cause of dissension, in other words, the inequality of wealth, by giving each an equal share of the cake. The trouble runs deeper. Just as the people are not really the people but actually the poor, the poor themselves are not really the poor. They are merely the reign of a lack of position, the effectivity of the initial disjunction that bears the empty name of freedom, the improper property, entitlement to dispute. They are themselves already the warped conjunction of what is proper to them that is not really proper to them and of the common that is not really common." (RANCIÈRE, *Disagreement*, pp. 13-14)

[32] FRASER, Nancy; "From Redistribution to Recognition? Dilemmas of Justice in a 'Post-Socialist' Age," in *New Left Review* I/212, July-August 1995, pp. 69-72.

[33] MARX, *The German Ideology*, p. 61.

against, and eventual elimination of, economic injustice would by itself also lead to the eradication of cultural injustice. The resilience of exclusionary processes and of prejudice directed at those who are culturally different, even in societies with strong egalitarian traditions, should suffice here as evidence of this. Economic equality is a necessary condition, although perhaps not a sufficient one, for multiple forms of life in their great plasticity to attain social recognition.

According to Nancy Fraser's view, an important challenge facing theories of recognition consists in adequately conceiving the regime of imbrication that exists between economic maldistribution and cultural misrecognition. In this regard, Fraser offers two distinct models of political action, stemming from the notion that there may in fact be *compensatory policies* associated with dynamics of recognition and redistribution, which are inseparable from what the author terms "mainstream multiculturalism" and from the perpetuation of the "liberal welfare state."

The scenario described above could also be interpreted as implying that there is a possible articulation between economic liberalism and multiculturalism that uses the affirmation of cultural difference as a form of compensation for political paralysis in relation to the social effects of liberal economic policies. To compensate for this paralysis, society's image is produced afresh as a network of atomized and strongly identitarian groups endlessly negotiating their recognition within a fragile dynamic of tolerance.

If we must speak of a "fragile dynamic of tolerance," that is because, at least in the present context, cultural identities are necessarily defensive constructs that define themselves by opposition and exclusion. Cultural identities – meaning those connected to the affirmation of specific forms of life structured on the basis of ethnicity, nationality, religion, sexual orientation, attachment to systematized consuetudinary practices, and so on – are invariably defined in terms of tension, as is evident to anyone who has not succumbed to "the typically liberal illusion of a pluralism without antagonism."[34] Most susceptible to this illusion are those who have forgotten that identities, whether political or psychological, are constructed within asymmetrical relations of power, and are therefore expressions of strategies of defense or domination.[35] The extreme politicization of the cultural sphere can do little to lessen this antagonism, a

---

[34] MOUFFE, Chantal; "Democratic Politics and the Question of Identity," in RAJCHMAN, *The Identity in Question*, p. 39.

[35] For a discussion of the nature of the asymmetry of power and its role in the formation of subjective identities and their intrinsic aggressiveness, cf. LACAN, "Aggressiveness in Psychoanalysis," in *Écrits*, pp. 82-101.

task which could only be accomplished, if at all, through the consolidation of an emphatically egalitarian space beyond any and all cultural differences.

Political multiculturalism thrives on the politicization of the field of cultural differences, however, which helps to explain why "tolerance" has been elevated to its significant position as a political affection. It is important to stress, then, that our specific historical moment does not allow for tolerance to be perceived as a political affection *endowed with transformative power*.[36] On the contrary, the politics of tolerance is what currently feeds a (negative) infinite cycle of conflicts occasioned by continual social regressions. It is for this reason alone that countries that were until very recently renowned for their highly "tolerant" cultural policies, such as Denmark and the Netherlands, currently stand out as those most deeply marked by forceful policies of cultural exclusion. It is as if the true function of multicultural societies has ultimately revealed itself to be the continuous blocking of politics through an extreme sensitization to the issue of cultural differences.

A politics based on tolerance is a politics that erects a field of tolerable differences, a practice that cannot help but feed the perpetual specter of "intolerable difference." In other words, the omnipresent feature of multicultural dynamics, the equalization of differences, is founded on the following question: to what extent can a certain difference be tolerated? As questions go, however, this is not a useful one. It presupposes that how one sees the other is primarily on the basis of the latter's differences in regards to one's own identity, as if one's identity were something fully determined that could be simply compared to the identity of the other. A better question might be: under what conditions can diversity appear as the modulation of a single universality *in a tense process of realization*? It may be regarded as a "better" question because it implies an understanding of the political not as a sphere conducive to the identification and recognition of differences, but as a sphere conducive to the *deconstruction* of differences.

There are some points of commonality between the above position and Fraser's belief in the possibility of *transformative strategies* that involve an articulation between what she views as practices connected to socialist redistribution and practices connected to the deconstruction of cultural differences. This deconstruction may be regarded as a necessity for two reasons. First, as long as recognition remains tied to the affirmation of cultural differences, and is thus dependent on the mobilization of existing bonds between itself and the production of identities, it will remain an impossible

---

[36] A theme addressed in BADIOU, *Ethics: An Essay on the Understanding of Evil* (Verso, 2001), as well as ZIZEK, *Violence: Six Sideways Reflections*. London: Profile Books, 2009.

task to prevent it from being used to justify practices that are not expressions of emancipatory processes.[37] As Craig Calhoun reminds us, questions pertaining to recognition and identity do not all produce the same consequences, an idea that may be easily grasped once one remembers how this applies to the multiple manifestations of religious fundamentalism, or to the Afrikaners resistance of a so-called "black supremacy," among several other examples.[38] Fraser has this ambivalence in mind when she remarks that, "from Rwanda to the Balkans, questions of 'identity' have fuelled campaigns for ethnic cleansing and even genocide – as well as movements that have mobilized to resist them."[39]

Secondly, new forms of solidarity and equality are created as soon as we become capable of seeing subjects as loci for deconstructive practices that alter the system of social representations at a structural level, through the constitution of a multiplicity of differences in unceasing motion. Judith Butler also explores this point through a reflection on the potential radicalization of the ethical dimension of the recognition of alterity, leading her to assert that:

> [We] might consider a certain post-Hegelian reading of the scene of recognition in which precisely my own opacity to myself occasions my capacity to confer a certain kind of recognition on others. It would be, perhaps, an ethics based on our shared, invariable, and partial blindness about ourselves.[40]

Thus, by refraining from imposing a strongly-structured identity upon oneself, and instead recognizing the need to deal with something within oneself that resists identitarian structures, one is led to a greater sense of solidarity with that which exists in the other yet cannot quite be integrated into one's own structures of recognition. If these new forms of solidarity worked, they could eliminate the merely compensatory character of policies directed at cultural recognition, mainly by not allowing political paralysis in regards to economic transformation to be hidden by the regressive dynamics of identitarian conflicts. In fact, from this perspective, these forms of solidarity could completely eliminate the regressive dynamics in question by making room

---

[37] As stressed by Mauro Basaure in BASAURE, Mauro; ¿Es la teoría de las luchas por el recono-cimiento una teoría de la política? (2012 conference, unpublished).

[38] CALHOUN, Craig; Critical Social Theory: Culture, History, and the Challenge of Difference. Oxford: Wiley Blackwell, 1995, p. 215.

[39] FRASER, "Rethinking Recognition," in New Left Review, 3 (May-June 2000), p. 107; in this regard, cf. also FRASER, "Social Justice in the Age of Identity Politics: Redistribution, Recognition, and Participation," in FRASER & HONNETH, Redistribution or Recognition, p. 38.

[40] BUTLER, Giving an Account of Oneself, p. 41.

for substantive sharing of subjective discomfort in relation to static identities. In other words, instead of the simple withdrawal of cultural discussions from the arena of political conflict, what instead emerges is a growing trend toward preventing the debate on culture from entering a state of regression because of its domination by problems related to the recognition of the production of identities.

However, it is not difficult to find positions that diverge from this one, yet are equally well-founded; for instance, in a text on the political power of the concept of recognition Emmanuel Renault and Jean-Philippe Deranty state that:

> there is no hard distinction to be made between the spheres of recognition and identity. Personal identity is the synthesis of the different strands of identity. [...] Recognition is therefore political in two interrelated senses: first, as delivering the grammar of political struggle, and second, as supporting the potentially political, integrating dimension of subjective identity.[41]

The authors contend that, for an individual, autonomy is incompatible with a generalized indifference in relation to all of his/her identities; but, not wishing to regress too much and be forced to argue in favor of the preservation of static identities, they suggest the recovery of the Hegelian notion of identity, understood as a form of "negative self-reference."[42] This is illustrated by remarks such as the following: "What individuals want to have recognized in the struggle for recognition is therefore, strictly speaking, not so much their positive identity, rather it is their identity as negative, their freedom to posit their own identity."[43]

To move beyond these two perspectives – which, incidentally, might converge if the former's deconstructive practices and the latter's suggested interpretation of the Hegelian notion of identity were integrated – it is worth considering the possibility of taking these matters in a slightly different direction. The solution to the problem might not consist in the mere dissociation of culture and identity, but could depend instead on a theory of recognition capable of dissociating politics from culture and cultural issues, which commonly pertain to the production of social identities. The debate

---

[41] DERANTY, Jean-Philippe, & RENAULT, Emmanuel; "Politicizing Honneth's Ethics of Recognition," in *Thesis Eleven*, Number 88, February 2007, p. 104.

[42] On this, cf. the discussion on the determinations of reflection in Hegel's "The Doctrine of Essence" (*Science of Logic*, pp. 337-505).

[43] DERANTY & RENAULT, *op. cit.*, p. 107.

on the relations between redistribution and recognition is one within which reflections on the nature of social relations are typically restricted to two spheres: the cultural and the economic. Politics could also be added to that list as an autonomous sphere, however, especially considering that we may never be able to fully dissociate culture from the production of defensive identities (something Nancy Fraser and Judith Butler appear to regard, each in her own way, as an actual possibility), but must instead investigate the possibility of affirming that politics was born out of the actualization of what may be termed the "power of depersonalization" – something that breaks into the dimension of shared existence and leads subjects to stop speaking as though they were the representatives of particular interests and identities.

## Politics of indifference

However much it may appear to fly in the face of the most elementary sociological truisms, it may be said that the true birth of the political sphere can only occur once it has been extricated from the spheres of both culture and economy.[44] Among the many consequences that may follow from this perspective is the affirmation that identities can and must find their proper space for development, with one *caveat*: there is nothing to suggest that it must be a politicized space. The hypothesis to be defended here, then, is that politics un-identifies subjects by stripping them of their cultural differences, and it de-localizes them by stripping them of their nationalities and geographic identities just as much as it de-individualizes them by stripping them of their psychological attributes. Thus, from this particular perspective, politics is above all a force of un-differentiation capable of opening subjects up to a productive sphere of indeterminacy; consequently, political subjects are not the bearers of individual demands representative of the interests of specific groups or classes. Under such conditions, the demands that appear in the political sphere merely emulate particularisms that seek a foothold in what is simply a network of power struggles, rather than a truly political confrontation endowed with concrete transformative power. In reality, politics has no regard for individuals, which is perhaps the most currently relevant among the many useful lessons imparted by Marx. The fact that from his perspective a revolution could only be undertaken by those belonging to a class bereft of

---

[44] This is my interpretation of statements such as the following, by Jacques Rancière: "Politics cannot be deduced from the necessity of gathering people into communities. It is an exception to the principles according to which this gathering operates." (RANCIÈRE, *Dissensus: On Politics and Aesthetics*, trans. by S. Corcoran. New York: Continuum Books, 2010, p. 35)

all predicates and completely dispossessed of all identity – a class composed, as we have seen, of "*world-historical,* empirically universal individuals in place of local ones" – is something that requires careful reflection. What such considerations suggest is that subjects only become political agents once their individual demands are de-individualized, which may even be interpreted as being the very condition that would allow rights to be generically extended.

It must be stated, therefore – and this is an important preliminary hypothesis, deserving of further investigation – that from a political perspective the space of cultural differences must be a space of absolute indifference.[45] Nonetheless, what exactly is meant by the proposition that cultural differences should be objects of political indifference? We should perhaps begin by defining what it *does not* mean. We cannot ignore the fact that the creation of specific policies favoring excluded, disadvantaged or discriminated-against social groups, or the enactment of laws to protect them, fulfils an important strategic function: in such cases, the affirmation of cultural differences increases social sensitivity to their plight as groups whose rights, historically, have been more vulnerable to attack than those of others. What often happens in these situations, however, is that the malleability of political action is used to impose the concrete conditions required to ensure that egalitarianism is affirmed, with one of the conditions in question being an increase in social awareness of the vulnerability of such historically dispossessed groups. This increase in awareness is a necessary stage of the societal transition towards a situation in which the proposed indifference to cultural differences is not rendered impossible by the violence continually perpetrated against specific groups. In other words, we can speak of a "strategically provisional" use of the notion of identity in such cases that is not unrelated to the perspective defended in the present chapter.

On the other hand, to state that cultural differences ought to be subjected to political indifference is to defend the autonomy of the political in relation to both culture and economy. This autonomy is derived from the belief that the political sphere alone possesses the required conditions to affirm itself as the sphere of radical equality, especially considering that the spheres of culture and economy are characterized by inequalities that may be minimized but never completely eradicated. If it is an undeniable fact that the social dynamics of culture are marked by a multiplicity of differences undergoing

---

[45] This is an exploration of the idea initially presented by Alain Badiou that "[d]ifferences can be transcended only if benevolence with regard to customs and opinions presents itself as an indifference that tolerates differences, one whose sole material test lies [...] in being able and knowing how to practice them oneself" (BADIOU, *Saint Paul: The Foundation of Universalism*, trans. by R. Brassier. Stanford: Stanford University Press, 2003, p. 99).

continuous reconfiguration, it is similarly true that fragmentation and differentiation blight the economic sphere. As early as the time of Hegel's *Elements of the Philosophy of Right* we have come to accept the idea that the circulation of goods and property between private individuals in civil society will never cease to produce inequality, despite it being a supposed function of the state to minimize and control inequality.[46] Of course, there are alternatives to the economics of the free market, with its affirmation of individualities and their respective interest systems and its lack of compunction about the economic pillaging of the most vulnerable; while more efficient social spaces may be created for the circulation of shared resources and for an affirmation of commonly-held property. Nonetheless, economic activity has at its core an accumulation principle which is a product of equating capital with performance, which is unlikely to be completely eliminated (and nor should it be), unless we collectively decide upon a complete statization of the means of production as a criterion for action. If, conversely, we come to accept that statizing the means of production is inextricable from insoluble problems connected to the blocking of demands for individual development, and that, precisely because of that, the historical moment in which it represented a viable political option has long gone, then we may reasonably affirm that a defense of the autonomy of the political may function as a means to ensure the existence of a space for radical equality in social life, a space that might even be strong enough to induce the economic sphere to meet demands for equality.

Let us now try to more clearly define what a political sphere autonomous in relation to both culture and economy might consist in. To do so, must we be forced to defend the existence of strictly political demands, which are by nature incapable of finding expression as demands for economic justice or demands for the recognition of cultural specificities? If that was the case, our efforts would come to nothing; demands of this nature are extremely unlikely to be met. Politics lacks a space of its own. Nonetheless, defending the autonomy of the political allows us to understand why certain social struggles perennially recur within the logic of economic gain and the defense of cultural particularities. The experience of the political does not take place at the margins of economy and culture, but makes use of both in the effort to push economic and cultural demands to the point at which a radical egalitarianism may be affirmed, one capable of unveiling "the universal function of private struggles when these are invested with a significance that transcends their own

---

[46] HEGEL, *Philosophy of Right*, § 243, p. 266.

particularity."[47] In this sense, assent must be given to Rancière's proposition that politics operate when the word "people" is not understood as meaning a race or population, or "poor" as meaning the disadvantaged segment of a population, or "proletarian" as meaning industrial workers. Politics exist when what is denoted by these terms are subjects that resist being inscribed as a part of society, and that must therefore be regarded as something that cannot be measured or circumscribed by the managerial logic of social life.

However, if that is the case, it is unclear why one should presuppose – and we have certainly done so at more than one point in this chapter – that the autonomy of the political is the condition that allows us to defend the existence of something that ought to be termed "anti-predicative recognition." To all appearances, what we have here is merely an understanding of the political as a sphere wherein universal rights are formed, an understanding that would therefore lead us to the idea that social demands become political demands the moment particular interests manifest as the expression of universal rights that have not yet been extended to disadvantaged groups. In this sense, far from their being affirmed in an "anti-predicative" manner, the opposite is true: subjects are predicated through determinations derived from legally established positive rights which those subjects had been hitherto denied. To speak of "anti-predicative recognition," then, would only make sense if we could affirm the need for something in the subject not to be determined by predicates, but to remain an indeterminate force of un-differentiation. Thus, it could be said that a deepening of the dynamics of recognition does not depend on an increase in the number of predicates attributed to a subject, but on the understanding that what a subject is actually defined by is precisely the fact that it carries within itself something that resists the process of predication.[48] This leaves us with a fundamental question, namely: how can this non-predicable force attain political recognition? Could we even conceive of political struggles whose concrete manifestation as particular demands unavoidably led us to recognize that which is radically anti-predicative?

---

[47] LACLAU, *La razón populista*, p. 305. Laclau suggestively proposes that the relation between the particular and the universal within political struggles should be thought of through the Lacanian notion of "objet petit a" as a partiality that functions as a totality; an incommensurable and irrepresentable totality relative to accepted representational standards would thus be uncovered.

[48] A strictly Hegelian perspective, one which, being fully conversant with Hegel's critique of the predicative structure of perception-based knowledge (as seen in the *Phenomenology of Spirit*), regarded this structure as a moment to be sublated into a theory of recognition, and thus had to arrive at similar conclusions.

Once the problem is stated in the terms described above, it becomes quite clear that we must avoid seeing it as a version of the need to recover the classic distinction between "citizen" and "bourgeois" so thoroughly explored by Marx in *On the Jewish Question*, with the sphere of what we understand as "culture" being regarded as a contemporary version of the field of interests of the bourgeois, property-owning individual (representing the "possessive individualism" described by Macpherson) to which the dimension of differentiated cultural attributes should now be added. The defense of "citizenship" normally encompasses an understanding that politics essentially advances through the institutionalization of acquired universal rights, which subsequently become predicates of all subjects without exception. While accepting that "citizenship" is a notion that merely reproduces those "contradictions that come into it the moment it is 'organically' inserted into 'bourgeois society,' whose conflicts, relations and processes it formalizes," the most we can do is be careful not to neglect the fact that it is also connected to "demands for 'real,' 'radical' equality and freedom, which is precisely whence its legitimacy comes."[49] However, perhaps the connection to demands for equality and freedom found in struggles for citizenship can only be preserved once we completely and totally reject its organic insertion into bourgeois society, as well as its tendency to be the juridical-institutional construction of a figure of "man" inseparable from the universalization and idealization of the material experience of the liberal individual. To a certain extent, then, the proposition advanced here takes some inspiration (as do several other mediations) from Marx's idea that "[h]uman emancipation will only be complete when the real, individual man has absorbed into himself the abstract citizen; when as an individual man, in his everyday life, in his work, and in his relationships, he has become a *species-being* [...]."[50]

## *The power of deinstitutionalization*

If we are to properly conceive of the conditions which would make such a recovery possible, it seems that further reflection is needed on what the affirmation of the existence of a necessarily "anti-predicative" dimension of recognition might actually entail. As has been stated above, we know that

---

[49] BALIBAR, *Citoyen sujet et autres essais*, p. 473. Considerations of the same nature led Marx to remark that "the so-called rights of man, as distinct from the rights of the citizen, are simply the rights of a member of civil society, that is, of egoistic man, of man separated from other men and from the community" (MARX, "On the Jewish Question," p. 42).

[50] MARX, *ibid.*, p. 46.

from a particular political perspective the inevitable endpoint of political struggles is the institutionalization of acquired rights; in other words, we struggle to have our rights recognized within the existing juridical ordering. Consequently, social life becomes increasingly institutionalized and regulated by clauses whose aim is to ensure that groups that had hitherto been extremely vulnerable are in full possession of their rights. The political principle in question has been very successful in promoting the extension of fundamental rights to ethnic, religious and sexual minorities, for example. It is clear that in such cases the specific demands at stake were directed at the state in its role as an agent capable of ensuring the *de facto* universalization of the conditions for freedom yearned for by its citizens. That this process has been and continues to be very important is undeniable; however, it has a significant side-effect, which is the strengthening of regulative strategies directed at what might be termed the "libidinal economy of capitalist societies."

Every time the juridical structure is strengthened, even when this is done in the name of defending vulnerable segments of the population, there is a concurrent increase in the disciplinary regulation of life, with the legal structure in question determining the possible forms that life may adopt, and the possible arrangements that may be devised by singularities. Forms of life are thus reduced to something molded in advance by the anticipatory measures of the legal structure. This process is not restricted to changing the juridical ordering, but also reinforces, at an institutional level, the circumscription of the production of difference within a cultural field where capitalist processes of exploitation are allowed to control the entire libidinal economy. The sensitization of the juridical sphere to difference is, after all, invariably accompanied by a naming process in which every social form attained by desire receives a different name. While this process provides greater visibility to groups commonly vulnerable to social violence, the allocation of names is restricted to a grammar of identities already in circulation, which is supposedly capable of accepting any and all identities, provided they can find a place for themselves within the general field of social difference management. In this sense, the *deactivation of names* may be said to be part and parcel of an important political strategy. Power can tell us nothing about difference, after all; it cannot exploit the economy of difference at a libidinal level, and must therefore free it from all institutionalized naming.[51] Hence, it would be helpful at this juncture to briefly recall Lacan's thoughts about naming, particularly his remarks on the radical inadequacy of subjects (conceived

---

[51] This is a point fully developed in the fourth chapter of SAFATLE, *Cinismo e falência da crítica* (Boitempo, 2008).

from a perspective in which desire is given complete centrality) in regards to the naming structures they are subjected to, as well as on the political consequences of this inadequacy and how, among other things, it leads us to seek a *non-predicable difference* endowed with strong political potential.

Faced with situations of this nature, we must attempt to develop recognition strategies that bypass any and all mechanisms of institutionalization, strategies that, on the contrary, involve far-reaching processes of de-institutionalization which, rather than enlarging the scope of the legal sphere, causes the latter to atrophy. There is a form of anti-predicative recognition attainable through de-institutionalization that reduces and even deactivates the power of juridical ordering, and thus creates "the possibility of a human existence beyond the Law."[52] This *topos* of a life lived beyond the reach of the law which appears throughout Giorgio Agamben's reflections on the possible form of a "destituent power" seems conducive to appropriation by a theory of recognition willing to cede space to the fundamental irreducibility of experiences of subjective indeterminacy, and to reflect on the political consequences of these experiences.[53] Furthermore, it is a *topos* that places us before a form of anomie that cannot simply be conceived of as the undermining of the capacity of social norms for cohesiveness and organization, as found in several models reminiscent of Durkheim's views on the matter[54] – a process believed to produce a costly deregulation of social norms, paid for in pathological conditions that manifest as feelings of emptiness and a complete incapacity for action.[55] What we are dealing with, instead, is an anomie that strengthens the political sphere by opening it up to that which lies beyond the law.

---

[52] AGAMBEN, Giorgio; *The Highest Poverty: Monastic Rules and Form-of-Life*, trans. by A. Kotsko. Stanford: Stanford University Press, 2013, p. 110.

[53] In this sense, one must give assent to a statement such as the following, by Giorgio Agamben: "[If] instead of continuing to search for a proper identity in the already improper and senseless form of individuality, humans were to succeed in belonging to this impropriety as such, in making of the proper being-thus not an identity and an individual property but a singularity without identity, a common and absolutely exposed singularity – if humans could, that is, not be-thus in this or that particular biography, but be only *the* thus, their singular exteriority and their face, then they would for the first time enter into a community without presuppositions and without subjects, into a communication without the incommunicable" (AGAMBEN, *The Coming Community*, trans. by M. Hardt. Minneapolis: University of Minnesota Press, 2007, p. 64).

[54] Cf. DURKHEIM, Émile; *Suicide: A Study in Sociology*, trans. by J. A. Spaulding & G. Simpson. New York: Routledge, 2002.

[55] Cf. e.g. HONNETH, *Das Ich im Wir: Studien zur Anerkennungstheorie*. Frankfurt: Suhrkamp, 2012, pp. 207-208.

When an idea of this kind is advanced, many are quick to denounce it as an insidious form of liberalism, meaning that they regard it as a practical application of that old mantra: the less state, the better. From this perspective, the implementation of practices of deinstitutionalization allows society to freely create forms of life while at the same time causing it to turn a blind eye to experiences of oppression and economic vulnerability. However, deinstitutionalization policies of a different sort, devoid of all liberal trappings, appear to us eminently conceivable; differently conceived, deinstitutionalization practices may involve the creation of "zones of cultural indifference," meaning zones within which society would be able to exercise its indifference in relation to cultural differences and their anthropological determinations. This could encompass the retraction, for instance, of laws pertaining to the family as an institution and to self-determination, with simultaneous efforts to increase juridical sensitivity to the detrimental effects of economic spoliation. After all, the recognition that problems related to redistribution are problems that must be approached in terms of their specificity ultimately prevents us from supporting any perspectives that might cause them to be submitted to the same logic that is commonly applied to questions of cultural difference. This would lead to the following state of affairs: strong regulation in regard to economic relations and weak regulation in regard to social relations. It may even be suggested that problems connected to redistribution should be sufficiently regulated within the juridical ordering, so that processes of recognition could develop within a zone of indifference in which legal structures had been rendered inoperative.

This conception of a process of deinstitutionalization capable of creating zones of indifference is the fruit of what is admittedly a rather heterodox appropriation of the notion that class struggle and the proletariat, as understood in Marx, are not only concepts that render the social struggle for economic justice operational, but also concepts that allow us to entertain the possibility of introducing an un-differentiating power into the political arena. However, the true extent of the productive potential of such power, which could be fundamental in producing true political subjects, can only become clear once the scope of the legal sphere has been reduced to the point where the indifferent production of singular forms of life is made possible.

A paradigmatic example of this concerns the potential deinstitutionalization of marriage. Contemporary societies are currently teeming with justified questions regarding the extension of the right to marry to same-sex couples, and this has given rise to demands for egalitarian juridical orderings in regard to an individual's right to enter into a marriage union. A more reasonable course of action, however, would be for such demands to be radicalized to the point of requiring the state to completely cease legislating on the subject of marriage, and instead obliging it to legislate exclusively on the economic relations between couples or other forms of "affective grouping." This would be one way to effect a radical opening of the institution of marriage to models unconnected to the disciplinary structure of the bourgeois heterosexual family and the attendant biopolitical management of life. Rather than extend the law to those cases it refused to contemplate (such as same-sex marriage) we should simply eliminate the legislation in question to create a deinstitutionalized zone of indifference.

The classic counterargument to this is that once the state ceases legislating on the subject of marriage, it leaves those who are most vulnerable without legal protection (in this case, women). This is a position that seems to underestimate the magnitude of the problem: in addition to legislating on matters that are within its purview (such as the economic relations within the family, the distribution of assets in the case of a divorce, the right to alimony, etc.) the state legislates on matters that legitimately fall outside its remit, specifically, the form of the affective choices made by subjects, or in other words the singular plasticity of forms of life being produced and transformed. Ideally, then, the state should only legislate on questions pertaining to the economic sphere, and refrain from legislating on questions pertaining to the sphere of affection. Obviously, this would have an impact on marriage, as marriage involves more than the establishing of an economic contract between parties: it is, or at least it should be, the recognition of an affective attachment produced as a singular expression of the reciprocal affections of emancipated subjects. In this sense, there is nothing to prevent the state from legislating on the strictly economic aspects of marriage and all other forms of civil union, provided it remains silent regarding the forms such unions take (whether they be between a man and a woman, two women, two women and a man, and so on). In other words, it is not up to the juridical ordering to predicate in advance which affective forms are to be understood as possible; what it must do instead is to embrace the multiple instantiations of what actually is possible. From a legal perspective, this multiplicity should be almost indiscernible.

Deinstitutionalization processes of this sort would allow societies to move incrementally towards a state of indifference in relation to questions of culture, as cultural questions will always be spaces for the affirmation of the multiple ordering of identities. Nonetheless, politics must strive to ultimately become detached from the previous remark: counterintuitive as it may seem, true politics always lies beyond the affirmation of identities. It inscribes into social structures broad, anti-predicative modes of recognition that manifest through the social dimensions of language and desire, which are dimensions singularly characterized by the production and circulation of that which refuses to offer itself to experience as having a proper form of its own.

*I therefore claim to show, not how men think in myths,*
*but how myths operate in men's minds*
*without their being aware of the fact.*
Claude Lévi-Strauss

One might say that the concept "game" is a concept with blurred edges [*verschwommenen Rändern*]. – "But is a blurred concept a concept at all?" – Is an indistinct [*unscharfe*] photograph a picture of a person at all? Is it even always an advantage to replace an indistinct picture with a sharp one? Isn't the indistinct one often exactly what we need?[1]

Such were the questions that confronted us at the beginning of this book. Through the constitution of a system of conceptual interpenetrations derived from a dialectical tradition which has Hegel, Lacan and Adorno as its central figures – a system designed to privilege questions set in motion by the notions of desire, drive, fantasy and action – the aim of the ensuing pages has chiefly been to demonstrate how, remarkably often, an indistinct picture is indeed the one we need. After all, the adoption of a sharp image in place of an indistinct one frequently leads to the loss of precisely the element one had been struggling to circumscribe. In terms of the notion of subject, more specifically, it appears that an indistinct picture is the *only kind* available; the only kind to be able to communicate something of that peculiar foundation that manifests as an *Abgrund*-engendering force, as an indeterminacy-producing experience.

A productive experience of this sort can only be adequately conceived once one abandons the illusion that the pre-philosophical language of common-sense has not been itself imbued with a naturalized metaphysics, that is, once one accepts that common-sense brings with it an anthropological figure of "man" to which we are expected to conform. This figure is in essence a *grammar*, a way of thinking and of guiding oneself in thought, yet it is also *therapeutic*; a way for us to extricate ourselves from anything which provokes anxiety and suffering because it forces us to "do things that we do not know that we know."

---

[1] WITTGENSTEIN, *Philosophical Investigations* I, § 71, p. 34.

Thus, at various points in the book attempts were made to show that any system of reflection for which the clarity provided by the egological reduction of the subject is an unquestionable and impassable dogma is a system that can only be seen as pathological. In a sense, it is as though the proposed treatment has side effects far more threatening than the original illness, given that the therapy in question prevents any form of reflection on what might constitute an individuality once it is freed from the bonds of what Michel Foucault once termed an "analytic of finitude." Indeed, the entire present book is structured as a critical movement directed precisely at this, which ought to be termed, for the sake of accuracy, the *egological reduction of the subject* (even when the ego in question has been given the form of a transcendental "I"), and at its consequences for the dimension of praxis.

The insistent recourse to Hegel throughout the book had the sole purpose of taking into consideration an extreme instance where the modern category of subject more obviously evinces its complete independence from any metaphysics of identity. The message implicit in such an approach is, one hopes, unmistakable: what is ultimately sought is not a radical reinvention of everything we are, but the questioning of deeply-held assumptions. To what an extent do we truly understand the movement of which we are the inheritors, of all that has taken place before our time and yet remains a palpable presence within our demands for change? What we have inherited is the full range of conflicts animating the very constitution of the category of subject within modernity. The overly-simplistic critique of the subject as a metaphysical delusion cannot even begin to address the profound development that the category of subject has undergone within each of the more central philosophical reflections of modernity; the category which this operates with – the so-called "modern subject" – simply does not exist as such. There is no such thing as a single invariant concept of subject unfolding throughout modern philosophy.

In fact, as the book nears its conclusion it strikes me all the more clearly as the end of a cycle. Starting with my Master's dissertation, defended in 1997, my work has consistently featured reflections on the possible outlines of a theory of subject freed from the constraints of identitarian thought, and from an anthropology with normative definitions of the humanity of human beings at its foundation. Such a release would have far-reaching consequences, not least of which would be a redimensioning of the theory of recognition, allowing it to approach, in a more structured manner, phenomena such as the nature of psychic conflict, the ontological insecurity of social normativity, and the need for non-reflexive conceptions of alterity, among others.

At this juncture, and with the benefit of hindsight, it is clear that the books I wrote were individual moments of the same overarching reflection, of a slowly growing awareness of the problem at hand. At least now it has been fully articulated. Hence, even if certain developments are yet to be undertaken – and they certainly will be, sometime in the future – the project seems to have more or less come to an end. There comes a point where one ought to admit as much. And yet, there is a cost: the end of a project throws into sharp relief just how little one's efforts ultimately achieve. At best one gets rid of a harrowing hypothesis that has imposed itself on one's mind as something deserving of careful reflection. In my case, almost a full fifteen years have been dedicated to this pursuit. There is something terrifying about this – the terror that comes with seeing that a human life may be little more than the occasion for an idea to think itself through.

ADORNO, Theodor. *Aesthetic Theory*. Trans. R. Hullot-Kentor. New York: Continuum, 2002.

————. *Against Epistemology: A Metacritique*. Trans. W. Domingo. Cambridge: Polity Press, 2013.

————. *Critical Models: Interventions and Catchwords*. Trans. H. W. Pickford. New York: Columbia University Press, 1998.

————. *Gesammelte Schriften, Band I: Philosophische Frühschriften*. Frankfurt: Suhrkamp, 1990.

————. *Hegel: Three Studies*. Trans. S. W. Nicholsen. Cambridge: the MIT Press, 1993.

————. *Kant's Critique of Pure Reason*. Trans. R. Livingstone. Stanford: Stanford University Press, 2001.

————. *Kierkegaard: Construction of the Aesthetic*. Trans. R. Hullot-Kentor. Minneapolis: University of Minnesota Press, 1989.

————. *Negative Dialectics*. Trans. E. B. Ashton. New York: The Continuum Publishing Company, 1983.

————. *Problems of Moral Philosophy*. Trans. R. Livingstone. Stanford: Stanford University Press, 2001.

————. "Sociology and Psychology – II." Trans. I. N. Wohlfarth. In: *New Left Review* I/47. January-February 1968: 79–97.

ADORNO, Theodor & HORKHEIMER, Max. *Dialectic of Enlightenment: Philosophical Fragments*. Trans. E. Jephcott. Stanford: Stanford University Press, 2002.

AGAMBEN, Giorgio. *The Coming Community*. Trans. M. Hardt. Minneapolis: University of Minnesota Press, 2007.

————. *The Highest Poverty: Monastic Rules and Form-of-Life*. Trans. A. Kotsko. Stanford: Stanford University Press, 2013.

ALMEIDA, Jorge. "Estilo." In: *Crítica dialética em Theodor Adorno: música e verdade nos anos vinte*. São Paulo: Ateliê Editorial, 2007: 79–100.

AMEISEN, Jean Claude. *La sculpture du vivant: le suicide cellulaire et la mort créatrice*. Paris: Seuil, 2003.

ARANTES, Paulo. *Hegel, a ordem do tempo*. São Paulo: Hucitec, 2001.

————. *Ressentimento da dialética*. São Paulo: Paz e Terra, 1996.

————. "Um Hegel errado, mas vivo." In: *Revista Ide* n. 21. São Paulo, 1991: 72–79.

ASSOUN, Paul-Laurent. *Introduction à l'épistémologie freudienne*. Paris: Payot, 1981.

ATLAN, Henri. *Entre le cristal et la fumée: essai sur l'organisation du vivant*. Paris: Seuil, 1979.

———— *L'organisation biologique et la theorie de l'information*. Paris: Seuil, 2006.

AVINERI, Schlomo. *Hegel's Theory of the Modern State.* London: Cambridge University Press, 1972.

BADIOU, Alain. *Being and Event.* Trans. O. Feltham. New York: Continuum, 2007.

———. *The Century.* Trans. A. Toscano. Cambridge: Polity Press, 2007.

———. *Deleuze: The Clamor of Being.* Trans. L. Burchill. Minneapolis: University of Minnesota Press, 2000.

———. *Ethics: An Essay on the Understanding of Evil.* Trans. P. Hallward. New York: Verso, 2001.

———. *Saint Paul: The Foundation of Universalism.* Trans. R. Brassier. Stanford: Stanford University Press, 2003.

BALIBAR, Etienne. *Citoyen sujet et autres essais d'anthropologie philosophique.* Paris: PUF, 2011.

BARTHES, Roland. *The Rustle of Language.* Trans. R. Howard. New York: Hill and Wang, 1986.

BASAURE, Mauro. "¿Es la teoría de las luchas por el reconocimiento una teoría de la política?" Paper presented at the International Society for Psychoanalysis and Philosophy's *5th International Conference on Psychoanalysis and Philosophy: Conflicts, Limits, Recognition.* Universidad Diego Portales, November 6-9, 2012.

BATAILLE, Georges. *Inner Experience.* Trans. L. A. Boldt. Albany: State University of New York Press, 1988.

BEBEE, Beatrice & LACHMANN, Frank. *Infant research and adult treatment: co-constructing interactions.* Hillsdale: Analytic Press, 2002.

BENJAMIN, Jessica. "The End of Internalisation: Adorno's Social Psychology." In: *Telos,* 32, 1977: 42–64.

BENJAMIN, Walter. *Illuminations.* Trans. H. Zohn. New York: Schocken Books, 2007.

BERNAYS, J. *Zwei Abhandlungen über die aristotelische Theorie des Drama.* Darmstadt: Wissenschaftliche Buchgesellschaft, 1968.

BOLTANSKI, Luc, & CHIAPELLO, Eve. *The New Spirit of Capitalism.* Trans. G. Elliott. New York: Verso, 2007.

BOOTHBY, Richard. *Freud as Philosopher: Metapsychology After Lacan.* New York: Routledge, 2001.

BRANDOM, Robert. *Tales of the Mighty Dead: Historical Essays in the Metaphysics of Intentionality.* Cambridge: Harvard University Press, 2002.

BRATEN, Stein (org.). *On being moved: from the mirrors neurons to empathy.* Philadelphia: John Benjamin Publisher House, 2007.

BUTLER, Judith. *Gender Trouble: Feminism and the Subversion of Identity.* New York: Routledge, 1999.

———. *Giving an Account of Oneself.* New York: Fordham University Press, 2005.

CALHOUN, Craig. *Critical Social Theory: Culture, History, and the Challenge of Difference.* Oxford: Wiley Blackwell, 1995.

CANGUILHEM, Georges. *Etudes d'histoire et de philosophie de la science.* Paris: Vrin, 2002.

————. *The Normal and the Pathological*. Trans. C. R. Fawcett & R. S. Cohen. New York: Zone Books, 1991.

————. "Vie", In: *Enciclopaedia universalis*, Paris: Enciclopaedia Universalis France, 1990.

————. *Writings on Medicine*. Trans. S. Geroulanos & T. Meyers. New York: Fordham University Press, 2012.

COHEN, G. A. *Self-Ownership, Freedom and Equality*. Cambridge: Cambridge University Press, 1995.

DAVID-MÈNARD, Monique. *Deleuze et la psychanalyse*. Paris: PUF, 2005.

————. "Les pulsions caractérisées par leurs destins: Freud s'éloigne-t-il du concept philosophique de Trieb?," § 14. In: *Revue Germanique Internationale* [Online Edition], 18 | 2002. Accessed on February 12, 2015. URL: http://rgi.revues.org/924.

DAVIDSON, Arnold. *The emergence of sexuality: historical epistemology and the formation of concepts.* Harvard: Harvard University Press, 2004.

DELEUZE, Gilles. *Bergsonism*. Trans. H. Tomlinson & B. Habberjam. New York: Zone Books, 1991.

————. *Difference and Repetition*. Trans. P. Patton. New York: Columbia University Press, 1994.

————. *The Logic of Sense*. Trans. M. Lester & C. Stivale. London: The Athlone Press, 1990.

————. *Nietzsche and Philosophy*. Trans. H. Tomlinson. London: Continuum, 2002.

DELEUZE, Gilles & GUATTARI, Felix. *Anti-Oedipus: Capitalism and Schizophrenia*. Trans. R. Hurley, M. Seem & H. R. Lane. Minneapolis: University of Minnesota Press, 1983.

————. *A Thousand Plateaus: Capitalism and Schizophrenia*. Trans. B. Massumi. Minneapolis: University of Minnesota Press, 1987.

DELEUZE, Gilles & PARNET, Claire. *Dialogues*. Trans. H. Tomlinson and B. Habberjam. New York: Columbia University Press, 1987.

DERANTY, Jean-Philippe, & RENAULT, Emmanuel. "Politicizing Honneth's Ethics of Recognition." In: *Thesis Eleven*, Number 88 (February). London: SAGE Publications, 2007: 92–111.

DERRIDA, Jacques. *Margins of Philosophy*. Trans. A. Bass. Chicago: Chicago University Press, 1982.

————. *Writing and Difference*. Trans. A. Bass. New York: Routledge, 2001.

DEWS, Peter. *Logics of Disintegration: Post-Structuralist Thought and the Claims of Critical Theory*. London: Verso Books, 1987.

————. "The Truth of the Subject: Language, Validity and Transcendence in Lacan and Habermas." In: DEWS, P. & CRITCHLEY, S. (eds.), *Deconstructive Subjectivities*. Albany: State University of New York Press, 1996: 149–168.

DRIGO, Larissa. *De la contingence dans la* Science de La Logique *de Hegel,* Mémoire, Université Paris I, 2010-2011.

DUNKER, Christian. *Mal-estar, sofrimento e sintoma*. São Paulo: Boitempo, 2015.

DURKHEIM, Émile. *Suicide: A Study in Sociology*. Trans. J. A. Spaulding & G. Simpson. New York: Routledge, 2002.

EHRENBERG, Alain. *La fatigue d'être soi*. Paris: Odile Jacob, 2000.

ELLENBERGER, Henri. *The Discovery of the Unconscious: The History and Evolution of Dynamic Psychiatry*. London: Fontana Press, 1994.

FASSIN, Didier, & RECHTMANN, Richard. *L'empire du traumatisme. Enquête sur la condition de victime*. Paris: Editions Flammarion, 2007.

FAUSTO, Ruy. "Dialética e psicanálise." In: SAFATLE, Vladimir (org.). *Um limite tenso: Lacan entre a filosofia e a psicanálise*. São Paulo: Unesp, 2003: 75–106.

———. *Marx: logique et politique*. Paris: Publisud, 1986.

FECHNER, Gustav. *Elements of Psychophysics, Vol. I*. New York: Holt, Rinehart and Winston, 1966.

FENICHEL, Otto. *The Psychoanalytic Theory of Neurosis*. New York: Routledge, 2005.

FITZGERALD, F. Scott. "The Crack-Up." In: WILSON, Edmund (ed.). *The Crack-Up*. New York: Quality Paperback Book Club, 1996: 69–84.

FLEISCHMANN, Eugène. *La philosophie politique de Hegel*. Paris: Gallimard, 1992.

FONAGY, Peter & TARGET, Mary. "Playing with reality: a theory of external reality rooted in intersubjectivity", *International Journal of Psychoanalysis*. 2007, n. 88, p. 917-937.

FOUCAULT, Michel. *Archaeology of Knowledge*. Trans. A. M. S. Smith. New York: Pantheon Books, 1972.

———. *The Birth of the Clinic: An Archaeology of Medical Perception*. Trans. A. M. S. Smith. New York: Routledge, 2003.

———. *The History of Sexuality, Vol. 1: An Introduction*. Trans. R. Hurley. New York: Pantheon Books, 1978.

———. *The History of Sexuality, Vol. 2: The Use of Pleasure*. Trans. R. Hurley. New York: Vintage Books, 1990.

———. *The Order of Things: An Archaeology of the Human Sciences*. New York: Routledge, 2002.

———. *Psychiatric Power: Lectures at the Collège de France 1973-74*. Trans. G. Burchell. New York: Palgrave Macmillan, 2006.

FRASER, Nancy. "From Redistribution to Recognition? Dilemmas of Justice in a 'Post-Socialist' Age." In: *New Left Review* I/212. July-August 1995: 68–93.

———. "Rethinking Recognition." In: *New Left Review* 3. May-June 2000: 107–20.

FRASER, Nancy, & HONNETH, Axel. *Redistribution or Recognition?: A Political-Philosophical Exchange*. Trans. J. Golb, J. Ingram & C. Wilke. New York: Verso, 2003.

FREUD, Sigmund. *The Standard Edition of the Complete Psychological Works of Sigmund Freud (24 Volumes)*. Trans. J. Strachey. London: The Hogarth Press and the Institute of Psycho-analysis, 1953-1974.

FROMM, Erich. "Arbeiter und Angestellte am Vorabend des Dritten Reiches. Eine sozialpsychologische Untersuchung." In: *Gesamtausgabe*, vol. 3. Stuttgart: Deutsche Verlag-Anstalt, 1981: 1–224.

FRÜCHTL, Josef. *Mimesis: Konstellation eines Zentralbegriffs bei Adorno*. Würzburg: Königshausen & Neumann, 1986.

GALLAGHER, Shaun & VARGA, Somogy. "Critical social philosophy, Honneth and the role of primary intersubjectivity", *European Journal of Social Theory*. 2012, 15: p. 243, p. 255).

GEYSKENS, Tomas & VAN HAUTE, Phillipe. *From Death Instinct to Attachment Theory*. New York: Other Press, 2007.

GOETHE, Johann Wolfgang Von. *Faust*. Trans. W. Kaufmann. New York: Anchor Books, 1962.

GOLDSCHMIDT, Victor. *A religião de Platão*. São Paulo: Difusão Européia do Livro, 1963.

GRANGER, Gilles-Gaston. *Essai d'une philosophie du style*. Paris: Éditions Odile Jacob, 2de. éd., 1988.

GUYOMARD, Patrick. *La jouissance du tragique. Antigone, Lacan et le désir de l'analyste*. Paris: Flammarion, 1998.

HABERMAS, Jürgen. *Moral Consciousness and Communicative Action*. Trans. C. Lenhardt & S. Weber. Cambridge: Polity Press, 2007.

———. *The New Conservatism: Cultural Criticism and the Historians' Debate*. Trans. S. W. Nicholsen. Cambridge: Polity Press, 1989.

———. *The Philosophical Discourse of Modernity: Twelve Lectures*. Trans. F. G. Lawrence. Cambridge: The MIT Press, 1990.

———. *Profils philosophiques et politiques*. Trans. F. Dastur, J.-R. Ladmiral & M. B. De Launay. Paris: Gallimard, 1980.

———. *Theory and Practice*. Trans. J. Viertel. Boston: Beacon Press, 1974.

———. *The Theory of Communicative Action, Volume 1: Reason and the Rationalization of Society*. Trans. T. McCarthy. Boston: Beacon Press, 1984.

———. *Truth and Justification*. Trans. B. Fultner. Cambridge: The MIT Press, 2003.

HACKING, Ian. *Historical ontology*. Harvard: Harvard University Press, 2004.

HEGEL, G.W.F. *Aesthetics: Lectures on Fine Art, Vol. II*. Trans. T. M. Knox. London: Oxford University Press, 1975.

———. *The Difference Between Fichte's and Schelling's System of Philosophy*. Trans. H. S. Harris & W. Cerf. Albany: State University of New York Press, 1977.

———. *Early Theological Writings*. Trans. T. M. Knox. Chicago: University of Chicago Press, 1948.

———. *Elements of the Philosophy of Right*. Trans. H. B. Nisbet. Cambridge: Cambridge University Press, 1991.

———. *Encyclopedia of the Philosophical Sciences in Basic Outline, Part 1: Science of Logic*. Trans. K. Brinkmann & D. O. Dahlstrom. Cambridge: Cambridge University Press, 2010.

———. *Encyclopedia of the Philosophical Sciences, Part III: The Philosophy of Mind*. Trans. W. Wallace, A. V. Miller & M. Inwood. Oxford: Oxford University Press, 2007.

————. *Hegel and the Human Spirit: A Translation of the Jena Lectures on the Philosophy of Spirit* (1805-6). Trans. L. Rauch. Detroit: Wayne State University Press, 1983.

————. *Hegel: the Letters*. Trans. C. Butler & C. Seiler. Bloomington: Indiana University Press, 1984.

————. *Introduction to the Philosophy of History*. Trans. L. Rauch. Cambridge: Hackett Publishing Company, 1988.

————. *Jenaer Realphilosophie: Die Vorlesungen von 1803/4 & 1805/6 (2 Volumes)*. Leipzig, 1932. Republished in a single volume under the title *Jenaer Realphilosophie*. Hamburg: Felix Meiner Verlag, 1967.

————. *The Jena System 1804-5: Logic and Metaphysics*. Trans. J. Burbidge & G. di Giovanni. Montreal: McGill-Queen's University Press, 1986.

————. *Lectures on the Philosophy of Religion*. Trans. E. B. Speirs & J. B. Sanderson. London: Kegan Paul, Trench, Trübner, & Co. Ltd., 1895.

————. *Phenomenology of Spirit*. Trans. A. V. Miller. Oxford: Oxford University Press, 1977.

————. *The Philosophy of History*. Trans. J. Sibree. Kitchener: Batoche Books, 2001.

————. *The Philosophy of Nature Vol. III*. Trans. M. J. Petry. London: George Allen & Unwin Ltd., 1970.

————. *Political Writings*. Ed. L. Dickey & J. B. Nisbet. Cambridge: Cambridge University Press, 2004.

————. *The Science of Logic*. Trans. G. di Giovanni. Cambridge: Cambridge University Press, 2010.

HEIDEGGER, Martin. *Being and Time*. Trans. J. Macquarrie & E. Robinson. Oxford: Basil Blackwell, 1985.

————. *Nietzsche, Volumes III & IV*. Trans. J. Stambaugh, D. F. Krell & F. A. Capuzzi. San Francisco: Harper Collins, 1995.

————. *Off the Beaten Track*. Trans. J. Young & K. Haynes. New York: Cambridge University Press, 2002.

HEINE, Heinrich. "Concerning the History of Religion and Philosophy in Germany." In: *Heinrich Heine: Selected Works*. Ed. & trans. H. M. Mustard. New York: Random House, Inc., 1973.

HOMER. *The Odyssey*. Trans. R. Fagles. New York: Viking, 1996.

HONNETH, Axel. *Das Ich im Wir: Studien zur Anerkennungstheorie*. Frankfurt: Suhrkamp, 2010.

————. *La societé du mépris: Vers une nouvelle Théorie critique*. Paris: Découverte, 2006.

————. *Pathologies of Reason: On the Legacy of Critical Theory*. Trans. J. Ingram. New York: Columbia University Press, 2009.

————. "Postmodern Identity and Object-Relations Theory: On the Seeming Obsolescence of Psychoanalysis." In: *Philosophical Explorations: An International Journal for the Philosophy of Mind and Action*, vol. 2 (3), 1999: 225–242.

————. *The Struggle for Recognition: The Moral Grammar of Social Conflicts*. Trans. J. Anderson. Cambridge: The MIT Press, 1995.

————. *Suffering from Indeterminacy: An Attempt at a Reactualization of Hegel's Philosophy of Right: Two Lectures*. Trans. J. Ben-Levi. Assen: Van Gorcum, 2000.

HORKHEIMER, Max. *Eclipse of Reason*. London: Continuum, 2004.

HÖSLE, Vittorio. *O sistema de Hegel: o idealismo da subjetividade e o problema de intersubjetividade*. Belo Horizonte: Edições Loyola, 2007.

HOULGATE, Stephen. *The Opening of Hegel's Logic*. West Lafayette: Purdue University Press, 2006.

HUHN, Tom (ed.). *The Cambridge Companion to Adorno*. Cambridge: Cambridge University Press, 2004.

HUME, David. *An Inquiry Concerning Human Understanding*. New York: Oxford University Press, 2007.

HYPPOLITE, Jean. *Genesis and Structure of Hegel's Phenomenology of Spirit*. Trans. S. Cherniak & J. Heckman. Evanston: Northwestern University Press, 1974.

JOUAN, Marlène. *Psychologie morale: autonomie, responsabilité et rationalité pratique*. Paris: Librairie Philosophique J. Vrin, 2008.

KANT, Immanuel. *Critique of Practical Reason*. Trans. W. S. Pluhar. Cambridge: Hackett Publishing Company Inc., 2002.

————. *Critique of Pure Reason*. Trans. P. Guyer & A. W. Wood. Cambridge: Cambridge University Press, 1998.

————. *Practical Philosophy*. Trans. M. J. Gregor. Cambridge: Cambridge University Press, 1996.

KEENAN, Dennis King (ed.). *Hegel and Contemporary Continental Philosophy*. Albany: State University of New York Press, 2004.

KEHL, Maria Rita. *Ressentimento*. São Paulo: Casa do Psicólogo, 2005.

KERNBERG, Otto. "The concept of death drive: a clinical perspective", *International Journal of Psychoanalysis*, 2009, vol. 90, n. 5.

KLEIN, Melanie. "The Origins of Transference." In: *The International Journal of Psychoanalysis*, 33, 1952: 433–438.

KOHLBERG, Lawrence. *The Psychology of Moral Development*. San Francisco: Harper and Row, 1984.

KOJÈVE, Alexandre. *Introduction à la lecture de Hegel*. Paris: Gallimard, 1947.

LACAN, Jacques. *Autres écrits*. Paris: Editions du Seuil, 2001.

————. *Écrits*. Trans. B. Fink, with H. Fink & R. Grigg. New York: W. W. Norton & Company, 2005.

————. "The Neurotic's Individual Myth." Trans. M. N. Evans. In: *Psychoanalytic Quarterly*, XLVIII (3), 1979: 405–425.

————. *The Seminar of Jacques Lacan, Book I: Freud's Papers on Technique, 1953-1954*. Ed. J.-A. Miller. Trans. J. Forrester. New York: W. W. Norton & Company, 1991.

————. *The Seminar of Jacques Lacan, Book II: The Ego in Freud's Theory and in the Technique of Psychoanalysis, 1954-1955*. Ed. J.-A. Miller. Trans. S. Tomaselli. New York: W. W. Norton & Company, 1991.

————. *The Seminar of Jacques Lacan, Book III: The Psychoses, 1955-1956*. Ed. J.-A. Miller. Trans. R. Grigg. New York: W. W. Norton & Company, 1997.

————. *Le séminaire, Livre IV: La relation d'objet et les structures freudiennes*. Ed. J.-A. Miller. Paris: Seuil, 1994.

————. *The Seminar of Jacques Lacan, Book VII: The Ethics of Psychoanalysis, 1959-1960*. Ed. J.-A. Miller. Trans. D. Porter. New York: W. W. Norton & Company, 1992.

————. *Le Séminaire, Livre VIII: Le Transfert*. Ed. J.-A. Miller. Paris: Seuil, 1994.

————. *The Seminar of Jacques Lacan, Book IX: Identification, 1961-1962* (Digital Version). Trans. C. Gallagher. Accessed on February 5, 2015. URL: http://www.lacaninireland.com /web/wp-content/uploads/2010/06/Seminar-IX-Amended-Iby-MCL-7.NOV_.20111.pdf.

————. *Le Séminaire, Livre X: L'Angoisse*. Ed. J.-A. Miller. Paris: Seuil, 2004.

————. *The Seminar of Jacques Lacan, Book XI: The Four Fundamental Concepts of Psychoanalysis*. Ed. J.-A. Miller. Trans. A. Sheridan. New York: W. W. Norton & Company, 1998.

————. *The Seminar of Jacques Lacan, Book XX, Encore: On Feminine Sexuality, the Limits of Love and Knowledge, 1972-1973*. Ed. J.-A. Miller. Trans. B. Fink. New York: W. W. Norton & Company, 1999.

LACLAU, Ernesto. *La razón populista*. Trans. S. Laclau. Buenos Aires: Fondo de Cultura Económica, 2005.

LAPLANCHE, Jean. *Life and Death in Psychoanalysis*. Trans. J. Mehlman. Baltimore: The Johns Hopkins University Press, 1990.

LAPLANCHE, Jean & PONTALIS, J.-B. "Fantasy and the Origins of Sexuality." In: BIRKSTED-BREEN, D., FLANDERS, S., & GIBEAULT, A. (eds.); *Reading French Psychoanalysis*. New York: Routledge, 2010.

LEAR, Jonathan. *Open minded: Working Out the Logic of the Soul*. Cambridge: Harvard University Press, 1998.

LEBRUN, Gérard. *A filosofia e sua história*. São Paulo: Cosac & Naify, 2006.

————. *L'envers de la dialectique*. Paris: Seuil, 2004.

LENIN, Vladimir. *One Step Forward, Two Steps Back: The Crisis in Our Party*. New York: Pathfinder, 1999.

LÉVI-STRAUSS, Claude. *The Raw and the Cooked: Mythologiques, Vol. 1*. Trans. J. & D. Weightman. New York: Harper and Row, 1969.

LOCKE, John. *Two Treatises of Government*. Cambridge: Cambridge University Press, 2005.

LOEWALD, Hans; *Collected Papers and Monographs,* Hagerstown, MD: University Publishing group, 2000.

LONGUENESSE, Béatrice. *Hegel's Critique of Metaphysics*. Trans. N. J. Simek. Cambridge: Cambridge University Press, 2007.

LOSURDO, Domenico. *Hegel and the Freedom of Moderns*. Trans. J. & M. Morris. Durham: Duke University Press, 2004.

LUKÁCS, György. *The Theory of the Novel: A Historico-philosophical Essay on the Forms of Great Epic Literature.* Trans. A. Bostock. Cambridge: The MIT Press, 1971.

MALABOU, Catherine. *L'avenir de Hegel: plasticité, temporalité, dialectique.* Paris: Vrin, 1996.

MARCUSE, Herbert. *Eros e civilização.* Rio de Janeiro: LTC,1999.

MARX, Karl. *Critique of Hegel's 'Philosophy of Right.'* Trans. A. Jolin & J. O'Malley. Cambridge: Cambridge University Press, 1971.

———. *The Eighteenth Brumaire of Louis Bonaparte.* Moscow: Progress Publishers, 1972.

———. "On the Jewish Question." In: TUCKER, Robert C. (ed.). *The Marx-Engels Reader.* New York: W. W. Norton & Company, 1978: 26–52.

MARX, Karl, & ENGELS, Friedrich. *The Communist Manifesto: A Modern Edition.* Trans. S. Moore. New York: Verso, 1998.

———. *The German Ideology, including Theses on Feuerbach and the Introduction to the Critique of Political Economy.* Amherst: Prometheus Books, 1998.

MAUSS, Marcel. "A category of the human mind: the notion of person; the notion of self." Trans. W. D. Halls. In: *The category of the person: Anthropology, philosophy, history.* Cambridge: Cambridge University Press, 1985: 1–25.

MERLEAU-PONTY, Maurice. *Signs.* Trans. R. C. McCleary. Evanston: Northwestern University Press, 1992.

MORTLEY, Raoul. *Désir et différence dans la tradition platonicienne.* Paris: Vrin, 1988.

MOUFFE, Chantal. "Democratic Politics and the Question of Identity." In: RAJCHMAN, John (ed.). *The Identity in Question.* New York: Routledge, 1995: 32–45.

MÜLLER, Marcos. "A liberdade absoluta entre a crítica à representação e o terror." In: *Revista Eletrônica Estudos Hegelianos*, 5 (9), dezembro de 2008: 75–99. Accessed on Feb. 6, 2015. URL: <http://www.hegelbrasil.org/reh9/muller9.pdf>

O'CONNOR, Brian. *Adorno's Negative Dialectic: Philosophy and the Possibility of Critical Rationality.* Cambridge: The MIT Press, 2004.

O'HARA, M. "Postpartum depression: what we know", *Journal of Clinical Psychology*, vol. 65, Issue 12, 2009.

PINKARD, Terry. *Hegel's Phenomenology: The Sociality of Reason.* Cambridge: Cambridge University Press, 1994.

PIPPIN, Robert. *Hegel's Idealism: The Satisfaction of Self-Consciousness.* Cambridge: Cambridge University Press, 1989.

———. *Hegel's Practical Philosophy: Rational Agency as Ethical Life.* Cambridge: Cambridge University Press, 2008.

PLATO. *Dialogues of Plato Vol. II.* Trans. B. Jowett. Oxford: The Clarendon Press, 1875.

POLITZER, Georges. *Critiques des fondements de la psychologie.* Paris: PUF, 2000.

PRADO JR., Bento. *Alguns ensaios.* São Paulo: Paz e Terra, 2000.

RANCIÈRE, Jacques. *Disagreement: Politics and Philosophy.* Trans. J. Rose. Minneapolis: University of Minnesota Press, 1999.

————. *Dissensus: On Politics and Aesthetics*. Trans. S. Corcoran. New York: Continuum Books, 2010.

————. "Politics, Identification and Subjectivization." In: RAJCHMAN, John (ed.). *The Identity in Question*. New York: Routledge, 1995: 63–70.

REICH, Wilhelm. *Análise do caráter*. São Paulo: Martins Fontes, 2001.

RENAULT, Emmanuel. *Souffrances sociales: philosophie, psychologie et politique*. Paris: La découverte, 2008.

RITTER, Joachim. *Hegel and the French Revolution*. Trans. R. D. Winfield. Cambridge: The MIT Press, 1982.

RORTY, Richard. "Is 'Cultural Recognition' a Useful Concept for Leftist Politics?" In: *Critical Horizons*, 1 (1), 2000: 7–20.

ROSENFIELD, Israel. *The Invention of Memory: A New View of the Brain*. New York: Basic Books, 1988.

SAFATLE, Vladimir. *Cinismo e falência da crítica*. São Paulo: Boitempo Editorial, 2008.

————. *Lacan*. São Paulo: Publifolha, 2007.

————. "Mirrors without images: mimesis and recognition in Lacan and Adorno." In: *Radical Philosophy*, n. 139, 2006: 9–19.

————. *A paixão do negativo: Lacan e a dialética*. São Paulo: Unesp, 2006.

SAFATLE, Vladimir, & TELES, Edson. *O que resta da ditadura*. São Paulo: Boitempo Editorial, 2010.

SARTRE, Jean-Paul. *Situations philosophiques*. Paris: Gallimard, 1990.

SAUSSURE, Ferdinand. *Course in General Linguistics*. Trans. W. Baskin. New York: McGraw-Hill Book Company, 1966.

SCHNEEWIND, J. B. *The Invention of Autonomy*. Cambridge: Cambridge University Press, 1998.

SCHOPENHAUER, Arthur. *The World as Will and Representation*, Volume II. Trans. E. F. J. Payne. New York: Dover Publications, Inc., 1958.

SEARLE, John. *Intentionality: an Essay in the Philosophy of Mind*. Cambridge: Cambridge University Press, 1983.

————. *Speech Acts*. Cambridge: Cambridge University Press, 1999.

SIEP, Ludwig. "Der Kampf um Anerkennung. Zur Auseinandersetzung Hegels mit Hobbes in den Jenaer Schriften." In: *Hegel-Studien*, Bd.9. Bonn, 1974: 155–207.

————. (org.). *Grundlinien der Philosophie des Rechts*. Berlin: Akademie Verlag, 2005.

SOPHOCLES. *Antigone*. Trans. R. Gibbons & C. Segal. New York: Oxford University Press, 2003.

————. *Oedipus at Colonus*. Trans. E. Grennan & R. Kitzinger. New York: Oxford University Press, 2005.

SOUCHE-DAGUES, Denise. *Liberté et négativité dans la pensée politique de Hegel*. Paris: Vrin, 1997.

————. *Recherches hégéliennes: infini et dialectique*. Paris Vrin, 1994.

STAROBINSKI, Jean. *Action and Reaction: The Life and Adventures of a Couple*. Trans. S. Hawkes & J. Fort. New York: Zone Books, 2003.

STEINER, George. *Antigones: The Antigone Myth in Western Literature, Art and Thought*. Oxford: Oxford University Press, 1984.

TAYLOR, Charles. *Hegel and Modern Society*. Cambridge: Cambridge University Press, 1980.

———. *Multiculturalism and the "politics of recognition"*. Princeton: Princeton University Press, 1992.

———. *Multiculturalism: Examining the Politics of Recognition*. Princeton: Princeton University Press, 1994.

THEUNISSEN, Michael. *Sein und Schein. Die kritische Funktion der Hegelschen Logik*. Frankfurt: Suhrkamp, 1994.

THOBURN, Nicholas. "Difference in Marx: the lumpenproletariat and the proletarian unnamable." In: *Economy and Society*, Volume 31, 3, August 2002: 434–460.

TOMASELLO, Michael. *The cultural origin of human cognition*. Harvard: Harvard University Press, 2003.

TRUDEAU, Pierre E. "Statement on Multiculturalism." In: FORBES, Hugh Donald (ed.). *Canadian Political Thought*. Toronto: Oxford University Press, 1985: 349–351.

VAN HAUTE, Philippe. "Antígona: heroína da psicanálise?" In: *Revista Discurso*, n. 36, 2006: 287–311.

VAN HAUTE, Philippe & DE VLEMINCK, Jens. "Aan genezijde van Freud: De grenzen en de mogelijkheden van een psychoanalytische pathoanalyse". In: Idem; *Freud als filosoof*, Kalmthout: Pelckmans, 2013.

VASSET, Philippe, & VIANNAY, Clotilde. "Abécédaire de la crise. Politiques du care. Micropolitique de l'habitat non-ordinaire." In: *Revue Multitudes*, 37, 38, 2009: 1–320.

WEBER, Max. *From Max Weber: Essays in Sociology*. Ed. & trans. H. H. Gerth & C. W. Mill. New York: Oxford University Press, 1946.

WHITEBOOK, Joel. *Perversion and Utopia: A Study in Psychoanalysis and Critical Theory*. Cambridge: The MIT Press, 1995.

———. "First nature and second nature in Hegel and psychoanalysis", *Constellations*, 2008, vol. 15, n. 3.

WILLIAMS, Bernard. *Moral Luck*. Cambridge: Cambridge University Press, 1991.

WILLIAMS, Robert. *Hegel's Ethics of Recognition*. University of California Press, 1998.

WINNICOTT, Donald Woods. *Da pediatria à psicanálise*. Rio de Janeiro: Imago, 2000.

———. *Playing and Reality*. New York: Routledge, 2009.

———. *Natureza humana*. São Paulo: Imago, 1990.

WITTGENSTEIN, Ludwig. *Philosophical Investigations*. Trans. G. E. M. Anscombe. Oxford: Basil Blackwell, 1986.

ZIZEK, Slavoj. "Introduction." In: ROBESPIERRE, Maximilien; *Virtue and Terror*. London: Verso, 2007.

————. "Multiculturalism, or, the Cultural Logic of Multinational Capitalism." In: *New Left Review* I/225, September-October 1997: 28–51.

————. *Violence: Six Sideways Reflections.* London: Profile Books, 2009.

ZUPANCIC, Alenka. "Sexuality and Ontology." In: *Why psychoanalysis? Three Interventions.* Uppsala: NSU Press, 20.

Lightning Source UK Ltd.
Milton Keynes UK
UKOW06f2338010817
306476UK00002B/5/P